Table of contents

Foreword

European countries today are faced with a significant threat from terrorism. None of the member states of the Council of Europe has yet the capacity to protect itself against attacks on the scale of those in Moscow or Madrid in 2004. With the rapid technological advances of the twentieth century, it is probably the first time in the history of mankind that such a small number of criminals has been able to inflict so much suffering on so many. For the authorities concerned, fighting against the threat of terrorism has become a priority.

Judicial and police authorities in particular have had to adapt their investigative measures in order to cope with the increasing complexity of terrorist networks which are often connected with other forms of serious crime, such as organised crime and drugs or arms trafficking. They have developed special investigation techniques, such as undercover operations, controlled delivery and electronic surveillance. These can been defined as techniques used to systematically gather information in such a way that they do not alert the persons investigated, and applied by law enforcement officials for the purpose of detecting and investigating crimes and suspects.

The European Court of Human Rights has endorsed the use of such techniques in the fight against terrorism, considering that:

> Democratic societies nowadays find themselves threatened by highly sophisticated forms of espionage and by terrorism, with the result that the State must be able, in order effectively to counter such threats, to undertake the secret surveillance of subversive elements operating within its jurisdiction. The Court has therefore to accept that the existence of some legislation granting powers of secret surveillance over the mail, post and telecommunications is, under exceptional conditions, necessary in a democratic society in the interests of national security and/or for the prevention of disorder or crime.
>
> (Klass and Others v. Germany)

It is indisputable that the use of special investigation techniques runs the risk of infringing upon fundamental rights and freedoms which are protected by the European Convention on Human Rights, such as the right to respect for private life (Article 8) or the right to a fair trial (Article 6). It is therefore of the utmost importance that the need to enhance the efficiency of the fight against terrorism runs in hand with the protection of fundamental rights and freedoms.

It is against this background that the Council of Europe is drawing up a Recommendation of the Committee of Ministers to member states that seeks to promote the use of special investigation techniques in relation to serious crimes, including acts of terrorism, whilst ensuring respect for the rights and freedoms of the individual.

This publication contains a survey of national practice in thrity-five Council of Europe member states and two observer states together with an analytical report, which examines special investigation techniques in relation to law enforcement and prosecution, the control of their implementation, human rights and international co-operation in this field.

The Council of Europe's mission is to ensure respect for human rights, pluralist democracy and the rule of law throughout its forty-six member states and these are values worth defending. Terrorism must be eradicated but it must be done in accordance with these values. This publication offers useful guidance and information to those concerned who are willing to contribute to this objective.

Guy DE VEL
Director General of Legal Affairs of the
Council of Europe

Part I
Analytical report

by Mr Philippe De Koster

Mr Philippe De Koster is Advocate-General seconded to the Supreme Court of Belgium. He is also Deputy Chairman of the Belgian Anti-Money Laundering Unit. From December 2001 to December 2002, he chaired the Multidisciplinary Group on International Action against Terrorism (GMT) in the Council of Europe.

Preamble

This analytical report is based on the replies provided by the member states of the Council of Europe to a general questionnaire on special investigation techniques (SIT) in relation to acts of terrorism. These replies appear in the Part II. They were gathered in the course of the year 2003 by the Secretariat of the Council of Europe and were subsequently updated in December 2004 by those member states that found such updating necessary.

The aim pursued by this report is not to compile and summarise the replies, but rather to try and pick out some major tendencies in the existence and use of special investigation techniques in connection with the fight against international terrorism. The analysis made is thus not intended to compare the different legal situations in order to discover a model, but rather to express a common denominator and the principles that govern the use and application of special investigation techniques, while bearing in mind the fundamental values championed by the Council of Europe in respect of safeguards for individual rights and freedoms. In this respect, the report also refers to landmark judgments of the European Court of Human Rights that have a bearing on this matter. In its final part, the report contains some observations on recent development in the use of SIT at the European level.[1]

The report is inspired by a previous report prepared by the author and adopted in September 2003 by the Committee of Experts on Special Investigation Techniques in relation to Acts of Terrorism.

---

1. For historical background on the use of SIT, see C. Fijnaut and G. Marx,"The normalisation of undercover policing in the West: historical and contemporary perspectives" in *Undercover police surveillance in comparative perspective*, Kluwer, 1995, pp. 3-5.

Introduction

At its 109th session on 8 November 2001, in the wake of the terrorist attacks on the United States of America on 11 September 2001, the Committee of Ministers of the Council of Europe "agreed to take steps rapidly to increase the effectiveness of the existing international instruments within the Council of Europe on the fight against terrorism, by, *inter alia*, setting up a Multidisciplinary Group on International Action against Terrorism (GMT)".

The tasks of the GMT included identifying appropriate measures that could be taken in the fight against terrorism and preparing a report for the Committee of Ministers, including the additional actions that the Council of Europe could implement in order to contribute to the international fight against terrorism.

In its final activity report, submitted to the Committee of Ministers at its 111th session in November 2002, the GMT set out a number of priority areas for action that the Council of Europe could begin to implement in 2003. Those priorities included special investigation techniques.

On the basis of those proposals, which were endorsed by the European Committee on Crime Problems (CDPC), the Committee of Ministers decided in February 2003 to set up a new committee, the Committee of Experts on Special Investigation Techniques in Relation to Acts of Terrorism (PC-TI).

On the expiry of the GMT's terms of reference, the Committee of Ministers set up a Committee of Experts on Terrorism (CODEXTER), whose tasks included co-ordinating the activities of the PC-TI and other priority activities.[1]

On 13 February 2003 at the 828th meeting of the Ministers' Deputies, the Committee of Ministers adopted the specific terms of reference of the PC-TI, which were revised at the 832nd meeting. They required the PC-TI Committee "to study the use of special investigation techniques respective of European criminal justice and human rights standards, with a view to facilitating the prosecution of terrorist offences and increasing the effectiveness of law enforcement, and to make proposals as to the feasibility of preparing an appropriate instrument in this field".

The Committee agreed that before addressing the question of the feasibility of preparing an instrument in this field, it should initially seek ways to:
a. define and draw up a list of special investigation techniques related to terrorist acts;
b. set standards concerning their use; and
c. provide safeguards to ensure that the techniques are used in compliance with the requirements of the European Convention on Human Rights.

In the light of the above, the Committee decided to draw up a questionnaire on the situation in member states concerning special investigation techniques, their regulation and use.

The Committee of Experts on Special Investigation Techniques in Relation to Acts of Terrorism concluded its work in September 2003 after having adopted its "Final report on special investigation techniques in relation to acts of terrorism" (document PC-TI (2003) 11).

At its plenary meeting in March 2004, the European Committee on Crime Problems (CDPC) approved revised draft specific terms of reference for a new Committee of Experts on Special Investigation Techniques (PC-TI) and submitted them to the Committee of Ministers, which adopted them at its 884th meeting at Deputies' level on 19 May 2004.

Pursuant to its specific terms of reference, the new PC-TI was called upon to draw up a recommendation on the basis of the conclusions of the above-mentioned Final Report, and with a view to the development of common principles governing the use of special investigation techniques and the improvement of international co-operation in matters related to them.

The new PC-TI started its work in October 2004 and completed it in February 2005.

The draft recommendation prepared by the PC-TI was transmitted in March 2005 to the CDPC for its approval, with a view to it being transmitted for adoption to the Committee of Ministers.

---

1. The other priority tasks were research on the concepts of *apologie du terrorisme* and "incitement to terrorism"; protection of witnesses and *pentiti*; international co-operation on law enforcement; action to cut terrorists off from sources of funding; and questions of identity documents that arise in connection with terrorism.

Chapter 1
Definition and typology of special investigation techniques

In order to combat serious crime, judicial and police authorities have had to adapt their investigative measures and develop what may be termed special investigation techniques.

Over the years the Council of Europe has organised a number of meetings at which special investigation techniques have been discussed in the specific context of the fight against organised crime. Following the work done by the Multidisciplinary Group on International Action Against Terrorism (GMT), the Council of Europe has initiated a number of activities focusing specifically on the use of special investigation techniques in the fight against terrorism.

For the purposes of the PC-TI's activities, special investigation techniques were defined as techniques for gathering information systematically in such a way as not to alert the target person(s), applied by law enforcement officials for the purpose of detecting and investigating crimes and suspects.[1]

Subsequent PC-TI discussions brought out the need, not only to try to define more precisely the concept of special investigation techniques in general, particularly on the basis of a number of common characteristics, but also to draw up a classification or typology of such techniques.

The questionnaire covers the following particular techniques:[2] undercover operations[3] (including covert investigations); front store operations (e.g. undercover company); informants; controlled delivery;[4] observation (including cross-border observation); electronic surveillance; interception of communications[5] (telephone, fax, e-mail, mail, public and private networks); searches (including premises and objects such as computers, cars, etc., by various means including scanning); cross-border (hot) pursuits; *agents provocateurs*; pseudo-purchases or other "pseudo-offences".

On the basis of the replies to the questionnaire, it seems worthwhile to draw up a typology of special investigation techniques, in order to better understand their characteristics.[6] Such a typology should also make it possible to set out standards applicable to those techniques. The standards derive from the duty to comply with the basic principles of fundamental rights and freedoms, which will be discussed later.

The classification of strategies for investigating and searching for evidence of offences developed by Professor G. Marx is a useful tool.[7] Two variables may be used: the use of subterfuge and the overt or secret nature of police or judicial action. However, it would be useful to add a third criterion: the interaction between, on the one hand, investigating or prosecuting authorities and, on the other hand, witnesses, suspects and third parties.[8]

The use of subterfuge involves a degree of deception: it is a procedure that seeks to lead an individual to perform certain acts or reveal certain information by generating a divergence between what is supposed to be the case and what is expressed in a conventional manner or otherwise.[9] Infiltration and pseudo-purchases or sales are good examples of this.

Secrecy is present where an attempt is made to conceal what is being done. Tailing, telephone-tapping and filming are by their nature secret. The aim of secrecy is not to alter the behaviour of the presumed offender but to deprive him or her of information. According to Professor de Valkeneer, secrecy can be distinguished from deception: the latter involves falsifying information; the former means deprivation of information.[10] The degree of secrecy varies: the accused may be informed of the results of telephone-tapping, tailing and filming at a later stage, while the identity of an infiltrated officer may be kept secret even at the trial stage.

As for interaction or personal communication with the individuals concerned, this is brought into play by the interrogation of a suspect, the questioning of a witness or a confrontation.

By combining these three variables, we arrive at the typology outlined by Professor de Valkeneer, which classifies criminal investigation procedures under eight headings.

- Overt investigations with interaction and without deception
  – Examination by a judge, interrogation, confrontation, reconstitution, searches of vehicles and baggage in the presence of their owners or keepers, body searches and identity controls fall into this category.

- Overt investigations without interaction and without deception
  – Scientific and technical police investigations, expert reports, visits to the home, consulting files and gathering information contained in open sources and judicial files fall into this category, as does surveillance of a public highway that results in observing the commission of offences.

- Overt investigations with interaction and with deception
  – Without concealing his or her identity, the police officer falsifies reality in order to obtain information or alter someone's behaviour. False promises and dissimulation, staged events and falsehood in the course of interrogation fit in with this definition.[11]

- Overt investigations without interaction but with deception
  – This covers cases where the powers conferred in a particular context are used for purposes other than those for which they were assigned, for example, subjecting a vehicle to a compulsory road-worthiness check in order to search it surreptitiously.

- Secret investigations with interaction and without deception.
  – The use of informants falls into this category.

- Secret investigations without interaction and without deception
  – This includes all the techniques used to monitor individuals, by tailing, observing, photographing and filming, tapping or monitoring telecommunications and the opening of mail.

- Secret investigations with interaction and with deception
  – This category includes undercover operations involving the establishment of a relationship between an investigator – or a person appointed by the police, who conceals his or her true identity – and suspected or potential offenders, in order to observe an offence or have it observed, in other words, gathering evidence and information through deception. Infiltration and front-store operations fall into this category.

- Secret investigations without interaction but with deception
  – The last category includes the use of enticements and traps to enable the commission of an offence to be observed or to gather evidence. The dissemination or transmission of false information in the absence of interaction, in order to lead a suspect into acting in such a way that he or she may be caught, is an example.

From this typology, it is clear that the last four categories of criminal investigation procedures are particularly relevant to special investigation techniques.

The above investigation strategies may be combined, and may be used either before a crime has been committed, or before or after the facts have been ascertained.

How are special investigation techniques to be defined? The concept is not easy to pin down since it is one that is constantly changing, as it has in the past and will certainly do in the future. For this reason it is more useful to highlight some of the intrinsic features of special investigation techniques.

Such special techniques are of a "particular" nature since their use may violate fundamental rights and freedoms, such as respect for private life, and impinge upon the fundamental principles of criminal procedure, such as fairness in the gathering of evidence. The secrecy of such techniques is another particularity. Unlike searches, for example, their very nature requires that they be secretly implemented; if they are not, their purpose is lost. Furthermore, such secrecy may in certain respects be absolute: for example, the identity of an informant or infiltrated officer may remain secret from suspects even at the trial.

Generally speaking, the special investigation techniques referred to in the questionnaire are either familiar to or applied in member states. There would appear to be no need here for a detailed comparative study. The replies show that the main special investigation techniques are used everywhere. There are no particular differences between member states. The Netherlands and Belgium can be considered as countries using the full panoply of such techniques.

These techniques are certainly useful in the fight against terrorism but their usefulness in the more general framework of combating organised crime is equally clear.

Special investigation techniques are used in the course of investigations into serious crime. There is no doubt that terrorism should be placed in the category of the most serious crimes, but the replies do not suggest that special investigation techniques have been reserved exclusively for the fight against terrorism.

Such techniques seem to have been developed first as part of the measures to combat drug-trafficking and then in combating organised crime. This being the case, is there a need to develop criminal procedural standards in connection with the fight against terrorism?

The experience of member states is mainly connected to combating organised crime in the context of the Council of Europe's work in this field. The conferences and other events organised under the Octopus programme have already emphasised the need to clarify the legal framework governing the use of special investigation methods. Terrorism clearly has one feature in common with organised crime: it is the work of structured criminal organisations and rarely of isolated individuals. It should also be noted that, at its third meeting on 10 and 11 April 2002, the GMT stressed that investigations of terrorist activities raised serious problems, aggravated by their links with other forms of crime.[12]

Examination of the replies to the questionnaire does not suggest that special investigation techniques should be specifically confined to the fight against terrorism, but rather that they should be seen in the more general context of combating certain serious forms of organised crime. Although the Court has considered that "terrorist crime falls into a special category",[13] its intention was not to endorse the setting-aside of the fundamental principles enshrined in the European Convention on Human Rights.

---

1. As defined in document PC-S-CO (2000) 3.
2. See the relevant provisions of the reference texts in document PC-TI (2003) Misc. 1 and, where applicable, other documents. The definitions referring thereto are intended for the purposes of clarification and the gathering of information and are not intended to be final. They imply no agreement on the part of the PC-TI.
3. "An undercover operation is a method of investigation where substantial information and evidence are gathered over a period of time, involving the use of lawful measures by law

enforcement agencies and by using undercover agents to obtain such information and evidence" – definition in document PC-TI (2003) Inf. 1.

4. "'Controlled delivery' shall mean the technique of allowing illicit or suspect consignments to pass out of, through or into the territory of one or more States, with the knowledge and under the supervision of their competent authorities, with a view to the investigation of an offence and the identification of persons involved in the commission of the offence" – Article 2 (i) of the United Nations Convention against Transnational Organized Crime.

"'Controlled delivery' means the technique of allowing illicit or suspect consignments of narcotic drugs, psychotropic substances ... or substances substituted for them, to pass out of, through or into the territory of one or more countries, with the knowledge and under the supervision of their competent authorities, with a view to identifying persons involved in the commission of offences ...". Article 1 (g) of the United Nations Convention against Illicit Traffic in Narcotic Drugs and Psychotropic Substances (Vienna, 1988).

5. "Interception of communication is: the covert monitoring of direct communication or telecommunication in which one or more suspects are taking part, in order to provide evidence or intelligence on their participation in crime", as defined by the PC-OC in document PC-S-CO (2000) 3.

6. See PC-TI (2003) 8 rev, 23/07/2003.

7. G. Marx, *Undercover Police Surveillance in America*, University of California Press, 1988, p. 11.

8. C. de Valkeneer, *La tromperie dans l'administration de la preuve*, Larcier, 2000, p. 24.

9. Ibid., p. 23.

10. Ibid., p. 24.

11. Of interest is the decision in Ebbinge v. the Netherlands, ECHR, 14 March 2000, 2000-IV, where the court considered that the use of certain mental stimulation techniques could be open to criticism in the context of a criminal pre-trial investigation.

12. See the reply of France, PC-TI (2003) 8, p. 73.

13. ECHR, 30 August 1990 Fox, Campbell and Hartley judgment, Series A, No. 182.

Chapter 2
Special investigation techniques, law enforcement and prosecution

The use of special investigation techniques in relation to pro-active or reactive investigations may help in investigating offences, gathering evidence in relation to them and bringing offenders before the courts competent to try them.

Police services may use special investigation techniques in order to gather and process data and information with the aim of investigating offences that have been or will be committed, gathering evidence and identifying and prosecuting those responsible.

Processing includes various operations, such as gathering, recording, organising, conserving, adapting or amending, consulting or extracting, dissemination, deletion, destruction and the like. Reference should be made to the relevant international instruments on the processing of personal data and protection of private life, as well as to the Council of Europe's evaluation reports on data protection.[1]

It can therefore be considered that both the decision to use special investigation techniques and the conditions for using them ultimately fall within the competence of the judicial authorities or any other independent *(ex post)* control, taking account of the specific characteristics of different systems of criminal procedure. It is always with the aim of preventing and punishing crime that such special techniques may, where necessary, be considered.

The question can be asked: Could special investigation techniques be used in the preparatory phase of a criminal investigation? The specific characteristics of the legal systems in member states do not immediately allow a clear, conclusive reply to this question. The concepts of pro-active investigation (preventing the commission of serious offences) and reactive investigation (elucidating the commission of serious offences) might offer the beginnings of a solution. The concept of pro-active investigation does not appear to exist in all legal systems, although the concept has been used in earlier research.[2]

What is meant by pro-active investigation? Professor Jean Pradel has usefully suggested that pro-active criminal investigations should be given a legal framework[3] and has also defined the concept. Taking as his starting-point the fact that new types of crime – consensual offences and organised crime – are now emerging alongside more traditional offences, he notes that these two types of repeated offences are rarely reported to the police. In order to demonstrate their existence or prevent their repetition, the police therefore use special techniques.

A police force that is not expressly informed of the identity of offenders is condemned to interminable investigations, which will only be concluded by chance.[4] According to Professor Pradel, the forms such investigations take are well-known: observation, infiltration, use of informants and the search for offenders using computer support. On the basis of these observations, he suggests defining pro-active investigation as "all investigations using special techniques to prevent the probable commission of offences or to detect offences that have already been committed but have not been identified".[5]

Since such investigations constitute a necessary danger, they need to be provided with a legal framework. They are a danger in that they interfere with the exercise of certain fundamental freedoms laid down in the European Convention on Human Rights. However, since according to the case-law of the European Court of Human Rights the prohibition on interference is not absolute, the following question must be addressed: What might the guiding principles of this new form of investigation be?[6]

This type of investigation should obey three principles, which are in a sense the counterpart of the principles surrounding possible exemptions from the full and complete exercise of fundamental freedoms:

- The lawfulness principle: criminal procedure must be governed by law. Since pro-active investigations constitute interference in private life, such interference can only be justified within the limits of a particularly precise law;[7]

- The principle of exceptional circumstances: pro-active investigations are aimed at offences that may be committed. There must be reasonable suspicion that an offence will be committed. This principle may therefore be subdivided into three sub-principles:
  1. the sub-principle of subsidiarity, according to which pro-active measures may be applied only if no other, less intrusive investigation method enables the offence to be detected or prevented;
  2. the sub-principle of proportionality, according to which pro-active techniques may be used only if safeguarding public order over-rides protecting the privacy of private life in general;
  3. the sub-principle of specificity, according to which the information gathered in the course of pro-active investigations may be used only in support of the charge which led to their being conducted.

- In addition to these principles, and where the investigation during which special investigation techniques are used is conducted autonomously by police forces or under the direct authority of a court, the judicial authorities or any other similar independent *(ex post)* control should assess whether or not pro-active measures are justified in order to investigate offences, gather evidence in relation to them and bring offenders before the courts competent to try them.

The sub-principle of specificity – in the sense that information in the pro-active phase can only be used for the purpose for which it has been gathered – should be interpreted with flexibility. The third evaluation (2000) of the Recommendation R(87)15 on data protection and police envisages the possibility of a linkage of different analysis files, set up as pro-active files for different purposes in order to find in one file possibly relevant information for the other file.

The use of special investigation techniques remains fundamentally linked to the existence of sufficient reason to believe that an offence has been committed, prepared or planned by one or more particular persons or an as-yet-unidentified group of individuals. This link justifies the use of investigatory methods that violate private life or individual freedom. The principle of prohibiting "fishing expeditions" remains intact.

One must not, however, lose sight of the difficulty in determining what is meant by "sufficient reason" and "reasonable evidence". It is the essentially factual nature of the two concepts that makes a legal definition of them almost impossible. The Court has interpreted the concept of reasonable suspicion within the meaning of Article 5 by stating that

> having a "reasonable suspicion" presupposes the existence of facts or information which would satisfy an objective observer that the person concerned may have committed the offence. What may be regarded as "reasonable" will however depend upon all the circumstances.[8]

On the other hand, it is clearly essential that there be proportionality between the infringement of individual rights and the nature of the suspicions or reasons; this may be easier to establish. Similarly, the existence of a criminal organisation may be deduced from a criminological analysis and result in sufficiently serious suspicion enabling certain offences to be imputed to a certain number of persons, without necessarily identifying all of them in advance.

It should be noted that the use of special investigation techniques for other purposes, such as the protection of national security, may also be problematic with regard to respect for human rights and, more particularly, the requirements of Article 8 of the European Convention on Human Rights.[9] The Court has also recognised that

> a democratic society based on the rule of law may call for institutions like [an internal security service] which, in order to be effective, must operate in secret and be afforded the necessary protection. In this way a State may protect itself against the activities of individuals and groups attempting to undermine the basic values of a democratic society.[10]

1. See Council of Europe Convention for the Protection of Individuals with Regard to Automatic Processing of Personal Data [ETS 108]; Report on the third evaluation of Recommendation R(87)15 regulating the use of personal data in the police sector, 2002; Report on the second evaluation of the relevance of Recommendation R(87)15 regulating the use of personal data in the police sector, 1998; Report on the Impact of Data Protection Principles on Judicial Data in the framework of Judicial Co-operation in Criminal Matters; Report containing guiding principles for the protection of individuals with respect to the collection and processing of data by means of video surveillance (2003). All the above reports have been published on the Council of Europe website.

2. P. Tak, *Heimelijke opsporing in de europese unie*, Intersential, 2000.

3. See Jean Pradel, *De l'enquête pénale proactive: suggestions pour un statut légal*, Dalloz, 1998, p. 57ff.

4. See J.-P. Brodeur, "La police: mythes et réalités", in *La police après 1984*, Montreal, p. 21.

5. Pradel, op. cit., p. 57.

6. The following comments are largely inspired by the work of the International Association for Penal Law in Guadalajara in October 1997. The framework for pro-active investigations was examined in depth. See RID pén., 1998.

7. ECHR, 24 April 1990, Kruslin and Huvig cases, Series A, Nos. 176A and B.

8. Fox, Campbell and Hartley, 30 August 1990; the Court considered that terrorist crime fell into a special category which forced the police to act quickly to exploit information in order to lessen the risk of suffering and loss of life.

9. Rotaru v. Romania, 4 May 2000, Series A, 2000-V, 59; a secret surveillance system designed to protect national security runs the risk of undermining, or even destroying, the democracy it is designed to defend.

10. ECHR, 9 February 1995, Vereniging Weekblad Bluff, Series A, No. 306.

Chapter 3
Special investigation techniques:
controlling their implementation

The defining characteristic of the measures at issue is their secrecy. The more secret an activity, the more difficult it is to control. In some cases, particularly infiltration, secrecy is inherent in the operation for security reasons.

Since they infringe individual rights, special investigation techniques have to be subject to control. Under the lawfulness principle, the nature of that control is also a matter for the law under the principle of legality. Such control may be exercised through prior authorisation, supervision during the investigation or *ex post facto* control.

It is difficult to make a judgment as to the appropriateness of the type of control since the European Court of Human Rights does not appear to have made any pronouncement on the question. It is, however, clear that the trial judge will exercise *ex post* control, but there is a danger that such control will result in some evidence being inadmissible or in the prosecution itself being inadmissible. In view of the principles of proportionality and subsidiarity, which should govern the use of special investigation techniques, the Committee considers that the most effective control would be a system of prior authorisation, although it is not always appropriate to establish such a control.

Whatever type of control (in the broad sense of the term) is adopted in advance, these types of control may or even must be complementary, depending on the degree of intrusiveness in the private sphere occasioned by the special investigation techniques. For example, in undercover operations, there may be control at the beginning, during and at the end of the operation. At the beginning, the launching of the operation is subject to there being sufficient reasons or suspicions; during the operation, regular reports will be made and, lastly, a precise description of the conduct of the operation will enable *ex post facto* control designed to resolve problems of provocation.

Generally speaking, authorisation and control of the use of special investigation techniques (in particular supervision and *ex post* control) should be the responsibility of a body independent of the individuals implementing the measures or carrying out the operations.

The type of control may differ according to whether prevention or punishment of a crime is concerned. However, in view of the guiding principles on the subject, the utmost caution and care is required in matters of crime prevention in order to avoid any kind of provocation on the part of the police.

Either *ex post* judicial control or independent *ex post facto* control of some other kind must be available to persons who have been the subject of special investigation techniques. This derives from application of Article 13 of the European Convention on Human Rights, which requires that everyone whose rights and freedoms are violated shall have an effective remedy before a national authority. In the Rotaru judgment[1] the Court set out what should be understood by the term "authority", stating that it may not necessarily in all instances have to be a judicial authority in the strict sense.

Alleged cross-border effects of the application of special investigation techniques could give rise to the question of which national authority is competent. Article 13 ECHR stipulates that there must be a remedy if there are such effects. The authority of the country where the decision to use the special investigation techniques has been taken would appear in a better position to investigate a complaint from abroad than the authorities of the country where the special investigation techniques have their effects. This implies that countries should give access to complaints from abroad on a non-discriminatory basis compared to complaints from their own citizens or residents on their territory.

---

1. Rotaru v. Romania, 4 May 2000, Series A, 2000-V, 59; with respect to secret surveillance, the Court considered that objective supervisory machinery may be sufficient as long as the measures remain secret. It is only once the measures have been divulged that legal remedies must become available to the individual.

Chapter 4
Special investigation techniques and respect of human rights

In a number of landmark cases, the European Court of Human Rights has underlined the need to combat terrorism. It has endorsed anti-terrorism measures by considering that

> Democratic societies nowadays find themselves threatened by highly sophisticated forms of espionage and by terrorism, with the result that the State must be able, in order effectively to counter such threats, to undertake the secret surveillance of subversive elements operating within its jurisdiction. The Court has therefore to accept that the existence of some legislation granting powers of secret surveillance over the mail, post and telecommunications is, under exceptional conditions, necessary in a democratic society in the interests of national security and/or for the prevention of disorder or crime.[1]

The Court has further considered that

> it is not for the Court to substitute for the assessment of the national authorities its own assessment of what might be the best policy in the field of investigation of terrorist crime .... A certain margin of appreciation in deciding what measures to take both in general and in particular cases should be left to the national authorities.[2]

Reading these two judgments, it may be inferred that the Court absolutely does not condemn the need to fight against terrorism, in that it allows states to use the most appropriate measures, even where they involve interference in fundamental rights and freedoms.

Nonetheless, it does not give states *carte blanche*. Thus it has ruled that

> [the Court] must, with due regard to the circumstances of each case and a state's margin of appreciation, ascertain whether a fair balance has been struck between the individual's fundamental right to freedom of expression and a democratic society's legitimate right to protect itself against the activities of terrorist organisations.[3]

Of interest here is a decision of the European Commission on Human Rights on the application of Article 17 of the Convention in which it stressed that

> the Convention recognises the principle that no group or person has the right to pursue activities which aim at the destruction of any of the rights and freedom enshrined in it.[4]

Here, the Commission was endorsing, under the prohibition of abuse enshrined in Article 17, the prohibition on broadcasting programmes containing statements made by persons connected with terrorist organisations.[5]

25

In a broader context, reference should also be made to the fundamental, inviolable right to life enshrined in Article 2 of the Convention, according to which the state has

> a primary duty ... to secure the right to life by putting in place effective criminal-law provisions to deter the commission of offences against the person, backed up by law-enforcement machinery for the prevention, suppression and punishment of breaches of such provisions.[6]

According to the Court, even the use of lethal force may be justified in the framework of anti-terrorist operations where it is based on an honest conviction deemed, for good reasons, to be valid at the time of the events.[7]

It may not, however, be inferred from the Court's express recognition of the necessity of the fight against terrorism that fundamental rights and freedoms may be jeopardised. In a number of judgments the Court,

> having taken notice of the growth of terrorism in modern society, has already recognised the need, inherent in the Convention system, for a proper balance between the defence of the institutions of democracy in the common interest and the protection of individual rights.[8]

Based on these judgments, the *Guidelines on human rights and the fight against terrorism* have identified limits on the interference with fundamental freedoms that measures to combat terrorism entail.[9]
The use of special investigation techniques in relation to terrorism therefore presupposes respect for the rights guaranteed by the European Convention on Human Rights.

Special investigation techniques should comply with the guiding principles of lawfulness, exceptional circumstances (a principle which includes the sub-principles of proportionality, subsidiarity and specificity) and they should be subject to a regime of independent control. The principle of specificity is to be regarded in a flexible way, allowing for further determination by domestic legislation. These guiding principles should be understood in tandem with the *Guidelines on human rights and the fight against terrorism*, particularly Guidelines III, VI, IX and XV. It is obvious that the interference in the exercise of fundamental rights inherent in the use of special investigation techniques is acceptable only if they are used in pursuit of a legitimate aim.

What are the principles to be observed when using special investigation techniques? In fact, the principles of lawfulness and proportionality should be observed wherever there may be interference in the rights enshrined in Article 8, regardless of the methods used. A balance has to be found between respect for individual rights and the need to safeguard the higher collective interest.

It is more appropriate to speak in terms of reconciling the effectiveness of measures on the one hand and respect for human rights on the other. Indeed, the objective of the European Convention on Human Rights is not to disarm the authorities responsible for prevention or prosecution in criminal matters. The Convention sets out criteria in order that the authorities' activities should constantly be guided by the rule of law and the pursuit of the democratic ideal.

The first criterion to be observed concerns the legal framework in which investigations should take place. Investigative means require a legal basis. According to ECHR case-law, the existence of a specific standard seems to be preferable to the simple enumeration of prohibited techniques. Not only must there be a legal basis in domestic law, but such legislation must be accessible to the person concerned and its effects foreseeable. In this connection, a legal provision is foreseeable where it is worded sufficiently precisely to enable an individual to adapt his or her behaviour accordingly,[10] without that implying that a person should be capable of foreseeing when the authorities will monitor telephone conversations.

The second criterion is reflected in the subsidiarity and proportionality principles: the investigation must be necessary and the result difficult to achieve by other means that interfere less with individual rights and freedoms. The criterion of proportionality is an element of the concept of necessity. Even where it is lawful and used in pursuit of a legitimate end, interference in protected rights can be justified only if it is necessary to safeguard a democratic society. The test of necessity requires that interference should be proportionate to the legitimate end pursued.[11]

The third and last criterion consists in distinguishing between the means implemented during the preliminary investigation and their use before the trial courts. The criteria of a fair criminal trial are more demanding than those for the preparatory investigation.[12] The duty to reconcile the effectiveness of investigations and respect for human rights will be assessed differently according to whether it is the private lives of individuals that are to be protected (Article 8 of the European Convention on Human Rights) or whether it is the right to a fair hearing that is to be ensured (Article 6).

In relation to special investigation techniques, an analytical interpretation of the Court's case-law is therefore required, according to which article is being applied.

Reconciliation with the respect to private life provided for in Article 8 of the European Convention on Human Rights (Guidelines III and VI)

A number of investigation methods and techniques may interfere with the rights guaranteed by Article 8. Indeed, any form of surveillance of an individual – in whatever place and by whatever means – constitutes interference in his or her right to respect for his or her private life.[13]

However, the Court has been called upon to examine only a limited number of situations. In view of the changing interpretation of the Convention, there is nothing to prevent the principles identified being applied *mutatis mutandis* to other specific cases.[14]

Telephone tapping

The Court has clearly laid down the principle that telephone tapping must comply with the law, considering that, where it does not, it is prohibited, regardless of whether it is for judicial purposes or for reasons of national security.[15] Lawful tapping must be provided for, in legislation which is accessible and whose consequences are foreseeable. At the very least, the law must set out the categories of persons whose telephones may be tapped, the nature of the offences justifying the use of tapping, the duration of the measure, the procedure for drawing up the summary reports containing intercepted conversations, the precautions to be taken in order to communicate the recordings intact and in their entirety for possible inspection by the judge and the defence, and the circumstances in which they are to be erased or destroyed (in particular following discharge or acquittal of the accused).[16]

It should be added that the Court has not ruled out "as a matter of principle and in the abstract that unlawfully obtained evidence of the present kind [a recorded telephone conversation] may be admissible" on the grounds that the Convention does not regulate the rules of evidence as such. The question arises only in relation to the concept of a fair hearing.[17]

Telephone tapping for the purposes of national security is lawful if it is not done for exploratory or general prevention purposes. This means that there must be suspicion of offences and contacts with probable offenders by the person concerned. The use of tapping for national security purposes appears to be compatible with Article 8 on condition that adequate guarantees in respect of (i) both the decision-making and implementing authorities and (ii) control by independent bodies with at least power to express an opinion, are provided for in law.[18]

These principles are applicable by analogy to recordings made in public places by directional microphones and in private places by installation of bugging devices or a microphone carried by an infiltrated officer.

Without appropriate safeguards, these techniques may be incompatible with Article 8. This could lead to arbitrary use which is in contradiction with Guideline II which prohibits any form of arbitrariness.[19]

Searches

These are governed by the protection afforded by Article 8 since they conflict with the right to respect for the home, considered as a place of habitation or work premises.[20] According to the scope of the measures and the guarantees provided by law, there can be a violation of the Convention in allowing a non-judicial authority alone to decide on such operations.[21]

In some circumstances, the Convention requires a judicial authority to decide on the appropriateness, number, duration and scope of search operations and for searches to be carried out within the limits of a warrant issued by a judge. In other circumstances, the Court has accepted as lawful a purely administrative search in view of the strict legal framework in which it took place and the proportionate scope of the action.[22]

Interception of mail

The Court has accepted the need for legislative provisions granting powers for the covert surveillance of correspondence and other items sent through the post as part of the fight against terrorism,[23] as long as appropriate and sufficient safeguards against abuse are provided. The Court's appreciation will depend upon the nature, extent and duration of any measures, the reasons required for ordering them, the authorities competent to authorise them, carry them out and review them, and the type of remedy provided for in domestic law.[24] Further protection is granted with respect to correspondence with a lawyer since this type of interference affects the rights of the defence.[25]

Electronic correspondence has introduced a new situation: if the investigation of criminal offences and the defence of public order are legitimate reasons for interference, a clearly defined legal framework is required. The particularity of such interference is that there is a violation of the secrecy of correspondence (information), the secrecy of communications (telephone lines) and the home (entering the hard disk of a computer installed in a home).

Photographing and filming

The Court has accepted the legitimacy of such techniques in the very particular context of the fight against terrorism and during questioning by the security forces.[26] It stressed that this context influenced its assessment of the fair balance between the rights of the individual and the needs of society.

However, it is clear that there must be a legal framework whose application is foreseeable, a legitimate aim and necessity. The use of visual recording is limited in some cases; for example, the Schengen Convention allows its use for cross-border observation of persons while committing an offence.

One must admit that we are in an evolving context that demands the outmost prudence; if it has been considered that the filming of a person in a public place with a camera that does not record visual data is not to be considered as interfering with the right to privacy,[27] the Court considered that, in a public place, there might be an interactive zone between individuals that falls within the scope of the right to privacy.[28]

Recording personal data

It may be necessary to record personal data in the course of a criminal investigation[29] or an investigation involving national security.[30] In the latter case, the secret nature of the surveillance requires that there be a strict legal framework: the nature of the data recorded, the authorities to which it is made available, the circumstances in which it is transmitted, and supervision by independent administrative or parliamentary authorities.

In the context of a criminal investigation, it is generally considered that the recording of identity-related data does not constitute disproportionate interference given the aims of preventing crimes or maintaining public order. The work of the Council of Europe through the Project Group on Data Protection (CJ-PD) should be taken into account.[31]

The use of informants and infiltrated officers

The Court has accepted that the needs of police action may require the use of informants without that being in violation of Article 8.[32] Under Article 8, the police do not have a duty to reveal the identity of persons who provide them with information, but using the testimony of such sources as evidence before the trial judge may nonetheless create problems in upholding the right to a fair hearing.

As for the use of infiltrated officers, the Court has considered that it does not present problems with regard to private life.[33] Neither observation by an officer nor his or her acts (telephone calls, pseudo-purchases or front store operations) is problematic. It even appears that there is no need to examine whether the infiltration was lawful and necessary. The Court has confirmed its case-law in respect of Article 6 of the European Convention on Human Rights, considering that an infiltrated officer who passively observes criminal activities is not infringing the offenders' rights.[34]

Reconciliation with the right to a fair hearing guaranteed by Article 6 of the European Convention on Human Rights

The principles connected with the right to a fair hearing, confirmed in Guideline IX, doubtless leave states with less margin of appreciation in terms of interference. The fairness of a criminal hearing is subject to more restrictive rules than is the preparatory investigation.[35] The purpose of special investigation techniques is to gather information and/or evidence that an offence has been committed or will be committed. While Article 6 does not govern the admissibility of evidence (a subject which is a matter for domestic law), the Convention authorities are required to establish whether or not the procedure as a whole, and therefore including how the prosecution and the defence evidence was presented, was fair.[36]

Provocation to commit an offence

While the Court accepts the use of infiltrated officers whose role is not entirely passive,[37] it condemns provocation to commit offences.[38] There is provocation where the behaviour of the authorities has been decisive in the commission of an offence. The Court also considers that a conviction based substantially on the testimony of *agents provocateurs* violates the right to a fair hearing.

In the particular circumstances of the Lüdi and Teixeira de Castro cases, the Court considers supervised operations and controlled operations are compatible with the rights of the accused, as long as those operations are conducted within a judicial investigation and the identity and role of the infiltrated officer are known to the judge. Conversely, action taken without judicial supervision would be unfair and taint the procedure from the outset. Therefore, there is no provocation where the criminal intention is latent and predates police enticement: there is no deception such as to undermine the offender's will.[39]

The right not to incriminate oneself

The Court has recognised the right of the accused not to incriminate him- or herself, not to be convicted for remaining silent, and for statements extracted under duress not to be used against him or her.[40] The right not to incriminate oneself may present problems with respect to special investigation techniques.[41]

Lack of cross-examination and the use of anonymous witnesses

The Court has often stated that the Convention does not prohibit the use of anonymous informants during a preliminary investigation, but that the use of information thus obtained at the trial presents a problem with respect to fairness.[42] The Court takes as its starting-point the principle that evidence must be presented at the trial and debated in the presence of both parties; this does not, however, prohibit the use at the trial of statements made during the investigation, provided that those who made them have been cross-examined by the defence prior to the trial. It is in this context that the use of anonymous testimony by witnesses who do not appear at the trial for security reasons and whose identity remains unknown to the defence, and sometimes even to the trial judge, has to be examined.

The admissibility of such anonymous testimony depends on the circumstances and three principles that emerge from the case-law: Is anonymity justified by a compelling reason? Have the resulting limitations on the effective exercise of the rights of the defence been adequately compensated for? Was the conviction exclusively or substantially based on such anonymous testimony?

The Court accepts that the anonymity of ordinary private citizens who are witnesses in a criminal case should be safeguarded where this is necessary to protect them and their families from reprisals by the accused.[43] The possibility of putting written questions to anonymous witnesses is not enough to offset the obstacles to the defence thus caused: the judge must be assured of their reliability and take their testimony in the presence of the accused's lawyer, who must have had the opportunity to question them.[44] The conviction must also have been based on other evidence, debated in the presence of both parties, from persons unconnected with the anonymous witnesses who confirm their statements.

The Court accepts anonymous testimony by police officers, either to ensure their personal safety and that of their families[45] or (with respect to an infiltrated officer) so that he or she may be used again.[46] It is particularly demanding in respect of the need to demonstrate the necessity of such a measure, considering the operational needs of the police not to be sufficient justification in themselves for limiting the rights of the defence. If the need for anonymity has been proven, the Court takes the view that the police officer must appear before the trial court, if necessary in disguise or made up in such a way as not to be recognised by the accused. Judge and defence must also be able to satisfy themselves as to the credibility of the testimony. The conviction must not be exclusively or even substantially based on the testimony of anonymous infiltrated police officers.[47]

Is it also necessary that all the evidence should be divulged to the defence? The Court has accepted that "there may be competing interests, such as national security or the need to protect witnesses at risk of reprisals or keep secret police methods of investigation of crime, which must be weighed against the rights of the accused". The Court considers as permissible only such measures restricting the rights of the defence as are strictly necessary.[48]

Reconciliation with the right guaranteed by Article 13 of the European Convention on Human Rights

One of the principles underlying the Convention – the rule of law – requires that interference by the authorities in an individual's rights is subject to effective control.[49] The principle relating to the right to an effective remedy must be upheld. Effective domestic remedies must be available through the courts, or independent administrative authorities or an ombudsman.[50]

The Court has, however, developed the concept of the arguable grievance and in each individual case it has to be assessed whether or not each alleged violation leading to a grievance under Article 13 is arguable. Only where there is an arguable grievance does an effective remedy have to be made available.[51] Wherever special investigation techniques constitute interference in guaranteed rights, they must be subject to effective control by bodies independent of the persons who implement them.

1. ECHR, 6 September 1978, Klass and Others v. Federal Republic of Germany, Series A 28.
2. ECHR, 28 October 1994, Margaret Murray and Others v. United Kingdom.
3. ECHR, 25 November 1997, Zana v. Turkey, 1997-VII.
4. E. Comm. HR, D 15404/89, Purcell and Others v. Ireland, DR 70, p. 262, particularly p. 295.
5. For a recent application of Article 17, see also ECHR, 13 February 2003, Refah Partisi and Others v. Turkey, §99.
6. ECHR, 28 March 2000, Cemil Kiliç v. Turkey, 2000-III, §62; for interference in order to protect the rights and freedoms of others, see ECHR, 29 April 1999, Chassagnou and Others v. France, 1999-III, §113.
7. ECHR, 27 September 1995, McCann and Others v. United Kingdom, Series A-324, 200; the Court went further, considering honest reasons to be an acceptable justification even where they later prove unfounded. The Court considers that an unrealistic burden may not be imposed on the state and its law enforcement personnel, perhaps to the detriment of their lives and those of others.
8. ECHR, 29 November 1988, Brogan and Others v. United Kingdom, 145-B; ECHR, 30 August 1990 Fox, Campbell and Hartley judgment, Series A, No. 182.
9. *Guidelines on Human Rights and the Fight against Terrorism*, adopted by the Committee of Ministers on 11 July 2002 at the 804th session of the Ministers' Deputies.
10. For a recent application of the principle of lawfulness, see ECHR, 16 February 2000, Amann v. Switzerland, 2000-II, §50; on the question of foreseeability, see ECHR, 4 June 2002, Oliveira v. the Netherlands, Application 33129.96.
11. On the criterion of proportionality, see ECHR, 27 June 2002, Butler v. United Kingdom; Application 41661/98. On the criterion of necessity, see in particular ECHR, 22 October 1981, Dudgeon v. United Kingdom, Series A- 45, §53; ECHR, 7 December 1976, Handyside v. United Kingdom, Series A-24, §48; ECHR, 16 December 1997, Cammerzind v. Switzerland, 1997-VIII; §44.
12. ECHR, 20 November 1989, Kostovski v. the Netherlands, Series A-166.
13. Hewitt and Harman v. United Kingdom, report of 9 May 1989 and Resolution DH (90) 36.
14. For the changing interpretation of the Convention, which has to be interpreted in the light of present-day conditions, see ECHR, 14 November 2000, Annoni di Gussola v. France, 2000-XI, §56.
15. ECHR, 27 November 1993, A. v. France, Series 277-B.
16. ECHR, 24 April 1990, Huvig and Kruslin v. France, Series 176-A; see also ECHR, 19 March 2002, Greuter v. the Netherlands, Application 40045/98 for an application of the proportionality test; see ECHR, 18 February 2003, Prado Bugalo v. Spain
17. ECHR, 12 July 1988, Schenk v. Switzerland, Series A-140; ECHR, 25 March 1999, Pélissier and Sassi v. France, 1999-II. It is for the national courts to decide on the admissibility of evidence. The French Court of cassation found that the recording of a private telephone conversation, carried out and kept without the person concerned knowing it, is an unfair process that makes inadmissible any evidence so obtained, see Ph. Bonfils, *Loyauté de la preuve au process équitable*, Dalloz, 2005, p. 122.
18. Klass and Others v. Germany, op. cit.
19. See *Guidelines on Human Rights and the Fight against Terrorism*, op. cit.
20. ECHR, 16 December 1992, Niemietz v. Germany, 251-B.
21. ECHR, 27 February 1993, Funke, Crémieux and Miailhe v. France, 256-A.
22. Camenzind v. Switzerland, op. cit.
23. Klass and Others v. Germany, op. cit.
24. ECHR, 26 March 1987, Leander v. Sweden, Series A-116; ECHR, 2 August 1984, Malone v. United Kingdom, Series A-82; on the foreseeability of the law authorising interference, see the Kahn judgment; on the condition of compliance with the law, ECHR, 25 June 1987, see Halford v. United Kingdom, 1997-III.
25. ECHR, 28 June 1988, Schonnenberger and Durmaz v. Switzerland, Series A-137, and ECHR, 25 June 1997, Halford v. United Kingdom, Series A-233, on the condition of lawfulness.
26. ECHR, 28 October 1994, Margaret Murray and Others v. United Kingdom, 300-A.
27. European Commission of Human Rights, 14 January 1998, Herbecq and Others v. Belgium, application Nos. 32200/96andt 32201/96.
28. ECHR, 17 July 2003, Perry v. United Kingdom.
29. Margaret Murray and Others v. United Kingdom, op. cit.

30. Leander v. Sweden, op. cit.; see also, ECHR, 16 February 2000, Amann v. Switzerland where the Court found that the gathering of personal data by a secret service agency interfered with the right to privacy, even though such data were not gathered through the use of SIT.

31. For the CJ-PD's work, see note 19.

32. Fox, Campbell and Hartley v. United Kingdom, op. cit; for a case where an informant used a video camera and a recorder, see ECHR, 5 November 2002, Allan v. United Kingdom.

33. ECHR, 15 June 1992, Lüdi v. Switzerland, Series A-238; see also commentary in RUDH, 1992, 497.

34. ECHR, 9 June 1998, Teixeira de Castro v. Portugal, 1998-IV.

35. Kostovski v. the Netherlands, op. cit.

36. See for instance, ECHR, 13 November 2003, Rachdad v. France; ECHR, 6 May 2003, Perna v. Italy; ECHR, 6 April 2004, Shannon v. United Kingdom; ECHR, 7 September 2004, Eurofinacom v. France.

37. Lüdi v. Switzerland, op. cit.

38. Teixeira de Castro v. Portugal, op. cit.; see also ECHR, 7 September 2004, Eurofinacom v. France; ECHR, 6 May 2003, Seoueira v. Portugal.

39. One may also wonder whether Article 5, paragraph 1, constitutes an independent basis for prohibiting provocation. By inciting citizens to commit offences, the state is indirectly infringing their freedom since it may have to use coercive measures against them.

40. Funke v. France, op. cit; and ECHR, 17 December 1996, Saunders v. United Kingdom, 1996-VI.

41. ECHR, 8 February 1996, John Murray v. United Kingdom, 1996-I; ECHR, 5 November 2002, Alan v. United Kingdom, 2002-IX.

42. Kostovski v. the Netherlands, op. cit.

43. Kostovski v. the Netherlands, op. cit.; ECHR, 23 April 1997, Van Mechelen v. the Netherlands, 1997-III; ECHR, 26 March 1996, Doorson v. the Netherlands, 1996-II; ECHR, 27 September 1990, Windisch v. Austria, Series A-186.

44. Kostovski v. the Netherlands; and Doorson v. the Netherlands, op. cit.

45. Van Mechelen v. the Netherlands, op. cit.

46. Lüdi v. Switzerland, op. cit.

47. Teixeira de Castro v. Portugal, op. cit.

48. ECHR, 16 February 2000, Fitt v. United Kingdom, 2000-II; see also ECHR, 22 July 2003, Edwards and Lewis v. United Kingdom; ECHR, 24 June 2003, Dowsett v. United Kingdom.

49. ECHR, 24 October 1983, Silver and Others v. United Kingdom, Series A-61.

50. See aforementioned Camenzind and Rotaru judgments.

51. Rotaru v. Romania, op. cit.

Chapter 5
Special investigation techniques in the framework of international co-operation

Democratic states and European states, particularly through the Council of Europe, rapidly realised the need to form an alliance against terrorism and to increase co-operation.[1]

Improvements in the fight against serious crimes led rapidly to the inclusion of special investigation techniques in various international instruments directly or indirectly dealing with international judicial co-operation. This has increasingly been the case in the Council of Europe, the starting-point being the Convention on Laundering, Search, Seizure and Confiscation of the Proceeds from Crime of 8 November 1990, which resulted in the Second Additional Protocol to the European Convention on Mutual Assistance in Criminal Matters of 8 November 2001.[2] Articles 17, 18 and 19 of the latter deal with the use of special investigation techniques, even if – at the time when the protocol was adopted (8 November 2001) – terrorism was not expressly included among offences that would allow cross-border observation to be used. Article 20 deals with joint investigation teams. These new powers need to be tested as soon as possible in order to demonstrate their value.

The importance attached to the protection of judicial data in the Second Additional Protocol should also be emphasised:[3] the data transmitted may be used only for the purpose of proceedings to which the 1959 Convention or any of its Protocols apply, for other judicial and administrative proceedings directly related to those proceedings, and for preventing an immediate and serious threat to public security.[4] If the country to which the data are transferred has not an adequate protection scheme, additional safeguards may be requested. This is a further expression of the principle of specificity, which limits use to specific, precise legitimate ends.

Judicial co-operation has been stepped up in the European Union, though it should be remembered that the European instruments developed in this forum are applicable only in the territory of the European Union.

Thanks to the Convention on Mutual Assistance in Criminal Matters of 29 May 2000, the formation of joint investigation teams, the introduction of the European Arrest Warrant and the setting-up of Eurojust, a complete overhaul of judicial co-operation has been undertaken.

The EU Convention on Mutual Assistance[5] seeks to remedy the main problems involved in mutual assistance in criminal matters. It lays down the principle that requests for assistance should be addressed directly by one judicial authority to another, without going through central government departments. It enables requests for assistance to be made in accordance with the formalities and procedures specified by the requesting state. It also provides a framework for controlled deliveries and joint investigation teams composed of police officers or officers of other services from several states.

These provisions were confirmed in a Council Framework Decision of 13 June 2002 specifically on joint investigation teams.[6] The convention of 29 May 2000 also establishes a legislative framework for investigations conducted by officers acting under covert or false identity (covert investigations) and for the interception of telecommunications relating to criminal matters.

Furthermore, the convention contains rules for the protection of personal data transmitted by one country to another prohibiting data gathered during an investigation from being used for other than judicial purposes.

The European Arrest Warrant was introduced in a Council Framework Decision of 13 June 2002[7] and is an innovation of the utmost importance. It seeks to transform the political act of extradition into an essentially judicial act. The warrant will enable wanted persons to be transferred directly from one judicial authority to another, with due regard for fundamental rights and freedoms.[8] The framework decision will completely change the nature of judicial co-operation in criminal matters, from conventional co-operation into the direct execution of a judicial decision throughout the European Union in the spirit of mutual recognition of court decisions.

The traditional principle, that the facts must constitute an offence in both the countries concerned, will be abandoned: the individual must be handed over even if the facts do not constitute an offence under the law of the state applied to, as long as that offence appears on the list of 32 offences for which an individual may be handed over, and which are subject to a three-year prison sentence in the applicant state. Terrorism appears on the list and harmonisation of the offence is, furthermore, the subject of a framework decision.[9]

Like Europol, the role of Eurojust is to act as an operational co-operation unit and is composed of prosecuting authorities responsible for co-ordination among national authorities and assisting investigations into organised crime, including terrorism. This European body may ask national judicial authorities to take specific measures, including the use of special investigation techniques, and to assist in the setting-up of joint investigation teams.[10]

Special investigation techniques are taking on greater importance in the process of overhauling international co-operation in criminal matters. However, this can only take place if fundamental rights and freedoms are respected and therefore must be carried out with reference to the guiding principles set out in the previous chapter. Legality, necessity and specificity remain the criteria legitimising the use of such techniques.

There may be international co-operation in criminal matters either at the investigation or the prosecution stage, in particular through conventional extradition or under the future European Arrest Warrant, and it may be worth examining the consequences of using special investigation techniques.

With respect to mutual legal assistance, two situations as regards the use of special investigation techniques can be seen from the replies to the questionnaire:
- If the law of the state to which the application has been submitted allows the use of all or some of those measures, it will provide judicial assistance in accordance with its law.
- If the law of the state to which the application has been submitted does not allow the use of all or some of those measures, judicial assistance will not be forthcoming.

Both situations are such as to present obstacles to satisfactory international judicial co-operation.

In the first case, the applicant state may provide assistance in accordance with the measures allowed by its domestic law. This means that what it is possible to request has to be known in advance, that proceedings will be more cumbersome and may even lead to prejudicial delays.

It then has to be asked whether it is still essential for the request for assistance to be carried out in compliance with the law of the applicant state. The EU Convention of 29 May 2000 allows a request to be executed in accordance with the procedural rules of the applicant state. The second additional protocol to the 1959 Convention provides the same possibility, in article 8, in accordance with certain formalities or procedures pursuant to the legislation of the requesting state.

In the second case, it is clear that refusal of assistance can only be prejudicial to the effectiveness of the fight against terrorism.

With respect to extradition, the effect of the use of special measures is less direct. Depending on the techniques used to gather the evidence on which a request for extradition can be based, the lawfulness of the extradition procedure might be challenged on the basis either of Article 5 of the European Convention on Human Rights (on the grounds of arbitrary or unlawful arrest) or Article 6 (lack of a fair hearing).

> When several persons work together to achieve the same goal over a sustained period of time, the idea that inspires them shapes their minds, and their individual consciences are interpreted in accordance with a common perception. Contact of those consciences with each other gradually creates a certain moral similarity and very soon they observe certain traditions and rules.[11]

However, the reality of international co-operation is very different: one expert of the Council of Europe considered that the mechanisms of mutual police and judicial assistance in criminal matters for the establishment of the common legal framework have not proved as efficient and expeditious as hoped, and have not made it possible to take the vigorous measures against the most dangerous international criminal organisations.[12]

For instance, the states from which assistance is requested may have little interest in the investigations where unilateral assistance is sought; in other cases the states may cling on to sovereignty in the administration of criminal justice.

By setting up common general principles on the use of SIT, the future recommendation of the Council of Europe will certainly be useful for the improvement of international mutual judicial assistance.

---

1. See Studia diplomatica, *Réaction collective des Etats européens contre le terrorisme*, 1988.

2. See Council of Europe texts on the work of the PC-TI (2003) 4, 26 March 2003. In addition to the two instruments cited, reference should be made to the Criminal Law Convention on Corruption of 27 January 1999, the Convention on Cybercrime of 23 November 2001 and Committee of Ministers Recommendation Rec(2001)11 concerning guiding principles on the fight against organised crime.

3. See Article 26 of the Second Additional Protocol.

4. The Committee has underlined that the transfer of police data is regulated in another manner; see the third evaluation of Recommandation(87)15 on data protection and the police and the Agreements between Europol and The United States.

5. EU OJ, No. C 197, 12 July 2000, p. 1.

6. EU OJ, No. L 162, 20 June 2002, p. 1.

7. EU OJ, 12 July 2002, No. L 190, p. 1.

8. The Charter of Fundamental Rights adopted at the European Council meeting in Nice in December 2000 notwithstanding, the Warrant falls within the scope of Article 5 of the European Convention on Human Rights.

9. Framework Decision dated 13 June 2002, EU OJ of 22 June 2002, No. L 164, p. 3.

10. Framework Decision dated 28 February 2002, EU OJ No. L 63, 6 March 2002, p. 1.

11. C. de Visscher, *Théories et réalités en droit international public*, Pédone, 1970, p. 257.

12. See PC-OC (2004) 2 of 16 February 2004, opinion by Mr Stefano Dambruso, a prosecutor in Milan.

Chapter 6
Intelligence services and the use of special investigation techniques

Some reflection on this subject could not be avoided because more and more often powers to include secret intelligence services into the judicial investigations are invoked.[1]

Following the attacks in Madrid in 2003, the Council of Europe expressed its intention to step up the fight against all forms of terrorism. On that occasion, the Council of Europe emphasised the importance of efficient co-operation in intelligence matters and a better evaluation of the threat and invited member states to promote efficient and systematic co-operation between the police and intelligence services.

The integration of the intelligence services into Europol or into common investigation teams is an interesting option, but such a choice will cause legal difficulties linked to the fundamental distinction between "law enforcement" and "intelligence".[2]

An interesting description of the possible confusion is provided by Mr Brodeur, of the Montreal School of Criminology, who states that

> the convergence of security intelligence and criminal intelligence ... is problematic and ... the interlinking of networks will not be achieved without difficulty, if it is ever achieved at all. ... The purpose of criminal intelligence is to arrest criminals and bring them before a court for trial. Owing to the public nature of the proceedings and to the cross-examination of witnesses, there is always a risk of confidential information being disclosed. It is for that reason that the security intelligence services are extremely reluctant to share their information with the police. The purpose of security intelligence is to prevent violence before it can be carried out, by various means. Recourse to the courts is one among a number of options and, in truth, a last resort.[3]

The WEU Assembly has stated that the gathering of intelligence will invariably run up against ethical issues and that there are therefore ethical limits to the kind of means that can be used to gather intelligence. It is an issue of democracy, requiring parliamentary control and perfect knowledge on the part of the services concerned of the relevant law and statute.[4] Admiral Lacoste, former Director of the French DGSE, said that

> at a time when democratic principles and human rights are increasingly recognised as universal values, citizens of all countries tend to require that their governments display transparency in conducting public affairs. Many are reluctant to accept that politicians and administrations can invoke 'Secret of State' to conceal certain information from their fellow citizens. Beyond the sensational aspects or arguments relating to individual cases, it is certainly a crucial subject, since it is eminently political, in the noble sense of the word. It is a debate involving society to which no one should be indifferent.[5]

Will that ethical limit to the gathering of intelligence be consistent with the principle of fairness in the admissibility of evidence, which is an element of a fair trial? The question must be asked, since the use of special investigation techniques for other purposes, such as the protection of national security, may also be problematic with regard to respect for human rights and, more particularly, the requirements of Article 8 of the ECHR.[6]

It is not only democratic control that is essential, but also respect for the fundamental principles of the European Convention on Human Rights. Thus, in relation to personal data that are needed in a criminal investigation[7] or in a security investigation,[8] it is necessary to reconcile the principles of Article 8 ECHR and the fight against terrorism. It will be necessary to ensure that the legal framework for the activities of the intelligence services is such that co-operation between the judicial services, the police and the intelligence services fully respects the provisions of Article 6 ECHR that guarantees the right to a fair trial without impeding the lawful action of the security services.

The work of the Council of Europe can certainly sustain discussions that are taking place at the European Union level where, in the framework of evaluation of national anti-terrorist measures, intelligence services were recommended to make use of special investigation techniques.[9]

---

1. On 13 and 14 January 2005 in Luxembourg, in the framework of the transatlantic dialogue, experts from the European Union and the United States launched a reflection on the proposal to use, before the courts for terrorist trials, information obtained in a secret manner.
2. See T. Coosemans, " Promouvoir l'Europe du renseignement: nécessité et perspectives", *Common Market and the European Union Review*, April 2004, p. 241.
3. See J.-P. Brodeur, *Les services des renseignement et les attentats de septembre 2001*, International Centre for Comparative Criminlogy, University of Montreal (available (in French) at www.unites.uqam.co); see also G. Treverton, *Reshaping Intelligence to Share with 'Ourselves'*, Commentary No. 82, publication of the Canadian Security Intelligence Service, 16 July 2003 (available at www.csis-scrs.gc.ca)
4. See WEU Assembly, *The new challenges facing European intelligence – reply to the annual report of the Council*, report submitted on behalf of the Defence Committee by Mr Lemoine, document A/1775, 4 June 2002.
5. Report of the symposium "Secret d'Etat ou transparence?", 20 January 1999 – Standing Committee for the supervision of the intelligence services, Activities Report 1999, Belgium.
6. See Euro Court HR, the Rotaru judgment of 4 May 2000, Reports 2000-V, 59: a system of secret surveillance designed to protect national security entails the risk of undermining or even destroying democracy on the ground of defending it.
7. See Euro Court HR, the Margaret Murray judgment, ECHR, 28 October 1994, Margaret Murray and Others v. United Kingdom, 300-A.
8. See Euro Court HR, the Leander v. Sweden judgment of 26 March 1997, Series A No. 116.
9. See Recommendation No. 4 on the interim report on the evaluation of national anti-terrorist measures of 23 November 2004, http://www.eu.int/politique/luttecontreleterrorism.

Conclusion

As early as 1990, Antonio Cassese said that "terrorism has a profoundly negative impact on the international community, in the sense that it upsets the rules of the game established by sovereign States".[1] In the face of terrorism, two possible options emerge: using the force or using the law.

It must be noted that the member states of the Council of Europe chose at the outset the option of the law, thus taking the view that "bringing terrorists before a judge is the worst punishment". Their decision to give preference to the rule of law in the fight against terrorism was no doubt made easier by the fact that the European Court of Human Rights has on numerous occasions, on the one hand, stated that member states must fight terrorism and, on the other hand, defined the democratic limits on the means to be employed in this fight.

Even if the use of SIT appears to be a means to safeguard the rule of law, it remains essential that these techniques are integrated into a legislative framework that fulfils the requirements of the European Convention on Human Rights.

The Council of Europe constitutes an appropriate forum to develop and supervise the means that are necessary and proportionate to fight against the most serious forms of crime, including acts of terrorism, and to continue its precursor role in the fight against crime and terrorism.

---

1. See A. Cassese, *Violence et droit dans un monde divisé*, P.U.F., Coll. Perspectives internationales, 1990, p. 115.

Part II
Situation in member and Observer states
of the Council of Europe

Questionnaire

1. Please indicate the SITs used in your country, the respective legal framework governing their use and their legal definition, if any.

2. When and under which circumstances (e.g. criminal investigation, preliminary stage, etc.) can SITs be used?

3. Are there any specific features governing the use of SITs in relation to acts of terrorism? If so, please specify.

4. How does the legal framework governing the use of SITs guarantee respect for human rights and individual freedoms, the principles of subsidiarity and proportionality? Is the authorisation to use SITs subject to time-imits? Which bodies and procedures are in place to supervise compliance with human rights standards and with the abovementioned principles in the use of SITs? Is supervision automatic/systematic?

5. Which institutions are involved in the use of SITs and what is their role (e.g. law enforcement agencies, prosecutor's office, judicial authorities, etc.)? Which institutions can order and/or authorise the use of SITs? How does co-operation between these institutions work in practice?

6. Are there any specialised counter-terrorism institutions? What is their role in the use of SITs?

7. Which measures have been adopted in order to facilitate international co-operation (e.g. joint investigation teams)? Can the SITs listed in reply to question 1 be used in cross-border settings?

8. What use can be made of SIT in the context of mutual legal assistance?

9. How can the use of SITs be improved? Please provide any comments/proposals concerning the implementation of the terms of reference of the PC-TI and in particular the use and regulation of SITs.

Armenia

1. Please indicate the SITs used in your country, the respective legal framework governing their use and their legal definition, if any.

Special investigative techniques used in the Republic of Armenia include the following:

Supervision of correspondence, mail, telegraph and other communication, tapping telephone conversations, search, seizure and confidential information of informants.

Supervision of correspondence, mail, telegraph and other communication, tapping telephone conversations, search, seizure, as special investigative techniques (means) may be executed only by court order, according to the articles 18, 20, 21 of the Constitution of the Republic of Armenia and provisions of the Criminal procedure code, in particular its Articles 14, 57 paragraph 4, 225-241, 279, 281 and 284.

2. When and under which circumstances (e.g. criminal investigation, preliminary stage, etc.) can SITs be used?

Special investigative techniques may be exercised only in the cases specified by the legislation of the Republic of Armenia as well as during investigations related to the fight against terrorism and preventive measures.

3. Are there any specific features governing the use of SITs in relation to acts of terrorism? If so, please specify.

There are no particular features concerning the implementation of special investigative techniques with regard to the acts of terrorism, in the Republic of Armenia.

4. How does the legal framework governing the use of SITs guarantee respect for human rights and individual freedoms, the principles of subsidiarity and proportionality? Is the authorisation to use SITs subject to time-limits? Which bodies and procedures are in place to supervise compliance with human rights standards and with the above-mentioned principles in the use of SITs? Is supervision automatic/systematic?

Article 14 of the Criminal procedure code specifies that supervision of correspondence, mail, telegraph and other communication, and tapping telephone conversations, is implemented only by court decision during criminal procedure.

However, Article 284 provides that in a case where the delay in the implementation of the operative-search measures could lead to a terrorist act or to threats to national security, military or environmental threats, based on the decision of the head of the operative-search body it is allowed to carry out such measures within 48 hours, notifying the court of that, and submitting documents envisaged in part 3 of this article. In a case where the court finds that the grounds for the implementation of the operative-search measures are insufficient, the implementation is immediately terminated, and the materials and data obtained as a result are liable to prompt elimination. Otherwise, the court rules to authorise the implementation of operative-search measures, as envisaged in this article.

When using special investigative techniques, fundamental human rights and freedoms are guaranteed and protected by the Constitution of the Republic of Armenia. In particular, Article 18 of the constitution lays down that "everyone is entitled to freedom and the right to be secure in their person. No one may be arrested or searched except as prescribed by law. A person may be detained only by court order and in accordance with legally prescribed procedures".

Paragraph 3 of Article 20 of the constitution determines that "Everyone has the right to confidentiality in his or her correspondence, telephone conversations, mail, telegraph and other communications, which may only be restricted by court order". Article 21 states that "It is prohibited to enter a person's dwelling against his or her own will except under cases prescribed by law. A dwelling may be searched only by court order and in accordance with legal procedures".

5. Which institutions are involved in the use of SITs and what is their role (e.g. law enforcement agencies, prosecutor's office, judicial authorities, etc.)? Which institutions can order and/or authorise the use of SITs? How does co-operation between these institutions work in practice?

The office of public prosecutor, the courts and law enforcement bodies are the institutions in the Republic of Armenia concerned in using special investigative techniques. A permit for the use of special investigative techniques is issued by a court, in compliance with reasoned grounds presented by the investigator.

6. Are there any specialised counter-terrorism institutions? What is their role in the use of SITs?

The specialised unit for fighting terrorism is the appropriate department within the National Security Service of the Republic of Armenia, which is entitled to implement special investigative techniques in conformity with the legislation of the Republic of Armenia.

7. Which measures have been adopted in order to facilitate international co-operation (e.g. joint investigation teams)? Can the SITs listed in reply to question 1 be used in cross-border settings?

The National Security Service of the Republic of Armenia according to respective international treaties, for facilitating international co-operation with corresponding foreign partner intelligence services, can carry out the exchange of information and the criminal search of offenders.

Special investigative techniques in the context of transfrontier co-operation cannot be carried out in the Republic of Armenia.

8.   What use can be made of SITs in the context of mutual legal assistance?

Special investigative techniques in the scope of mutual assistance in judicial matters may be used for establishing an evidentiary database on the committed crimes.

9.   How can the use of SITs be improved? Please provide any comments/proposals concerning the implementation of the terms of reference of the PC-TI and in particular the use and regulation of SITs.

Currently, draft laws on the operative-search activity and on combating terrorism are under consideration by the National Assembly of the Republic of Armenia. The passage of the abovementioned laws will make more effective the implementation of special investigative techniques in the Republic of Armenia.

Appendix

Articles of the Criminal Procedure Code of the Republic of Armenia
relating to the response to the questionnaire

Article 14 – Confidentiality of correspondence, telephone conversations, mail, telegraph and other communications

1. Everyone has the right to confidentiality of correspondence, telephone conversations, mail, telegraph and other communications. No one can be unlawfully deprived of the said right or limited in that right in the course of criminal proceedings.

2. Imposition of arrest on postal and telegraph correspondence, its examination, wire-tapping and interception of conversations over the telephone or other means of communication, may be ordered in the course of criminal proceedings only upon a decision of the court and in the manner prescribed by law.

Article 56 – Bodies of inquiry

The following are the bodies of inquiry:

1. the police;

2. the commanders of military units, the heads of military institutions, regarding cases of military crimes, and also deeds committed on the territory of military units or incriminated to conscripts;

3. the bodies of state fire control: regarding cases on fires;

4. the state tax bodies: regarding tax crimes;

5. the customs bodies: regarding cases on smuggling;

6. national security bodies: regarding cases within their competence.

Article 57 – Powers of the body of inquiry

1. The head of the body of inquiry personally, and also with the assistance of the officer of the body of inquiry, ensures the exercise of the powers of the body of inquiry.

2. The body of inquiry executes the following:

a. undertakes the necessary operative-investigatory and criminal procedure measures for detection of the crime and the persons who committed it, or for prevention and suppression of the crime;

b. prior to institution of the criminal case, implements examination of the crime site based on prepared materials, and appoints expert inquiry;

c. Institutes a criminal case, undertakes the proceeding of the case or sends it by subordination, or rejects the institution of the criminal case, as envisaged in this Code, with the copy of the decision to institute or reject the case being forwarded to the prosecutor within 24 hours;

d. Immediately informs the prosecutor or the investigator about the crime discovered and the inquest initiated;

e. After having instituted the criminal case, in order to to discover the criminal and traces of the crime, implements urgent actions, examination, searches, monitoring of correspondence, mail, telegrams, etc., wire-tapping, seizures, investigation, arrest of the suspect and interrogation, questioning of the injured and witness(es) with cross-examination, and appoints expert inquiry;

f. Within 10 days after the start of the criminal case, and if the criminal is found and impleads, the case is forwarded to the investigator;

g. The instructions of the prosecutor are carried out based on the cases under consideration by the investigator;

h. Registers statements made about committed crimes;

i. Brings to the investigation the persons suspected in the crime, examines and searches them, and sets free the persons detained without sufficient grounds;

j. Allows the prosecutor to inspect the activities of the inquest body;

k. Provides the prosecutor and the investigator, within their authority, with necessary information demanded by them;

l. Takes measures to compensate the damages inflicted by the crime;

m. Interviews the witnesses in the case, familiarises themself with the circumstances of the case, and documents and cases that may contain information on the incident and persons related to it;

n. Demands information on the incident and persons related to it;

o. Demands to conduct checks, inventarisations and the like;

p. Suspends the proceedings of the criminal case, and forwards a copy of the decision to the prosecution within 24 hours;

q. Organises the implementation of the legitimate instructions of the court; and

r. Carries out other actions which are authorised by this Code.

3. Only the head of the body of inquiry can use the authorities of the body of inquest, institute the criminal case, reject institution of the criminal case, suspend the criminal case proceedings, arrest the suspect, or apply means of securing the presence of the suspect, to eliminate or change these means, to apply to the court with a motion to implement operative-investigatory measures.

4. The head of the body of inquest is entitled to instruct the officer of the inquest body to conduct inquest of the case, to give him mandatory written instruction for implementation of certain investigatory actions, to transfer the case from one officer to another, to instruct several officers to investigate the case, to participate in the inquest, and to conduct the inquest personally.

5. The instructions of the prosecutor on the criminal cases, given pursuant to the rules established by this Code, are obligatory for the head of the body of inquiry.

6. The body of inquest implements other authorities envisaged in this law.

Chapter 31 – Search and seizure

Article 225 – Grounds for conducting search

The investigator, having sufficient ground to suspect that in some premises or in some other place or in possession of some person, there are instruments of crime, articles and valuables acquired in a criminal way, as well as other items or documents, which may be significant for the case, conducts a search in order to find and take the latter.

The search can also be conducted to find searched-for persons and corpses. The search is conducted only by a court decree.

Article 226 – Grounds for seizure

When it is necessary to take articles and documents significant for the case, and provided it is known for certain where they are and in whose possession, the investigator conducts seizure.

The seizure of documents that contain state secrets is conducted only by permission of the prosecutor and with the agreement of the administration of the given institution.

No enterprise, institution or organisation, no official or citizen has the right to refuse to give the investigator the articles, documents or their copies that he or she demands.

Article 227 – Persons present at search and seizure

Search and seizure is done in the presence of attesting witnesses.

When necessary, an interpreter and an expert take part in the search and seizure.

When performing search and seizure, one must provide for the presence of the person or the full-age members of his family where the search or seizure is conducted. If their presence is impossible, a representative of the apartment maintenance office or local administration is invited.

Search and seizure at premises owned by enterprises, institution, organisations and military units is done in the presence of their representative.

The persons whose premises are searched and whose items are seized, as well as the attesting witnesses, experts, interpreters, representatives and lawyers, are entitled to be present during all actions of the investigator, and make statements which must be recorded in the protocol.

Article 228 – Procedure of search and seizure

Based on a search or seizure warrant, the investigator is entitled to enter apartments or other buildings.

Prior to the search or seizure the investigator must familiarise the searched person, or the one from whom property is seized, with the warrant, for which a signature is taken from the latter.

When conducting a search, the investigator or the expert can use technical devices about which a record is made in the search protocol.

The investigator is obliged to take measures not to publicise the fact of the search and seizure, as well as their results and the facts of the private life of the searched person.

The investigator is entitled to prohibit persons present at the search or seizure site from leaving the site, as well as to prohibit communication between them until the investigatory actions are over.

When conducting a seizure, after presenting and announcing the warrant, the investigator proposes to hand over the articles and documents subject to seizure of the person's own accord; in case of refusal, compulsory seizure is done. If the searched-for articles are not discovered at the place indicated in the warrant, by discretion of the investigator and by court decree, a search can be conducted.

When conducting a search, after presenting and announcing the decree, the investigator proposes to hand over the articles and documents or the hiding person subject to seizure. If the latter are handed over of the person's own accord, this is recorded in the protocol. If the searched-for items and documents are not handed over or are handed over partially, or the hidden person does not surrender, a search is conducted.

All taken items and documents are presented to the participants of investigatory actions, are described in detail in the protocol and, when necessary, are sealed with the investigator's seal.

When conducting a search and seizure, the investigator is entitled to open closed premises and warehouses, if their owner refuses to open the latter of his or her own accord. The investigator must avoid fdamaging locks, doors and other objects without need.

Article 229 – Personal search

When conducting searches in the premises, in case of sufficient grounds, the investigator is entitled to conduct personal search and take items and documents possessed by the person at whose premises the investigatory actions are conducted, found in his or her personal effects, clothes or on the body, which can have evidentiary value.

Personal search can be conducted without warrant in the following cases:
1.   when arresting the suspect, and bringing him to the police or other law enforcement institution;
2.   when using arrest as a measure to secure the appearance of the suspect or the accused;
3.   when there are sufficient grounds to suspect that the person, in the given premises where the search is made, may conceal documents or other items which have evidentiary value for the case.

Personal search can be conducted by the investigator, with the expert and attesting witness, provided they are of the same sex as the searched person.

Article 230 – Search and seizure protocol

When the search and seizure are over, the investigator writes an appropriate protocol, which must indicate the place where investigatory actions were conducted, the time, the considerations, whether the searched-for items and persons were surrendered of the person's own accord, the name, surname and position of the person who conducted the search, the names, surnames and addresses of attesting witnesses, and the surnames, position and legal status of other participants in the search.

All the seized articles must be indicated in the protocol of investigatory activities, mentioning their quantity, size, weight, individual features and other peculiarities.

If attempts were made to eliminate or hide the articles or documents found during investigatory actions, this fact is indicated in the protocol.

The investigator is obliged to familiarise all participants of investigatory actions with the protocol and they are entitled to demand that their comments be incorporated in the protocol.

Article 231 – The mandatory presentation of the copy of the search and seizure protocol

The copy of the search and seizure protocol with a signature is presented to the person in whose premises the investigatory actions had been conducted, or to the full-age members of his or her family, and in case of their absence to a representative of the apartment maintenance office in whose area the investigatory actions were conducted.

If the search or seizure were done in the territory of an enterprise, institution, organisation or military unit, the copy of the protocol is presented to their representatives.

Chapter 32 – Arrest of property

Article 232 – Arrest of property

Arrest of property is used as a remedy to secure property in a civil claim and to prevent possible seizure and for coverage of court expenses.

Arrest of property is imposed on the property of the suspect and the accused as well as those persons whose actions can cause financial responsibility, regardless who possesses what property.

The arrest of property commonly shared by spouses or the family is imposed on the part owned by the accused. In case of sufficient evidence that the commonly shared property increased or was acquired in a criminal way, the arrest can be imposed on the whole property of the spouses or the family or on a larger part of it.

Seizure cannot be imposed on a property that according to law can not be seized.

Article 233 – Grounds for arrest of property

Arrest of property can be applied by bodies conducting criminal proceedings only where the materials collected for the case provide sufficient ground to believe that the suspect, the accused or another person who has the property, may hide, spoil or consume the property liable to seizure.

Arrest of property is carried out based on the decree of the investigating body, the investigator or the prosecutor.

The decision on the seizure of property must indicate the property subject to seizure, the value of the property on which it is intended to impose arrest being based on what is sufficient to secure the civil claim and court expenses.

When necessary, if there is ground to suspect that the property will not be surrendered for seizure of the person's own accord, the prosecutor appeals to the court for search permission, as established in this Code.

Article 234 – Valuation of the property to be arrested

The value of property to be arrested is determined at market prices.

The value of the property that is arrested as provision for civil claim or court expenses initiated by the prosecutor or civil plaintiff must be adequate to the amount of the claim.

When determining the portion of property to be arrested from a number of accused or persons responsible for the actions of the latter, the degree of participation in the crime is taken into account; however, to provide for a civil claim, the property of one of the relevant persons can be seized in full amount.

Article 235 – Procedure of implementation of the decree for property arrest

The investigation body, the investigator or the prosecutor hands over the property arrest decree to the property owner or manager and demands the submission of property. When the demand is rejected, an enforced seizure is done.

After the end of the preliminary investigation, by court ruling, the marshal of the court implements the arrest of property.

When imposing property arrest, when possible, an expert in the commodity is involved who determines its approximate value.

The owner or manager of the property is entitled to decide which articles or valuable items should be seized first to provide for the amount indicated in the property arrest decree.

The investigating body, the investigator or the prosecutor writes a protocol on property arrest and the court marshal compiles other documents envisaged in law. The protocol (document) enumerates the whole seized property, accurately indicating the name, quantity, means, weight, degree of wear and tear, other individual features and when possible the value; it indicates what property was seized and what property was left for keeping; the seized property is described, together with the statements of persons who were present about ownership by other people.

The copy of the appropriate protocol (document) with a signature is handed over to the owner or manager of the seized property, and in case of their absence, to the full-age members of their family, to the apartment maintenance office or local self-government representative. When seizing the property of an enterprise, institution or organisation, the copy of the appropriate protocol (document) with signature is given to the administration representative.

Article 236 – The preservation of seized property

Except real estate and large-sized items, seized property as a rule is taken away.

Precious metals and stones, diamonds, foreign currency, cheques, securities and lottery tickets are handed for safe keeping to the Treasury of the Republic of Armenia, cash is paid to the deposit account of the court that has jurisdiction over this case, other taken items are sealed and kept at the body which made a decision to seize the property or are given for safe keeping to the apartment maintenance office or local self-government representative.

The arrested property that has not been taken away is sealed and kept with the owner or manager of the property or the full-age members of his or her family, who are advised as to their legal responsibility for spoiling or alienation of this property, for which they undersign.

Article 237 – Appeals against arrest of property

The property seizure decree can be appealed against to the prosecutor; however, the submitted complaint does not prevent the execution of the decision.

Article 238 – Release of property from seizure by criminal proceedings

The property is released from seizure by criminal proceedings ruling if, as a result of recalling of the civil action, the qualification of the criminal act incriminated to the suspect or the accused has changed, and the necessity to seize property has disappeared.

By petition of the civil plaintiff or other interested party, who wish to claim the property through civil proceedings, the court is also entitled to preserve the imposed property seizure after the end of criminal proceedings, within a month.

Chapter 33 – Monitoring of correspondence, mail, telegrams and other communications

Article 239 – Monitoring of correspondence, mail, telegrams and other communications

When there are sufficient grounds to believe that there is evidentiary value in the mail or other correspondence, mail, telegrams and other communications (referred to below as correspondence) sent by the suspect or by the accused, or to them by other persons, the investigator can make a grounded decision to impose monitoring on the correspondence of these people.

The decision must indicate the name of the post office responsible for withholding the correspondence, the name(s) and surname(s) of the person(s) whose correspondence will be withheld, the exact address of these persons, the type of correspondence to be monitored and the period of monitoring.

The correspondence that can be arrested, in particular, concerns the following items: letters, telegrams, radiograms, parcels (printed matter), cases, post containers, transmissions, fax and e-mail messages.

A decision on the monitoring of correspondence is sent to the appropriate post office director, for whom it is mandatory.

The director of the post office withholds the correspondence indicated in the decision of the investigator and advises the latter about that.

The monitoring of correspondence is lifted by the investigator, prosecutor or court which took the decision.

Article 240 – Examination and seizure of correspondence

The investigator familiarises the director of the post office, and when necessary, other employees of the given office, with the seizure decree and its signature, and, with the participation of selected attested witnesses from the employees of the office, opens up and examines the correspondence.

When revealing documents and items that may be significant for the case, the investigator seizes the appropriate articles or confines themself to copying them. In case of absence of any data that may be significant for the case, the investigator gives instructions to hand the examined correspondence to the addressee or to withhold it within the established period.

A protocol is written about each case of examination or withholding, which indicates: by whom, where, when and exactly what correspondence was withheld or examined, why it was withheld, what should be handed over to the addressee or temporarily withheld, what correspondence was copied, what technical means were used and what was revealed in the given case. All persons who participated in the investigatory actions must be familiarised with the protocol, which they confirm with their signatures and, when necessary, are entitled to incorporate their comments into the protocol.

Article 241 – Supervision of conversation

If there are sufficient grounds to suspect that the telephone conversations of the suspect or the accused, or their conversations conducted by other means of communication, may contain significant information for the case, the court makes a decision to permit the supervision and recording of these conversations.

The investigator makes a grounded decision on initiating an application to the court, which indicates the criminal case and grounds on which the appropriate investigatory actions must be taken, the surnames and names of the persons whose conversations are subject to supervision, the supervision period, and the institution instructed to conduct the technical implementation of supervision and recording. The decree is forwarded to the court.

In case of approval by the judge, the conversation supervision and recording decision is forwarded by the investigator to the appropriate institution for implementation.

Conversation supervision and recording can be limited to no longer than six months. They are lifted when the necessity for them is over, but in any case no later than the end of the preliminary investigation.

The investigator is entitled to demand the record at any time for examination and listening within the established period. The record is handed to the investigator in the sealed form with an accompanying letter, which must indicate the time of beginning and end of the record of conversations, and any necessary technical description of devices used.

Examination of and listening to records by the investigator is done in the presence of attesting witnesses, and when necessary, experts, about which a protocol is written, which must reproduce verbatim the part of the conversation concerning the case. The record is attached to the protocol, and the irrelevant part of it is eliminated after the court verdict becomes *res judicata* or after suspension of the case.

Article 279 – Investigatory actions conducted by court decree

The court decrees the implementation of apartment search, as well as investigatory actions concerning the restriction of privacy of correspondence, telephone conversations, telegram and other communications.

Article 281 – Implementation of operative and search actions by court decree

Operative and search actions concerned with restricting the confidentiality of correspondence, telephone conversations, mail, telegrams and other communications are implemented by court decree.

Based on court decree, operative and search actions mentioned in the law on "Operative and search actions" are conducted.

Article 284 – Discussion procedure of appeals against operative-searching measures

Operative-searching activities concerned with the restriction of the individual's right to confidentiality of correspondence, telephone conversations, mail, telegrams and other communications, except in cases where one of the interlocutors gave his or her consent to supervision, are carried out only with a court ruling.

The authorisation to conduct operative-search measures envisaged in this Code is granted by the court located in the same district as the body carrying out such measures or the one that requests such measures.

The ground for the authorisation of operative-searching measures envisaged in this Code is a decree of the body in charge of operative-searching actions containing a request to obtain authorisation for such activities. The decision indicates the grounds for operative-searching measures, the data which it is planned to obtain as a result of these measures, the venue and deadline of the measures, and all data substantiating the necessity of the operative-searching measures. The decision and attached materials are submitted to the court by the head of the body in charge of operative-search measures or by his or her deputy.

The judge considers the appeal sitting alone, in a closed-door court session with participation of the official who submitted the appeal, or his representative. The appeal must be considered and a ruling made within 12 hours after its receipt.

At the request of the judge, other materials grounding the need for the operative-searching measures are submitted to him, except in those cases where there is danger of breaching a state or official secret, or when this might expose the secret agents of the operative-searching body and persons who secretly collaborate with this body, certain sources of information and the methods of receiving the information. The judge can demand additional materials and explanations from officials to verify the sufficiency of the grounds for implementation of operative-searching measures.

Based on the results of the discussion of the issue, the court makes a decision to authorise or turn down the application, indicating the grounds for approval or dismissal. The relevant materials are returned by the court to the body in charge of operative-searching measures.

The period of validity of the court order is calculated from the day of its adoption and it can not exceed six months, unless otherwise envisaged in the ruling. The deadline for the implementation of operative-searching measures can be extended, based on an application contained in the decision of the head of the operative-search body, as established in this article.

In cases where delay in the implementation of the operative-search measures may lead to a terrorist act or to threats to national security, military or environmental threats, based on the decision of the head of the operative-search body it is allowed to carry out such measures within 48 hours, advising the court of that, submitting documents envisaged in part 3 of this article. In cases where the court finds that the grounds for the implementation of the operative-search measures are insufficient, the implementation is immediately terminated, and the materials and data obtained as a result are liable to prompt elimination. Otherwise, the court rules to authorise the implementation of operative-search measures, as envisaged in this article.

Austria

1. Please indicate the SITs used in your country, the respective legal framework governing their use and their legal definition, if any.

The following SITs are used in Austria:

Undercover operations (including covert investigations)

With regard to the prevention of criminal offences, covert investigations are defined as the collection of information without referring to the official character of, and the voluntary nature of participating in the investigation (Section 54 paragraph 3 of the Code of Police Practice). The use of covert investigations is permissible if otherwise the prevention (defence) of dangerous offences or criminal associations would be endangered or significantly hampered. For the purpose of the prevention of criminal associations, covert investigations are permissible only if the commission of criminal offences punishable by substantial penal sanctions is suspected. With regard to prosecution of criminal offences, neither a definition nor legal requirements for the use of undercover operations are embodied in current Austrian criminal procedure.

Informants

The conduct of covert investigations into serious crime by police informers was admitted by several decisions (e.g. in cases of drug trafficking) of the Austrian Supreme Court, if the prerequisites of a fair trial and hearing mentioned in the decision of the ECHR from 9 June 1998 in the case of Teixeira de Castro v. Portugal, App. No. 00025829/94, are fulfilled. Especially, there must be good reasons to suspect that the individual is a drug trafficker. Furthermore the police informers (as well as officers who lead covert investigations under covert or false identity) have to confine themselves to investigating the individual's criminal activity in an essentially passive manner, without exercising an influence such as to incite commission of an offence. The identity of such police informers is a subject of secrecy, if there are no circumstances that give reasons for suspicion that the police informer themself is involved in criminal activities.

Controlled deliveries are carried out. For the time being, the existing provisions of international law in combination with Sections 3 ff. of the Code of Police Co-operation (which provide for cross-border administrative assistance) are considered as sufficient legal basis (e.g. Article 73 of the Convention implementing the Schengen Agreement; Article 12 of the Convention on Mutual Assistance in Criminal Matters between the Member States of the European Union; Article 22 of the Convention on Mutual Assistance and Co-operation between Customs Administrations).

Observation (including cross-border observation)

Section 54 paragraph 2 of the Code of Police Practice defines "observation" as investigation of personal data by means of monitoring. According to this provision, observations can be carried out to prevent a criminal offence against life and limb, sexual freedom, liberty, property or environment, planned by a specific person, during its preparation. In addition to that, observations are permissible if otherwise the prevention (defence) of dangerous offences or criminal associations would be endangered or significantly hampered. With regard to criminal procedure (investigation and prosecution of already committed offences) observations are considered permissible, but have currently no specific legal basis, with the exception of a regulation of the competent court contained in Section 55 paragraph 1 of the Law on Extradition and Mutual Legal Assistance (and following Article 40 of the Schengen Agreement).

Electronic surveillance and bugging

Rules on requirements and execution regarding electronic surveillance (bugging and video recording) are contained in Sections 149d ff., Code of Criminal Procedure. It is defined as surveillance of non-public behaviour or non-public communications by technical (electronic) means without informing the person concerned.

According to these provisions a distinction has to be made between surveillance restricted to the non-public behaviour or the non-public communication, intended for a person informed of the surveillance (e.g. an undercover agent or a police informer equipped with bugging devices). In this case it is admissible to order such surveillance, if it seems to be necessary for the clearing up of an intentionally committed penal offence punishable by a prison sentence for a term exceeding three years.

Surveillance of non-public behaviour or non-public communications by technical (electronic) means without informing a person participating (e.g. the equipment of private rooms with bugging devices), however, is admissible only if it seems otherwise impossible to clear up an intentionally committed penal offence punishable by a prison sentence for a term exceeding ten years or the offences of a criminal organisation or terrorist association, and the person concerned is highly suspected to have committed the offence in person, or there are reasons to believe that a person highly suspected of the offence will establish a connection with him or her. Surveillance is only admissible if the proportionality for the purpose of the measure is observed. In this connection it shall be particularly taken into consideration that the success aimed at is justifiably proportionate to the presumed infringement upon the rights of third parties, and the possibility must be examined whether there could be also a reasonable chance of success by taking less intrusive measures.

The video surveillance of non-public behaviour only in order to clear up crimes is also admissible if objects or places outside homes are observed, or if the tenant expressly agrees to surveillance inside his or her home and this is necessary to clear up an intentionally committed penal offence punishable by a prison sentence for a term exceeding one year.

Interception of communications

Interception of a telecommunication is defined as tracing of the local area where a final device being characterised by a certain subscriber's line is situated or has been situated (Section 149a paragraph 1 no. 1 lit. a, Code of Criminal Procedure), tracing what subscribers' lines are or have been the origin or destination of a telecommunication (Section 149a paragraph 1 no. 1 lit. b, Code of Criminal Procedure) and the listening, interception, controlling, recording and any other monitoring of information being transmitted or received through telecommunication (Section 149a paragraph 1 no. 1 lit. c, Code of Criminal Procedure). Requirements and provisions for the execution of interception of telecommunications are contained in Sections 149a ff., Code of Criminal Procedure (a court warrant is required without exception, etc.). Interception of communication not transmitted by means of tele-communication is subject to the provisions on electronic surveillance and bugging or the rules regarding observation.

Searches

Searches of premises are defined in Section 139 of the Code of Criminal Procedure as the search of a residence or other rooms belonging to a house or comparable dwelling. A search of premises is permissible if there are reasonable grounds to assume that a person suspected of having committed a criminal offence is concealed therein or that evidence may be found therein. Precise instructions for the execution of searches of premises are given by Sections 140 ff., Code of Criminal Procedure.

Cross-border (hot) pursuits

Officers who are pursuing an individual apprehended in the act of committing one of the offences referred to in Article 41 Section 4 of the convention implementing the Schengen Agreement, or involved in one of those offences, are authorised to continue their pursuit on the territory of another state, where because of the particular urgency of the situation the authorities of that state cannot be informed about the pursuit or are unable to reach the scene in time to take over the pursuit. The pursuit has to cease as soon as the authority in whose territory the pursuit is taking place so requests.

Agents provocateurs and pseudo-purchases or other pseudo-offences

A pseudo-purchase is permissible if carried out in compliance with Section 25 of the Code of Criminal Procedure, which forbids inciting the perpetrator to commit, continue or finalise criminal offences. Thus, pseudo-purchases are limited to cases where the perpetrator is already determined to committing a criminal offence and is searching for a potential buyer. The Austrian Criminal Procedure does not explicitly define pseudo-purchases.

2. When and under which circumstances (e.g. criminal investigation, preliminary stage, etc.) can SITs be used?

Special investigation techniques that are subject to a court decision (electronic surveillance and bugging, interception of a telecommunication, searches of premises except in cases of danger in delay) can only be applied during a judicial investigation *(Voruntersuchung)* or during an investigation which is initiated by or conducted with the knowledge of the prosecutor and following a judicial decision requested by the prosecutor. Only in cases of "danger in delay" (requiring immediate action) may the police conduct searches without submitting the case to the prosecutor's office or to court.

3. Are there any specific features governing the use of SITs in relation to acts of terrorism? If so, please specify.

Generally no. But pursuant to Section 149d paragraph 1, Code of Criminal Procedure, electronic surveillance (bugging and video recording) of non-public behavior and non-public communication without knowledge of the person concerned is (among other cases) admissible in cases where the clearing up or the prevention of crimes in the frame of a terrorist association (Section 278b Austrian Criminal Code) would otherwise be endangered or significantly hampered and if there is a strong suspicion that the person concerned is a member of such an association or if there are good reasons to assume that the person concerned will establish a connection with the person highly suspected.

4. How does the legal framework governing the use of SITs guarantee respect for human rights and individual freedoms, the principles of subsidiarity and proportionality? Is the authorisation to use SITs subject to time-limits? Which bodies and procedures are in place to supervise compliance with human rights standards and with the above-mentioned principles in the use of SITs? Is supervision automatic/systematic?

Electronic surveillance (bugging and video recording) of non-public behavior and non-public communications without knowledge of the person concerned is admissible in cases of hostage-taking, but limited to the time and place of the offence. In other cases the surveillance is admissible subject to authorisation by a court.

The electronic surveillance and bugging can only be ordered for the time period presumed to be required to reach the targeted purpose, but not exceeding one month. The order has to contain the supposed beginning and ending of the SIT. It is admissible to prolong such an order if there are well-founded reasons to believe that a prolonged surveillance will be successful.

Upon termination of monitoring, the orders shall be served at once on the holder of the room monitored and of the distributor's line as well as the accused. But the service may be suspended as long as that could endanger the purpose of the investigation.

Rooms of defence counsels, lawyers, notaries, fiduciaries, psychiatrists, psychotherapists, psychologists, probation officers or mass media bodies may be surveyed only with special permission of an independent official charged with the protection of legality and proportionality *(Rechtsschutzbeauftragter)*. An "automatic supervision" of the execution of a SIT takes place in cases where the electronic surveillance is subject to authorisation by court. The official (the *Rechtsschutzbeauftragter*) has the right to appeal against judicial orders and to apply for the deletion of data, recordings and videotapes gained via the use of such SITs.

5. Which institutions are involved in the use of SITs and what is their role (e.g. law enforcement agencies, prosecutor's office, judicial authorities, etc.)? Which institutions can order and/or authorise the use of SITs? How does co-operation between these institutions work in practice?

The public prosecutors (upon request of the law enforcement agencies) can apply for the use of interception or electronic surveillance at the court. Generally, the Council Chamber, a chamber of three judges *(Ratskammer)*, has to authorise the use of the SIT; in cases of "danger in delay" the investigating judge *(Untersuchungsrichter)* is empowered to order the interception of communications (and electronic surveillance), but has to inform the Council Chamber immediately so they can reach their decision about the admissibility. After the termination of the conduct of the SIT, the police authorities have to report in detail about the measures taken, the place, the number of persons concerned and the reasons for success or failure of the SIT.

6. Are there any specialised counter-terrorism institutions? What is their role in the use of SITs?

There is a special department for the protection of the constitution and the countering of terrorism *(Bundesamt für Verfassungsschutz und Terrorismusbekämpfung)*, which is part of the general law enforcement agencies (Ministry of Internal Affairs).

7. Which measures have been adopted in order to facilitate international co-operation (e.g. joint investigation teams)? Can the SITs listed in reply to question 1 be used in cross-border settings?

There are no restrictions to the types and techniques of legal assistance in criminal matters under Austrian law. It is also the understanding that, despite the principle of reciprocity, the European Convention on Mutual Legal Assistance in Criminal Matters can be used as a basis for the application of SITs in the requested state based on the general provision of Article 1 of this convention. The same principle applies to the Austrian Extradition and Mutual Legal Assistance Act (*Auslieferungs- und Rechtshilfegesetz – ARHG*), but specific provisions concerning cross-border observation and interception of telecommunication traffic have been introduced in recent years.

The Austrian Police Co-operation Act (*Polizeikooperationsgesetz – PolKG*) provides a legal and flexible framework for police co-operation. Joint investigation teams can be established under the provisions of this Act to the extent permitted by any multinational or bilateral instrument of international law.

8. What use can be made of SIT in the context of mutual legal assistance?

Austria can apply SITs in the context of legal assistance to the extent that these SITs are also admissible in Austrian criminal proceedings. In cases where a SIT requires intrusive or coercive measures, a decision of the competent court of the requesting state is necessary. In the absence of such a decision, the requesting authority has to confirm that the requested SIT is admissible under the law of the requesting state and that this authority is empowered to conduct this SIT without any court decision.

The Austrian Extradition and Mutual Legal Assistance Act (*Auslieferungs- und Rechtshilfegesetz – ARHG*) already contains a few specific provisions with regard to SITs, especially where cross-border activities are requested.

9. How can the use of SITs be improved? Please provide any comments/proposals concerning the implementation of the terms of reference of the PC-TI and in particular the use and regulation of SITs.

The recommendations should contain certain common (minimum) standards regarding judicial decisions, the principles of subsidiarity, proportionality and the special protection of human rights (especially the rights of third parties and persons who are subject to professional secrecy).

Azerbaijan

1. Please indicate the SITs used in your country, the respective legal framework governing their use and their legal definition, if any.

According to Article 14, paragraph 4 of the Law of the Republic of Azerbaijan on "Operative-Investigation Activity", any information on the management, means and methods of operative-investigation activity, on the source of operative data or on the private life of persons, that is considered as a matter of state, military or official secrecy, shall not be declassified. Furthermore, in accordance with Article 4 of the Law of the Republic of Azerbaijan on "State Secrecy", information regarded as state secrecy includes information in the area of operative-investigation activity. Due to the aforementioned reasons, answering this question is not considered appropriate.

2. When and under which circumstances (e.g. criminal investigation, preliminary stage, etc.) can SITs be used?

Rules for the application of Special Technical Means (STM) are regulated by Article 10 of the Law of the Republic of Azerbaijan on "Operative-Investigation Activity" and by Article 445 of the Criminal Procedure Code of the Republic of Azerbaijan. Accordingly, STM applies both in the process of crime prevention and for the purpose of detecting a crime in the process of crime investigation.

3. Are there any specific features governing the use of SITs in relation to acts of terrorism? If so, please specify.

Legislation of the Republic of Azerbaijan does not provide for any specific features of STM related to terrorist acts.

4. How does the legal framework governing the use of SITs guarantee respect for human rights and individual freedoms, the principles of subsidiarity and proportionality? Is the authorisation to use SITs subject to time-limits? Which bodies and procedures are in place to supervise compliance with human rights standards and with the above-mentioned principles in the use of SITs? Is supervision automatic/systematic?

Article 8 of the Law of the Republic of Azerbaijan on "Operative-Investigation Activity" as well as Articles 12-36, 199 and 201 of the Criminal Procedure Code of the Republic of Azerbaijan provide for the protection of human rights and liberties stipulated in the Constitution of the Republic of Azerbaijan in the process of the application of STM. At the same time, according to the requirements of Article 259.2 of the Criminal Procedure Code of the Republic of Azerbaijan, the application of STM shall not last longer than six months. As a rule, the application of STM is carried out upon a court decision. Control over the application of STM in the process of operative-registration work or investigation is carried out by prosecutors and judicial authorities in a systematised way.

5. Which institutions are involved in the use of SITs and what is their role (e.g. law enforcement agencies, prosecutor's office, judicial authorities, etc.)? Which institutions can order and/or authorise the use of SITs? How does co-operation between these institutions work in practice?

Application of STM is carried out by investigation agencies conducting operative-investigation activity in accordance with the Law of the Republic of Azerbaijan on "Operative-Investigation Activity" and the Criminal Procedure Code of the Republic of Azerbaijan. In accordance with the relevant decree of the President of the Republic of Azerbaijan, operative activities dealing with terrorist crimes and the conduct of investigation of such cases are within the competence of the Ministry of Internal Affairs and the Ministry of National Security. Authorisation for the application of STM is given by a court decision based on the well-grounded request of an investigation agency and on the report of the prosecutor accepting that request and carrying out the procedural supervision of the preliminary investigation. An official from the requesting investigation agency or investigator, along with the prosecutor, defends the request as well as the report before the court. If the court agrees with their arguments, it makes the decision on the application of STM. Otherwise, if the court is not satisfied, it decides to reject their requests.

7. Which measures have been adopted in order to facilitate international co-operation (e.g. joint investigation teams)? Can the SITs listed in reply to question 1 be used in cross-border settings?

Azerbaijan Republic has joined some international conventions dealing with combating terrorism and the financing of terrorism. In this connection, by the Law of the Republic of Azerbaijan of 17 May 2002, relevant additions were made to the Law of the Republic of Azerbaijan on "Combating Terrorism", while the new Article 214-1 (the financing of terrorism) was added to the Criminal Code of the Republic of Azerbaijan. The application of STM may be carried out throughout Azerbaijan in accordance with the legislation of Azerbaijan Republic.

8. What use can be made of SIT in the context of mutual legal assistance?

Azerbaijan Republic has signed international agreements with some countries, including the CIS countries, the Republic of Bulgaria, the Islamic Republic of Iran and the Republic of Turkey. Furthermore, on 7 November 2001, Azerbaijan Republic joined the European Convention on Combating Terrorism 1977, and in December 2001 *Milli Mejlis* (the parliament) of the Republic of Azerbaijan ratified the European Convention on Mutual Assistance in Criminal Matters of 1959. Azerbaijan Republic is guided by the remedial legislation in the investigation and legal proceedings conducted within the territory of Azerbaijan Republic, including the fulfilment of requests dealing with the application of STM sent by countries with which Azerbaijan Republic has signed international agreements on mutual assistance in criminal matters.

Belgium

1. Please indicate the SITs used in your country, the respective legal framework governing their use and their legal definition, if any.

Act of 6 January 2003

The Belgian Act of 6 January 2003 on special investigation techniques and a number of other investigation techniques was published in the *Moniteur Belge* on 12 May 2003. Two royal enforcement decrees were published at the same time. The first concerns the rules of operation of national and local informant managers and contact officers; the second regulates police investigation techniques.

The distinction between "special investigation techniques" (SITs) and "police investigation techniques" (PITs) is important. The SITs regulated by the Act of 6 January 2003 are observation, infiltration and the use of informants. Police investigation techniques are techniques that may be applied in the framework of a SIT and are used in support of it. They are applied in the same legal framework as SITs and all the principles concerning proportionality and subsidiarity are applicable without exception or exemption.

The Act does not give any overall definition of the notion but simply lists the three investigation techniques and describes their objectives. The important point is that all the special investigation techniques used – observation, infiltration and the use of informants – must have the purpose of helping the judicial authorities or trial courts to rule in the framework of criminal procedure; they therefore pursue the same judicial purpose.

The Act nonetheless allows the police to apply SITs in order to gather and process data and information but, again, only for the purpose of investigating offences that have been or will be committed, to gather evidence and identify and prosecute the perpetrators. Where the police have obtained the approval of the judicial authorities to use a SIT, they must bear this judicial purpose in mind and act accordingly throughout the operation.

The use of SITs must take place in the framework of a police investigation or a preliminary judicial investigation. Since under Article 28bis, §2, of the Criminal Investigation Code, investigation includes pro-active investigation, SITs may also be used in the framework of a pro-active investigation.

The definition of the notion explicitly provides that the use of SITs should be supervised by the State Counsel's Department. Such supervision is necessary at all times, even if the techniques are applied in the framework of a judicial investigation. The law also stipulates that the public prosecutor must supervise SITs authorised by an investigating judge.

As indicated above, SITs are divided into three major categories: observation, infiltration and the use of informants, defined as follows.

Observation

Article 47sexies, §1 of the Criminal Investigation Code says:

> For the purposes of this Code, observation shall mean the systematic observation by a police officer of one or more persons, their presence or behaviour, or of specific things, places or events.

> For the purposes of this Code, systematic observation shall mean observation for more than five consecutive days or more than five non-consecutive days within a one-month period, observation entailing the use of technical means, observation of an international nature, or observation carried out by specialised units of the federal police.

> For the purposes of this Code, a technical means is a configuration of components that detects and transmits signals, activates their recording and records the signals, to the exclusion of technical means used to execute a measure under Article 90ter.

Infiltration

Article 47octies, §1 of the Criminal Investigation Code states:

> For the purposes of this Code, infiltration shall mean a police officer, known as an infiltrator, who, using a false identity, sustains a relationship with one or more persons who, there is serious reason to believe, has/have committed or will commit offences in the framework of a criminal organisation under Article 324bis of the Criminal Code or offences under Article 90ter, §§ 2 to 4.

> The infiltrator may in exceptional circumstances and with the express authorisation of the competent judge, use briefly, in the framework of a specific operation, the expertise of a person from outside the police if it proves absolutely indispensable to the success of his or her mission.

Use of informants

Article 47decies, §1 of the Criminal Investigation Code, says:

> For the purposes of this Code, the use of informants shall mean a police officer maintaining regular contact with a person, known as an informant, who is believed to have close contacts with one or more persons who, there is serious reason to believe, has/have committed or will commit offences, and who provides the police officer with information and data

concerning them, whether or not he or she has been requested to do so. This police officer is known as a contact officer.

Police Investigation Techniques

The royal decree on police investigation techniques of 9 April 2003 lists the techniques that may be used in the framework of infiltration. Where they are used, the legal framework is the same as for infiltration: all the principles applicable to infiltration (such as the principles of proportionality and subsidiarity, and the principle of fairness and legality) also apply in their entirety to the use of police investigation techniques. This is essential and no exception can be made. Police investigation techniques are never used outside the framework of SITs. Police investigation techniques are as follows.

Pseudo-purchase

This consists of introducing oneself or being introduced to an individual as a potential purchaser of one of the services or goods referred to in Article 42, 1 to 3, of the Criminal Code, whose ownership that individual wishes to transfer, either on his or her own account or on behalf of another person.

Trust-winning purchase

This consists of introducing oneself or being introduced to an individual as a potential purchaser of one of the services or goods referred to in Article 42, 1 to 3, of the Criminal Code, whose ownership that individual wishes to transfer, either on his or her own account or on behalf of another person, in which ownership is actually transferred in order to gain the vendor's trust or gather further information.

Test purchase

This consists of introducing oneself or being introduced to an individual as a potential purchaser of one of the services or goods referred to in Article 42, 1 to 3, of the Criminal Code, whose ownership that individual wishes to transfer, either on his or her own account or on behalf of another person, in which ownership is actually transferred in order to check the vendor's allegations and the authenticity of the goods offered.

Pseudo-sale

This consists of introducing oneself or being introduced to an individual as a potential vendor of a service or goods.

Trust-winning sale

This consists of introducing oneself or being introduced to an individual as a potential vendor of a service or goods, where ownership is actually transferred in order to gain the purchaser's trust or gather further information.

Controlled delivery

This means allowing the transportation, under constant police control, of an illegal consignment of goods or persons that is known to the police, that police officers transport and deliver themselves or for which they provide assistance, and where police intervention is deferred until the final destination in Belgium or abroad.

Assisted controlled delivery

This means allowing the transportation, under constant police control, of an illegal consignment of goods that is known to the police, that police officers transport and deliver themselves or for which they provide assistance, where there is no police intervention at the final destination. Assisted controlled delivery of persons is not permitted.

Front store

This technique allows the police to create or actually run one or more businesses, possibly using false identities, which supply goods and services to the criminal community.

The Act of 6 January 2003 also covers "other investigation techniques". These techniques include the interception and opening of mail, "discreet visual checks", bugging, deferred intervention, and gathering information on bank accounts and bank transactions. These investigation techniques are distinguished from SITs by the fact that no "confidential" file is opened: all the documents are included in the judicial file, which may be consulted by the parties to the case. They are not, therefore, "special" investigation techniques in the strict sense of the term. These techniques follow the ordinary procedural rules of the Criminal Investigation Code.

Definitions

Interception and opening of mail

This is covered by Articles 46ter and 88sexies of the Criminal Investigation Code:

> In connection with criminal investigations, the public prosecutor may intercept mail entrusted to a postal operator that is addressed to, has been sent by, or concerns a suspect, if there are reasonable grounds for believing an offence may result in at least one year's imprisonment.

> In the execution of the measure provided for in Article 46ter, only the investigating judge may open intercepted mail and read its contents.

76

Where someone is caught in the act, the public prosecutor also has this power.

Discreet visual checks

Article 89ter of the Criminal Investigation Code states:

The investigating judge may, by a written order giving reasons communicated to the public prosecutor, authorise the police to enter private property without the knowledge of the owner or his or her representatives or the occupier or without their consent if there is reason to be believe offences under Article 90ter, §§ 2 to 4, have been or may be committed by a criminal organisation as defined in Article 324bis of the Criminal Code and if the truth cannot be uncovered by other investigation techniques.

Bugging

See below, under Other investigation techniques: interception of communications.

Deferred intervention

Art 40bis of the Criminal Investigation Code says:

The public prosecutor may in the interests of the investigation authorise the police to defer the arrest of those presumed to have committed offences and the seizure of all the items referred to in Article 35.

Gathering information on bank accounts and banking transactions

Article 46quater of the Criminal Investigation Code states that:

When investigating offences, the public prosecutor may, if there is reason to believe that those offences may result in at least one year's imprisonment, request the following information:
a. a list of the bank accounts of whatever nature of which the suspect is the holder, representative or true beneficiary and, if necessary, all related information;
b. the transactions that have taken place during a particular period concerning one or more of these bank accounts, including information on all payer and payee accounts.

When the needs of the investigation so require, the public prosecutor may request that that for a renewable period of a maximum of two

77

months the transactions made in relation to one or more of the suspect's bank accounts are observed.

Other investigation techniques

Electronic surveillance

Electronic surveillance is a type of observation and is regulated by the provisions on observation in the Criminal Investigation Code.

Interception of communications

Belgian law does not consider the interception of communications (including telephone, fax, e-mail, mail, public and private networks) to be a SIT. Articles 90ter §1 ff of the Criminal Investigation Code treat bugging in the context of judicial investigations. Article 90ter §1 reads as follows:

> Where the needs of the preliminary investigation so require, the investigating judge may exceptionally bug, listen to and record private communications or telecommunications during their transmission if there is reason to believe that the fact referred to him or her is an offence under one of the provisions listed in §2 and if the truth cannot be uncovered by other investigation techniques.

> The measure may be ordered only with respect either to persons suspected, on the basis of precise evidence, of having committed an offence, or to means of communication or telecommunication regularly used by the suspect, or to premises presumed to be frequented by him or her. It may also be ordered with respect to persons presumed, on the basis of precise evidence, to be in regular communication with a suspect.

The Act of 6 January 2003 amended this article by inserting a paragraph on bugging, worded as follows:

> In order to make it possible to bug, listen to or record private communications or telecommunications with the aid of technical means, the investigating judge may also, without the knowledge or consent of the occupier, owner or his or her representatives, order entry into a home or private place.

The addition of this regulation to Articles 90ter ff of the Criminal Investigation Code now makes it possible to enter a home without the occupier's knowledge or consent in order to plant a microphone or to enter the home legally with a microphone concealed on one's person or clothes in order to record the discussions that take place there.

Searches

These can be of places or objects (such as computers or cars), by various means including scanning.

Searches of persons and cars

Articles 28 and 29 of the Act on the police of 5 August 1992 provide for searches of persons and cars in the performance of administrative and judicial police duties. These articles read as follows:

Article 28 §1. Police officers may, in the routine performance of their duties and in order to ensure that a person is not carrying a weapon or an object endangering public order, conduct a security search of the person in the following circumstances:

1. where the behaviour of a person subject to an identity check in the cases and circumstances provided for in Article 34 or material evidence or circumstances give the officer reasonable grounds for believing that he or she is carrying a weapon or an object endangering public order;

2. where a person is subject to administrative or judicial arrest;

3. where persons are taking part in public gatherings that are a real threat to public order;

4. where persons enter premises where public order is threatened.

A security search shall be carried out by patting the body and clothes of the person searched and by checking his or her bags. It may not last longer than the time needed to carry it out, and the person may not be detained for more than an hour for this purpose.

In the cases referred to in points 3 and 4, the search shall be conducted on the order and under the responsibility of an officer of the administrative police; it shall be conducted by a police officer of the same sex as the person searched.

§2. In the exercise of their judicial duties, police officers may conduct a judicial search of persons under judicial arrest as well as of persons who, there is reason to believe, are carrying evidence of an offence.

A judicial search may last no longer than the time needed to carry it out, and the person may not be detained longer than six hours for this purpose.

A judicial search shall be conducted in accordance with the instructions and under the responsibility of a senior police officer.

§3. Police officers may conduct a body search of persons before they are placed in a cell.

The purpose of this search is to ensure that the person is not in possession of objects or substances dangerous to him- or herself or to others, or of a nature to facilitate escape, and may last no longer than the time needed to carry it out. It shall be carried out by a police officer or another person of the same sex as the person searched, in accordance with the instructions and under the responsibility of an officer of the administrative or judicial police forces, as appropriate.

§4. (…)

Article 29. Police officers may search a vehicle or any other means of transport that is travelling or parked on a public highway or in a place accessible to the public, where the behaviour of the driver or passengers, material evidence or circumstances of time and place give reason to believe that the vehicle or means of transport has been, is being or may be used:
1. to commit an offence;
2. to harbour or transport persons who are wanted or who are trying to evade identity control;
3. to store or transport objects presenting a danger to public order or evidence of an offence.

The same shall apply if the driver refuses to allow the vehicle's compliance with the law to be checked.

A search of a vehicle may last no longer than the time required by the circumstances justifying it. The vehicle may not be detained for more than one hour for the purpose of a search conducted in the framework of administrative police duties.

The search of a vehicle permanently fitted out as housing and actually used as such at the time of the search shall be treated in the same way as a house search.

Search of premises

In connection with facts referred to him, an investigating judge may search any place or issue a search warrant giving reasons in which he or she delegates his or her power of search to a police officer. Where someone has been caught committing a crime the public prosecutor may at any time of the day or night, search the home of the accused (Article 36 of the Criminal Investigation Code). The law also authorises house searches at the request of the person who actually has the usufruct of the place or with his or her consent. Such a search may take place at any time.

The Act on computer crime of 28 November 2000 inserted new provisions in the Criminal Investigation Code *inter alia* on searches of computer systems.

Cross-border pursuit

Cross-border pursuit is not specifically regulated in Belgian law. However, Article 41 of the Schengen Agreement provides that officers who in their own country are pursuing a person seen committing an offence may continue the pursuit on the territory of another contracting party without prior authorisation.

Agents provocateurs

Police provocation is prohibited under Belgian law. Article 47ter of the Criminal Investigation Code, inserted by the Act of 6 January 2003, is worded as follows:

> In the framework of a special investigation technique, a police officer may not lead a suspect to commit offences other than those he or she intended to commit.
>
> In the event of contravention of the preceding paragraph, any case brought in relation to those facts shall be declared inadmissible.

2. When and under which circumstances (e.g. criminal investigation, preliminary stage, etc.) can SITs be used?

For this and the following questions, replies are limited to SITs and the other investigation techniques provided for by the Act of 6 January 2003. None of these techniques may be used other than in the framework of a criminal investigation.

Observation

The public prosecutor may authorise observation in the framework of an investigation when the needs of that investigation so require and if other investigation techniques are not sufficient to uncover the truth (principle of subsidiarity).

Observation effected with the aid of technical means may only be authorised where there is reason to believe the offences are such as to result in at least one year's imprisonment (principle of proportionality).

Only the investigating judge may, in connection with an investigation, order observation effected with the aid of technical means in order to see inside a home where there is reason to believe that offences under Article 90ter, §§ 2 to 4, are being or will be committed in the framework of a criminal organisation referred to in Article 324bis of the Criminal Code.

Infiltration

The public prosecutor may, in the framework of an investigation, authorise infiltration if the needs of the investigation so require and if other investigation techniques are not sufficient to uncover the truth (subsidiarity). Infiltration may be authorised if there is good reason to be believe that the persons subject to infiltration are committing or will commit offences in the framework of a criminal organisation referred to in Article 90ter, §§ 2 to 4.

The public prosecutor may also authorise the police to apply certain police investigation techniques in the statutory framework of infiltration and taking the purpose of the infiltration into account.

If there is justification for doing so, he or she will authorise the necessary measures to be taken to guarantee the infiltrator's physical, mental and moral safety.

Use of informants

The use of informants is not connected with a particular investigation. The law does not link the use of informants to any requirement of subsidiarity or proportionality since it is difficult to accept that information provided should be removed from a file because it concerns an offence that does not meet the requirement of proportionality. In some cases it is not yet clear at this stage what offence is concerned. The law first has to seek to curb unregulated contacts between police officers and "professional" informants by creating a clear legal and regulatory framework within which such contacts should take place. There is no reason not to make this framework as satisfactory as possible, and it should therefore also be applicable to contacts concerning all offences about which the informant is able to provide information.

3. Are there any specific features governing the use of SITs in relation to acts of terrorism? If so, please specify.

There are no specific features governing the use of SITs in relation to acts of terrorism for the simple reason that terrorism is not (yet) established as a separate offence in Belgian criminal law. It goes without saying that in investigations into terrorist acts SITs may be used, provided those acts fall within other criminal categories and that those categories are within the scope of application of special techniques.

4. How does the legal framework governing the use of SITs guarantee respect for human rights and individual freedoms, the principles of subsidiarity and proportionality? Is the authorisation to use SITs subject to time-limits? Which bodies and procedures are in place to supervise compliance with human rights standards and with the above-mentioned principles in the use of SITs? Is supervision automatic/systematic?

Subsidiarity and proportionality

Subsidiarity means that SITs are so intrusive that it must be ensured that the same result cannot be obtained by other investigation techniques. A principle generally adopted in the context of police investigations or preliminary (judicial) investigations is that the most intrusive techniques are used only if other less intrusive measures produce insufficient results. The judge concerned interprets the principle of subsidiarity *ex abstracto*. The starting-point is that, if other techniques are likely to lead to the same result, they must be preferred.

It is not, however, necessary for classic investigation techniques to be used before the judge orders observation. A judge who, in certain circumstances, considers that other techniques will not be (sufficiently) effective to uncover the truth or advance the case may, for example, immediately order observation. In other words, observation may be used if it is reasonable to suppose that, in the circumstances, the use of classic investigation techniques will not enable satisfactory results to be achieved.

Subsidiarity is formulated in the same way. The terminology used in the act to describe the principle of subsidiarity, namely "if the needs of the investigation so require and if other investigation techniques are insufficient to uncover the truth", and its interpretation are taken from Article 90ter, §1, paragraph 1, of the Criminal Investigation Code, where the regulations on bugging, listening to and recording private communications or telecommunications formulate the principle of subsidiarity in the same terms.

Proportionality requires that the measure used should be proportionate to the gravity of the offence. The principle of proportionality means that the technique selected should be proportionate to the objective and that a restriction of individual freedoms and rights can only be tolerated if there is a serious breach of the peace. In view of the great diversity of SITs, the law has opted not to give the principle of proportionality a general formulation but to use different thresholds according to each technique (see above).

The use of informants is not subject to any requirement of subsidiarity or proportionality.

The authorisation itself is not subject to a particular time-limit. There are, however, time-limits with respect the length of time SITs may be used.

The definition of the notion expressly provides that the use of SITs must be subject to supervision by the State Counsel's Department. Such supervision is required at all times, even if the SITs are being used in the framework of a preliminary judicial investigation. Moreover, the law provides in this respect that it is the public prosecutor who has power to execute authorisations to use SITs issued by an investigating judge.

The public prosecutor executes and supervises authorisations to use SITs. This takes nothing away from the supervisory task of the investigating judge, who may for this purpose consult the confidential file and modify, supplement or extend the authorisation at any time. He or she may also withdraw authorisation if he or she observes any irregularities.

All the supervisory mechanisms of criminal procedure are applicable to cases in which SITs have been used. However, Article 47undecies of the Criminal Investigation Code provides further guarantees.

A public prosecutor who has used observation and infiltration during an investigation and wishes to bring charges must apply to the investigating judge. Following this procedure, the latter reports to the court in chambers without having power to take any investigative action on his or her own initiative.

At least every three months, the public prosecutor transmits to the Principal State Counsel all the cases in which observation or infiltration have been used and concerning which he or she has decided not to bring charges, so that the lawfulness of the techniques used may be reviewed.

The Principal State Counsel writes a report on this which is transmitted to the College of State Counsel, which includes an overall assessment and statistics on these reports in its annual report.

The Principal State Counsel also publishes in his or her annual report an overall assessment and statistics on cases where the federal prosecuting authorities have opened an investigation and proceedings have been discontinued.

5. Which institutions are involved in the use of SITs and what is their role (e.g. law enforcement agencies, prosecutor's Office, judicial authorities, etc.)? Which institutions can order and/or authorise the use of SITs? How does co-operation between these institutions work in practice?

The police

Only the Belgian police as defined in Section 2 of the Act on the police of 5 August 1992 may be charged with implementing SITs. This does not exclude the possibility that, in application of international treaties on the subject, foreign police must, in the context of a cross-border or international operation necessitating the use of SITs in Belgian territory, be able to work in Belgium under the authority, direction and supervision of the relevant Belgian authorities. Where this is the case, all the legal provisions and regulations applicable to the Belgian police also apply to them.

Within each decentralised judicial department, as defined in Section 105 of the Act of 7 December 1998 organising a two-level integrated police force, an officer is responsible for the constant supervision of SITs in the district.

With regard to the use of informants, the law has established a number of specific posts in police forces: the national informant manager, the local informant manager and the contact officer. These persons' operating regulations are governed by the royal decree of 26 March 2003.

The public prosecutor and the federal prosecutor

It is the public prosecutor who may authorise the use of SITs in the framework of an investigation.

The public prosecutor exercises constant supervision over police implementation of such techniques within his or her judicial district.

The public prosecutor informs the federal prosecutor of the SITs implemented in his or her district.

Where the use of such techniques extends over several judicial districts or is under the authority of the federal prosecutor, the relevant public prosecutors and the federal prosecutor immediately inform one another and take all necessary measures to ensure that operations run smoothly.

Investigating judges

They may authorise the application of SITs within the framework of their preliminary investigations. The public prosecutor is nevertheless responsible for execution of such authorisations. In the course of preliminary investigations, investigating judges have the right to consult the confidential file on execution of SITs at any time, but may not mention its content in the context of preliminary investigations. They may at any time amend, supplement or extend authorisation, giving reasons for their decision. They may withdraw authorisation at any time. Each time an authorisation is amended, supplemented or extended, they must ascertain whether the conditions concerning the SIT are being fulfilled.

6. Are there any specialised counter-terrorism institutions? What is their role in the use of SITs?

As yet there is no "specialised" counter-terrorism institution, though State Security, Military Intelligence and the federal police all have counter-terrorism responsibilities.

The federal police have a Terrorism Unit, which is particularly concerned with terrorism-related investigations. SITs may be used in connection with such investigations, provided the legal conditions are in place.

7. Which measures have been adopted in order to facilitate international co-operation (e.g. joint investigation teams)? Can the SITs listed in reply to question 1 be used in cross-border settings?

With respect to observation, Article 40 of the Schengen Agreement enables police officers of one of the contracting parties who, in the context of a criminal investigation, are keeping under observation in their country a person who is presumed to have taken part in a criminal offence to which extradition may apply, to continue their observation in the territory of another contracting party where the latter has authorised cross-border observation in response to a request for assistance which has previously been submitted.

8. What use can be made of SITs in the context of mutual legal assistance?

SITs may be used in the context of mutual legal assistance under the general regulations on mutual legal assistance, that is, on the basis of requests for such assistance by other countries where a multilateral or bilateral agreement includes provisions on such techniques (e.g. the European Convention on Mutual Assistance in Criminal Matters of 29 May 2000).

9. How can the use of SITs be improved? Please provide any comments/proposals concerning the implementation of the terms of reference of the PC-TI and in particular the use and regulation of SITs.

The Act of 6 January 2003 is a new regulation of SITs in Belgium. The Act now has to be assessed in practice. For this reason it would be premature to say that the use of such techniques could be improved.

In the context of the Council of Europe, Belgium supports the PC-TI's terms of reference to study the use of SITs in order to facilitate the prosecution of the perpetrators of acts of terrorism and increase the efficacy of law enforcement agencies in this field.

Bosnia and Herzegovina

1. Please indicate the SITs used in your country, the respective legal framework governing their use and their legal definition, if any.

The texts of reference are: Criminal Procedure Code of Bosnia and Herzegovina (BH CPC), and the Law on Intelligence and Security Agency of Bosnia and Herzegovina (Law on ISA).

According to Article 116 of the BH CPC, "special investigative actions" are:
- surveillance and technical recording of telecommunications,
- access to computer systems and computerised data-processing,
- surveillance and technical recording of premises,
- covert following and technical recording of individuals and objects,
- use of undercover investigators and informants,
- simulated purchase of objects and simulated bribery, and
- supervised transport and delivery of objects of criminal offence.

2. When and under which circumstances (e.g. criminal investigation, preliminary stage, etc.) can SITs be used?

Conditions under which special investigative techniques may be used are defined in Article 116 paragraph 1 of BH CPC, during criminal investigation and for the purpose of obtaining evidence.

3. Are there any specific features governing the use of SITs in relation to acts of terrorism? If so, please specify.

Article 117, paragraph 1, item c) of BH CPC stipulates that criminal offences for which special investigative techniques may be ordered include the criminal offences of terrorism. There are no specific characteristics that regulate the use of SITs in cases of terrorism.

4. How does the legal framework governing the use of SITs guarantee respect for human rights and individual freedoms, the principles of subsidiarity and proportionality? Is the authorisation to use SITs subject to time-limits? Which bodies and procedures are in place to supervise compliance with human rights standards and with the above-mentioned principles in the use of SITs? Is supervision automatic/systematic?

The legal framework for the application of SITs is contained in Article 118 of BH CPC, which stipulates the procedure for application of SITs, and in Article 77 of the Law on Intelligence and Security Agency of Bosnia and Herzegovina.

The principle of subsidiarity is guaranteed by Article 116 of the BH CPC.

Article 118, paragraph 3 of BH CPC stipulates that SITs referred to in item a) to c) of Article 116, paragraph 2 of BH CPC may last no longer than six months, and SITs referred to in items d) and g) may last no longer than three months.

Article 119, paragraph 3 of BH CPC stipulates the obligation of the BH Court, upon request by the person against whom SITs were undertaken, to review the legality of the order to apply SITs and of the method by which the order was enforced.

Article 77 of the Law on Intelligence and Security Agency of Bosnia and Herzegovina stipulates the conditions for covert obtaining of information that requires court authorisation. Court authorisation must be obtained *a priori* from the president of the Court of Bosnia and Herzegovina or from a judge of the said court designated by the president of the court. Upon approval of the measures, the director general of the agency must inform the judge of the BH Court immediately.

5. Which institutions are involved in the use of SITs and what is their role (e.g. law enforcement agencies, prosecutor's office, judicial authorities, etc.)? Which institutions can order and/or authorise the use of SITs? How does co-operation between these institutions work in practice ?

Institutions that apply SITs are courts and prosecutor's offices (in accordance with the Criminal Procedure Code of Bosnia and Herzegovina). Article 6 of the Law on Intelligence and Security Agency of BH precisely stipulates which BH bodies may use information obtained in accordance with this Law.

6. Are there any specialised counter-terrorism institutions? What is their role in the use of SITs?

The Group for counter-terrorism and strengthening capacities for counter-terrorist activities was established by the Decision of the Council of Ministers dated 19 February 2004. The Group operates under the supervision of the BH Ministry of Security and under the leadership of the BH Prosecutor's Office, which is the official head of the Group.

Article 3 of the Decision stipulates that the Group, upon an order by a prosecutor from BH Prosecutor's Office, "shall collect information about all terrorist cases" which implies the right to use SITs.

7. Which measures have been adopted in order to facilitate international co-operation (e.g. joint investigation teams)? Can the SITs listed in reply to question 1 be used in cross-border settings?

The BH Prosecutor's Office has no answer to this question, apart from the fact that the Council of the European Union on 20 June 2002 adopted the framework Decision dated 13 June 2002, regarding the establishment of joint investigative teams.

The Council's Decision of 30 November 2000 provided Recommendations to member countries regarding the assistance of European Police (Europol) in the establishment of investigative teams by member countries.

8. What use can be made of SITs in the context of mutual legal assistance?

Use of SITs in the context of mutual legal assistance cannot be separated from the broader context of mutual co-operation and admissibility of evidence in other countries.

9. How can the use of SITs be improved? Please provide any comments/proposals concerning the implementation of the terms of reference of the PC-TI and in particular the use and regulation of SITs.

The BH Prosecutor's Office (for now) has no proposals to improve the application of SITs.

Appendix

Additional Information from the Intelligence and Security Agency of Bosnia Herzegovina

The legal basis for the application of SITs by the Intelligence and Security Agency of Bosnia and Herzegovina (ISA) and other authorised bodies consists of the Criminal Procedure Code of BH, the Criminal Procedure Code of RS, the Criminal Procedure Code of FBH, and the Law on Intelligence and Security Agency of BH.

Article 74 of the Law on ISA defines SITs that may be applied, as follows: physical following of persons and surveillance of objects in public places for which there are grounds for suspicion that they are included in any activities or preparation of activities within the scope of work of ISA; search of moveable and immovable property, provided that conditions referred to in Articles 77 and 78 of the Law on ISA have been met; surveillance of electronic media, provided that conditions referred to in Articles 77 and 78 of the Law on ISA, have been met; and using other sources believed to have information that ISA needs, provided that conditions referred to in Article 75 of the Law on ISA have been met.

The Criminal Procedure Code of BH and Entity CPCs specify which activities are considered to be SITs, against whom and for what crimes they may be applied, who is charged with approving the application of SITs, the procedure of court approvals and periods of application, and the treatment of and the procedure for obtained evidence. The code specifies that evidence obtained without legal procedure of approval by the respective judge would not be admissible.

According to the Criminal Procedure Code, SITs may be applied against persons for whom there are grounds for suspicion that they committed, personally or as accessories, crimes against the integrity of BH, against humanity and values protected under international law, terrorism, and other crimes that carry a minimum sentence of three years in prison, according to the code.

SITs are ordered by the preliminary proceeding judge in a written order according to the procedure stipulated by the code, upon a written request by the prosecutor. Conditions for the application of SITs, the filing of requests, issuance of the order by the authorised judge, duration, and the cessation of application of SITs, are all stipulated by the BH CPC, Articles 116 to 121, and the CPC of FBH, Articles 130 to 136.

Articles 74 and 74 of the Law on ISA stipulate conditions under which ISA obtains information.

We would like to stress that there are no specific provisions regulating the application of SITs in cases of terrorism, but the same criteria apply to all enumerated crimes.

The Law on BH ISA, as *lex specialis* dealing with specific methods and the scope of work of the Agency, elaborates in detail the manner and conditions for application of SITs by the Agency, and the manner of obtaining and preserving information. Application of SITs by the Agency is stipulated in Articles 77-80 of the Law on ISA.

All conditions and limitations of applying SITs by the Agency are in accordance with the provisions of the Criminal Procedure Code, with additional elaboration of measures for storing and protecting the confidentiality of collected data. Only the Court of Bosnia and Herzegovina may issue order for application of SITs by the Agency. The Law on ISA and Agency by-laws elaborate in detail the procedures for applying SITs and for destruction of information upon cessation of conditions for their use, as well as the accountability of ISA employees for possible violations of prescribed procedures, all with the view to preventing violations of human rights and freedoms.

Apart from the above, there is also "external control" by bodies and institutions that monitor the mentioned procedures, such as the BH Parliament, BH Council of Ministers, BH Ombudsperson, RS and FBH Ombudspersons, and the Human Rights Court of BH.

Institutions involved in application of SITs are the Court of BH and the BH Prosecutor's Office, while approval for application of SITs by ISA may be granted only by the Court of BH.

Co-operation between the mentioned institutions so far has been limited to exchange of information, though the co-operation could certainly be improved.

The BH Ministry of Security has a counter-terrorist co-ordination team, but their role in the application of SITs is unknown to us.

In order to facilitate international co-operation, an agreement on exchange of secret information has been signed between BH and the EU. The second part of the question regards the State Border Service.

In the context of mutual legal assistance, BH ISA may extend legal assistance by providing technical assistance with obtaining evidence to other institutions that may use SITs under the law, provided that all legal procedures mentioned are observed.

From the point of view of BH ISA, in order to improve the results of using SITs, it would be necessary to modernise technical equipment and methods of application. It would be also necessary to train personnel that would work with the new equipment and apply new methods. Prosecutors and judges involved in investigations should be informed about the technical capacities of equipment used for SITs, in order for the equipment to be used efficiently, while reducing human rights violations to the minimum.

To achieve success with SITs, it is necessary to use a small number of experienced, successful and trustworthy staff, who would be able to protect the confidentiality of technology and methods. Also, it would be necessary to keep the procurement of modern special equipment confidential, unknown to criminals in BH. It would also be useful if methods of applying special investigative techniques were not revealed during court proceedings. Bearing in mind all of the above and in order to ensure efficient surveillance of equipment and application of SITs, a solution might be to have only one institution applying SITs, which would require adoption of appropriate legislation.

Bulgaria

1. Please indicate the SITs used in your country, the respective legal framework governing their use and their legal definition, if any.

The use of Special Investigation Techniques in the Republic of Bulgaria is governed by the Special Investigation Techniques Act (SITA) and the Criminal Procedure Code (CPC).

Under Article 2, paragraph 1 of SITA, Special Investigation Techniques are the technical means and the operative techniques for their application, used for preparing material evidence – filming, video recording, sound recording, photos and marked objects. The technical means are listed under Article 2 and the operative techniques under Article 3.

SITA gives a legal definition of the operative techniques (Articles 5 to 10):

Article 5
Under surveillance – both visual and through technical means, various aspects of the activity and behavior of persons and targets, their sojourn at different places or when changes occur in the concrete situation, are established and documented.

Article 6
Under bugging, using technical, auditory or other means, verbal, telephone or electronic communication of target persons is intercepted.

Article 7
Under surveillance – visual and through technical means, the movement of the target persons is established, uncovered and documented.

Article 8
Under penetration, by the use of technical means, actual facts, found in premises and belongings used by the target persons, are established.

Article 9
Under marking, through the use of technical means and substances, objects and belongings are marked for the purpose of establishing their movement, acquisition or place of storage.

Article 10
Under mail control, through the use of chemical substances and technical means, the contents and the addressees of the correspondence of the target persons and objects are established.

2. When and under which circumstances (e.g. criminal investigation, preliminary stage, etc) can SITs be used?

93

Under Article 3, paragraph 1 of SITA, Special Investigation Techniques are used in cases when needed for the prevention and uncovering of grave crimes governed by the Penal Procedure Code, when the necessary data cannot be collected in another way. The Bulgarian legislator has provided legal opportunities for the use of SITs both for completed crimes and for the preparation and organising of the crime, there being two basic limitative listed requirements:

- It must concern a heavy, premeditated crime under the Criminal Code, for which it envisages imprisonment for 5 years or more.
- When the data needed cannot be gathered in any other way.

3. Are there any specific features governing the use of SITs in relation to acts of terrorism? If so, please specify.

There are no specific features in the acting legislation in the Republic of Bulgaria regulating the use of special investigation techniques in relation to terrorist acts, as the Criminal Code considers these to be grave crimes.

4. How does the legal framework governing the use of SITs guarantee respect for human rights and individual freedoms, the principles of subsidiarity and proportionality? Is the authorisation to use SITs subject to time-limits? Which bodies and procedures are in place to supervise compliance with human rights standards and with the above-mentioned principles in the use of SITs? Is supervision automatic/systematic?

and

5. Which institutions are involved in the use of SITs and what is their role (e.g. law enforcement agencies, prosecutor's office, judicial authorities, etc.)? Which institutions can order and/or authorise the use of SITs? How does co-operation between these institutions work in practice?

In the SITA from 1997 the legislator for the first time envisages the restriction of the rights and freedoms of the citizens when using Special Investigation Techniques to be performed only after judicial sanction and only for the prevention and detection of grave crimes or for the defence of national security.

By this principle, accepted by the SITs Act, the rights of citizens are guaranteed completely by supreme judicial control.

The accepted regulation for the SITs Act of preliminary and follow-up control, while restricting the rights according to Article 34 of the Constitution, not only corresponds to the international standards for preserving the right of inviolability of freedom and secrecy of correspondence and other kinds of messages but also ensures to a greater extent this defence.

The parallel of Article 8 of the European Human Rights and Basic Liberties Convention and Article 17 of the International Civil and Political Rights Pact with Bulgaria's SITA shows that this Act is more demanding in the conditions required for infringing the rights of citizens by using SITs and so it ensures more complete defence of the above rights. By adopting the SITA the Republic of Bulgaria has not deviated from European standards in this area.

The following have the right to require the use of Special Investigation Techniques and to use the data and material evidence gathered through them according to their level of competence:
- National services with the exception of the National Fire and Emergency Safety Service and the local services of the Ministry of Interior;
- The Services "Military Information" and "Security – Military Police and Military Counterintelligence" to the Minister of Defence;
- the National Intelligence Service;
- the National Investigation Service, the Sofia City Investigation Service and the regional investigation services;
- the Chief Prosecutor, the Supreme Cassation Prosecutor's Office, the Supreme Administrative Prosecutor's Office, the Military Appellative Prosecutor's Office, the Appellative Prosecutor's Offices, the Sofia City Prosecutor's Office, the District and Military District Prosecutor's Offices.

Other authorities apart from those listed in Article 1 cannot request and cannot make use of the Special Investigation Techniques.

These are services directly engaged in counteracting criminality and the defence of National Security. The limiting approach chosen by the Bulgarian legislator is an additional guarantee for the defence of the rights and liberties of the citizens. In compliance with this approach, the services within the Ministry of Interior, which can only apply Special Investigation Techniques, are imperatively specified in Article 111 b of the CPC and Article 20 of SITA.

Under Article 14 the requisites, which must be included in the request for the use of Special Investigation Techniques, are specified.

The filled-in and signed request is handed over to the services under Article 15 of SITA who are the only competent authority to permit the use of SITs and they are:
- the chairpersons of the Sofia City Court and the District Courts or a deputy chairperson authorised by them;
- for the military, the chairpersons of the corresponding District Military Courts or a deputy chairperson authorised by them;
- in cases where the authorities under the abovementioned refuse to grant the requested permission, the chairperson of the corresponding Appellative Court or a deputy explicitly authorised by him or her.

According to Article 16 of SITA, after receiving written permission under Article 15, the Minister of the Interior or a Deputy Minister of the Interior, authorised in a written form, gives a written order for the application of Special Investigation Techniques by the services that operate them and it is only then that the use of SITs starts

Alongside this procedure, the legislator has provided two special hypotheses, which provide legal opportunity for the use of SITs to start immediately in emergency cases or in cases of immediate danger of grave premeditated crimes or a threat to national security,

The first one is described in Article 17 of SITA. In emergency cases the use of SITs can begin immediately on receiving the written permission by the chairperson of the corresponding District Court or a deputy chairperson explicitly authorised by him or her.

In this case the Minister of Interior, or a deputy minister authorised by him or her in a written form, should be informed immediately about the received written permission. After the minister, or the deputy authorised, has given permission, the operative-technical service is informed in order to start the immediate application of SITs.

The second hypothesis is described in Article 18 of SITA. In cases of immediate danger of grave, premeditated crimes or a threat to national security, the Special Investigation Techniques could be used without the permission of the authority under Article 15 for 24 hours after an order of the Minister of Interior or a deputy minister authorised by him or her.

The use of SITs is terminated if within 24 hours the authority under Article 15 (the chairperson of the corresponding District Court or a deputy chairperson authorised by him or her) has not issued permission and the same authority stipulates the storage and the destruction of the collected information.

If written permission is issued, it confirms the performed activities up to that time. Otherwise the gathered information is destroyed in accordance with Article 31 paragraph 3 of SITA (within a 10-day period).

The procedure for the use of SITs provides the performance of automatic control by the court authorities and the government, and a systematic one by the Parliament of the Republic of Bulgaria by standing or especially constituted commissions, and the Prosecutor's Office of the Republic of Bulgaria when data are acquired for a committed crime.

6. Are there any specialised counter-terrorism institutions? What is their role in the use of SITs?

Under the Ministry of Interior Act, the specific bodies to counteract terrorism are the –National Service Combating Organised Crime, the National Security Service and the National Intelligence Service. According to the Ministry of Interior Act, the officers from these services can request the use of SITs.

7. Which measures have been adopted in order to facilitate international co-operation (e.g. joint investigation teams)? Can the SITs listed in reply to question 1 be used in cross-border settings?

Bulgarian Legislation (SITA, CPC) gives a legal opportunity for the use of SITs by the services under Article 13 of SITA, including joint work teams for investigation when it is technically possible.

To facilitate international co-operation in the framework of the EU, we consider that the technical facilities of the special services that exploit SITs should be synchronised.

8. What use can be made of SIT in the context of mutual legal assistance?

The acting Bulgarian legislation permits, provided there are signed agreements, to perform court orders also through the úse of SITs, when as a result of their use material evidence means should be prepared.

9. How can the use of SITs be improved? Please provide any comments/proposals concerning the implementation of the terms of reference of the PC-TI and in particular the use and regulation of SITs.

In order to facilitate the efficiency of the combat against terrorism and cross-border criminality, we consider that the following should be equalised:
- Time-limits for the use of SITs in compliance with the best European practices;
- Time-limits for all member countries concerning the storage of the information collected through SITs, as well as the mechanism for its declassification and destruction.
- Unification of the standards for the targets that are subjects to SITs. For example, for the purposes of criminal justice these are individuals, but for the purposes of investigation SITs are applied to communication means, premises and other objects;
- The obligations of the telecommunication operators and internet providers for the provision, installation and implementation of intercepting interfaces at their own expense should be defined clearly.

Cyprus

1. Please indicate the SITs used in your country, the respective legal framework governing their use and their legal definition, if any.

Certain SITs are used by the police as a means of gathering information and of investigating criminal offences. Such SITs include undercover operations, the use of informants, observation, the use of *agents provocateurs* and the commission of pseudo-offences.

The use of these methods is not regulated by specific legislation; however, it is governed by the principles of the rule of law and it is scrutinised in the manner explained herein below in the context of Question 4.

Specific reference needs to be made to the use of the following SITs.

Controlled Delivery

The use of this SIT is regulated by specific legislation, namely, the Suppression of Crime (Controlled Delivery and Other Specific Provisions) Law of 1995 (Law 3(1)/95).

In this context, controlled delivery means the method whereby the state authorities knowingly allow the transport of prohibited things or substances to or from or through the territory of a state or states in order to identify the persons involved in the commission of certain prescribed offences.

The law specifies the circumstances in which this SIT may be utilised. It provides that the decision to use this technique in any given case can be made either by the Chief of Police or the Director of Customs and Excise (or their designated representative). Any such decision is, prior to its implementation, communicated to the Attorney General who may give any relevant orders in this respect.

Interception of communications

The matter is regulated by the provisions of the Protection of the Confidentiality of Private Communication (Interception of Communications) Law of 1996 (Law 92(1)/96).

Interception means the securing of the content of any private communication through the use of any mechanical, electronic or other such method. The rule is that interception of private communications is prohibited. Any act in contravention of the prohibitive provisions of the Law constitutes a criminal offence.

Thus, it is illegal for any state authority to intercept private communications. (The rule is subject to certain specific exceptions, which however are of very limited scope.)

It must be noted that Law 92(1)/96 incorporates constitutional principles. The constitution itself safeguards the right to confidentiality of one´s private communications, and does not allow interference with such right, even if such interference is justified for facilitating crime prevention and detection.

Bugging (private or public premises)

This SIT cannot be utilised. Any attempt to use such a method would amount to a violation of the right for respect of the private life of any individual concerned. This right is safeguarded by the constitution and any interference with the exercise thereof must be specifically authorised by a law made in the interests of, *inter alia*, public order.

Since no legislation has been enacted authorising bugging of premises in the context of crime prevention and crime detection, any such activity would constitute a violation of constitutional provisions.

Searches

Searches of premises and vehicles (as well as of objects found therein) are conducted in pursuance of respective search warrants issued by the court.

The Criminal Procedure Law, Cap. 155 (and other legislations dealing with specific crimes) set out the procedure that is to be followed and the conditions that need to be satisfied before a search warrant is issued. Adequate material must be put before the court justifying a reasonable suspicion that the premises, vehicles and so on are connected with the commission of an offence.

2. When and under which circumstances (e.g. criminal investigation, preliminary stage, etc.) can SITs be used?

The answer to this question depends on the nature of each individual SIT. For example, the use of informants is not confined to criminal investigation but extends also to the gathering of information. On the other hand, for controlled delivery to be applied, there must be some information that an offence is about to be committed.

It must be repeated that a search warrant in not issued unless the court is satisfied that there is a reasonable suspicion of connection between the premises, vehicles or the like, and the commission of an offence.

Thus generally speaking, SITs are used both in the context of criminal investigation as well as in the context of gathering intelligence depending, of course, on the circumstances.

3. Are there any specific features governing the use of SITs in relation to acts of terrorism? If so, please specify.

There are no specific features governing the use of SITs in relation to acts of terrorism.

4. How does the legal framework governing the use of SITs guarantee respect for human rights and individual freedoms, the principles of subsidiarity and proportionality? Is the authorisation to use SITs subject to time-limits? Which bodies and procedures are in place to supervise compliance with human rights standards and with the above-mentioned principles in the use of SITs? Is supervision automatic/systematic?

In this context, one has to bear in mind that the provisions of the European Convention on Human Rights, which guarantee human rights and individual freedoms, have been incorporated into the Cyprus Constitution. In Part II thereof, under the title "Fundamental Rights and Liberties", the relevant provisions of the Convention are virtually reproduced.

The case-law of the Supreme Court of Cyprus has established, ever since 1982, that evidence obtained in violation of human rights and individual freedoms guaranteed by the constitution, is not admissible in any judicial proceedings.

It must be noted that the rule excluding the admission of such evidence in judicial proceedings, is absolute. No discretion is allowed to the court to admit the evidence.

This rule operates effectively in discouraging the police from abusing their powers because any evidence obtained through methods violating human rights and individual freedoms cannot, at the end of the day, be used in any subsequent prosecution.

Furthermore, the Supreme Court, through its case-law, has established that any act of a state organ which amounts to a breach of rights and liberties guaranteed by the constitution (and, in effect, the Convention) gives rise to an actionable right in damages. Thus, where SITs are used in a manner amounting to a breach of such rights, the person affected is entitled to bring proceedings against the state for damages, and the officers who have exposed the state to such liability have to face the consequences.

It must be added that all state officers concerned (police officers, customs officers, etc.) operate within the established structure of the respective state institutions under the supervision of superior officers, within a structure of hierarchy and are subject to disciplinary rules and procedures.

5. Which institutions are involved in the use of SITs and what is their role (e.g. law enforcement agencies, prosecutor's office, judicial authorities, etc.)? Which institutions can order and/or authorise the use of SITs? How does co-operation between these institutions work in practice?

Generally speaking, SITs are predominantly used by the police.

Other institutions may be involved in the process. For example, the police may seek the advice of the Office of the Attorney General on legal questions arising in connection with the use of a SIT in a particular case. Furthermore, as has already been said, any decision made for controlled delivery is communicated to the Attorney General in advance.

As for search warrants, they are issued by the court upon an application filed by the police.

6. Are there any specialised counter-terrorism institutions? What is their role in the use of SITs?

By decision of the Council of Ministers, a Co-ordinating Body Against Terrorism was set up. It is chaired by the Deputy Attorney General and is composed of representatives of the Police, the Customs Department, the Anti Money-Laundering Unit, the Ministry of Foreign Affairs and the Ministry of Justice and Public Order.

It is a body with administrative and co-ordinating functions and it is not involved in the use of SITs.

7. Which measures have been adopted in order to facilitate international co-operation (e.g. joint investigation teams)? Can the SITs listed in reply to question 1 be used in cross-border settings?

International co-operation is regulated by the provisions of the relevant legal instruments such the relevant conventions.

A classic example of a SIT used in cross-border settings is controlled delivery, where it is possible for authorities of different states to watch and, eventually, control an illegal operation that takes place in more than one country.

8. What use can be made of SIT in the context of mutual legal assistance?

Usually, and depending on the specific provisions of the legal instrument whereby legal assistance is requested (convention, protocol, bilateral agreement etc.), the state authorities responsible for gathering the information requested are empowered to secure the information utilising methods they would have used had they themselves been engaged in the investigation.

9. How can the use of SITs be improved? Please provide any comments/proposals concerning the implementation of the terms of reference of the PC-TI and in particular the use and regulation of SITs.

The regulation of the use of SITs should be a very important aspect of the work of this committee. In the terms of reference themselves, emphasis is placed on "human rights standards".

A SIT is, by definition, an investigation technique which is used without the knowledge of the targeted person. This entails an inherent risk of abuse by the state organs.

A fair balance must be struck between the need to combat terrorism and the necessity to maintain and reinforce respect for fundamental human rights such as the right to one´s private life.

In this context, it would be desirable for national legislation to:
- prescribe preconditions, which must be satisfied before the authorities embark on the use of SITs in any given case, for instance, that there is at least some evidence supporting the suspicion that the targeted person(s) is connected with the commission of an offence, and
- provide for relief in cases where the unreasonable use of a SIT by the state authorities results in violation of individual rights and freedoms.

Czech Republic

1. Please indicate the SITs used in your country, the respective legal framework governing their use and their legal definition, if any.

The general legal framework for the SITs used in the Czech republic is given by two instruments: Code of Criminal Procedure/Act No. 141/1961 Coll. as amended; and Act No. 283/1991 Coll. on Police of the Czech Republic as amended.

The acts mentioned above stipulate for the following SITs mentioned in the questionnaire:
1. undercover operations (including covert investigations),
2. operational search techniques – agents, pretended transfer, monitoring of persons and things,
3. front store operation (e.g. undercover company),
4. informants,
5. monitoring of a consignment (including controlled delivery),
6. electronic surveillance, bugging (private or public premises), interception of communications,
7. searches,
8. cross-border (hot) pursuit, cross-border observation, covert investigation and joint investigative teams.

There is no legal basis for so-called "provocation".

The legal framework

Undercover operations (including covert investigations)

According to Czech law this is not one of the special techniques; it is rather a main category. All the special investigation techniques fall under this category.

Operational search techniques

The operational search techniques used in the Czech republic include agents, feigned transfer, surveillance of persons and things, which are regulated by § 158b, 158c, 158d, 158e, 158f of the Criminal Proceedings Code.

If the law does not provide otherwise, the body entitled to use investigative tools (pretended transfer, monitoring persons and things, use of agents) in proceedings concerning serious intentional crime is the police unit that has been authorised by the competent minister (units of the Czech Police should be authorised by the police president; units of the Czech Security Information Service should be authorised by the director of this service).

Use of these tools can follow no other objective than to learn facts important for the criminal proceeding. By the use of these tools, information is acquired which helps to reveal crime and its perpetrators, and to prevent crime.

With the help of these tools it is possible in pre-trial proceedings to ascertain whether or not an intentional crime has been committed. The use of these tools is not limited to the pre-trial proceedings, although they are governed by the provisions systematically placed in part of the Criminal Proceedings Code dealing with pre-trial proceedings, in course of which they are used the most. They can be used from the start of the criminal prosecution and during the trial.

These tools may be used only when the objective cannot be achieved otherwise or if it would be considerably complicated. Rights and freedoms of persons can be limited only if it is of prime necessity. Video, audio or other records gained by these investigative tools according to the relevant provisions may be used as evidence.

Agents

The use of agents in the sense of § 158e is permitted only in criminal proceedings concerning especially a serious crime, a crime committed on behalf of a criminal organisation or other intentional crime, which should be prosecuted according to a promulgated international treaty that is binding on the Czech Republic (§ 158e/1). The conditions are thus stricter than those for the pretended transfer and monitoring of persons and things.

Especially serious intentional crimes are defined in §§ 41 and 62 of the Criminal Code; § 62 of the Criminal Code contains a list of extremely serious crimes; § 41/2 deals with intentional crimes for which the term of imprisonment is at least eight years.

Section 158e
Use of an Agent

1. If the criminal proceeding is conducted with regard to an especially grave and wilfully committed criminal offence perpetrated in favour of a criminal association, or another criminal offence the prosecution of which results from the international treaty which the Czech Republic is bound with, the police agency if it is a unit of the police of the Czech Republic, is entitled to use an agent.

2. The agent is a member of the Police of the Czech Republic who fulfils the tasks charged by the police agency and who acts, as a rule, while hiding the actual purpose of his/her activity. If it is necessary with regard to using, preparing or protecting the agent, the following measures are allowed for the purpose of hiding his/her identity:

106

a. creating a cover story of another personal life and introducing personal data resulting from such cover story into the information systems operated in accordance with specific laws;

b. performing businesses and trades, the performances of which require special licences, permits or registrations;

c. hiding their relationship with the Police of the Czech Republic.

3. Governmental bodies of public administration are obliged to provide their assistance to the Police of the Czech Republic without unnecessary delay when it exercises the authorisations referred to under letters a to c.

4. Use of the agent is allowed based on the proposal of the public prosecutor of the High Public Prosecutor´s Office by the judge of the High Court within the circuit of which the public prosecutor giving the suggestion performs his/her office. The permission must indicate the purpose of the application and the time for which the agent is to be used, and data enabling identification of the agent. Based on a new proposal, including evaluation of the existing performance of the agent, the period of permission may be extended, even repeatedly.

5. The agent does not need any other licence to trace the persons and things within the scope mentioned under Section 158 subsection 2.

6. The agent is obliged to select such tools when performing his/her duties as are convenient for compliance with his/her official tasks and which are not to the detriment of other persons´ rights. The agent has no other obligations in accordance with the specific law providing the positions of members of the Police of the Czech Republic.

7. The public prosecutor is obliged to ask from the respective police agency for the information required for assessment whether the grounds for use of an agent continue, and whether the agent´s activities are in compliance with the law. The public prosecutor is obliged to consider and evaluate such grounds for justification of the agent´s use on a regular basis, however at least once in three months, and if the reasons for use of the agent disappear, to give the police agency an instruction promptly to terminate the agent´s activity. The police agency is obliged to submit the public prosecutor the record of using the agent.

8. The agent may fulfil his/her tasks also in the geographic area of another country. The police president decides on the agent´s mission, after the prior approval of the appropriate bodies of the country in the geographic area of which the agent is scheduled to operate, and based on the permission of the judge referred to under subsection 4, unless provided otherwise by the international treaty the Czech Republic is bound with; provisions of subsections 1 to 7 shall apply accordingly.

Pretended transfer

The Criminal Proceedings Code (§ 158c) enables an authorised police body to pretend the purchase, sale or any other method of transfer of a subject of performance, including transfer of an object
a. for possession of which a special permit is necessary,
b. the possession of which is impermissible,
c. that comes from a crime, or
d. that is intended for committing a crime.

Therefore it is possible to pretend a purchase or sale contract or any other method of transfer of the subject of performance, including the transfer of an object, without taking into account other restrictive conditions for acquisition of a property of an object.

The pretended transfer may be performed by the authorised police body on the basis of a written permit of the public prosecutor only. The approval is issued in the form of a measure (not as a decision) and therefore it is not possible to appeal against it or to deliver it.

The amendment which entered into force on 1 November 2004 and which implemented Article 14 of the Convention of 29 May 2000 on Mutual Assistance in Criminal Matters between member states of the European Union and Article 19 of the 2001 Protocol thereto, which regulate covert investigations, provides in § 437 that in accordance with a promulgated international treaty binding on the Czech Republic, a policeman from another state may operate as an agent (in the sense of § 158e Criminal Proceedings Code) or perform a pretended transfer (in the sense of § 158c Criminal Proceedings Code) on the territory of the Czech Republic, on request from the competent authorities of that state or from the authorities responsible for criminal prosecution. To avoid competence problems, and having regard to prompt decision-making and confidentiality, one public prosecutor's office has been made responsible for decision-making about these requests from a foreign state. It will be the High Public Prosecutor's Office in Prague.

Monitoring of persons and things

Monitoring of persons and things is regulated by Section 158d of the Code of Criminal Procedure – Act No. 141/1961 Coll. as amended

Monitoring of persons and things means, according to this paragraph, the collection of information on persons and things executed by technical and other means.

If it is found during monitoring that the accused is communicating with his/her attorney, the police are obliged to destroy the record of the communication. Police cannot use any information contained in such a record, unless when criminal proceeding is conducted for an intentional offence.

Section 158d distinguishes three types of monitoring:
   a. monitoring of a person,
   b. monitoring with recording of sound and video and other recording by technical means, and
   c. monitoring that breaches some substantial citizen's rights guaranteed by the constitution (inviolability of the home, secrecy of letters etc.)

These three types of monitoring differ in the permission process:
   a. can be executed without permission. It is a jurisdiction of police.
   b. must be permitted by the prosecutor (in written form), unless the matter allows no delay. If so, the police are obliged to apply for the permission immediately. If the permission is not granted within a 48-hour period, police must cease the monitoring and destroy all records; information resulting from the observation cannot be used in any way.
   c. must be permitted in advance by a judge.

The permission in cases b and c is issued for a limited time period (at most six months) that has to be explicitly specified. The authority that issued the permission can extend it, but only by six months at most.

The permission in cases b and c is not required if the observed person explicitly agrees.

Section 158d
Monitoring persons and things

1. Monitoring persons and things (hereinafter referred to as "tracking") is understood to be obtaining knowledge of persons and things in a hidden manner by technical or other means. If the police agency finds in the course of tracking that the defendant communicates with his/her defence counsellor, it is obliged to destroy the record of such communication and not to use in any manner whatsoever the information it has gained in that connection.

2. Tracking when audio, video, or other recordings are to be made may be implemented based on the written approval of the public prosecutor only.

3. If tracking should interfere with inviolability of domicile or confidentiality of correspondence, or if the content of the other written documents and records kept in private is to be investigated while applying technical equipment, it may take place based on the prior approval of the judge only. When entering an apartment, no other acts may be executed than those which are directed at installation of the technical equipment.

4. The permission in accordance with subsections 2 and 3 may be issued based on a written request only. The application must be justified

by a suspicion of the criminal activity in particular, and if known, also by information on persons or things who or which are to be traced. The permission must specify the time over which tracking is to be implemented, which cannot be more than six months. This period may be extended at all times by the person who has allowed the tracking, based on a new application, for the maximum time of six months only.

5. If the matter cannot be postponed, and if the cases are not those as referred to under subsection 3, tracking may be initiated also without permission. The police agency is however obliged promptly to ask for a permission additionally and if it does not receive the same within 48 hours, it is obliged to terminate the tracking and not to use in any manner whatsoever the information it has gained in that connection.

6. Tracking may be implemented without compliance with the conditions referred to under subsections 2 and 3 if it has been explicitly agreed with by the person whose rights and liberties are interfered with. If such consent is additionally withdrawn, tracking is promptly terminated.

7. If the record made during tracking is used as evidence, the record distinguished for the prerequisites referred to under Sections 55 and 55a has to be attached.

8. If no circumstances significant for the criminal proceedings have been found during tracking, the records must be destroyed in the specified manner.

9. Operators of telecommunications services, their employees and other persons which or who participate in telecommunications services, as well as the post office and a person carrying consignments, are obliged to provide the police agency performing the tracking the required assistance according to its instructions, free of charge. The duty to secrecy provided under specific laws cannot be then referred to.

10. The record made during tracking and the attached certificate may be used as evidence in another criminal case than that which has been tracked under the conditions referred to under subsection 2, only if in such other case are also conducted the proceedings of the willfully committed criminal offence or if agreed with by the person the rights and liberties of which have been interfered with by tracking.

Front store operation

An agent (see above) is allowed to create a cover story of another personal life and introduce personal data resulting from such a cover story into the information systems operated in accordance with specific laws and also to perform businesses and trades, the performance of which requires special licences, permits or registrations.

The police are also allowed to use clandestine documents according to provisions contained in the Act on the Police of the Czech Republic.

Informants

The conditions for the use of informants are stipulated by the Police Act (No. 283/1991). The police are allowed to use an informant for preventing criminal offences and in the course of criminal proceedings. There is also a Mandatory Instruction of the Police President on the use of informants.

An informant means any natural person who provides the police with information and services in such a way that his/her collaboration with the police is kept confidential. It is possible to provide a financial reward to an informant.

There is an analogous measure (to the institution of informant) also in the Act on the Security Intelligence Services (under special conditions).

Monitoring of a consignment

Monitoring of a consignment is regulated by the § 87, 87a, 87b Criminal Proceedings Code (No. 141/1961 Coll., as amended).

Section 86
Detention of consignment

1. If it is necessary to ascertain the contents of undelivered mail consignments, other consignments or telegrams to clarify the facts important for criminal proceedings in a particular matter, the presiding judge and in pre-trial proceedings the public prosecutor shall order the post office or the person performing their transport to deliver consignments to the presiding judge and in pre-trial proceedings either to the public prosecutor or police body.

Section 87
Opening of consignment

The consignment issued under Section 86, paragraph 1 may only be opened by the presiding judge and in pre-trial proceedings by the public prosecutor or police body with the consent of the judge.

Section 87a
Consignment Substitution

1. In the interest of ascertaining the persons participating in disposing of a consignment containing narcotics, psychotropic substances, precursors, toxins, radioactive materials, forged money and forged securities, firearms or weapons of mass destruction, ammunition and explosives or any other thing for possession of which a special permit is

required, things intended for committing a crime or things coming from a crime, the presiding judge and in pre-trial proceedings the public prosecutor with the consent of the judge may order to substitute the contents of such a consignment with another and such an altered consignment to be given over for further transport.

Section 87b
Monitored Consignment

1. The public prosecutor may order in the preliminary proceedings that a consignment in respect of which there is a justified suspicion that it contains things referred to under Section 87a is monitored if it is necessary to clarify a criminal offence or discovery of all its offenders and ascertaining the required circumstances in another manner would be ineffective, or substantially more difficult. The police agency will arrange monitoring of the consignment according to the public prosecutor's instruction; no acts aimed at surrendering or withdrawing the thing are executed with regard to persons who handle the monitored consignment. A record is made of monitoring the consignment, and an audio or another record is made as required.

2. The police agency may initiate monitoring of a consignment without the order referred to under subsection 1 if the matter cannot be postponed, and the order cannot be obtained in advance. The police agency advises the public prosecutor thereof without delay and proceeds further according to the instructions of the latter.

3. The police agency may take up required measures to achieve that end such that consignment of the things referred to under Section 87a subsection 1, or the things replacing the same, passes with the knowledge and under the supervision of the customs authorities from the geographic area of the Czech Republic abroad, and vice versa, or from abroad via the geographic area of the Czech Republic to another third country.

4. The police agency terminates monitoring of the consignment based on the order of the public prosecutor, and if it is obvious that handling the consignment results in a grave danger to life or health, or considerable damage to property, or if there threatens a grave danger that such consignment cannot be monitored further, even without such order. The police agency takes up at the same time as termination of monitoring the consignment such steps directed against further holding of things contained in the consignment; this does not apply if the monitored consignment crosses the state border and the appropriate body of the foreign country takes over its monitoring within the framework of international collaboration.

Electronic surveillance, bugging (private or public premises), interception of communications

Interception, recording and transcription of telecommunications

The legal conditions for the use of interception and recording of telecommunication are explained in Act No. 141/1961 Coll. The authorisation of the relevant bodies and the liabilities of operators in connection with telecommunication recording and interception are dealt with by Act No. 141/1961 Coll., the Act 283/1991 Coll., on the Police of the Czech Republic, and Act No. 151/2000 Coll., on e-telecommunications.

The natural and legal persons that provide telecommunication services are obligated to provide for connection for interception and recording of telecommunication. The Ministry of Informatics of the Czech Republic is drafting a new Act on electronic communication that will replace (amend) existing Act No.151/2000 Coll. on telecommunications.

The interception and the recording of telecommunication are carried out by the Police of the Czech Republic for all bodies active in criminal proceedings.

The interception can be authorised by a judge on the basis of a summons of the state prosecutor in the case of an especially serious intentional crime or in cases of any other intentional crime that is being pursued under the terms of an international treaty.

Interception and recording of telecommunications may be ordered only if there is a justified assumption that any fact significant for the criminal proceedings would be communicated through them.

If the owner of the telecommunication station that is monitored agrees with the interception, it is also possible to record the telecommunication (without authorisation).

The term "telecommunication operation" is an operation by a phone, fax, mobile phone, transmitter or any other telecommunication device, e.g. a modem-equipped computer.

According to the provisions of Section 86 of the Act No.151/2000 Coll., on telecommunications, the legal or natural person that provides the telecommunication services is obligated (at their own expense) to inform the authorities about the information that is the subject of keeping of the telecommunications secret, whether the subject of the legal protection is personal details or transmission details. These details must be archived for two or six months (according to the request of relevant authorities).

Section 88
Intercepting and recording the telecommunication operation

1. If criminal proceedings are conducted for an extremely serious intentional crime, or for any other intentional crime the prosecution of which is a covenant resulting from a declared international agreement, the presiding judge and in pre-trial proceedings the judge based on motion of the public prosecutor may order the interception and recording of the telecommunication operation, provided that there is a justified assumption that any fact significant for the criminal proceedings would be communicated to them. It is not allowed to execute any interception or record of telecommunication operation between the counsel and the charged person. If the police body ascertains from the interception and records of the telecommunication operation that the charged person communicates with his/her counsel, the police body shall be obliged to discontinue the intercepting immediately, destroy the record of the contents, and be prevented from from using in any way the information it has ascertained in this respect.

2. An order for the tapping and registration of phone communications should be issued in written form and justified. At the same time should be stipulated the duration of the tapping and registration of phone communications, which can not be longer than 6 months, with the possibility of prolongation for 6 months by a judge. The judge immediately forwards a copy of the order to a public prosecutor. The Police of the Czech Republic carry out tapping and recording of the telecommunication operations for the needs of all agencies involved in the criminal proceedings.

3. Without an order under subsection 1 of this provision, the agency can order tapping and recording of the telecommunication operations or carry this out itself even in the cases not mentioned in subsection 1, if the user of the tapped telecommunication station agrees.

4. If the tapping and registration of telecommunication is to be used as evidence, it is necessary to annex to it a protocol with data on the place, time, ways and content of registration, and about the person who made the registration as well. Other registration shall be marked and reliably saved and it is necessary to write down in the protocol where the registration is saved. It is possible to use as evidence the registration of telecommunication in another criminal case than in the case within which the tapping has been made, if a prosecution in this another case is conducted also for the crime mentioned in subsection 1 of this provision or if the user of the tapped telecommunication station agrees.

5. If during the tapping and registration of telecommunications no facts important for penal proceedings were found out, it is necessary to destroy in the prescribed way the registration of telecommunication tapping.

Section 88a

1. If it is necessary to clarify circumstances significant for the criminal proceedings, to identify data of the telecommunication operation implemented, which are otherwise subject to telecommunication secrecy and to which the protection of personal and mediation data applies, the chairman of the bench, and the judge in the preparatory proceedings, orders that legal entities or natural persons performing the telecommunications services disclose this information to a chairman of the bench, or to a public prosecutor or to a police agency in preliminary proceedings. The order to identify data of the telecommunication operation must be issued in writing and on justified grounds.

2. No order in accordance with subsection 1 is required if the user of the telecommunication device, which the data of the telecommunication operation are to apply to, gives consent to disclose the data.

Searches

Act No. 141/1961 Coll, regulates three types of searches – house search, search of other premises and land, and body search.

The conditions of house search are: House search can be carried out if there is reasonable suspicion that in a flat or other premises used for living, or premises belonging to them, is a thing or person important for criminal proceedings.

A search of premises not serving as a dwelling and a search of land can be carried out for the same reasons, if they are not accessible to the public.

A body search can be carried out if there is reasonable suspicion that a person is carrying something important for criminal proceedings.

§ 83
Search warrant

1. The presiding judge and in pre-trial proceedings the judge based on motion of the public prosecutor are authorised to order the search of closed premises. In exigent cases this can be done by the presiding judge or the judge, in the district of whom the search is to be carried out, instead of the appropriate presiding judge or judge (§ 18). The search warrant must be issued in writing and justified. It shall be served on the person, in whose premises the search is to be carried out, during the search, and if this is not possible, within 24 hours at the latest from elimination of the obstacle preventing the service.

§ 83a
Search warrant for other premises and land

1. The presiding judge, or in pre-trial proceedings the public prosecutor or police body, is authorised to order the search of other premises or land. The police body needs prior consent of the public prosecutor for this. The warrant must be issued in writing and justified. It shall be served on the user of the concerned premises or land, and, if not served during the search, immediately after elimination of the obstacle preventing the service.

§ 83b
Body search warrant

The presiding judge, or in pre-trial proceedings the public prosecutor or police body with the public prosecutor's consent, is authorised to order a body search.

Cross-border (hot) pursuit, cross-border observation, covert investigation and joint investigative teams

Czech legislation also provides for cross-border observation, cross-border hot pursuit, covert investigation and joint investigative teams (Act 141/1961 Coll.). These techniques have been included in the Criminal Procedure Code by Act No. 539/2004 Sb., which was adopted on 24 September 2004 by the Parliament of the Czech Republic and came into force on 1 November 2004.

Cross-border observation {Section 436}

In compliance with the conditions of a ratified international treaty that is binding on the Czech Republic, the police can, during observation, enter into the territory of a foreign state and continue the observation on that territory. Equally the authorities of a foreign state can, during observation, enter into the territory of the Czech Republic and continue the observation on that territory. While carrying out these tasks in the territory of the Czech Republic, these authorities are bound by legal order of the Czech Republic and the instructions of the Czech police body.

Unless an international treaty, by which the Czech Republic is bound, states differently, the authority of a foreign state, while carrying out observation on the territory of the Czech Republic, is not entitled to carry out a house search (§ 82), search of other premises and lands (§ 83a), nor enter housing premises, other premises or lands, nor detain or interrogate the observed person.

The regional state prosecution office in Prague is entitled to permit observation and pursuance of actions connected with observation of persons and items across the borders of the Czech Republic. Permission is valid also for the competent authorities of the Czech Republic, if they take over, from

116

the authorities of a foreign state, observation in the same matter on the territory of the Czech Republic.

If the matter cannot be delayed, the authorities of a foreign state can carry out observation in the territory of the Czech Republic even without previous permission. However, the authority of a foreign state is obliged to ask for permission without delay, at latest at the time of crossing the state border. If the authority does not receive permission within 5 hours, it should cease observation.

The state prosecutor is competent to file a request to carry out observation in the territory of a foreign state.

Cross-border hot pursuit {Section 435}

In compliance with the conditions of a ratified international treaty that is binding on the Czech Republic, members of police forces can, while carrying out hot pursuit, enter the territory of a foreign state and continue hot pursuit of a person in the territory of this state. Equally the authorities of a foreign state can, while carrying out hot pursuit, enter into the territory of the Czech Republic and continue with hot pursuit of a person. While carrying out these tasks in the territory of the Czech Republic, the authorities of a foreign state are bound by legal order of the Czech Republic and the instructions of the Czech police body.

Unless the international treaty by which the Czech Republic is bound states differently, the authority of a foreign state, while carrying out hot pursuit in the territory of the Czech republic, is not entitled to carry out a house search (§ 82), search of other premises and lands (§ 83a), nor enter housing, other premises or lands, nor detain or interrogate the observed person.

Provided that the pursued person has been retained in the territory of a foreign state after the hot pursuit, and the person is not a citizen of this state, the state prosecutor will ask for her/his preliminary retention for the purpose of extradition or hand-over in the period of six hours after her/his retention in the territory of a foreign state. The hours between midnight and 9 a.m. do not count for this purpose.

The pursued person, who has been caught in the territory of the Czech Republic based upon hot pursuit by police of a foreign state, if they have permission for long-term residence in the territory of the Czech Republic, will be released within the period of six hours after her/his retention, unless the competent authority of a foreign state delivers in this period a request for taking this person into preliminary custody for the purpose of extradition or hand-over. The hours between midnight and 9 a.m. do not count for this purpose.

117

Covert investigation (Section 437)

This article sets out the conditions under which the competent authorities of a foreign state can carry out pretended transfer (Section 158c) and use an agent (Section 158e) on the territory of the Czech Republic. The conditions are: a ratified international treaty that is binding on the Czech Republic, and the request of the competent authorities of the foreign state or request of the body active in criminal proceedings, as well as an authorisation given by a judge.

Joint investigation team

If the international agreement by which the Czech Republic is bound so states, it is possible, for the fulfilment of tasks in criminal investigation, to conclude with the appropriate authorities of one or more foreign states an agreement about the creation of a joint investigative team.

A request to conclude such an agreement, according to Section 1, is filed by the appropriate state prosecutor via the highest state prosecution office to the competent authority of a foreign state. In the request he/she will state in which criminal matter the joint investigative team is to be be created, including a description of the act and its legal qualification, the aim of the joint investigative team and the period for which the team shall be created, with the possibility to prolong this period, which police forces or other forces will be participating in the joint investigative team on behalf of the Czech republic, the specific competence of the participating police forces of the Czech Republic and other participants of the team, information about the possible criminal and civil responsibility of the team's participants, provisions about data protection, the working language of the joint investigative team, provisions of the Criminal Procedure Act of the Czech Republic to be applied by the team, and methods of command and communication. An agreement, according to Section 1, on behalf of the Czech Republic always includes the highest prosecution office, and this is based upon the state prosecutor's request as well as the foreign state authority's request. Requirements of the agreement have to be fulfilled, according to Section 2 of this paragraph.

If the joint investigative team shall be acting in the territory of the Czech Republic, then the commander of the joint investigative team shall be always a person in service of the Czech Republic's police forces.

Any evidence found by any member of the team in the territory of states where this team is active, if procedures were carried out according to the legal order of that state or according to the legal order of the Czech Republic, are effective in criminal proceedings held in the Czech Republic.

Actions to be carried out in a state whose police forces were not sent to the joint investigative team have to be always requested via request (§425).

For designation of competence, delegated from more competent state prosecutions for acts in criminal proceedings carried out by members of the Czech Republic's police forces sent to the joint investigative team, if it is necessary in the interests of speeding up the proceedings or in other serious interests, the provisions of §431 section 3 can be used accordingly.

If the competent state prosecution office shall carry out an act of criminal proceedings outside its territory, it shall act according to §§53 and 54.

§443 Powers of foreign members of the joint investigative team

If an agreement on a joint investigative team has been concluded according to §442, the employees of competent authorities of a foreign state who have been seconded to this team can in the context of the joint investigative team, in the territory of the Czech Republic and under the command of a person active in the service of the Czech Republic police authority, take part in:
- extradition and confiscation of items (§§78 and 79);
- house searches and searches of other premises and lands, mainly according to Chapter IV, Section 4;
- examination (§§113 and 114);
- investigation attempts (§104c);
- reconstructions (§104d); and
- checks on the place (§104e).

While carrying out tasks according to Section 1 in the territory of the Czech Republic, employees of competent authorities of a foreign state are obliged by legal order of the Czech Republic and commands of the Czech Republic police authority.

The employees of competent authorities of a foreign state sent into the joint investigative team can be present at a defendant's interrogation (§90 to §94), interview of witnesses (§97 to §104), confrontation (§104a), recognition (§104b) or giving an explanation according to §158. They can make an additional query only with the approval of the investigation authority, that is, carrying out the interrogation. The investigation authority carrying out the interrogation can make a query only if it is in harmony with the legal order of the Czech Republic.

The commander of the joint investigative team is entitled, in harmony with the legal order of the Czech Republic, to delegate performance of separate acts in a foreign state to employees of competent authorities of the foreign state sent into the joint investigative team.

2. When and under which circumstances (e.g. criminal investigation, preliminary stage, etc.) can SITs be used?

See above.

119

3. Are there any specific features governing the use of SITs in relation to acts of terrorism? If so, please specify.

In the Czech criminal law there are no special features governing the use of SITs in relation to acts of terrorism. The general rules on SITs are applicable also in such cases.

4. How does the legal framework governing the use ot SITs guarantee respect for human rights and individual freedoms, the principles of subsidiarity and proportionality? Is the authorisation to use SITs subject to time-limits? Which bodies and procedures are in place to supervise compliance with human rights standards and with the above-mentioned principles in the use of SITs? Is supervision automatic/systematic?

See Section 1.

5. Which institutions are involved in the use of SITs and what is their role (e.g. law enforcement agencies, prosecutor's office, judicial authorities, etc.)? Which institutions can order and/or authorise the use of SITs? How does co-operation between these institutions work in practice?

See Section 1.

6. Are there any specialised counter-terrorism institutions? What is their role in the use of SITs?

The Police Unit for detecting organised crime contains a group specialising in terrorism. The rules for using SITs are the same for all authorised forces.

7. Which measures have been adopted in order to facilitate international co-operation (e.g. joint investigation teams)? Can the SITs listed in reply to question 1 be used in cross-border settings?

See Section 1. Some of the SITs mentioned above (cross-border observation, cross-border hot pursuit and joint investigative teams, controlled delivery) can be used in cross-border settings. Others can be used under the conditions of international treaties.

8. What use can be made of SITs in the context of mutual legal assistance?

See question 7.

Denmark

1. Please indicate the special investigation techniques (SITs) used in your country, the respective legal framework governing their use and their legal definition, if any.

The legal framework governing the use of special investigation techniques (SITs) in Denmark is primarily the Administration of Justice Act, cf. Consolidation Act No. 961 of 21 September 2004, as amended in Act No. 1436 of 22 December 2004

Denmark is however a party to a wide range of international conventions and agreements concerning the fight against terrorism, mutual assistance in criminal matters and so on, where the use of special investigation technique are described. Some of these investigation techniques are not specifically defined or mentioned in the Administration of Justice Act, but are regulated in government orders, departmental circulars and the like, in accordance with Chapter 67 – general rules of investigation.

According to the Administration of Justice Act, as well as the practice concerning special investigation techniques laid down in accordance with the general rules on investigation in government orders and the like, and by the courts, the following SITs can be used:

Undercover operation

An undercover operation is a method of investigation where substantial information and evidence is gathered over a period of time, involving the use of lawful measures by law enforcement and by using undercover agents to obtain such information and evidence, cf. definition in PC-TI (2003) Inf.1.

Undercover operations are not defined or regulated specifically in the Administration of Justice Act, but the use of agents (undercover agents) is strictly regulated, see the description below under 'Agents'.

It shall be mentioned that Denmark, while ratifying the second additional protocol to the European Convention on Mutual Assistance in Criminal Matters, made a reservation to Article 19 (covert investigation).

Agents

According to Section 754 a in the Administration of Justice Act, the police may not, as part of the investigation of an offence, prompt that assistance is offered or measures are taken with the purpose of inciting someone to commit or continue the offence, unless:

1. a particularly confirmed suspicion is present that the offence is about to be committed or attempted;

2. other investigative measures will not be suitable for securing evidence in the case; and
3. the investigation concerns an offence that under the law can be punished by imprisonment for six years or more, or a violation of the criminal code Section 289, 2nd period (smuggling of a particularly serious nature).

The measures mentioned in Section 754 a must not cause an aggravation of the extent or seriousness of the offence, and the measures may only be conducted by police officers, cf. Section 754 b.

The measures are implemented following a court order. The court order shall state the specific circumstances in the case upon which it is based, and that the conditions for the implementation of the measures are fulfilled. The court order can at any time be reversed, cf. Section 754 c, subsections 1 and 2.

If the purpose of the measures would be jeopardised if the court order were to be awaited, the police can take the decision of implementing the measures. In that case the police shall as soon as possible, and at the latest within 24 hours from initiation of the measures, bring the case before the court, cf. Section 754 c, subsection 3.

On 23 April 2003 the Danish Government presented a bill to the Danish Parliament containing initiatives aimed at combating biker gang members and other types of organised crime. In order to improve the investigative possibilities of the police, it is proposed that it shall be possible to use civil agents (persons outside the police force) with the sole purpose of introducing a police agent, cf. the insertion of a provision in Section 754 b. Furthermore it is proposed, that the provision in Section 754 a, no. 1, "particularly confirmed suspicion" is modified to "reasonable suspicion", and that the provision in Section 754 a, no. 2, "Other investigative measures will not be suitable for securing evidence in the case" is modified to "the investigation measure is presumed to be of crucial importance for the investigation". Parliament passed the bill on 5 June 2003 and the bill entered into force on 12 June 2003.

Informants

The concept "informant" is not defined and the uses of informants are not regulated in the Administration of Justice Act. It is however possible for the police to use informants in accordance with the general rules of investigation in the Administration of Justice Act.

According to the practice in relation to investigation techniques, an informant is defined as a person, often anonymous and from a criminal environment, who passes on information on projected offences to the police or provides the police with general information about the activities in a special group or environment. The informant cannot take an active part in the offences.

Controlled delivery

The concept "controlled delivery" is not defined, and the uses of controlled delivery are not regulated in the Administration of Justice Act. According to the practice on investigation techniques laid down by the courts, however, the use of controlled delivery is possible in accordance with the general rules of investigation in the Administration of Justice Act and the general rules in government orders.

In the Act passed by the Parliament on 5 June 2003 a special section has been inserted in the Administration of Justice Act concerning controlled delivery. According to Section 754 a, subsection 2, the police can make minor changes in carrying out a controlled delivery without being covered by the rules on agents.

Observation

According to Section 791 a, the police can photograph or observe by means of binoculars or other devices persons who are at a place not freely accessible (observation), if:
1. the measure must be presumed to be of significant importance for the investigation; and
2. the investigation concerns an offence that under the law can result in imprisonment.

Observation as mentioned above by means of a remote-controlled or automatically functioning television camera, photographic camera or similar device may, however, only be conducted if the investigation concerns an offence that under the law can result in imprisonment for one year and six months or more, cf. subsection 2.

Observation of persons who are in a residence or other dwelling, by means of remote-controlled or automatically functioning television camera, photographic camera or similar device, or by means of a device employed in the residence or the dwelling, may however only be conducted if special provisions are absorbed, cf. subsection 3.

Observation must not be conducted if – considering the purpose of the measure, the significance of the case, and the offence and inconvenience that the measure is presumed to cause the concerned person or persons – it would be a disproportionate measure, cf. subsection 5.

As stated above, Denmark is a party to different international conventions and agreements. According to some of these conventions, for example Section 40 in the Schengen convention, it is possible to follow a person under observation into another country – cross-border observation – when special conditions are observed.

It shall however be mentioned that Denmark, while ratifying the second additional protocol to the European Convention on Mutual Assistance in Criminal Matters, made a reservation to Article 17 (cross-border observation).

Interception of communications, electronic surveillance and bugging

According to the provisions of Chapter 71 in the Administration of Justice Act, the police may intervene in the secrecy of communications by:
1. intercepting telephone conversations or similar telecommunications (telephone interception)
2. intercepting other conversations or statements by means of a device (other interception)
3. obtaining information about which telephones or other similar communication devices are connected with a certain telephone or other communication device, although the owner thereof has not granted permission (tele-information)
4. obtaining information about which telephones or other similar communication devices within a specific area are connected to other telephones or communication devices (expanded tele-information)
5. withholding, opening, and becoming informed of the contents of letters, telegrams, and other mail deliveries (letter opening), and
6. stopping the forwarding of mail as mentioned in no. 5 (letter stopping), cf. Section 780, subsection 1.

Invasion of the secrecy of communication may only be conducted if there are specific reasons to presume that messages are given or mail is delivered by the means in question to or from a suspect, if the investigation is presumed to be of crucial importance for the investigation, and if the investigation concerns a specific offence mentioned in Section 781, subsection 1, no. 3.

An invasion of the secrecy of communication takes place according to an order of the court. The court order shall state the telephone numbers, locations, addresses or mail deliveries that the measure concerns. The court order lays down the period of time within which the measure can be implemented. This time period shall be as short as possible and must not exceed four weeks. The time can be extended but at the most by four weeks at a time, cf. Section 783, subsections 1 and 2.

If the purpose of the measure would be jeopardised if a court order were to be awaited, the police can take the decision of implementing the measure. In that case the police shall as soon as possible, and at the latest within 24 hours from initiation of the measure, bring the case before the court, cf. Section 783, subsection 3.

Mail enterprises and providers of telecommunications networks or services shall assist the police in implementing invasions of the secrecy of communication, including by establishing interception of telephone conversations, etc., by giving the information referred to in Section 780, subsection 1 (iii) and (iv) and by withholding and surrendering consignments and mail, etc. to the police, cf. Section 786, subsection 1.

According to Section 786, subsection 4 the providers of telecommunications network or services shall record and store traffic data ("log") for one year for the purpose of investigation and prosecution of criminal offences. The recording and storage only concern traffic data and not the actual contents of the communication. Furthermore, only the companies have a duty to record and store the traffic data in question.

Moreover, the section includes rules on the access for the police to the nationwide directory enquiry service, which contains name and address data concerning all telephone subscribers listed by name in Denmark, including unlisted telephone numbers, regardless of the subscriber's telecommunications provider.

In June 2002 (The Anti-Terrorism Act) a new provision was inserted in the Administration of Justice Act. According to Section 791 b, the police in cases of very serious offences can obtain a court warrant allowing them to capture data in an information system not available to the public by means of software or other equipment (data capture) without being present at the location where the information system (a computer or another data system) is being used. This provision makes it possible for the police to use the so-called "sniffer programs" that provide the police with a copy of all data input by the data system user.

With the Act of 5 June 2003 the provision for data capture was extended, making it possible for the police to use data capture after a court order in all cases, when the investigation concerns an offence that under the law can be punished by imprisonment for six years or more or a violation of the Criminal Code Section 286, subsection 1 (theft of a particularly aggravated nature), and Section 289 (smuggling of a particularly serious nature).

Searches

According to Section 793 in the Administration of Justice Act, the police can conduct searches of:
1. residences or other dwellings, documents, papers and similar, as well as the contents of locked objects, and
2. other objects as well as premises other than dwellings.

The law does not regulate searches of premises or objects that are freely accessible to the police.

A search to locate a suspect, who is to be arrested, or a person, who is to be taken into custody for the purpose of enforcing a punishment or the alternative penalty in default of payment of a fine, can furthermore take place pursuant to Sections 759 and 761. As for examination of a person and the search of a person's clothes, the rules of Chapter 72 apply. As for examination of letters, telegrams, and similar mail deliveries, the rules of Chapter 71 apply; cf. subsection 3.

Searches of dwellings, other premises or objects, of which a suspect has possession, can only be conducted if:
1. the individual is on reasonable grounds suspected of an offence, which is indictable by the state, and
2. the search must be presumed to be of significant importance for the investigation.

As for searches of the kinds mentioned in Section 793, subsection 1, no. 1, it is furthermore required that the case concerns an offence that under the law can result in imprisonment, or there are specific reasons to presume that evidence in the case or objects that can be seized may be found by the search, cf. Section 2.

According to Section 796, subsection 1, the decision to search for the objects or premises mentioned in Section 793, subsection 1, no. 2, of which a suspect has possession, is made by the police.

A decision to search in other situations is made by court order, unless the individual grants written consent to the search being conducted, or the search is in connection with the detection or report of an offence and a search of the scene of the crime is to be conducted. In these cases the police can also make the decision to search.

The court order shall state the specific circumstances in the case upon which it is based, and that the conditions for the measures are fulfilled. The court order can at any time be reversed.

A search must not be conducted if, considering the purpose of the measures, the significance of the case, and the offence and inconvenience that the measure can be presumed to cause, it would be a disproportionate measure. Furthermore it shall be taken into consideration if the search involves destruction or damage of objects, cf. Section 797.

If it is of crucial importance for the investigation that the search is conducted without the knowledge of the suspect or others, the court in special cases can in the form of a court order make a decision to this effect and of deviating from the rules of Section 798, subsection 2, 1st-4th period, and Section 3. This does however not apply as for searches of dwellings, other premises or objects in possession of somebody, who pursuant to the rule of Section 170 is excluded from, or who pursuant to the rule of Section 172, is exempted from testifying as witness in the case, cf. Section 799.

In June 2002 (The Anti-Terrorism Act) Section 799 was amended so the court can allow the police, with only one warrant, to carry out several individual searches without immediate notification (repeated secret searches) within a period not exceeding four weeks. This may be necessary where, for example, no drugs or weapons were found at the first search, but where it is still suspected that delivery at the location in question will take place within a short time, or where a search has had to be interrupted owing to the risk of discovery of the investigation. The court has to fix the number of searches in connection with the search warrant. In special cases the court may decide, however, that the police may carry out an indeterminate number of searches within the specified period (not exceeding four weeks).

Cross-border (hot) pursuits

The concept "cross-border pursuit" is not defined and the use of cross-border pursuits is not regulated in the Administration of Justice Act. But as stated above Denmark is a party to the Schengen convention, and according to Section 41 in the Schengen convention, cf. Act on Denmark's accession to the Schengen convention, it is possible to follow a person into another country, when special conditions are observed.

In accordance with the Schengen convention, Denmark has made special agreements on police co-operation in the border district with Sweden and Germany.

2. When and under which circumstances (e.g. criminal investigation, preliminary stage, etc.) can SITs be used?

Some of the special investigation techniques can be used in the preliminary stage, where no offence has been committed, but where the police are aware that criminal activities are planned. Please refer to the answer to question 1.

3. Are there any specific features governing the use of SITs in relation to acts of terrorism? If so, please specify.

The Danish Security Intelligence Service is an integral part of the police and employs the same law enforcement activities or investigative methods as the Danish police in general. These are more precisely defined in the Administration of Justice Act.

The special investigation techniques mentioned above apply equally to the Danish Security Intelligence Service, except for the rules regarding agents. The law does not regulate the use of agents by the Security Service. Furthermore, the Security Service can keep material gathered during an investigation concerning counter-terrorism as long as it is deemed relevant, without court authorisation, even though the investigation does not turn into a criminal case.

Before undertaking intrusive measures or SITs, the specific measure is laid before the court for *a priori* authorisation. When the case concerns the Security Service, a specially appointed defence lawyer views the case and has opportunity to comment on use of the measure prior to the court's decision to authorise the measure in question.

4. How does the legal framework governing the use of SITs guarantee respect for human rights and individual freedoms, the principles of subsidiarity and proportionality? Is the authorisation to use SITs subject to time-limits? Which bodies and procedures are in place to supervise compliance with human rights standards and with the above-mentioned principles in the use of SITs? Is supervision automatic/systematic?

The European Convention on Human Rights and Fundamental Freedoms (ECHR), with the additional protocols, was incorporated into Danish law in 1992. The convention applies to the state and is binding for all state organs below this: the Danish Government, the courts, the executive and so on.

The Danish Government assures conformity of draft legislation with the European Convention on Human Rights and Fundamental Freedoms and with other international human rights instruments by means of a general procedure working at the inter-ministerial level.

Rules and procedures for the drafting of legislation have been laid down in government circular 159/1998. In pursuance of Section 24 herein, all legislation must be put before the Ministry of Justice upon drafting and prior to its introduction before Parliament, for examination of issues concerning law technique. These issues are stated, in the Guidelines on Law Quality as issued by the Ministry of Justice, to include aspects of general international human rights conventions such as the European Convention on Human Rights and Fundamental Freedoms. The prescribed general consultation with the Ministry of Justice ensures that all legislation will undergo a certain examination of general human-rights-related aspects.

The Danish courts are furthermore obliged *ex officio* to ensure that the rules and procedures laid down in the use of SITs according to the legislation are in conformity with the principles in the ECHR.

The principles of subsidiarity and proportionality are basic principles in the Administration of Justice Act. The principles are set out specifically in the majority of the sections concerning the use of SITs.

Yes, please refer to the answer to question 1.

The Danish courts are obliged to take into account human rights, when they are presented in the use of intensive measures /SITs.

5. Which institutions are involved in the use of SITs and what is their role (e.g. law enforcement agencies, prosecutor's office, judicial authorities, etc.)? Which institutions can order and/or authorise the use of SITs? How does co-operation between these institutions work in practice?

Intrusive methods of investigation such as telephone interceptions, observations and the like are only carried out by police authorities. They are undertaken with caution and have to be approved by the head of the police department/police district/the Security Service – the head always has a legal background – before being laid before the court for *a priori* authorisation. The court gives a warrant for, say, telephone interception or bugging for a period of up to four weeks. This period may be prolonged, but at the most for four weeks at a time and only following a court decision, cf. the answer to question 1.

If an intrusive method such as telephone interception is so urgent that it cannot await court authorisation, it will be undertaken on the orders of the police following the approval of the head of the police department/police district/the Security Service. Within 24 hours after the interception has been carried into effect, the case will be laid before the court for subsequent approval. There is always a legal adviser on call in the various police departments/districts and the Danish courts have a corresponding "on call"-system, which minimises the number of cases where, for instance, a telephone interception is carried into effect without *a priori* court authorisation.

The combination of legal control within the police department/police district/the Security Service, the specially appointed defence lawyer and the court ensures the legality of the intrusive measures carried out, and the co-operation between said institutions in general works in a smooth and efficient way.

6. Are there any specialised counter-terrorism institutions? What is their role in the use of SITs?

In Denmark counter-terrorism lies within the work carried out by the Security Intelligence Service whose main task is "to monitor, prevent and combat any plans or actions which may be assumed to endanger the Nation's independence and Security and the legitimate social order and thus first and foremost the offences detailed in Chapters 12 and 13 of the Penal Code."

Terrorism falls under Chapter 13 of the Danish Penal Code, and counter-terrorism is one of the major tasks carried out by the Security Service. As mentioned in the reply to question 3, the Danish Security Intelligence Service is an integral part of the police and SITs are used by the service following the procedure outlined in the reply to question 5.

7. Which measures have been adopted in order to facilitate international co-operation (e.g. joint investigation teams)? Can the SITs listed in reply to question 1 be used in cross-border settings?

In the wake of 11 September 2001 the bilateral and multilateral co-operation between law enforcement agencies and security services worldwide has intensified.

Denmark has ratified the Council of Europe Convention on Mutual Legal Assistance and the additional protocol to the convention. Furthermore, Denmark has ratified the EU Convention of 28 May 2000 on Mutual Legal Assistance. By Act No. 258 of 8 May 2002 Denmark has incorporated into Danish law the EU Convention of 28 May 2000 on Mutual Legal Assistance, the additional protocol to the Council of Europe Convention on Mutual Legal Assistance and the EU Framework Decision on joint investigation teams.

Joint cross-border investigations are set up ad hoc if needed in a specific case and participation in international working groups has increased.

Investigative methods can be used in cross-border settings under the same conditions as in national investigations.

8. What use can be made of SIT in the context of mutual legal assistance?

Investigative methods that can be used nationally can also be used in the context of mutual legal assistance.

9. How can the use of SITs be improved? Please provide any comments/proposals concerning the implementation of the terms of reference of the PC-TI and in particular the use and regulation of SITs.

As described above in the answer to question no. 7, the bilateral and multilateral co-operation between law enforcement agencies and security services has intensified worldwide. A wide range of international conventions and agreements therefore already deals with the subject of special investigation techniques in relation to mutual legal assistance.

Appendix

The Danish Administration of Justice Act

Chapter 68 – Interrogation and special investigations measures

Section 754 a

(1) The police may not, as part of the investigation of an offence, prompt that assistance is offered or measures are taken with the purpose of inciting someone to commit or continue the offence, unless:
1. a reasonable suspicion is present that the offence is about to be committed or attempted,
2. the investigative measure is presumed to be of crucial importance for the investigation, and
3. the investigation concerns an offence that under the law can be punished by imprisonment for six years or more, or a violation of the criminal code Section 289, 2nd period.

(2) Measures carried out in order to incite somebody to commit or continue an offence, are not covered by subsection 1, if the police by these means do not affect substantially the circumstances of the offence.

Section 754 b

(1) The measures mentioned in Section 754 a must not cause an aggravation of the extent or seriousness of the offence.

(2) The measures may only be conducted by police officers. Civil persons may upon agreement with the police assist in committing or continuing an offence being investigated, if the assistance given is extremely modest in comparison with the offence.

Section 754 c

(1) Measures under Section 754 a are implemented following an order of the court. The matter thereof is brought before the court where prosecution is or can be expected to be initiated or otherwise where the decision is made by the police to seek implementation of the measures.

(2) The court order shall state the specific circumstances in the case upon which it is based, and that the conditions for the implementation of the measures are fulfilled. The court order can at any time be reversed.

(3) If the purpose of the measure would be jeopardised if a court order were to be awaited, the police can take the decision of implementing the

131

measures. In that case the police shall as soon as possible, and at the latest within 24 hours from initiation of the measures, bring the case before the court. The court decides in the form of an order if the measures can be approved and whether they can be upheld. If, in the opinion of the court, the measures should not have been conducted, the court shall give notice thereof to the Ministry of Justice.

Section 754 d

If measures as mentioned in Section 754 a are implemented and an indictment for the offence is filed, the defence counsel shall be given notice of the measures. If considerations of foreign powers, the safety of the state, the solving of the case or a third party exceptionally require it, the police can order the defence counsel not to pass on the information received pursuant to the 1st period.

Section 754 e

The rules of Sections 754 a to 754 d do not apply to investigations of violations of the Criminal Code Chapter 12, Sections 111-115 and 118.

Chapter 71 – Invasions of the secrecy of communication and observation

Section 780

(1) The police can pursuant to the rules of this chapter invade the secrecy of communication by

1. intercepting telephone conversations or similar telecommunications (telephone interception),

2. intercepting other conversations or statements by means of a device (other interception),

3. obtaining information about which telephones or other similar communication devices are connected with a certain telephone or other communication device, although the owner thereof has not granted permission (tele-information),

4. obtaining information about which telephones or other similar communication devices within a more specific area are connected to other telephones or communication devices (expanded tele-information),

5. withholding, opening and becoming informed of the contents of letters, telegrams and other mail deliveries (letter opening), and

6. stopping the forwarding of mail as mentioned in no. 5 (letter stopping).

(2) The police can make recordings or take copies of the conversations, statements, mail deliveries and the like mentioned in subsection 1, to the same extent that the police are entitled to become informed of the contents thereof.

Section 781

(1) Invasion of the secrecy of communication may only be conducted if:

1. there are specific reasons to presume that messages are given or mail is delivered by the means in question to or from a suspect,

2. the invasion is presumed to be of crucial importance for the investigation, and

3. the investigation concerns a specific offence that under the law can be punished with imprisonment for six years or more, an intentional violation of the Criminal Code Chapter 12 or 13 or a violation of the Criminal Code Sections 124, subsection 2; 125; 127, subsection 1; 193, subsection 1; 228, 235; 266; 281; 286, subsection 1; or 289, or a violation of the Law of Aliens Section 59, subsection 5.

(2) If the conditions of subsection 1, nos. 1 and 2 are fulfilled, telephone interception and tele-information can further take place if the suspicion concerns offences against certain individual rights of the kind described in the Criminal Code Section 263, subsection 2, or Section 263, subsection 3, relating to subsection 2.

(3) If the conditions of subsection 1, nos. 1 and 2 are fulfilled, tele-information can further take place if the suspicion concerns repeated offences against certain individual rights of the kind described in the Criminal Code Section 265. The same applies if the suspicion concerns a violation of the Criminal Code Section 279 a or Section 293, subsection 1, committed by the use of a telecommunication service.

(4) Letter opening and letter stopping can furthermore take place if there is a particularly substantiated suspicion that the mail delivery contains objects that should be confiscated, or those that, by a crime, have been purloined from somebody, who can claim them back.

(5) Interception pursuant to Section 780, subsection 1, no. 2, and Section 780, subsection 1, no. 4 can only take place when the suspicion concerns an offence that has caused or that can cause endangerment of human life or welfare or for significant values of society. Interception pursuant to Section 780, subsection 1, no. 1 can be done, irrespective that the provision in subsection 1, no. 1 is not fulfilled.

Section 782

(1) An invasion of the secrecy of communication must not be conducted if, considering the purpose of the measure, the significance of the case, and the offence and inconvenience that the invasion can be presumed to cause the concerned person or persons, it would be a disproportionate measure.

(2) Telephone interception, other interception, letter opening, and letter stopping must not be conducted with regard to the relations of the suspect with persons, who, pursuant to the rules of Section 170, are excluded from giving testimony as witnesses.

Section 783

(1) An invasion of the secrecy of communication takes place according to an order of the court. The court order shall state the telephone numbers, locations, addresses and mail deliveries that the measure concerns. Further, the specific circumstances of the case upon which it is based, and that the conditions for the measure are fulfilled, shall be stated. The court order can at any time be reversed.

(2) The court order lays down the period of time within which the measure can be implemented. This time period shall be as short as possible and must not exceed four weeks. The time period can be extended, but at the most by four weeks at a time. The extension is issued in the form of a court order.

(3) If the purpose of the measure would be jeopardised if a court order were to be awaited, the police can take the decision of implementing the measure. In that case the police shall as soon as possible, and at the latest within 24 hours from initiation of the measure, bring the case before the court. The court decides in the form of an order if the measure can be approved as well as whether it can be upheld, and if so for which period of time, cf. subsection 1, 2nd-3rd period, and subsection 2. If in the opinion of the court, the measure should not have been implemented, the court shall give notice thereof to the Ministry of Justice.

(4) (Information according to Article 20 in the Convention of 29 May 2000 on Mutual Assistance in Criminal Matters between the member states in the European Union).

Section 784

(1) Before the court makes a decision pursuant to Section 783, an attorney shall be appointed for the person whom the measure concerns, and the attorney shall have the opportunity to make a statement. If the investigation concerns a violation of the Criminal Code Chapters 12 or

13, the attorney is appointed from among the special group of attorneys mentioned in subsection 2. A decision of the court to the effect that the attorney shall not be appointed from among this special group can be appealed to the higher court.

(2) The Minister of Justice engages for the area of each high court a number of attorneys, who can be appointed in the cases mentioned in subsection 1, 2nd period. The Minister of Justice issues further rules about when the attorneys concerned are on call, about compensation for being on call, and about issues of security, including approval of secretarial assistance.

Section 785

(1) An attorney appointed pursuant to Section 784, subsection 1, shall be notified of all court meetings in the case and is entitle to attend these as well as to become informed of the material obtained by the police. The attorney is further entitled to receive a copy of the material. If the police find that the material is of a particularly confidential nature, and that a copy thereof should not be given, the police shall, upon request from the attorney, bring this question before the court for decision. The attorney must not forward the received information to others or without the consent of the police make contact with the person against whom it was petitioned that the measure be implemented. The appointed attorney must not be represented by another attorney or by an assistant.

(2) The rules of appointed defence counsels in Chapter 66 and Section 746, subsection 1, as well as the rules in Chapters 91 and 92 about costs and fines for contempt of court, similarly apply to the appointed attorney. The court can rule that the appointed attorney cannot later during the case function as defence counsel for any accused.

Section 786

(1) Mail enterprises and providers of telecommunications networks or services shall assist the police in implementing invasions in the secrecy of communication, including by establishing interception of telephone conversations, etc., by giving the information referred to in Section 780, subsection 1, nos. 3 and 4, and by withholding and surrendering consignments or mail.

(2) In cases other than those referred to in Section 780, subsection 1, no. 3, the court may, at the request of the police and with the consent of the owner of a telephone or other communication device, order the companies, etc., referred to in subsection 1 hereof to state what other devices are connected with the device in question.

(3) The provision of Section 178 applies correspondingly to any person who fails to provide the assistance referred to in subsection 1 hereof or

to comply with an order made under subsection 2 hereof without any lawful cause.

(4) Providers of telecommunications networks or services shall record and store traffic data for one year for the purpose of investigation and prosecution of criminal offences. Upon negotiation with the Minister for Science, Technology and Innovation, the Minister of Justice will lay down detailed rules on such recording and storing.

(5) Upon negotiation with the Minister for Science, Technology and Innovation, the Minister of Justice may lay down rules on the practical assistance to the police by providers of telecommunications networks and services in connection with invasions in the secrecy of communication.

(6) Any person is liable to a fine if he or she violates subsection 4, first sentence, hereof. Criminal liability may be imposed on companies, etc. (legal persons) under the rules of Part 5 of the Criminal Code.

(7) Provisions on fines may be laid down for violation of provisions in regulations laid down pursuant to subsection 4, second sentence, and subsection 5 hereof. Provisions may also be laid down on the imposition of criminal liability on companies, etc. (legal persons) under the rules of Part 5 of the Criminal Code.

(8) The Minister of Justice may lay down rules on financial compensation to the enterprises referred to in subsection 1 hereof for expenses in connection with assistance to the police for implementation of invasions in the secrecy of communication.

Section 787

(1) The appointed attorney can demand to witness the opening of letters and other sealed mail deliveries. This does not, however, apply if the opening cannot be postponed.

(2) The rule of subsection 1 also applies to a defence counsel.

Section 788

(1) Upon conclusion of an invasion of the secrecy of communication, notification shall be given about the measure, cf., however subsection 4. If the person, to whom notification pursuant to subsection 2 shall be given, has been a suspect in the case, notification shall also be given hereof and which criminal offence the suspicion has concerned.

(2) Notification is given

1. of telephone interception and tele-information to the owner of the telephone concerned,

2. of other interception to the person who has possession of the place or the room where conversation took place or the statement was made, and

3. of letter opening and letter withholding to the sender or the recipient of the mail delivery.

(3) The notification is given by the lower court, which has made the decision pursuant to Section 783. The notification is given as soon as possible, unless the police within 14 days after the expiration of the time period, for which the measure has been permitted, have put forward a request of omission or postponement of notification, as described in subsection 4. If, pursuant to Section 784, subsection 1, an attorney has been appointed, a copy of the notification shall be sent to him.

(4) If notification as mentioned in subsections 1-3 will be harmful to the investigation, or to the investigation of another pending case concerning an offence, which under the law can be subject to an invasion of the secrecy of communication, or if the circumstances otherwise speak against notification, the court can, upon request from the police, decide that notification shall be omitted or postponed for a specified period of time, which can be extended by a subsequent decision. If, pursuant to Section 784, subsection 1, an attorney has been appointed, he shall have the opportunity to make a statement, before the court makes a decision about omission or postponement of the notification.

Section 789

(1) If, during an invasion of the secrecy of communication, the police obtain information about an offence that has not formed and which according to Section 781, subsection 1, no. 3, or Section 781, subsection 5, could not form the basis for the measure, the police can use this information as part of the investigation of the criminal offence concerned.

(2) Information obtained during an invasion of the secrecy of communication must not be used as evidence in court in regard to an offence that has not formed, and according to Section 781, subsection 1, no. 3, or Section 781, subsection 5, could not form the basis for the measure.

(3) The court can decide that subsection 2 does not apply, if

1. other investigative measures will not be suitable for securing evidence in the case,

137

2. the case concerns an offence that under the law can result in imprisonment for one year and six months or more, and

3. the court otherwise finds that it does not cause concern.

Section 790

Mail deliveries that have been withheld for the purpose of letter opening shall as soon as possible be forwarded to their destination. If the police wish to block the forwarding, a request of letter stopping shall be submitted to the court within 48 hours after initiation of the suppression.

Section 791

(1) Tape recording, photocopies or other reproductions that the police have obtained as a result of the measure shall be destroyed if no charges are brought against anybody for the offence that formed the basis for the measure, or if prosecution is later dismissed. The police notify an attorney appointed under Section 784, subsection 1, when the destruction has taken place.

(2) If the material continues to be of investigative importance, destruction can be omitted or postponed for a specified period of time. The police submit the question thereof to the court, which before decision is made shall allow the appointed attorney the opportunity to make a statement. The rules of 2nd period do not apply to material obtained as part of an investigation of violations of the criminal code Chapter 12, Sections 111-115 and 118.

(3) If, in connection with telephone interception or letter opening, invasions have occurred of the relations of the suspect with persons, who according to the rules of Section 170 are excluded from testifying as witnesses, material about such invasions shall be destroyed immediately. However, this does not apply if the material causes charges for a criminal offence to be brought against the person concerned, or for the defence counsel to be removed from his assignment pursuant to Sections 730, subsection 3, and 736.

(4) Otherwise, the police shall destroy material that is obtained during invasion of the secrecy of communication, if it proves to be without investigative importance.

Section 791 a

(1) The police can photograph or observe by means of binoculars or other devices persons who are at a place not freely accessible (observation), if:

1. the measure must be presumed to be of significant importance for the investigation, and

2. the investigation concerns an offence that under the law can result in imprisonment.

(2) Observation as mentioned in subsection 1 by means of a remote-controlled or automatically functioning television camera, photographic camera or similar device may, however, only be conducted if the investigation concerns an offence that under the law can result in imprisonment for one year and six months or more.

(3) Observation of persons in a residence or other dwelling, by means of remote-controlled or automatic television camera, photographic camera or similar device or by means of a device employed in the residence or the dwelling, may however only be conducted if:

1. there are specific reasons to presume that evidence in the case can be obtained by the measure,

2. the measure must be presumed to be of crucial importance for the investigation,

3. the investigation concerns an offence that under the law can be punished with imprisonment for six years or more, an intentional violation of the Criminal Code Chapter 12 or 13 or a violation of the Criminal Code Sections 124, subsection 2; 125; 127, subsection 1; 193, subsection 1; 266; 281; 286, subsection 1; 289, or a violation of the Law of Aliens Section 59, subsection 5, and
the investigation concerns an offence that has caused or can cause endangerment of human life or welfare or for significant values of society.

(4) Observation of a place not freely accessible as mentioned in subsections 1-3, of which the person, who claims to be victimised by the offence, has possession, is not regulated by the rules of this section, if the individual in writing consents to the observation.

(5) Observation must not be conducted if, considering the purpose of the measure, the significance of the case, and the offence and inconvenience that the measure is presumed to cause the concerned person or persons, it would be a disproportionate measure.

(6) The rules of Section 782, subsection 2; Sections 783-785; Section 788, subsection 1, subsection 2, no. 2, and   subsections 3 and 4; Section 789 and Section 791 similarly apply as for the cases dealt with in subsections 2 and 3.

Section 791 b

(1) Data in an information system not available to the public may be captured by means of software or other equipment (data capture), if:

1. there are specific reasons for assuming that a suspect is using the information system in connection with an offence, either planned or committed, as referred to in no. 3 hereof;

2. the measure must be assumed to be decisive to the investigation; and

3. the investigation concerns a specific offence that under the law can be punished with imprisonment for six years or more, an intentional violation of the Criminal Code Chapter 12 or 13 or a violation of the Criminal Code Section 289.

(2) Measures referred to in subsection 1 hereof may not be carried out if the measure would be disproportionate in view of the purpose of the measure, the importance of the case, and the infringement and inconvenience presumably inflicted on the person or persons subject to the measure.

(3) Any decision on data capture is made by the court by order. Such order must state the information system subject to the measure. In other respects, the rules of Section 783, subsection 1, third and fourth sentences, and subsections 2 and 3 apply correspondingly.

(4) Subsequent notice of a measure carried out will be given under the rules of Section 788, subsection 1, 3 and 4. The notice will be given to the person who disposes of the information system subject to the data capture under subsection 1 hereof. In other respects, the rules of Section 782, subsection 2, and Sections 784, 785, 789 and 791 apply correspondingly.

Chapter 73 – Search

Section 793

(1) Pursuant to the rules of this chapter the police can conduct searches of:

1. residences or other dwellings, documents, papers and similar, as well as the contents of locked objects, and

2. other objects as well as premises other than dwellings.

(2) Searches of premises or objects freely accessible to the police are not regulated by the rules of this chapter.

(3) A search to locate a suspect who is to be arrested, or a person who is to be taken into custody for the purpose of enforcing a punishment or the alternative penalty in default of payment of a fine, can furthermore take place pursuant to Sections 759 and 761. As for examination of the body of a person and searching the clothes, which the individual is wearing, the rules of Chapter 72 apply. As for examination of letters, telegrams, and similar mail deliveries, the rules of Chapter 71 apply.

Section 794

(1) Searches of dwellings, other premises or objects, of which a suspect has possession, can only be conducted if:

1. the individual is on reasonable grounds suspected of an offence indictable by the state, and

2. the search must be presumed to be of significant importance for the investigation.

(2) As for searches of the kinds mentioned in Section 793, subsection 1, no. 1, it is furthermore required that the case concerns an offence that under the law can result in imprisonment, or there are specific reasons to presume that evidence in the case, or objects which can be seized, may be found by the search.

(3) If during the search of the possessions of a suspect, written messages or similar are found, which originate from a person, who pursuant to the rules of Section 170 is excluded from giving testimony as a witness in the case, searches hereof must not be conducted. The same applies to material, which originates from a person who is included in Section 172, when the material contains information that the individual pursuant to Section 172 is exempted from testifying about as a witness in the case.

Section 795

(1) Searches of dwellings, other premises or objects in the possession of a person who is not a suspect are not regulated by the rules of this chapter, if the individual grants written consent to the search or if, in connection with the detection or report of an offence, consent is granted by the individual. Otherwise, a search of the possessions of a person who is not a suspect may only take place, if:

1. the investigation concerns an offence that under the law can result in imprisonment, and

2. there are specific reasons to presume that evidence in the case, or objects that can be seized, may be found by the search.

(2) As for the possessions of persons, who pursuant to the rules of Section 170 are excluded from giving testimony as witnesses in the case, written messages and similar between the suspect and the person concerned, as well as notes and similar by this person concerning the suspect, are not subject to search. As for the possessions of persons who are included in Section 172, material containing information about matters that the individuals pursuant to Section 172 are exempted from testifying about as witnesses in the case are not subject to search.

Section 796

(1) The decision to search the objects or premises mentioned in Section 793, subsection 1, no. 2, of which a suspect has possession, is made by the police.

(2) The decision to search in other situations is made by court order, cf., however, subsections 5 and 6. The court shall state the specific circumstances in the case upon which it is based, and that the conditions for the measure are fulfilled. The court order can at any time be reversed.

(3) If the purpose of the measures would be jeopardised if a court order were to be awaited, the police can take the decision to conduct the search. If the person who has possession of the dwelling, premises or objects against which the search is directed puts forward a request hereof, the police shall as soon as possible, and at the latest within 24 hours, bring the case before the court, which in the form of a court order decides if the measure can be approved.

(4) Before the court makes a decision pursuant to subsection 3, 2nd period, the person in possession of the dwellings, premises or objects against which the search is directed shall be given the opportunity to make a statement. Section 748, subsections 5 and 6 similarly apply.

(5) If the search is directed against dwellings, premises or objects of which a suspect has possession, and this individual grants written consent to the search being conducted, the decision to search can also be made by the police.

(6) A decision to the effect that, in connection with the detection or report of an offence, a search of the scene of the crime is to be conducted, can, regardless of the rule in subsection 2, also be made by the police if the person who has possession of the dwelling, premises or object concerned is not a suspect and it is not possible to come into contact with this individual immediately. In this case, notification of the search shall be given to the individual as soon as possible.

Section 797

(1) A search must not be conducted if, considering the purpose of the measures, the significance of the case, and the offence and inconvenience that the measure can be presumed to cause, it would be a disproportionate measure.

(2) In making the decision pursuant to section 1 it shall be taken into consideration if the search involves destruction or damage of objects.

Section 798

(1) Searches shall be conducted with the utmost leniency as allowed under the circumstances, including, to the extent possible, without causing destruction or damage, and without the measure, due to the time or the way in which it is conducted, causing unnecessary attention.

(2) If a person who has possession of the dwelling, the premises or the object or, in his or her absence, other persons are encountered, these individuals shall be informed of the conduct of the search and the grounds therefore as well as being invited to witness the search. If the search is conducted based on a court order, this shall, upon request, be shown. If the search is conducted pursuant to the rule in Section 796, subsection 3, the police shall advise the individual of the access to bring the matter before the court. The person who has possession of the dwelling, the premises or the object can demand that another person of his or her choice witness the search unless time-based or investigative reasons speak against this. If the search requires it, including if obstacles are put in the way of the conduct of the search, the police can decide that the persons encountered shall be removed while the search is taking place.

(3) If nobody is encountered when a search as described in Section 793, subsection 1, no. 1, is to be conducted, two housemates or other witnesses shall, to the extent possible, be summoned to witness the search. After the conduct of a search as described in Section 793, subsection 1, no. 1, the person who has possession of the dwelling or the object shall be notified hereof and, if the search has been conducted pursuant to the rule in Section 796, subsection 3, of the access to have the matter brought before the court; a possible manner is for the police to leave a notice in writing at the location.

Section 799

(1) If it is of crucial importance for the investigation that the search is conducted without the knowledge of the suspect or others, the court can, if the investigation concerns an intentional violation of the Criminal Code Chapter 12 or 13 or a violation of the Criminal Code Sections 180; 183, subsection 1 and 2; 183 a; 186, subsection 1; 187, subsection 1; 191;

192 a or 237, in the form of a court order make a decision to this effect and deviating from the rules of Section 798, subsection 2, 1st-4th period, and subsection 3. However, this does not apply to searches of dwellings, other premises or objects in possession of somebody who pursuant to the rule of Section 170 is excluded from or who, pursuant to the rules of Section 172, is exempted from testifying as a witness in the case.

(2) The rules in Section 783, subsections 2 and 3, and Sections 784, 785 and 788 apply to the cases described in subsection 1, 1st period.

(3) The court can decide, that within the time period fixed in subsection 2, pursuant to the rule in Section 783, subsection 2, repeated searches can be made. The court shall in that connection fix the number of searches. If special grounds speak therefore, the court may decide that there can be conducted an indeterminate number of searches.

Section 800

(1) If, during a search, the police obtain information about an offence, which has not formed and which according to the rules of Section 794, subsection 1, no. 1, and subsection 2; Section 795, subsection 1, no. 1; or Section 799, subsection 1, respectively, could not form the basis for the measure, the police can use this information as part of the investigation of the criminal offence concerned, but not as evidence in court in regard to the offence.

(2) The court can decide that subsection 1 does not apply as for information obtained by the police during a search conducted pursuant to Section 799, subsection 1, if:

1. other investigative measures will not be suitable for securing evidence in the case,

2. the case concerns an offence that under the law can result in imprisonment for six years or more, and

3. the court otherwise finds that it does not cause concern.

Estonia

The Surveillance Act regulates the general principles for using SIT. The use of SIT for collecting evidence in criminal procedures in regulated by the Criminal Procedure Act (CPA).

1. Please indicate the SITs used in your country, the respective legal framework governing their use and their legal definition, if any.

Chapter 3 division 8 of the CPA prescribes the possibilities of collecting evidence by surveillance activities. In criminal procedure the following surveillance activities are allowed for collecting evidence:

- Covert surveillance, (bugging[1] if necessary), § 115;

- Covert examination of postal items, § 116;

- Collecting information on the fact of messages being sent via a technical communication channel, duration and type of communication, and personal data and location of senders and receivers of such messages from providers of technical communication services, § 117;

- Wiretapping and recording of data forwarded by telephone, telegraph or other technical communication channel, § 118;

- Covert observing and recording of data (not sent by technical communication channel) (bugging if necessary), § 114 section 3, § 118;

- Staging of criminal offence, (bugging if necessary), § 119 (including pseudo-offences, pseudo-purchases, etc.);

- Police agent or official collecting evidence using changed identity, §120;

- Searches: the CPA foresees the possibility to carry out searches. In § 91 it is allowed to search persons, buildings, premises and vehicles with the aim to find:
  1. physical evidence;
  2. objects belonging to confiscation;
  3. documents, objects or persons, which are important for the case;
  4. property, which will be seized for compensation of material loss;
  5. wanted persons;
  6. corpses.

Controlled delivery is possible under the Customs Code in order to combat organised crime. A customs office has the right to allow goods that are being or have been carried across the customs frontier to arrive unhindered at their destination under customs surveillance and if necessary, to co-operate with other surveillance agencies.

2. When and under which circumstances (e.g. criminal investigation, preliminary stage, etc.) can SITs be used?

SITs can be used for collecting evidence in criminal investigations if it is impossible or seriously difficult to collect evidence using other procedural methods and if the investigations concern a crime of the first degree, or an intentionally committed crime of the second degree for which imprisonment of up to at least three years is prescribed as punishment.

3. Are there any specific features governing the use of SITs in relation to acts of terrorism? If so, please specify.

No special features.

4. How does the legal framework governing the use of SITs guarantee respect for human rights and individual freedoms, the principles of subsidiarity and proportionality? Is the authorisation to use SITs subject to time-limits? Which bodies and procedures are in place to supervise compliance with human rights standards and with the above-mentioned principles in the use of SITs? Is supervision automatic/systematic?

Surveillance activities can be conducted according to the *ultima ratio* principle. The CPA permits surveillance activities only if it is impossible or seriously difficult to collect evidence using other procedures. To attain proportionality, the CPA foresees that surveillance activities can be used only in investigations of first-degree crime or an intentionally committed second-degree crime for which imprisonment of at least three years is prescribed; § 110.

Permission of the court is required to conduct covert examination of postal items, wiretapping and recording of information sent by communication channels, and staging of a criminal offence. Separate permission of the court also has to be applied for if covert entry into housing, other buildings and constructions and other premises, data banks, workplaces and means of transport is necessary for the purpose of installing or removing technical appliances. The head of the appropriate office should submit a reasoned application in writing to the court. A judge can grant permission with a term of validity up to two months. The permission can be prolonged in the aforementioned way (§ 110, § 114). The basis for the commencement of other surveillance activities is an order issued by the head of the surveillance agency which conducts a surveillance proceeding.

In addition to the supervision exercised by the court, while granting leave for surveillance, the prosecutors' office supervises the legality of the whole pre-trial investigation, including surveillance. The pre-trial investigation agency must inform the prosecutors' office about court permission for surveillance activities within three days; § 114, § 213. The State Prosecutor's Office receives a monthly overview of all conducted surveillance activities and they are empowered to carry out on-the-spot inspections.

The independent body for supervising surveillance activities is the security authorities' supervisory committee of Parliament. It oversees agencies of executive power in questions relating to the activities of security authorities and surveillance agencies, including ensuring fundamental rights and efficiency in their work. The committee controls the activities of the Security Police Board, Police Board, Board of Border Guard, Tax Board and Board of Customs. It receives an overview of all conducted surveillance activities every four months and is also authorised to arrange on-the-spot inspections.

Searches can be carried out on the basis of a prosecutor's or court's ruling. The CPA does not provide certain circumstances under which searches can be conducted as in the case of surveillance activities. It is up to a prosecutor or a judge to weigh in each case whether the restriction of an individual's fundamental rights is reasoned or not, taking into account also the principles of proportionality and subsidiarity. That kind of system follows the principles of subsidiarity and proportionality and grants supervision over the legality of performing SITs.

5. Which institutions are involved in the use of SITs and what is their role (e.g. law enforcement agencies, prosecutor's office, judicial authorities, etc.)? Which institutions can order and/or authorise the use of SITs? How does co-operation between these institutions work in practice?

SIT	Bodies with the right to use the SIT
Covert surveillance	Security Police Board, Police Board, Tax Board, Board of Border Guard, Board of Customs
Covert examination of postal items	Security Police Board, Police Board
Collecting data on the fact of messages being forwarded via technical communication channel	Security Police Board, Police Board, Tax Board, Board of Border Guard, Board of Customs
Wiretapping and recording of data	Security Police Board, Police Board,
Covert observing and recording of data	Security Police Board, Police Board
Staging of criminal offence	Security Police Board, Police Board
Police agent	Security Police Board, Police Board
Bugging	Security Police Board, Police Board
Controlled delivery	Customs Board
Searches	All law enforcement authorities

The authorisation of SITs was described in the previous answer.

6. Are there any specialised counter-terrorism institutions? What is their role in the use of SITs?

In Estonia, counter-terrorism activity is within the responsibility of the Security Police Board. It can carry out all the aforementioned SITs for collecting evidence in a criminal matter. But in order to facilitate suppression of terrorism at an early stage, the Security Police Board is empowered to conduct exceptional operations outside judicial procedure. Conditions for such activities are prescribed in the Security Authorities Act.

7. Which measures have been adopted in order to facilitate international co-operation (e.g. joint investigation teams)? Can the SITs listed in reply to question 1 be used in cross-border settings?

Estonia has ratified all international conventions related to the suppression of terrorism.

According to the CPA, surveillance activities can be carried out on the basis of an international request for legal assistance; § 110 section 2.

SITs listed in reply to question one can't be conducted by Estonian authorities outside Estonian territory.

8. What use can be made of SIT in the context of mutual legal assistance?

As mentioned in the previous answer, the surveillance activities prescribed in the CPA can be conducted on the basis of an international request for legal assistance.

9. How can the use of SITs be improved? Please provide any comments/proposals concerning the implementation of the terms of reference of the PC-TI and in particular the use and regulation of SITs.

It is considered that the range of available SITs in Estonian legislation can satisfy the needs of judicial procedure in the cases of terrorist acts.

---

1. Covert entry into housing, other buildings and constructions and other premises, data banks, workplaces and means of transport for the purpose of installing or removing technical appliances.

Finland

1. Please indicate the SITs used in your country, the respective legal framework governing their use and their legal definition, if any.

The Security Police and NBI, and the local police, have the right to use specific investigation means such as technical observation, surveillance, technical surveillance, use of undercover agents and the right of access to call-associated data.

The investigation means and procedures of the police are regulated in the Police Act and in the amended Coercive Measures Act, which both came into force on 1 March 2001. See here below a summary of the new Police Act, the regulations of which may be of interest to you.

The new Police Act contains regulations on, for example, interception of telecommunications, technical surveillance, security clearances related to trials and other events requiring special protection, use of undercover agents and simulated transactions.

From 1 March 2001, a policeman is entitled to make use of interception of telecommunications in a situation where information gathered by interception of telecommunications is necessary to prevent a threat against a person's life or health. In case of urgency, a policeman pertaining to the officers may make the decision. The court shall be informed within 24 hours.

Interception of telecommunications may also be used in order to prevent or expose crimes, on condition that there is a reasonable cause for suspicion that a person, on account of his or her utterance, threats or behaviour, will commit a drugs or an IT offence, an illegal threat or a threat against a person who is being heard in court, or a crime the sentence enacted in law of which is at least 4 months' imprisonment. The police are also entitled to temporarily close an extension or a data terminal.

Along with the amendments in the Police Act, the field of application of technical surveillance has enlarged as well. A permanent residence – exclusive of a cell – remains still outside the application of technical surveillance. Elsewhere, the police may use technical listening and visual monitoring, on condition that there is a reasonable cause for supposing that information necessary to prevent a crime will be gathered by its means.

Regulations on the use of undercover agents and simulated transactions are now for the first time included in the Police Act. According to the Act in question, a policeman is entitled to use undercover agents if it is necessary to prevent, expose or clear up a criminal activity described in Chapter 5 a Section 2 of the Coercive Measures Act, and if there is a reasonable cause for suspicion that the subject of information-gathering, on account of his or her behaviour or for some other reason, will commit the offence concerned. Undercover agents may also be used in a residence, on the condition that it can be effected in active co-operation with the user of the residence.

A policeman is entitled to make a simulated transaction if it is necessary to prevent, expose or clear up a receiving offence or a crime the maximum sentence of which is at least two years' imprisonment. A policeman is also entitled to make a simulated transaction in order to find an object, a substance or a property being kept in illegal possession on account of an aforesaid crime, or to recover the profit gained by committing such a crime.

Regulations entitling the police to run security checks on persons seeking to attend a trial are incorporated in the new Police Act as well. The police are also entitled to ensure the security of persons taking part in a public meeting, a public gathering or another similar event requiring special protection, by checking the participants and the goods these people are bringing with them.

Definitions

In the Police Act, this is what is meant.

- Technical observation is visual observation or listening as well as automatic recording of voice or picture, practised by means of technical devices, directed towards the public, drivers or pedestrians;

- Surveillance is constant or frequent gathering of information about a particular person or his/her activity;

- Technical surveillance is constant or frequent listening and recording of voice (technical listening), visual control and video-taping (technical visual control), as well as following-up movements of a vehicle or goods (technical follow-up), all by means of technical devices;

- Use of undercover agents is constant or frequent gathering of information about a particular person or a group of persons or his/their activity and infiltration, in which misleading or covert information or register records are used, or false documents are made or used, in order to prevent revelation of the information-gathering and infiltration concerned;

- Simulated transaction is a purchase offer made by the police in order to prevent possession of or bargaining with an object, a substance or a property held in illegal possession or forming the target of the bargain, or to prevent or expose illegal production of an object, a substance or a property, or to find the aforesaid object, substance or property, or to recover the profit gained by committing a crime;

- Interception of telecommunications is the obtaining of confidential ID information through telemessages sent from an extension or data terminal connected to a public or other Telnet within the Finnish Telecommunications Market Act, or received by an aforesaid extension or data terminal, as well as temporary closing of such an extension or data terminal.

2. When and under which circumstances (e.g. criminal investigation, preliminary stage, etc.) can SITs be used?

See above.

3. Are there any specific features governing the use of SITs in relation to acts of terrorism? If so, please specify.

No.

4. How does the legal framework governing the use of SITs guarantee respect for human rights and individual freedoms, the principles of subsidiarity and proportionality? Is the authorisation to use SITs subject to time-limits? Which bodies and procedures are in place to supervise compliance with human rights standards and with the above-mentioned principles in the use of SITs? Is supervision automatic/systematic?

The chief of the Security police unit assigned by the Ministry of the Interior decides on the use of undercover agents and the eventual making of false register records and documents to be used in the matter. A policeman pertaining to the officers decides on use of a simulated transaction. In case of urgency, a policeman pertaining to the officers can make the decision to intercept telecommunications. The court shall be informed within 24 hours. Listening to telecommunications requires always a court order.

A policeman who has decided on technical surveillance referred in the Police Act shall inform the person subject to it of the measure, after concluding the measure, unless notification endangers the purpose of gathering information or pre-trial investigation of the offence.

A policeman who has conducted intercepting shall without delay prepare a protocol on intercepting, in regard to which more specific provisions have been enacted by the Police Decree. The protocol shall be delivered to the Ministry of the Interior, which prepares an annual report on the use of technical surveillance for the parliamentary Ombudsman. The police unit concerned, after having decided to use undercover agents, shall draw up a report on the activity to the Ministry of the Interior, the latter giving annually a report on use of undercover agents to the Parliamentary Ombudsman. Use of undercover agents requires special training.

Furthermore the security police are accountable to the Ministry of the Interior and to the parliamentary Ombudsman. An annual report of the activities of the Security police shall be prepared for the Ministry of the Interior.

5. Which institutions are involved in the use of SITs and what is their role (e.g. law enforcement agencies, prosecutor's office, judicial authorities, etc.)? Which institutions can order and/or authorise the use of SITs? How does co-operation between these institutions work in practice?

The Security Police carry out preliminary investigations of, for example, crimes manifesting themselves in terrorist and sabotage acts committed in Finland.

As soon as the preliminary investigations are advancing, the investigation of the affair shall be referred without delay to the National Bureau of Investigation or the local police.

6. Are there any specialised counter-terrorism institutions? What is their role in the use of SITs?

The Finnish Security Police have a unit specialising in counter-terrorism, which consists of policemen specialised in terrorism. They can use the same SITs as the NBI and the local police.

7. Which measures have been adopted in order to facilitate international co-operation (e.g. joint investigation teams)? Can the SITs listed in reply to question 1 be used in cross-border settings?

The SITs listed in reply to question 1 can be used in cross-border settings, but this normally requires a request for legal assistance. However, for example in pursuit, it is possible to authorise the authority of another state to extend the pursuit to Finland when the situation is so urgent that a formal procedure cannot be followed. The pursuit also requires that it is not possible for the Finnish police to continue the pursuit in their own territory.

Finland can establish or participate in the work of joint investigation teams.

8. What use can be made of SITs in the context of mutual legal assistance?

The SITs enable more effective co-operation between different countries. As crime is becoming more and more international, the investigation methods used by the police must also be effective, and independent of borders between different countries. The SITs also enable more persistent police work to fight against international crime.

9. How can the use of SITs be improved? Please provide any comments/proposals concerning the implementation of the terms of reference of the PC-TI and in particular the use and regulation of SITs.

The specific means stated above in the current Police Act do not give the police the right of access to call-associated data necessary for preventing terrorist offences, nor do they allow the police to bug with a view to prevent or uncover preparations for terrorist offences. This is due to the fact that the punishments stated in the amended Penal Code (comes into force 1 January 2003) for preparations for terrorist offences are too low. Neither is it possible to use interception of telecommunications in order to prevent or uncover terrorist offences

Due to the international development of terrorism, the police cannot effectively act with a view to preventing terrorist offences exclusively by means of traditional methods, the object of which is to clear up terrorist offences already committed. Preventing social damage brought about by terrorist acts requires that the police have sufficient powers to gather information on terrorist activities and their grounds, so that specific terrorist acts can be prevented.

France

1. Please indicate the SITs used in your country, the respective legal framework governing their use and their legal definition, if any.

The legal regulation of SITs in France was recently profoundly modified through the adoption of the Law of 9 March 2004, on adapting the criminal justice system to changes in crime. One of the major innovations of this Law is the creation of a specific section of the Code of Criminal Procedure applicable to "organised crime" offences, which include acts of terrorism. In addition, France is preparing to ratify the Council of Europe Convention on Cybercrime and plans to introduce legislation for this purpose shortly.

The presentation of the SITs used in France must therefore take these developments in domestic law into account.

Controlled delivery

Controlled delivery is allowed in investigations into drug-related offences (criminal or customs). It is provided for in Article 706-32 of the Code of Criminal Procedure and Article 67bis of the Customs Code. It is defined as "monitoring (surveillance) of the transport of narcotics or the proceeds of the commission of the offences" in question.

In controlled delivery, police officers, gendarmes and customs officers play a passive role consisting of following the members of a network in order to identify other members or to be able to seize goods. Consequently its use requires simply that the relevant public prosecutor be given notice of it.

Since the adoption of the Law of 9 March 2004, the provisions on controlled delivery are no longer confined to drug-trafficking offences. This Law indeed incudes a new Article 706-80 on "monitoring" ("surveillance") in the Code of Criminal Procedure. This provision enables senior police officers and police officers acting under their authority, subject to the public prosecutor's being informed and not opposing the measure, to conduct surveillance throughout the country of the delivery or transportation of objects, goods or proceeds resulting from or furthering the commission of offences falling within the scope of organised crime.

Infiltration

In certain circumstances the provisions of Article 706-32 of the Code of Criminal Procedure and Article 67bis of the Customs Code give investigators "legal permission" to commit acts that may be classed as criminal, provided they receive prior authorisation from the public prosecutor or investigating judge.

This is the case when persons committing drug-trafficking offences are afforded the legal means as well as the means of transporting, delivering, storing, conserving and communicating. Similarly, investigators may acquire, be in possession of, transport or deliver drugs or the proceeds of the commission of the offences in question. It should be emphasised that this list of authorised acts is restrictive in order to exclude any provocation to commit an offence.

The Law of 9 March 2004 on adapting the legal system to changes in crime inserted seven new articles on "infiltration" in the Code of Criminal Procedure (Articles 706-81 to 706-87).

According to the definition as it stands, infiltration consists of a specially authorised police officer keeping under surveillance persons suspected of committing an offence by posing as one of them or as an accomplice or receiver. For this purpose, the officer is authorised to use a false identity and if necessary commit certain specified acts, which may never, however, constitute incitement to commit an offence.

These acts are the following:
- acquiring, being in possession of, transporting, delivering or supplying substances, goods, products, documents or information deriving from or being used for the commission of offences;
- using or making available to persons committing such offences legal or financial means, or means of transport, delivery, storage, accommodation, conservation and telecommunication.

Infiltration operations are subject to the following strict conditions:
- they must be justified by the needs of an investigation into offences defined as the most serious forms of organised crime;
- they must be authorised by the public prosecutor or investigating judge in charge of the case and conducted under their supervision. Authorisation must be in writing and the grounds for it given, otherwise it is null and void, and it can be withdrawn at any time. It must mention the false identities of the officers in question;
- the judge must set a time-limit for the operation, which may not exceed a renewable period of four months. It may be ended at any time before the expiry of this period.

Observation (including cross-border observation)

As indicated above, the Law of 9 March 2004 included a new Article 706-80 on "surveillance" in the Code of Criminal Procedure. Subject to the public prosecutor's being informed in advance and not opposing the measure, police officers may place under surveillance throughout the country persons "whom there is one or more reasons to suspect[1] of committing an offence falling within the scope of 'organised crime'".

Moreover, the new Article 694-6 of the Code of Criminal Procedure permits pursuit abroad of a surveillance that has already started in France.

With respect to cross-border observation, France applies the provisions of Article 40 of the Convention Applying the Schengen Agreement, which enables police officers of one of the contracting parties who, within the framework of a criminal investigation, are keeping under observation in their country a person who is presumed to have taken part in an extraditable criminal offence, to continue their observation in the territory of another contracting party, where the latter has authorised cross-border observation in response to a request for assistance which has previously been submitted.

Article 40 further provides that where, for particularly urgent reasons, prior authorisation cannot be requested, the officers may continue the observation beyond the border, provided that the authorities of the second country are notified immediately that the border has been crossed and a request for assistance is submitted without delay. In these circumstances, observation may not exceed five hours if authorisation has not been obtained from the requested state within that time.

Interception of communications

French law distinguishes two categories of interception of correspondence sent by telecommunications:

- first, security interceptions (known as "administrative") under the supervision of the National Security Interceptions Committee. They are authorised by the Prime Minister and their purpose is to seek information on national security, the safeguarding of elements essential to the scientific and economic potential of France, or the prevention of terrorism, crime and organised crime and the re-forming or continuing existence of groups dissolved by application of the Act of 10 January 1936 on fighter groups and private vigilante groups;
- second, judicial interceptions regulated by Articles 100 ff of the Code of Criminal Procedure.

Judicial interceptions are an investigation technique that may only be ordered by an investigating judge to whom offences carrying a sentence of at least two years' imprisonment have been lawfully referred. The investigating judge may also order the recording and transcription of those communications.

Under Article 32 of the Posts and Telecommunications Code, "telecommunications" are "any transmission, broadcast or reception of signs, signals, writings, images, sounds or information of any kind by wire, optics, radio-engineering or other electromagnetic systems". Therefore, remote computer networks, Minitel, telex and other services using the terrestrial network (in particular, radiotelephones) are covered, in addition to public and private telephone services.

A decision to intercept is limited to a four-month period, though this may be renewed. Furthermore, only correspondence useful to uncovering the truth may be transcribed as evidence. No interception may take place of the line of a deputy or senator unless the president of the Assembly to which he or she belongs has been informed, while a line belonging to a lawyer's office may only be intercepted if the investigating judge has informed the President of the Bar.

The Law of 9 March 2004 makes it possible to intercept correspondence sent by telecommunications in the course of investigations supervised by the public prosecutor (investigations of an offence discovered while it is being committed and preliminary investigations), provided they concern facts connected with organised crime (which includes terrorist acts).

Such interception is, however, subject to prior authorisation by the *juge des libertés et de la détention* (a member of the bench) on the application of the public prosecutor. The conditions to which such interception is subject are identical to those in Articles 100 ff of the Code of Criminal Procedure but may not exceed a period of 15 days, which may be renewed once.

With the imminent ratification of the Convention on Cybercrime, France is already or will soon be able to require the immediate preservation of all types of computerised data stored, in particular by service providers. With respect to traffic data, it will be possible to order disclosure of the chain of communication of such technical data, if they have passed through several providers. It will also be possible to order that such frozen data should be handed over to the authorities.

Searches

In principle, Article 76 of the Code of Criminal Procedure makes all searches, house searches and seizures conducted in the course of a preliminary police investigation (investigation of offences not discovered while being committed) subject to the express consent of the person on whose property the operation takes place, as they may not be conducted during the night (between 9 p.m. and 6 a.m.).

However, Articles 706-89 and 706-90 of the Code of Criminal Procedure make it possible to disregard these provisions with respect to the fight against organised crime and to the fight against terrorism if this is justified by the needs of the investigation and under certain conditions. With the prior authorisation of the *juge des libertés et de la détention*, on the application of the public prosecutor, searches, house searches and seizures may be conducted:

- without the express consent of the person on whose property they take place,
- and at night, if they do not concern residential accommodation.

Cross-border pursuit

France implements the provisions of Article 41 of the Convention Applying the Schengen Agreement as follows:
- borders with the Kingdom of Belgium and the Federal Republic of Germany: pursuit is unlimited in space and time;
- borders with the Kingdom of Spain, the Grand Duchy of Luxembourg and Italy: pursuit is limited to a distance of 10 km from the border.

France has not allowed any of its partners' police officers to take people in for questioning on French territory.

The provisions of Article 73 of the Code of Criminal Procedure may be applied only if all the following apply:
- being observed in the act of committing an offence punishable by imprisonment;
- which the foreign police officer involved has witnessed or of which he or she has been the victim;
- on condition that this offence has been committed on French territory;
- the person taken in for questioning must immediately be taken to the nearest police officer.

In this case the person is therefore arrested not on the basis of the offence that justified the right of pursuit, but on the basis of a distinct offence.

2. When and under which circumstances (e.g. criminal investigation, preliminary stage, etc.) can SITs be used?

As indicated above, SITs may only be used in connection with criminal investigations (investigation of offences discovered while being committed, preliminary police investigation or judicial investigation) conducted by police officers under the supervision of a law officer (whether a prosecutor, investigating judge or *juge des libertés et de la détention*) into serious offences such as drug-trafficking or terrorist acts.

The Law of 9 March 2004 henceforth enables them to be used for a broader range of offences referred to as "organised crime".

3. Are there any specific features governing the use of SITs in relation to acts of terrorism? If so, please specify.

There is no specific feature governing the use of SITs as regards investigation into acts of terrorism. The Law of 9 March 2004 aims to enable SITs to be used in relation to all organised crime offences and acts of terrorism. As the GMT noted at its third meeting (10-11 April 2002), "by their complex and secret nature ... investigations into terrorist activities raise serious problems. These are accentuated still further by the frequent links between terrorism and other forms of crime".

4. How does the legal framework governing the use of SITs guarantee respect for human rights and individual freedoms, the principles of subsidiarity and proportionality? Is the authorisation to use SITs subject to time-limits? Which bodies and procedures are in place to supervise compliance with human rights standards and with the above-mentioned principles in the use of SITs? Is supervision automatic/systematic?

The legal framework governing the use of SITs in France is based on the essential principle of supervision of police officers by law officers representing the judicial authority, "the guardian of individual liberty" in the words of Article 66 of the Constitution.

As indicated in the reply to question 1, the use of SITs is always placed under the supervision of law officers. SITs used during the investigative phase that are likely to infringe fundamental freedoms more seriously are supervised by a member of the Bench (the *juge des libertés et de la détention*), as well as members of the public prosecutor's office.

Moreover, use of SITs is also subject to:
- the requirement of proportionality, in that it must always be justified by the needs of the investigation,
- reasons being given for decisions (searches at night),
- controlled time-limits (cf reply to question 1).

5. Which institutions are involved in the use of SITs and what is their role (e.g. law enforcement agencies, prosecutor's office, judicial authorities, etc.)? Which institutions can order and/or authorise the use of SITs? How does co-operation between these institutions work in practice?

See reply to question 1.

6. Are there any specialised counter-terrorism institutions? What is their role in the use of SITs?

Prosecution, investigation and trial of terrorist offences are centralised in Paris. The public prosecutor's office of the regional court of Paris includes a central counter-terrorism department (Section A6) composed of six prosecutors and six specialised investigating judges.

This rule of centralisation is applied in the framework of the principle of concurrent jurisdiction of the Paris court and the local court. It is a supplementary, optional power exercised after agreement with the courts concerned. Application of this rule takes into account, in particular, the

160

regional, national or international nautre of the individual or collective terrorist undertaking concerned.

There are also specialised central police units responsible for counter-terrorism. In addition to UCLAT (*Unité de Coordination et de Lutte Anti-Terroriste* – Anti-terrorism Co-ordination and Combat Unit), which is responsible for co-ordinating the various units, three units are more particularly responsible for investigations: the DNAT (*Division Nationale Anti-Terroriste* – National Anti-Terrorist Division), the Crime Squad Counter-Terrorism Section (SAT) and the DST (*Direction de la Surveillance du Territoire* – Counter-Intelligence Directorate).

These various specialised units have no particular role in the use of SITs.

7. Which measures have been adopted in order to facilitate international co-operation (e.g. joint investigation teams)? Can the SITs listed in reply to question 1 be used in cross-border settings?

One of the major advances in the European Union with respect to international judicial co-operation has been the adoption of the Convention on Mutual Assistance in Criminal Matters of 29 May 2000 and the Framework Decision on joint investigation teams of 13 June 2002.

France incorporated into domestic law the mechanisms provided for by these instruments and created new possibilities for mutual assistance in criminal matters through the Law of 9 March 2004.

This will be done, in particular, through:
* joint investigation teams,
* simplifying the channels through which requests for mutual assistance within the European Union are transmitted,
* using telecommunications (videoconferencing) in connection with international mutual assistance, and
* the possibility of authorising the continuation in French territory of infiltration operations conducted by foreign police officers (under the supervision of French police officers and with the agreement of the Minister for Justice).

In addition, the setting-up of the Eurojust unit (decision of the Council of the European Union, 28 February 2002) should make it possible to promote and improve co-ordination and co-operation between the relevant authorities of EU member states with respect to investigations into the most serious forms of crime, including terrorist acts.

With the adoption of the Law of 9 March 2004, France also incoporated into its legislation the mechanisms provided for in the Council of the European Union's Framework Decision of 13 June 2002 on the European arrest warrant and the surrender procedures between member states, which is the first practical expression of the principle of mutual recognition and is intended to replace often cumbersome extradition mechanisms.

The Ministry of Justice is at present examining the possibility of ratifying the Second Additional Protocol to the European Convention on Mutual Assistance in Criminal Matters adopted on 8 November 2001, which will make it possible to extend a higher level of mutual assistance mechanisms to states that are not members of the EU.

8. What use can be made of SITs in the context of mutual legal assistance?

In principle, where the use of a SIT is provided for in French law, it can be implemented at the request of a third country in response to a lawfully formulated request for mutual assistance.

Furthermore, certain instruments explicitly provide for the use of SITs in the context of mutual assistance in criminal matters. For example, the Convention of 29 May 2000 (see above) and the Council of Europe Convention on Cybercrime, which France is on the point of ratifying.

9. How can the use of SITs be improved? Please provide any comments/proposals concerning the implementation of the terms of reference of the PC-TI and in particular the use and regulation of SITs.

Recently France has profoundly modified its law on criminal procedure, as described above. Moreover, important instruments such as the Convention of 29 May 2000 and the Council of Europe Convention on Cybercrime will soon be entering into force. It would therefore be premature to envisage ways of improving SITs at this stage.

---

1. Statutory criterion enabling a person to be taken into police custody.

Germany

1. Please indicate the SITs used in your country, the respective legal framework governing their use and their legal definition, if any.

Undercover operations

a.   In accordance with German criminal procedure law, "undercover agents" may be used to investigate serious criminal offences, including amongst others criminal offences (such as trafficking in arms) which constitute offences against national security – including terrorist activities.

An "undercover agent" is a police officer investigating under an assumed identity assigned to him/her for an extended period (cover).

b.   The deployment of an "undercover agent" requires the consent of the public prosecution office. If deployment targets a specific accused person – which is the case as a rule – or if one must anticipate that the "undercover agent" will enter a private dwelling, the consent of a judge is required.

Undercover companies

German law does not make express provision for "front store operations". In individual cases, such operations may occur in the context of the deployment of an "undercover agent". The law therefore provides that "undercover agents" may participate in legal transactions using the cover given them, and may be provided with appropriate documents which they may make use of.

Informants

a.   German law distinguishes between "co-operating witnesses" and "informants". An "informant" is a person who is prepared in an individual case to provide information to the criminal prosecution authorities in return for an assurance that it will be kept confidential. A "co-operating witness" is a person who without belonging to a criminal prosecution authority is willing to support the latter for an extended period in solving criminal offences, and whose identity on principle is kept secret.

German criminal procedure law includes no special rules for the treatment of "co-operating witnesses/informants" in criminal proceedings. They are regarded as witnesses.

b.   Since "informants" and "co-operating witnesses" may be placed at risk if their co-operation with the criminal prosecution authorities is revealed, they can be assured of "confidentiality".

163

This confidentiality is assured by the head of the respective public prosecution office carrying out the investigation. The consequence of assurance is that the name of the "informant" or "co-operating witness" does not appear in the files, their information is introduced into the court proceedings via a police officer as "hearsay testimony" and the latter, as well as every investigating officer dealing with this matter, may and indeed must refuse to reveal it if, for instance, asked in court as to the origin of the information.

Controlled delivery

With illegal transport runs monitored by the criminal prosecution authorities (controlled delivery) over national borders, German law distinguishes between controlled importation, controlled exportation and controlled transit. On principle, controlled delivery requires the consent of the public prosecution office, whilst with controlled importation and controlled exportation, additionally, the participating foreign states must agree and give their consent to constantly monitor the transportation, and investigate the couriers, ringleaders and recipients with the aim in mind of punishing them by seizure of the prohibited articles, and to continually inform the German authorities of the progress of the case.

Observation

a. German law distinguishes between long-term and short-term observation, observation being defined as "planned monitoring".

Whilst short-term observation may be ordered and implemented by the investigating police officers, long-term observation (defined as observation carried out for an uninterrupted period of more than 24 hours or on more than two days) must be ordered by the public prosecution office. This order must be time-limited to a maximum of one month. Any extension over and above one month must be ordered by the investigating judge.

In the case of criminal offences of considerable significance, "special technical aids intended for the purposes of observation" may be used in observation. These include for instance night-vision equipment, tracking systems, and the Global Positioning System (GPS) satellite-guided positioning system. Furthermore, photographs may be taken and video recordings made in the context of observation, but only outside dwellings. Since dwellings are particularly protected by law, photographing and filming into dwellings from outside is not permitted either. The use of these means is ordered by the public prosecutor or the investigating police officers.

b. Cross-border observation is possible in the context of Article 40 of the convention applying the Schengen Agreement. Accordingly, it is necessary on principle for a request for assistance to have previously been submitted and authorised. For particularly urgent reasons, with specific suspicion of serious criminal offences (including assassination, murder, arson, kidnapping and hostage-taking, trafficking in arms and explosives, but not "mere" membership of a terrorist association) observation may also be continued over a border without the prior authorisation of the other state. The other state must however be informed without delay, and observation is to cease as soon as the other state so requests or where authorisation has not been obtained five hours after the border was crossed.

Electronic surveillance

Surveillance using electronic means takes place either in support of observation or in the framework of acoustic surveillance. Reference is therefore made to the information provided re Nos. 5, 7 and 8.

Optical surveillance (photographs or video recordings) within dwellings or other private premises is not permissible in accordance with German criminal procedure law.

Bugging

German law distinguishes between bugging inside and outside dwellings, also including office and commercial premises that are not generally accessible, but not motor vehicles. In both cases, bugging is permissible only in the case of those particularly serious criminal offences listed in the law, including membership of and support for a terrorist association, as well as "typical" terrorist criminal offences such as murder, explosives and arson attacks, arms trafficking and kidnapping.

Bugging outside dwellings is ordered by the investigating judge; only where a delay is likely to jeopardise the success of the investigation may the order be given by a public prosecutor or the police, in which case this order must be confirmed by a judge within three days.

Bugging within dwellings must be ordered by a chamber responsible for offences against national security consisting of three judges of the regional court. Bugging the dwellings and office premises of clergy, physicians and lawyers is not permissible on principle if they are not suspected of participating in the indictable offence in question.

The ordering of bugging within dwellings is to be time-limited to a maximum of four weeks, although extensions – by not more than four weeks at a time – are possible. Bugging outside dwellings must be limited to three months at a maximum. Extensions are possible by not more than three months at a time.

Interception of communications

German law permits monitoring of the accused's posts, as well as monitoring of telecommunication. Over and above the definition mentioned in the questionnaire, telecommunication facilities of uninvolved persons may also be monitored if they accept and pass on information from or for the accused (messengers) or if the accused uses their telecommunication facilities.

a.   The seizure of the accused's posts is ordered by a judge, or by the public prosecutor where a delay is likely to jeopardise the success of the investigation. Only the judge is entitled to open and monitor the content of the postal items. However, the judge may transfer the right to open seized postal items to the public prosecutor to the extent necessary where a delay would jeopardise the success of the investigation.

b.   Interception of communications (including mobile communications, fax and e-mail) is permissible with specific serious criminal offences expressly named by the law (including participation in a terrorist organisation and the abovementioned "typical" terrorist criminal offences). An order permitting the content of telecommunications to be monitored and recorded and obliging the network operators to provide the connection data related to the telecommunications is issued by a judge, in urgent cases by the public prosecution office. The order must be confirmed by the judge within three days. Ordering and confirmation by a judge applies for a maximum of three months and may be extended.

Searches

Only searches of persons, their dwellings and other premises at their disposal are regulated by law, as are articles belonging to them, including motor vehicles.

German law distinguishes between searches of suspects and searches of third parties. Whilst a search of the suspect is already permissible if it is anticipated that it may lead to the discovery of evidence, other persons not under suspicion may only be searched if facts exist revealing that the specific evidence searched for is on the premises that are to be searched.

Looking through documents found during searching, including documents and other recordings contained on data carriers, is effected on principle by the public prosecution office. Other officials, in particular police officers, are only permitted to search if the owner expressly permits this or if the public prosecutor so decides.

Hot pursuit

The pursuit over national borders of a person apprehended in the act is permitted in the context of Article 41 of the convention applying the Schengen Agreement with specific criminal offences listed therein (including murder, arson, kidnapping and hostage-taking, trafficking in arms and explosives, but not "mere" membership of a terrorist association).

The modalities of hot pursuit are determined by the individual states for their sovereign territory (declaration in accordance with Article 41 paragraph 9 of

166

the Convention applying the Schengen Agreement), so that German officials in hot pursuit must adhere to different rules in the various neighbouring states. By virtue of its declaration, Germany has granted the competent officers of the bordering "Schengen" states the right of hot pursuit on German sovereign territory without limit in space or time for all extraditable criminal offences, and has also granted the right of apprehension.

Agents provocateurs

The use of police *agents provocateurs* is not governed by law. However, case-law has formed rules on their use and in particular the limits imposed on their deployment. For instance, the deployment of an *agent provocateur* is permissible if an existing strong suspicion of serious criminal conduct is to be tested for its veracity, but not to encourage persons who would not dream of committing a crime to do so. Co-operating witnesses and undercover agents can be deployed as *agents provocateurs*.

Pseudo-purchases

Pseudo-purchases, considered namely on suspicion of trafficking in narcotics and arms, are a special form of the activities of an *agent provocateur*. For this reason, please refer to the previous paragraph.

Other special investigation methods

DNA analysis

German law permits molecular genetic testing of traces found at the scene of a crime and their comparison with the suspect's DNA material. Molecular genetic tests may only be ordered by a judge.

Search by screening

In solving specific serious crimes, including terrorist criminal offences, automatic data comparison between specific characteristics directly applying to the offender with data stored elsewhere for other reasons is permissible. As an example: Since it is known that terrorists are not properly registered with the police, and that electricity utilities for the dwellings where they conspire are not paid for by bank transfers, but in cash, it is permissible to screen out from the billing files of the electricity utilities those persons who do not pay their bills by transfer or direct debit, and to filter out from the persons identified thereby those who are officially registered. As to the remaining persons, the named criteria are met, and they need to be more closely investigated.

Search by screening may only be ordered by a judge, although where a delay is likely to jeopardise the success of the investigation also by a public prosecutor, whose order must however be confirmed within three days by a judge. Once the measure has been concluded, the competent data protection authority is to be informed.

2. When and under which circumstances (e.g. criminal investigation, preliminary stage, etc.) can SITs be used?

In the context of criminal prosecution, the application of special investigation methods can only be considered if initial suspicion exists. "Initial suspicion" means in accordance with the statutory definition that sufficient factual indications exist for a criminal offence.

3. Are there any specific features governing the use of SITs in relation to acts of terrorism? If so, please specify.

There are no special investigation methods for terrorist criminal offences or special conditions for their application to terrorist criminal offences under German law. Several investigation methods are only permissible, as stated above, with particularly serious criminal offences. These always include terrorist criminal offences.

4. How does the legal framework governing the use of SITs guarantee respect for human rights and individual freedoms, the principles of subsidiarity and proportionality? Is the authorisation to use SITs subject to time-limits? Which bodies and procedures are in place to supervise compliance with human rights standards and with the above-mentioned principles in the use of SITs? Is supervision automatic/systematic?

Adherence to the above principles is guaranteed firstly by the fact that Parliament has already made the use of the individual investigation means – graduated by the seriousness of the encroachment on the rights of the person concerned – available only subject to various preconditions. For instance, relatively minor encroachments on the rights of the person concerned may already be made if the results of the investigation reached by these means "may be useful for the investigation". The acoustic monitoring of a dwelling, by contrast, may only be considered if research into the facts would be made "disproportionately more difficult or devoid of prospects for success" with other means.

Furthermore, the lion's share of investigation methods involving encroachments on the rights of the accused or of third parties must be ordered or at least confirmed by an independent judge; indeed, in the case of acoustic monitoring of dwellings, which is considered to be the most serious, by a college of judges (criminal chamber with three professional judges). Serious encroachment is time-limited by law.

Finally, undercover investigation measures are linked to far-reaching information duties – as soon as this is possible without endangering the investigation – enabling those concerned to have the lawfulness of the measure examined by an independent court even after the fact.

5. Which institutions are involved in the use of SITs and what is their role (e.g. law enforcement agencies, prosecutor's office, judicial authorities, etc.)? Which institutions can order and/or authorise the use of SITs? How does co-operation between these institutions work in practice?

The institutions on principle called on to criminally prosecute are the police, the public prosecution office and the courts. The actual investigation authority is the public prosecution office, which may avail itself of the services of the police to investigate the facts. In practice, in cases of small and medium-scale crime, the investigations are carried out independently by the police.

The public prosecution office only hears of the criminal offence when the files are submitted once the police investigations have been concluded. With serious criminal offences – also including terrorist criminal offences – by contrast the public prosecution office carries out the investigation from the outset, in which case the individual investigation measures as a rule are carried out by the police in co-ordination with the public prosecution office.

In the context of the investigations, an independent court in the shape of an investigating judge only acts in cases in which a special investigation method is required whose use the law has expressly made dependent on the consent of a judge.

6. Are there any specialised counter-terrorism institutions? What is their role in the use of SITs?

In Germany, the prosecution of terrorist criminal offences is a matter exclusively for the Federal Public Prosecutor General. In less significant cases, he/she may hand over the case to the chief public prosecution office with local competence.

The Federal Public Prosecutor General commissions the police investigations as a rule to the Federal Criminal Police Office or – less often – to the Land Criminal Police Office with local competence. In principle, however, he/she may also give the investigation mandate to any other police unit.

The investigating judge of the Federal Court of Justice is competent for the court rulings necessary in the context of investigations carried out by the Federal Public Prosecutor General.

7. Which measures have been adopted in order to facilitate international co-operation (e.g. joint investigation teams)? Can the SITs listed in reply to question 1 be used in cross-border settings?

a.   The Federal Criminal Police Office has liaison officers stationed in many capital cities, and in return there are liaison officers from many foreign states at the Federal Criminal Police Office in Wiesbaden. The exchange of information between police forces has been much improved by this measure.

As yet, there have been no formal joint investigation teams – as far as we know – involving participation by German investigation officers, at least not in the field of terrorist criminal offences.

b.   The German Federal Ministry of Justice has stationed a liaison officer (staff member of the Federal Public Prosecutor General) at the French Ministry of Justice. Co-operation with the French judiciary, namely with investigating judges at the Paris Regional Court, which is competent in France for terrorist criminal offences, has improved considerably as a result of this.

c.   In the case of requests for mutual assistance, the deployment of Eurojust has proved to be extremely helpful. Specifically approaching the Eurojust representative of the country in question by the German Eurojust representative (staff member of the Federal Public Prosecutor General) has made it possible not only to send the request immediately to the right unit, but has made carrying out the requests much simpler and faster.

8.   What use can be made of SITs in the context of mutual legal assistance?

A number of special investigation methods can be requested across borders and carried out on the basis of the European Convention on Mutual Assistance in Criminal Matters, of the convention applying the Schengen Agreement, of the Convention on Mutual Assistance in Criminal Matters between the member states of the European Union, which Germany has signed but not yet ratified, and of the Second Additional Protocol to the European Convention on Mutual Assistance in Criminal Matters.

Where Germany has not yet ratified the convention in question, corresponding requests from foreign states may be carried out on a non-contractual basis, using domestic law on international mutual assistance in criminal matters as a foundation. With special investigation methods that depend on the use of coercive measures, dual criminality must exist as regards the criminal offence on which the request is based. This is likely to be the case as a rule with criminal offences from the field of terrorism.

9.   How can the use of SITs be improved? Please provide any comments/proposals concerning the implementation of the terms of reference of the PC-TI and in particular the use and regulation of SITs.

a.   Within Europe, with cross-border measures in the context of the fight against terrorism the problem frequently exists that - in contradistinction to German law – the law of several states does not have the offence of support for and/or membership of a terrorist association. This leads to difficulties with the international criminal law prosecution of a group planning terrorist activities which has not yet provably started to make concrete preparations.

b.   Problems are caused in many cases by hot pursuit. The difficulties are to be found on the one hand in the limit in space or time set by many states, and on the other in the list of criminal offences facilitating hot pursuit. This may be given different legal priority in the individual countries. It would be desirable to have a power of hot pursuit with a right to apprehend applying to all criminal offences without limit in space or time.

Hungary

1. Please indicate the SITs used in your country, the respective legal framework governing their use and their legal definition, if any.

Undercover operations (including covert investigations)

According to Hungarian law this is not one of the special techniques; it's rather a main category. All the special investigation techniques fall under this category. (The title of Chapter VII of the Police Act is "Covert information gathering", which in other words is "Undercover operations".)

Front-store operations

Hungarian authorities are entitled to use front companies and shell documents during covert operations (Police Act Chapter VII., Article 64. (1) a.; National Security Act Article 54. (1) g., h.).

Informants

There are three kinds of co-operating persons:
- informants,
- confidential agents (not members of the authority), and
- others.

They differ from each other in the frequency of helping the authority. The informant constantly provides information; the others do not (Police Act Ch.VII. Article 64. (1) a.).

The national security services "can enter into secret connection with private persons" to gather information (National Security Act Article 54. (1) c.).

Informants, confidential agents and other co-operators can be paid for providing information. Termination of the criminal proceedings can also be offered to those who have committed crime (except for homicide) (see XII).

Joint investigation teams (or "common criminal intelligence groups") can employ informants, according to the Act on International Co-operation between Law Enforcement Agencies:

Employment of a Person Co-operating with the Law Enforcement Agency

Section 24

(1) The member seconded to a common criminal intelligence group operating in the territory of Hungary may employ a person who co-

operates with a foreign law enforcement agency in the territory of Hungary.

(2) The Hungarian member seconded to a common criminal intelligence group operating in a foreign state may employ a person who co-operates with the Hungarian law enforcement agency if such a person or the data he/she supplies are provided with a protection by the foreign state that is at least identical to that stipulated in Hungarian laws.

Controlled delivery

The Police Act Chapter VII Article 64. (1) f. deals with controlled delivery. The definition written in the United Nations Convention against Transnational Organised Crime goes for this category too.

The National Security Act doesn't deal with controlled delivery, but according to it the services can observe or monitor any vehicle (National Security Act Article 54 (1) h.).

The Act on International Co-operation of Law Enforcement Agencies Section 17 deals with controlled delivery:

Section 17

(1) Based on the request sent to the International Law Enforcement Co-operation Centre (ILECC) and according to the ad hoc agreement of the Hungarian central law enforcement agency and the foreign authority, controlled delivery may be carried out in the territory of Hungary.

(2) If a delay jeopardises law enforcement interests, the Hungarian law enforcement agency may accept the request of the responsible agency of the foreign state directly and/or of the Hungarian law enforcement agency of the foreign state which has the same authority. The Hungarian law enforcement agency shall inform the agency defined in Section 19 Subsection (1) or the ILECC immediately.

Section 18

When making an ad hoc agreement on controlled delivery, the following should be provided for:
   a. the content, expected route and duration of the consignment, the mode of transport, the data eligible for identification of the transport means;
   b. the person managing the controlled delivery;
   c. the mode of communications of participants;
   d. the mode of escorting;
   e. the number of persons participating in escorting;
   f. the circumstances of transferring and accepting the consignment;
   g. the measures to be taken in the case of an arrest;

h. the measures to be taken in the case of a contingency.

Section 19

(1) The authorised and responsible Hungarian law enforcement agency shall be entitled to manage and control the operation in course of a controlled delivery carried out in the territory of Hungary.

(2) A member of a foreign authority may also take part in escorting a controlled consignment in accordance with an ad hoc agreement as defined in Section 17, subsection (1). An undercover detective may take part in escorting a controlled consignment with the consent of the public prosecutor according to Section 64, subsection (4) of the Police Act.

Observation

The person suspected with reason of a criminal offence or a person who has relations with him/her, and also any premises, buildings, other real estate, area, route, vehicle, or any event can be monitored and recorded (Police Act Chapter VII. Article 64. (1) d.; National Security Act Article 54. (1) h.).

The Act on International Co-operation of Law Enforcement Agencies declares:

Section 27

(1) The foreign authority may continue surveillance – of the person suspected with reason of a criminal offence and/or a person who has relations with him/her during its law enforcement activity pursued in its own territory – also in the territory of Hungary, if the ILECC has given its prior consent to such surveillance by setting a time-limit.

(2) In the event the foreign authority so specifies in its request, the Hungarian agency authorised for surveillance may render assistance in the surveillance carried out in the territory of Hungary.

(3) The Hungarian law enforcement agency may continue the surveillance commenced in the territory of Hungary in the territory of a foreign state according to the conditions defined in the international treaty.

Section 28

(1) If any delay involved a danger or otherwise infringed the law enforcement interest, the member of the foreign authority who carries out surveillance may carry out surveillance also without the prior consent of the ILECC if he/she notifies:
    a. the Hungarian authority indicated in the international treaty, at the time of crossing of the border, and

b. the ILECC of the reasons supporting the necessity of crossing the border without prior consent, at the time of crossing the border.

(2) Surveillance must be immediately terminated if it is requested so by the responsible Hungarian law enforcement agency after such notification or if the ILECC fails to give its consent within five hours following communication of the request.

Section 29

(1) Surveillance is allowed if suspicion arises of a criminal offence that qualifies as a serious criminal offence as defined in Section 97, subsection (1), paragraph i) of the Police Act for which surveillance is allowed by Article 40 of the convention implementing the Schengen Agreement on gradual elimination of border controls and by the European Union Convention adopted on Mutual Assistance and Co-operation between Customs Administrations (Naples II Convention).

(2) The criminal offences set out in subsection (1) paragraph b) are included in the schedule to this Act.

Section 30

Without prejudice to the provision of Section 28, surveillance in the territory of Hungary may be carried out by the member of a foreign authority who has a document certifying that such surveillance is permitted provided, however, that he/she has a document certifying his/her official capacity and that he/she belongs to the foreign authority.

Electronic surveillance, bugging

The observation mentioned in the previous section can be carried out by means of technical equipment (technical surveillance). If the technical surveillance is carried out in a private house, the operation needs authorisation by a judge (Police Act Article 69. (1) b.; National Security Act Article 56. b.).

Interception of communications

This covert operation needs authorisation by a judge and can be carried out only in the case of serious crimes or other crimes mentioned in the Act, including terrorism.

Letters, wire and mobile telecommunications, e-mail and computer communications, e.g. via the Internet, can be intercepted (Police Act Article 69 (1) c., d., National Security Act Article 56. c., d.). There is no distinction between public and private networks.

Searches

Searches can be used in open investigations without any authorisation (Criminal Procedure Code Article 103). Searches can be carried out in premises, houses, areas connected to premises or houses, and vehicles. (On 1 July 2003 a completely new criminal procedure code enters into force. The rules concerning searches, however, won't be modified significantly.)

If searches are used as special investigation techniques (secret house searches), they need authorisation by a judge. Secret house searches can be carried out only in private premises (Police Act Article 69. (1) a.; National Security Act Article 56. a.). There are no separate rules concerning searches of objects, of computers and so on, by various means including scanning.

Cross-border (hot) pursuits

Since it is not recognised as a special (secret) investigative tool, but rather a form of international co-operation in criminal matters, the Act on International Co-operation of Law Enforcement agencies deals with it:

Hot pursuit

Section 31

(1) A member of a foreign authority may, without prior consent, pursue a person in the territory of Hungary who
  a. may be suspected of committing or attempting to commit a criminal offence in the territory of a foreign state as defined in Section 29, and who was caught in committing of such an offence;
  b. has escaped from detention, provisional arrest or execution of imprisonment,

and any delay involved by notifying the Hungarian law enforcement agency would make arrest of the perpetrator significantly more difficult or would seriously jeopardise law enforcement interests of the foreign state and it can be substantiated that the Hungarian law enforcement agency is not capable of assuming pursuit in due course.

(2) The Hungarian law enforcement agency may continue the hot pursuit commenced in the territory of Hungary in the territory of the foreign state according to the conditions defined in the international treaty,

(3) The member of the foreign authority defined in subsection (1) must immediately notify the Hungarian authority indicated in the international treaty.

(4) The pursuit must be immediately terminated when it is requested by the responsible Hungarian law enforcement agency.

177

Section 32

Without prejudice to the provisions of Section 31, a hot pursuit may be carried out in the territory of Hungary by a member of a foreign authority who has a document certifying his/her official capacity and that he/she belongs to the foreign authority.

Section 33

Subsequent to termination of the hot pursuit, the member of the foreign authority who carried out pursuit shall act in accordance with the international treaty.

Agents provocateurs

Provoking the commission of a crime is forbidden in Hungary. To persuade or induce anyone to commit a crime is also forbidden. However, it is possible for a covert agent while infiltrating a criminal organisation to commit a crime (but not homicide) under certain circumstances. In these cases the prosecutor terminates the criminal proceeding against the secret agent (Police Act Article 67/A). There are no such rules in the National Security Act.

An undercover agent (a member of the authority) therefore can be used in order to infiltrate a criminal organisation, to carry out (or to take part in) controlled delivery, and to carry out pseudo-purchase, purchase of confidence or purchase of a sample. (see XII.)

The Act on International Co-operation between Law Enforcement Agencies also deals with undercover agents (but not with agents provocateurs):

Employment of Undercover Detectives

Section 25

(1) If a Hungarian undercover detective should be employed in the territory of a foreign state or a foreign undercover detective should be employed in Hungary for the success of law enforcement carried out in Hungary, it may be initiated by the ILECC with the foreign authority.

(2) If a foreign undercover detective should be employed in the territory of Hungary or a Hungarian undercover detective should be employed in a foreign state for the success of law enforcement carried out by the law enforcement agency of a foreign state, upon the request of the foreign authority, with the permit of the public prosecutor in the case set out in Section 64, subsection (1), paragraph f) of the Police Act, a foreign undercover detective may be employed in Hungary and a Hungarian undercover detective may be employed abroad.

(3) The Hungarian law enforcement agency or the ILECC shall immediately inform the foreign authority if a foreign undercover detective commits an offence that is punishable according to the laws of his/her own state.

Section 26

(1) An undercover detective may be employed according to the ad hoc agreement between the Hungarian central law enforcement agency and the foreign authority.

(2) Such agreement shall include:
- the duration of intelligence gathering;
- the conditions of employment;
- the rights and obligations of the undercover detective;
- the measures to be taken if the undercover detective becomes detected;
- information about the rules of responsibility for any damage caused by the undercover detective within the scope of his/her operation.

Pseudo-purchases or other pseudo-offences

There are three separate forms of buying things with hidden intention: pseudo-purchase, purchase of confidence and purchase of sample. Using the definitions of the Police Act, pseudo-purchase is a purchase carried out by an undercover detective in order to secure evidence or to catch the suspect.

Purchase of confidence is a purchase carried out by an undercover detective in order to inspire confidence with the intention of a future pseudo-purchase.

Purchase of sample is a purchase of materials, objects, instruments, or samples or components of these things, in order to secure them for further inspection during the intelligence work. Purchase of sample can be carried out not only by an undercover detective, but also by an informant, by a confidential agent, or by another co-operator.

Besides the pseudo-offence described under the *agent provocateur* title, there is another way of avoiding punishment once a crime has been committed. According to the Police Act Article 67, powers exist to offer the possibility of the termination of a criminal proceeding if the perpetrator agrees to provide information to the authority. If an agreement is settled, the police recompense the damages caused by the perpetrator, prepare shell documents, and prepare the necessary agreement on keeping state secrets and service secrets. This special investigative tool needs the consent of the county deputy chief prosecutor.

Other special investigative tools

According to the Police Act Article 64. (1) e., the police, in order to disclose a crime or to provide evidence, can set up a so-called technical trap. Causing injury or death must be avoided under all circumstances. The same regulation can be found in the National Security Act Article 54. (1) e.

The definition of a technical trap is not included in the Acts. By way of example, a banknote, soaked with chemical material and used in order to mark a perpetrator, is a technical trap.

The National Security Services are entitled to build up an information network in order to make information-gathering easier (National Security Act Article 54. (1) d.).

According to the Police Act Article 64. (1) g. a policeman can take over the role of an injured party in order to avoid his/her physical injury or death, if there is no other way to prevent the continuation of a crime, or to catch the perpetrator or to identify the perpetrator or to reveal a crime. In this case the Act mentions "policeman" instead of "undercover detective".

The Police Act Article 64 (8) entitles the police to enter bogus information in public registries, if it is needed to defend undercover detectives, informants, confidential agents, other co-operators, front companies or shell documents.

The Police Act Article 68. entitles the police to request access to information containing banking secrets, portfolio secrets, tax secrets, financial secrets, trade secrets and information provided by telecommunication companies or health institutions. These measures can be carried out by the consent of the public prosecutor.

All the detailed rules about how to use SITs are in a strictly confidential ministerial decree.

2. When and under which circumstances (e.g. criminal investigation, preliminary stage, etc.) can SITs be used?

Special investigative tools can be used by the police in the intelligence stage and in the criminal investigation too.

The national security services can use special investigative tools in order to carry out their own tasks, described respectively in the National Security Act. For example, the National Security Bureau is to reveal and eliminate any attempt to commit terrorist acts. Criminal investigation is outside the National Security Bureau's sphere of authority. Whenever enough evidence is collected against a perpetrator preparing to commit a terrorist act, the National Security Bureau passes the case to the police for carrying out the investigation.

SITs can be used in relation to any criminal act, except for those SITs which need authorisation by the judge:
- secret house search in private premises;
- technical surveillance in private premises;
- interception of letters and of wire and mobile telecommunication;
- interception of e-mails and computer network communication.

These SITs can only be used in the case of serious crimes and other crimes listed by the Act.

3. Are there any specific features governing the use of SITs in relation to acts of terrorism? If so, please specify.

According to specialists of the prosecutory service, the police and the national security services, there are no specific features governing the use of special investigative tools in relation to acts of terrorism. Our laws answer to the scale of terrorist threat in the country and this is low. (The international agreements concerning terrorism are nevertheless implemented.) Therefore there are no special SITs or special ways of using them in cases with relation to terrorism.

4. How does the legal framework governing the use of SITs guarantee respect for human rights and individual freedoms, the principles of subsidiarity and proportionality? Is the authorisation to use SITs subject to time-limits? Which bodies and procedures are in place to supervise compliance with human rights standards and with the above-mentioned principles in the use of SITs? Is supervision automatic/systematic?

The authorisation to use SITs is subject to time-limits. According to the Police Act Articles 71-72, if judicial authorisation is needed, the judge has to decide within 72 hours following the receiving of the request for authorisation. The time-limit of the authorisation is 90 days, and on proper request this can be extended by another 90 days.

The Police Act declares that any personal data concerning persons indifferent to the case must be immediately deleted and must not be used in the criminal proceeding.

The Police Act does not mention the principle of subsidiarity, but the National Security Act does: "Special Investigative Techniques can only be used if the information cannot be gathered by any other way" (Article 53 (2)). The principle of proportionality is not mentioned by either of the two laws.

The use of SITs is supervised systematically by the competent leaders of the police units. It is possible however to conduct financial supervision by independent bodies, but the appropriateness and effectiveness cannot be examined by these financial supervision bodies. There was an interesting case when the police used a special SIT, the side-effect of which was the slight violation of third persons' human rights. Although the action was a great success, the policemen responsible for the operation had to suffer the consequences.

5. Which institutions are involved in the use of SITs and what is their role (e.g. law enforcement agencies, prosecutor's office, judicial authorities, etc.)? Which institutions can order and/or authorise the use of SITs? How does co-operation between these institutions work in practice?

The institutions involved in the use of SITs are:
- The police, who use special investigative techniques in the intelligence and criminal investigation phases; decide on the use of SITs, if this does not require consent or authorisation by a prosecutor or a judge;
- The national security services;
- National Security Bureau (internal intelligence agency);
- Intelligence Bureau (foreign intelligence agency);
- Military Security Bureau (internal military intelligence);
- Military Intelligence Bureau (foreign military intelligence);
- National Security Special Service (provides technical equipment and experts in secret intelligence work);
- The Prosecutory Service, which authorises the police to carry out pseudo-purchases, purchases to gain trust, infiltration of a criminal organisation by an undercover detective and controlled delivery, can allow the termination of criminal proceedings against an undercover detective and others;
- The judge authorises the police and the national security services to carry out secret searches in private premises, technical surveillance in private premises, interception of letters and telecommunication, e-mails and other data stored on computer or the Internet.

Co-operation between these institutions is quick and effective. The major problem is the lack of enough equipment and trained experts .

6. Are there any specialised counter-terrorism institutions? What is their role in the use of SITs?

The national security services are involved in anti-terrorist activities. One of the National Security Bureau's main tasks is to eliminate any threat arising from terrorist activities.

There is a Sub-Department for Explosives and Arms Trade cases inside the Budapest Police Organisation, Department against Organised Crime. This unit deals also with cases of a terrorist character.

There is an Anti-terrorist Department in the Central Police Organisation. This department is a relatively new unit. Since offensive terrorist activities are rare in Hungary, this unit's main task is fighting international crime.

There is a Counter-Terrorism Special Unit, which has no investigative power. This is a highly trained commando unit, fighting in the front line against dangerous criminals and terrorists.

There is some parallelism between the spheres of authorities of these institutions, and all of them have the right to use SITs. However, only the police have the right to investigate openly.

(Some other authorities are empowered with secret intelligence powers, for example the Border Guard Service, or the Financial Investigative Unit, which is now integrated into the police, or the Prosecutory Service. The latter has the right to use SITs during investigations, but is not allowed to take part in intelligence work.)

7. Which measures have been adopted in order to facilitate international co-operation (e.g. joint investigation teams)? Can the SITs listed in reply to question 1 be used in cross-border settings?

There are some 200 laws and other regulations concerning international co-operation in criminal matters, including international treaties, most of them bilateral treaties. The most important law is the Act on International Co-operation of Law Enforcement Agencies, which enters into force at the time of the accession to the European Union, in 2004.

It deals exclusively with the SITs used by the police in the intelligence phase. The SITs mentioned in this Act are:
- controlled delivery,
- set up of a common criminal intelligence group,
- employment of an undercover detective,
- cross border surveillance, and
- hot pursuit.

Further forms of international co-operation are:
- direct exchange of information, and
- set-up of a common criminal intelligence group (comparable to a joint investigation team).

8. What use can be made of SITs in the context of mutual legal assistance?

All the experts say that for the time being there is no way of using SITs in mutual legal assistance.

9. How can the use of SITs be improved? Please provide any comments/proposals concerning the implementation of the terms of reference of the PC-TI and in particular the use and regulation of SITs.

The new Criminal Procedure Code enters into force on 2 July 2003. It brings a lot of changes. For example, the papers containing the decision of the authority concerning the use of an SIT must be put into the file; therefore the defendants and the defence attorneys can see them. It makes the use of SITs far less efficient.

The Law on mutual legal assistance has no regulations concerning SITs. The Act 1999/54, on The Exchange of Information with Interpol, Europol and the Schengen Information System, however, says that the information gathered by using SITs must be forwarded on the proper request of the abovementioned institutions.

Working out rules concerning SITs in mutual legal assistance could help to provide stronger evidence for the courts.

Strengthening the active role of the Prosecutory Service seems to be necessary. In Hungary, for example, the most important corruption cases are investigated exclusively by public prosecutors. They are authorised by the law to use SITs, but in fact they have to ask for technical help from the police or the National Security Special Service, because of the lack of equipment and specialists. This can be a security risk, if the suspect is a high-ranking police officer. Moreover, the bilateral international agreements, as well as the Act on International Co-operation between Law Enforcement Agencies, leave out the prosecutors of the international co-operation.

Ireland

1. Please indicate the SITs used in your country, the respective legal framework governing their use and their legal definition, if any.

The following SITs are used in Ireland:
- informants,
- controlled delivery,
- observation, excluding cross-border observation,
- interception of communications, and
- searches, excluding scanning.

Some of the above are used in accordance with police procedures, whereas other SITs are employed in observance of the legislative boundaries imposed by various Acts of the *Oireachtas* (Parliament). Searches of persons or properties are carried out within the parameters of various Acts such as the Offences against the State Acts 1939/98, the Misuse of Drugs Acts 1977/84, the Criminal Law Act 1976 and the Child Trafficking and Pornography Act 1998. Other powers of arrest and search are encompassed in the plethora of legislation covering assaults, theft, fraud etc. Controlled deliveries are carried out in accordance with the Europol Convention.

The interception of communications is strictly governed by the Interception of Postal Packets and Telecommunications Messages (Regulation) Act, 1993. Interception is defined as

(a) an act that consists of the opening or attempted opening of a postal packet addressed to any person or the delaying or detaining of any such postal packet or the doing of anything to prevent its due delivery or the authorising, suffering or permitting of another person (who is not the person to whom the postal packet is addressed) to do so, and
(b) an act that consists of the listening or attempted listening to, or the recording or attempted recording, by any means, in the course of its transmission, of a telecommunication message, other than such listening or recording, or such an attempt, where either the person on whose behalf the message is transmitted or the person intended to receive the message has consented to the listening or recording.

2. When and under which circumstances (e.g. criminal investigation, preliminary stage, etc.) can SITs be used?

SITs can be used to obtain intelligence, determine the path to be followed in an investigation and in furtherance of a criminal investigation.

3. Are there any specific features governing the use of SITs in relation to acts of terrorism? If so, please specify.

No.

4. How does the legal framework governing the use of SITs guarantee respect for human rights and individual freedoms, the principles of subsidiarity and proportionality? Is the authorisation to use SITs subject to time-limits? Which bodies and procedures are in place to supervise compliance with human rights standards and with the above-mentioned principles in the use of SITs? Is supervision automatic/systematic?

Irish Courts vigorously enforce the human rights safeguards enshrined in the Irish constitution.

Legislation in Ireland does not allow police officers to operate independently of the law. There are no exemptions in place to allow police officers to breach the legal provisions of the state, either of their own volition or by direction.

A warrant allowing the interception of communications is issued by the Minister for Justice, Equality & Law Reform on receipt of a written request from the Commissioner of the *Garda Síochána* (the national police force). The warrant is valid for a period not exceeding three months, at which stage a new application to retain the interception must be made by the Commissioner. In the absence of such application the interception will be ceased. A judge of the High Court is appointed to regularly review the general operation of the Act and forward any relevant reports to the Minister for Justice, Equality & Law Reform.

5. Which institutions are involved in the use of SITs and what is their role (e.g. law enforcement agencies, prosecutor's office, judicial authorities, etc.)? Which institutions can order and/or authorise the use of SITs? How does co-operation between these institutions work in practice?

The *Garda Síochána* use the SITs listed above. The defence forces are entitled to intercept communications in the interests of national security

6. Are there any specialised counter-terrorism institutions? What is their role in the use of SITs?

The role of the *Garda Síochána* includes counter-terrorism, both domestic and international. The deployment of SITs is ultimately at the behest of the Commissioner of the *Garda Síochána*.

7. Which measures have been adopted in order to facilitate international co-operation (e.g. joint investigation teams)? Can the SITs listed in reply to question 1 be used in cross-border settings?

Ireland is a signatory to the Schengen Agreement Article 39 dealing with joint investigation teams, but is limited to matters than can be dealt with on a police-to-police basis. The topic is currently being discussed at European level. Ireland has not signed up to Articles 40 to 43 of the Schengen Agreement, on cross-border matters. As the situation stands at present, the SITs listed at 1 above may not be used in a cross-border setting.

8.   What use can be made of SITs in the context of mutual legal assistance?

Each mutual assistance request is considered on its own merits, where SITs can be deployed if required.

9.   How can the use of SITs be improved? Please provide any comments/proposals concerning the implementation of the terms of reference of the PC-TI and in particular the use and regulation of SITs.

The increased threat to society from terrorist groups cannot be ignored and must be vigorously counteracted. There is a duty of care on all countries to protect the lives of their citizens, whether affiliated to a terrorist organisation or not. The means deployed to counteract the terrorist groups must be proportionate to the perceived threat and take cognisance of the rights of the individuals. National legislation must be such as to allow law enforcement agencies to operate efficiently and effectively for the common good.

Italy

1. Please indicate the SITs used in your country, the respective legal framework governing their use and their legal definition, if any.

The Italian legal system currently in force generally enables law-enforcement officers investigating, either before or after criminal proceedings have been started, to engage in a series of intelligence-gathering activities which, broadly speaking, can be classified as typical or atypical.

As requested, investigative tools which can be used in the fight against terrorism will be mentioned herein.

All typical efforts must be expressly laid down in and governed by the code of criminal procedure and/or other pieces of special legislation. In particular, the following measures are allowed which are prescribed by the relevant legislation:

Interception of communications

This covers telephone, fax, e-mail and conversations between persons physically present at a place ("bugging" of premises). This investigative tool is governed by the code of criminal procedure and Section 3 of Law No. 438/2001. It consists of electronic surveillance conducted in the course of criminal proceedings. It is authorised by the judge whenever it is deemed necessary for investigative purposes and the available evidence is sufficient for prosecution. The contents of the said communications can be used evidentially in court.

Interception of communications for preventive purposes

The possibility of telephone conversations, computer-based conversations and conversations between persons physically present at a place being intercepted in the context of terrorism investigation – as is the case with organised crime investigations – is provided for in Section 5 of Law No. 438/2001, whenever this measure is necessary to acquire information relating to the prevention of offences for terrorist purposes. In other words, specific intelligence is needed in order for the interception of such communications to be justified. Although administrative in nature, this measure requires nevertheless the supervision of the competent judicial authority. It serves the purpose of obtaining information (which cannot be used in criminal proceedings, however) to step up both investigative and intelligence activities.

Undercover activities

Section 4 of Law No. 438/2001 provides for the non-punishability of law enforcement officers who, in the course of specific and previously authorised police operations and with the exclusive aim of obtaining evidence relating to those terrorist crimes they are investigating – including acts of international terrorism – directly or indirectly acquire, receive, replace or conceal money, weapons, documents or other material representing the object, result, proceeds of a crime or the means to commit it, or who hamper efforts to trace the origin of said items, or who allow them to be used.

The law has also provided for the possibility of "using indications that have emerged in the course of undercover activities to establish contacts with individuals and sites on the Net". Basically, this is a case of resorting to the agent provocateur. Undercover activities are also allowed for offences concerning sexual exploitation of children and trafficking of human beings (article 14, Law 3 August 1998, n. 269 and article 10, Law 11 August 2003, n. 228).

Cross-border surveillance

Section 40 of the Schengen Convention introduces a provision whereby law-enforcement personnel from a state signatory to the Schengen Treaty may keep monitoring/watching a person whom they have been monitoring in their own country in the context of a criminal investigation in connection with an extraditable offence on the territory of another Schengen state. Both routine and urgent procedures are provided for – with and without the previous authorisation of the competent authorities of the foreign state concerned.

Moreover, the judicial authorities may allow law-enforcement agencies to conduct a series of other activities, such as gathering information and documents concerning current accounts, financial transactions and flows of money from banks and finance houses, as well as telephone billing records from public telephone companies.

Law-enforcement officers may gather information from public records (real estate, car, ship or aircraft registration) on their own initiative and without the previous authorisation of the judicial authorities.

Unlike the intelligence-gathering measures mentioned above, no specific statutory provisions govern atypical investigative tools such as moving surveillance operations (e.g. shadowing) using audio-visual aids or electronic or satellite tracking.

Forensic examination techniques based on state-of-the-art technology may also prove instrumental in conducting successful investigations, both when prosecuting the perpetrators of a crime and in preventing crimes from being committed.

Front store operations

These are allowed under the same conditions and requirements explained for undercover activities.

Informants

Although informants are largely used in police practice, there is no explicit regulation on their status or direct protection. However, under the Code for Penal Procedure (Article 203 CPP) the role of informants is acknowledged as a privileged relationship with the police and security services, while information provided by them cannot be utilised during investigations or at trial, unless they are heard as witnesses:
- police forces' or security services' witnesses cannot be compelled to reveal the names of their informants;
- information provided by informants can neither be acquired nor utilised in the proceedings, unless informants become witnesses;
- if informants have not been questioned or interviewed by the police or the prosecutor, the information provided by them before trial cannot be used at trial.

Controlled delivery

In cases of delivery of money and other property or assets:

(a) in the event of kidnapping or hostage taking, the payment of any ransom is forbidden and property, assets and money which can be used for that purpose are seized. However, under the authority of a judicial Decree, upon request of the Prosecutor, may be authorised the controlled delivery of ransoms. (Article 7, Law 15 March 1991, n. 82, as amended by Law 13 February 2001, n. 45)

Observation

Observation is widely used in police and investigation practice. Its admissibility is founded on the contingency power of the police to ascertain crimes and seek evidence (including video and audio tape of persons), when the prosecutor cannot, at the appropriate time, direct investigations (Article 354 CPP).

Searches

Different types of searches are regulated in the domestic legislation:
- body or local searches may be decided for evidentiary purposes by a reasoned Decree of the Prosecutor and conducted personally or through police officers. No validation is needed under prior authorisation (Article 247-252 CPP). However, in case a seizure is made for evidentiary purposes, without prior Decree and under contingency

circumstances directly by the police, validation of the seizure has to be subsequently approved by the Prosecutor (Article 355 CPP);

- searches of buildings or a block of buildings are allowed for the recovery of firearms;
- search and seizure of real estate where firearms were held by organised criminal or terrorist groups, or when the real estate is pertinent to the crime (Article 3, Law 8 August 1977, n. 533);
- search on board and seizure of ships and aeroplanes used for the transport of drugs (Article 99, Presidential Decree 9 October 1990, n. 309);
- body and vehicle searches, by law-enforcement officials, under exceptional and contingent circumstances for the maintenance of public order and in relation to the suspected possession of firearms or explosives (Article 4, Law 22 May 1975, n. 152);
- body search on persons temporarily held by the police as suspected of involvement in the possible commission of serious crimes, including terrorist crimes (Article 6, Law 6 February 1980, n. 15);
- ships and vehicles searches, by law enforcement officials and agents, under contingent circumstances, in relation to the suspect of smuggling of migrants (Article 12.7, Legislative Decree 25 July 1998, n.286); search is operated without prior Decree directly by the police, but has to be subsequently approved by the Prosecutor (Article 352 CPP).

Agents Provocateurs

Although controversial, criminal liability for the conduct of an *agent provocateur* may be excluded on the ground of accomplishment of a legal duty (Article 51, CP).

Pseudo-purchases or other pseudo-offences

Pseudo-purchase of firearms

Law-enforcement officials are not liable for prosecution, if the operation was previously planned by the appropriate authority and for evidentiary purposes. The seizure of firearms may be delayed up to the closure of investigation, upon decision of the Prosecutor (Article 12 *quater*, Law 7 August 1992, n. 356);

Pseudo-money laundering

Law-enforcement officials are not liable for prosecution, if the operation (laundering of money, property or assets resulting from money-laundering activities or other interference with tracking of the origin or else allowing those monies, property or assets to be utilised) was previously planned by the appropriate authority and for evidentiary purposes. The seizure of money, property or assets may be delayed up to the closure of investigation, upon decision of the Prosecutor (Article 12 *quater*, Law 7 August 1992, n. 356);

Pseudo-purchase of drugs

Law-enforcement officials are not liable for prosecution, if the operation was previously planned by the appropriate authority and for evidentiary purposes. The seizure of drugs may be delayed upon decision of the Prosecutor (Article 97, Presidential Decree 9 October 1990, n. 309).

Pseudo-offences concerning sexual exploitation of children

Law enforcement officials are not liable for prosecution, if the operation (purchasing of pornographic material, participation to sexual travel, etc.) was previously planned by the appropriate Authority and for evidentiary purposes; the seizure of the pornographic material may be delayed up to the closure of investigation, upon decision of the Prosecutor (article 14, Law 3 August 1998, n. 269);

Pseudo-trafficking of human beings

Law enforcement officials are not liable for prosecution, if the operation (purchasing, receiving, counterfeiting, etc. of things resulting from trafficking of human beings activities) was previously planned by the appropriate Authority and for evidentiary purposes (article 10, Law 11 August 2003, n. 228); the seizure of money, property or assets may be delayed up to the closure of investigation, upon decision of the Prosecutor (article 8, Law 11 August 2003, n. 228).

2. When and under which circumstances (e.g. criminal investigation, preliminary stage, etc.) can SITs be used?

As stressed above, a number of special investigation techniques (SITs) – mostly typical in nature – can only be used in the course of criminal proceedings and after the green light from the judicial authorities.

An exception to the rule is the "preventive" interception of communications, whose results cannot be used evidentially in court and only serve intelligence purposes.

3. Are there any specific features governing the use of SITs in relation to acts of terrorism? If so, please specify.

All the SITs listed can be used in enquiries into crimes perpetrated for terrorist purposes. Some of them can be used only to prevent and repress acts of terrorism or organised crime. This is the case for the above-mentioned preventive interception and undercover activities – operational instruments of an exceptional character introduced by the law-making body to counter the most serious and dangerous threats posed by organised crime and terrorism.

4. How does the legal framework governing the use of SITs guarantee respect for human rights and individual freedoms, the principles of subsidiarity and proportionality? Is the authorisation to use SITs subject to time-limits? Which bodies and procedures are in place to supervise compliance with human rights standards and with the above-mentioned principles in the use of SITs? Is supervision automatic/systematic?

According to the legal system presently in force, and as already mentioned in point 1, almost all SITs have to be authorised by judicial authorities. This ensures inspection of both the legitimacy and the merits of the investigations. The authorisations issued by magistrates are in their turn subject to inspection of both their legitimacy and the merits, at various levels, on the part of judicial supervisory bodies.

Similarly those SITs for the use of which no magistrates' preventive authorisation is requested can be adopted by police forces, provided that they respect human rights and individual freedoms – the principles sanctioned by the Italian Constitution. In addition to the crime of "abuse of power"[1] (on the basis of which, punishment is envisaged for a public official who intentionally in the line of duty carries out activities aimed at obtaining undue profits or at causing unfair damage to other people), a series of offences peculiar to public officials is provided for by the Criminal Code. In particular, punishments are envisaged for law-enforcement officers who carry out acts that abuse and/or injure personal freedom and dignity.

Those SITs that must be authorised by a magistrate are subject to time-limits, as envisaged by law. For example, telephone interception is authorised for a period of up to 40 days, but extensions (20 more days) can be granted by a decree detailing the specific reasons for it, in cases where the grounds that induced the judge to give such authorisation persist.

Furthermore, the rights of the defence are protected. As a matter of fact, the results of interception are shown to the counsels, who are also served notice on filing the recordings and relevant notes with the court clerk's office.

5. Which institutions are involved in the use of SITs and what is their role (e.g. law enforcement agencies, prosecutor's office, judicial authorities, etc.)? Which institutions can order and/or authorise the use of SITs? How does co-operation between these institutions work in practice?

Law-enforcement agencies, prosecutors' offices and judicial authorities are all involved in the use of SITs, with different roles and tasks. In particular,
- law-enforcement agencies are in practical charge of carrying out investigations and supervise the use of human resources and specific technologies;

- prosecutors' offices, according to the legal system presently in force, have the function to supervise investigations, co-ordinate the activities of law-enforcement agencies and delegate the carrying out of investigations to them. Prosecutors' offices also issue authorisations that are anyway subject to inspection with regard to both their legitimacy and their merits;
- specific judicial authorities – the investigating magistrates, the court competent to review the legality and legitimacy of an arrest, and the supreme court – are responsible for inspection of both the legitimacy and the merits of the measures adopted.

As for the institutions that can issue authorisations, in particular:
- Interception of communications is carried out if there is a specific order by the Prosecutor's office (PM), upon authorisation of investigating magistrates (GIP). Only in cases of emergency, when there are reason to believe that to delay an order might result in serious damage to the investigations, the PM can authorise interception activities also in the absence of preventive authorisation by the GIP, who however must ratify this measure within the next 48 hours;
- Preventive interception, as requested by the Interior Minister or, upon his/her delegation, by the *Questore* or the officials in charge of the ministry's Central Directorates, is authorised by the public prosecutor operating in the district where this measure has to be adopted;
- Undercover activities are authorised, depending on the membership of personnel conducting such operations, by the chiefs of police forces (e.g., the chief of police, the general officers commanding the *Arma dei Carabinieri* or the *Guardia di Finanza)*. The body authorising undercover activities must notify the PM of such move, of later developments and results;
- The acquisition of printouts relating to bank accounts and telephone traffic is authorised by the PM and this measure must be always based on solid reasons.

Other SITs are authorised by those in charge of law-enforcement agencies dealing with investigations and/or enquiries.

As to co-operation between law enforcement, the Public Prosecutor's Office and other judicial authorities, it can be observed that a subordination role only exists between police and the Public Prosecutor's Office under whose authority the former come when carrying out criminal investigations. Technically speaking, no relationship exists between the Public Prosecutor's Office and the GIP or any other judicial authority, since they operate at totally different levels: the first one is entrusted with the task of officially charging someone with a crime on the basis of evidence collected, whereas the other judicial bodies judge the case on its merits, check the legitimacy and validity of the activities carried out during preliminary investigations and assess the evidence collected with a view to the judgment.

6. Are there any specialised counter-terrorism institutions? What is their role in the use of SITs?

A number of specialised services have been set up within police forces (State National Police, *Carabinieri* and *Guardia di Finanza*) to counter terrorism, both in terms of prevention and suppression of criminal activities.

In particular, the *Direzione Centrale della Polizia di Prevenzione* (Directorate of Prevention Police) is the central office within the National Police, dealing with counter-terrorism activities. It is assisted by the *Divisioni Investigazioni Generali ed Operazioni Speciali* (DIGOS), local prevention offices set up in every Italian province.

The *Carabinieri* also have specialised offices all over the national territory, namely the *Raggruppamento Operativo Speciale* (ROS) and the *Nuclei Operativi*, at provincial level. So has the *Guardia di Finanza*, that is specifically responsible for countering terrorist financing.

Both central and local offices may use the above-mentioned SITs while carrying out criminal police activities.

7. Which measures have been adopted in order to facilitate international co-operation (e.g. joint investigation teams)? Can the SITs listed in reply to question 1 be used in cross-border settings?

An analysis is currently being conducted in Italy of the provisions designed to fully and effectively implement the decisions made at European level.

A number of significant initiatives have been taken within the EU. Of particular importance is Enfopol 19, adopted by the JHA Council of 25/26 April 2002, relating to the setting-up of multinational ad hoc teams entrusted with the task of collecting and exchanging information on terrorists. A project on forming "Joint Investigation Teams" has also been approved (Outline Decision 2002/465/JHA of the JHA Council of 13.6.2002). Of considerable interest is the subsequent Decision 2003/48 JHA on implementation of specific measures on police and judicial co-operation in the fight against terrorism, under Section 4 of the Common Position 2001/931/PESC.

Of the SITs listed under point 1, only cross-border surveillance can be used abroad by police forces of the Schengen countries. However, foreign police personnel may co-operate with colleagues from national agencies, by virtue of agreements between specialised services, and take part in investigations and activities, such as shadowing.

8. What use can be made of SITs in the context of mutual legal assistance?

Data acquired thanks to SITs can be shared between the police forces of the various countries by virtue of and in conformity with the international conventions and/or bilateral/multilateral agreements currently in force between the countries involved.

9. How can the use of SITs be improved? Please provide any comments/proposals concerning the implementation of the terms of reference of the PC-TI and in particular the use and regulation of SITs.

As to this last point, it is observed that a harmonisation of SITs would be advisable in the field of increased police co-operation between EU member states. Concerted action against the terrorist threat would then be possible, also allowing the multinational ad hoc teams and joint investigation teams to become fully operational.

---

1. Article 323 of the Criminal Code (Abuse of power) states: "Unless the act committed is envisaged as a more serious crime, the public official or the person in charge of public services, who in the line of duty or while in service, in violation of laws or regulations, or failing to abstain if there is an interest for him/her or for a close relative, or in the other cases as prescribed by law, intentionally obtains undue property profits for him/her or for other people, or causes unfair damage to other people, is punished with a prison term of 6 months to 3 years. The punishment is increased in those cases when the profit or damage are significantly extensive".

Latvia

1. Please indicate the SITs used in your country, the respective legal framework governing their use and their legal definition, if any.

The respective legal framework concerning SITs, their regulation and use, is the Law of Investigatory Operations (undercover investigations).

The legal basis of investigatory operations is the Constitution, the Criminal Procedure Code of Latvia, and other laws and international agreements which regulate the functions, rights and obligations of the authorities that ensure state security, defence and economic sovereignty and public order (Section 3).

In compliance with the Law of Investigatory Operations (LIO), investigatory operations are: the overt and covert legal activities of specially authorised – pursuant to the procedures prescribed in this Law, and by law – officials of state authorities, the objectives of which are the protection of the life and health, rights and freedoms, honour, dignity and property of persons and the safeguarding of the constitution, the political system, national independence and territorial integrity, the capabilities of the state regarding defence, the economy, science and technology, and state official secrets, against external and internal threats.

The LIO also governs undercover activities, as follows.

Enquiries

This is covert activity of officials of bodies performing undercover activities in the course of which, with the help of questioning, ascertainment and determination, information is obtained regarding facts, persons and things. Determination is performed by finding out information from persons, where there is reason to believe that such information is available to the relevant persons but they do not wish to provide it directly.

Observation (shadowing)

If a body performing undercover operations has available well-founded information regarding a crime in preparation or having been committed by persons, or regarding other unlawful acts, or a threat to interests of importance to the state, the observation (shadowing) of such persons, and persons associated with them, is permitted; that is, observation of various stationary and mobile facilities, observation (shadowing) of persons associated, and preventive investigatory observation of facilities.

Inspection

Officials of bodies performing operations are entitled, without disclosing their official affiliation and the true reason, to inspect the premises, territory and other publicly accessible property of enterprises, institutions and organisations. Property which is not accessible to the public may be inspected by entering or approaching such only with the consent of the relevant possessor.

Acquisition of samples and research

Officials of bodies performing operations are entitled to obtain samples of the handwriting, voice and odours of persons, their fingerprints, things and parts and copies thereof, materials, substances and products, traces of the actions of persons and animals, excretions of persons and animals, and other samples, samples of finished goods, partly processed goods, raw and other materials, documents and copies thereof and other things. Research is performed by comparison and other techniques.

Examination of a person

Investigatory examination of a person is performed without revealing to the person the interests of the body performing the operations and the purpose of the examination, and by specially creating such conditions as will cause the person to be in a situation that would make feasible the performing of such operations.

Entry

Entry is performed by covertly gaining access to an apartment, premises, transport vehicles or other facilities not open to the public, in order to ensure the carrying out of undercover operations activities. Investigatory entry is permitted only in cases of undercover activities.

Experiment

The purpose is to create special circumstances (situations) in order to determine the persons or things of interest, or to determine the actions of persons regarding whom the process is being conducted or the movement of things, in such circumstances, and to determine the motivation (subjective aspect) of such persons for their actions. An experiment, the purpose of which is to record how persons, in relation to whom the investigatory process is being conducted, act in a situation eliciting a criminal or other illegal act, is performed only with the approval of a prosecutor.

The LIO also covers monitoring of correspondence; the acquisition of information through technical means; and wiretapping of conversations.

In the course of undercover activities, video, audio, cinematograph and photographic equipment, various information systems and technical, chemical and biological means may be utilised. Such means shall be used so as to not cause harm to the health of the population or the environment (Chapter 2, Section 6).

Investigatory activities, in the course of which there is significant infringement of the constitutional rights of persons, are conducted in accordance with the special method. Investigatory monitoring of correspondence, investigatory acquisition of information by technical means, investigatory covert monitoring of non-public conversations (including by telephone, electronic or other means of communication) and investigatory entry are performed only in accordance with the special method and with the approval of a judge.

2. When and under which circumstances (e.g. criminal investigation, preliminary stage, etc.) can SITs be used?

Investigatory operations may begin before criminal proceedings are initiated, may take place during the period of investigation of a criminal matter and continue after termination thereof (Chapter 3, Section 18). All SITs can be used before criminal proceedings are begun. The aim of using SITs at this stage is to prevent a presumptive offence. The legal framework for using SITs at this stage is the LIO. The functions of operations at this stage are:

1. to protect persons against criminal threats;

2. to prevent, deter and detect the crime, and to determine the persons committing crimes and the sources of evidence;

3. to obtain, accumulate, analyse and utilise, in accordance with procedures prescribed by law, political, social, military, economic, scientific and technical, criminal and other information related to the criminal sphere and its infrastructure, and threats against state security, defence and economic sovereignty;

4. to protect state secrets and other interests important to the state, and, in cases prescribed by law, to provide special protection to persons.

During the period of investigation of a criminal matter and after this period the legal basis of using SITs is the LIO and Criminal Procedure Code.

3. Are there any specific features governing the use of SITs in relation to acts of terrorism? If so, please specify.

There are no specific features governing the use of SITs in relation to acts of terrorism.

4. How does the legal framework governing the use of SITs guarantee respect for human rights and individual freedoms, the principles of subsidiarity and proportionality? Is the authorisation to use SITs subject to time-limits? Which bodies and procedures are in place to supervise compliance with human rights standards and with the above-mentioned principles in the use of SITs? Is supervision automatic/systematic?

Respect for human rights and individual freedoms, the principle of subsidiarity and proportionality, are guaranteed and embodied in the principles of investigatory operations (Section 3).

The principles of investigatory operations are as follows:

1. Investigatory operations shall be organised and performed on a lawful basis, observing overall human rights, and in co-operation with and relying on the assistance of the general public.

2. In performing investigatory operations activities it is prohibited to cause physical harm or material damage to persons, to endanger the life and health of people; to threaten the use of or use physical means of coercion; to incite people to criminal acts, and to cause significant harm to the environment.

3. Investigatory operations actions, and the manner, scope and intensity of the conducting thereof shall be commensurate with the form and danger level of the threat. Investigatory duties shall be conducted so as to interfere as little as possible in the sphere of human rights.

4. Investigatory operations activities shall be performed in accordance with the general method if the tactics, form and scope of their performance do not significantly infringe on the constitutional rights of persons. Such activities shall be initiated by an official with the approval of his or her immediate manager (supervisor) or the deputy manager (Section 7).

5. Investigatory operations activities shall be initiated and performed only if fulfilling the functions mentioned in Section 2 of this Law and only if achieving the objectives is not possible by other means or is significantly more difficult.

6. Investigatory operations activities shall be performed without regard to the citizenship, gender, nationality, age, residence, education, or social, employment or financial status and office of persons, their political and religious views, or affiliation with parties or other public organisations. The factors mentioned shall not influence investigatory operations, unless such are specially set out in law.

7. The bodies performing investigatory operations and their officials are prohibited from acting directly or indirectly in the interests of political parties,

organisations and movements or persons, and from being involved with state authority and administrative bodies, the Office of the Prosecutor and court institutions, and the activities of public, political and religious organisations in order to influence or affect them, except in cases where such is necessary to prevent or uncover crimes.

If a person believes that a body performing investigatory operations has through its actions infringed the lawful rights and freedoms of the person, such a person is entitled to submit a complaint to a prosecutor who, after conducting an examination, shall provide an opinion with regard to the conformity with law of the actions of the officials of the body performing the investigatory operations, or the person may bring an action in court (Section 5).

If in the course of investigatory operations the rights and interests of persons have been unlawfully infringed, and as a result thereof harm has been caused, the obligation of the relevant official, prosecutor or court shall be to restore such rights and to compensate for or allay the inflicted material and moral harm in accordance with procedures prescribed by law (Section 29).

The authorisation to use SITs is subject to a time-limit. Before criminal proceedings are initiated, the LIO prescribes ("investigatory activities which are conducted in accordance with the special method") that monitoring of correspondence, acquisition of information by technical means, covert monitoring of non-public conversations (including by telephone, by electronic or other means of communication) and entry are performed only in accordance with the special method and with the approval of of a judge. Permission to perform such investigatory operations activities is issued for a period of up to three months and may be extended where it is substantiated that it is necessary, but only for the period of time that the investigatory process is being carried out with respect to the person.

If the body performing investigatory operations has at its disposal information with respect to specific persons (including information obtained as a result of an investigatory examination) and it provides a sufficient basis to suspect such persons of planning or committing a crime or threatening interests of importance to the state, or such persons are being sought with respect to a crime already committed, an investigatory process is initiated with respect to such persons.

The term for an investigatory process in such matters is six months, which may be further extended for six months with the approval of the head or deputy head of the body performing the investigatory operations. A further extension of the term may be done only with the approval of the Prosecutor General or a prosecutor specially authorised by the Prosecutor General, but it shall not be for more than the limitation period of the crime in relation to which the investigatory process is being conducted (Section 22).

The main direction of investigatory operations is determined by the National Security Council, but parliamentary monitoring is performed by the *Saeima*. The National Security Committee of the *Saeima* is entitled to hear the reports and accounts of the heads of institutions performing investigatory operations, and to acquaint itself with the official documents and information of such institutions, except documents regarding sources of covert information.

The performance of the functions of bodies performing investigatory operations is monitored in accordance with procedures prescribed by law and the Cabinet.

Monitoring procedures in the investigatory operations of institutions are determined, in accordance with the LIO and other laws, by the heads of such institutions who are personally responsible for the organisation of the work of subordinate units.

Monitoring regarding the conformity to law with investigatory operations is performed by the Prosecutor General and by prosecutors specially authorised by the Prosecutor General. In performing monitoring; they are entitled to acquaint themselves with such documents, materials and information at any stage of investigatory operations as are available to the investigatory operations institution. Covert information and its sources are revealed only to the Prosecutor General; they may be revealed to the prosecutors specially authorised by the Prosecutor General only with the permission of the head of the investigatory operations institution.

In order to take a decision with respect to investigatory operations activities mentioned in the LIO, the performance of which requires approval by a judge, the judge is entitled to acquaint himself or herself with those documents, materials and information available to the investigatory operations institution, upon which the necessity for the specific investigatory operations activities is based. The covert information and the sources of such are revealed to the judge only with the permission of the head of the investigatory operations institution.

The Code of Criminal Proceedings (Section 176) prescribes that correspondence by mail and telegraph can be put under arrest and withdrawn. The arrest of correspondence by mail and telegraph and its retention in post and telegraph institutions can be performed only in examining serious crime and exclusive serious crime, and only on the basis of the decision of a judge or a court.

The abovementioned code (Section 176.1) also prescribes that undercover monitoring of telecomunications and the acquisition of information from hardware can be accomplished on the basis of a decision of the judge or the court and examined for a period of up to six months.

The LIO provides for the respect for the principles of subsidiarity and proportionality, and determines that the use of these SITs is permissible only on occasions when the use of other (ordinary) means and solutions is impossible.

5. Which institutions are involved in the use of SITs and what is their role (e.g. law enforcement agencies, prosecutor's office, judicial authorities, etc.)? Which institutions can order and/or authorise the use of SITs? How does co-operation between these institutions work in practice?

Undercover operations are the overt and covert legal activities, of specially authorised – pursuant to the procedures prescribed in the LIO, and by law – officials of state authorities, the objectives of which are the protection of the life and health, rights and freedoms, honour, dignity and property of persons and the safeguarding of the constitution, the political system, national independence and territorial integrity, the capabilities of the state regarding defence, the economy, science and technology, and state official secrets, against external and internal threats.

Investigatory operations may also be performed in accordance with:
- a separate assignment submitted in writing by the Office of the Prosecutor and pre-trial investigation (preliminary investigation) and court institutions, with respect to such criminal matters as are entered in the records of these institutions;
- a written request by another body performing investigatory operations; and
- a request from or agreement with an international or foreign law enforcement body, or a state security or defence body (Section 19).

Institutions involved in the use of SITs are: the Bureau of Defence of *Satversme*, the Armed forces of Counterintelligence, the operations department of State Criminal police; Financial Police; Military Police and Security department, the Border Guard of the State, and specially authorised authorities of the customs institutions; the Security department of the Prison Board and the Bureau of Preventing and Combating Corruption. These institutions in their terms of reference are using SITs. If the use of SITs is essential, the permission of a prosecutor is needed. All these institutions are working within their competency, and co-operation between these institutions in exchanging information occurs only as stated by the law.

Where the permission of the court and the prosecutor to use SITs is not required, this use is determined by the authorities responsible for operative activities, i.e. Bureau of Defence of *Satversme* is the co-ordinating institution.

6. Are there any specialised counter-terrorism institutions? What is their role in the use of SITs?

No, there are no specialised counter-terrorism institutions. The fight against terrorism is within the scope of the Security police.

7. Which measures have been adopted in order to facilitate international co-operation (e.g. joint investigation teams)? Can the SITs listed in reply to question 1 be used in cross-border settings?

The Republic of Latvia is party to a number of international conventions on terrorism, including the International Convention for the Suppression of Terrorist Bombings, the International Convention for the Suppression of the Financing of Terrorism, and the European Convention on the Suppression of Terrorism. The Criminal Procedure Code (Chapter 15) determines the formation of joint international investigation teams, their principles of action etc. and, in conformity with this chapter, operative action is possible.

8. What use can be made of SITs in the context of mutual legal assistance?

The Criminal Procedure Code (Section 603) provides that SITs may be used upon foreign request only where this would be tolerated in ongoing criminal action for the same offence in Latvia. Criminal action provides justification for a form of co-operation with or assistance to a foreign institution to acquire the permission of the court to intercept communications.

9. How can the use of SITs be improved? Please provide any comments/proposals concerning the implementation of the terms of reference of the PC-TI and in particular the use and regulation of SITs.

A new law on Criminal Procedure has been drafted. Most SITs provided for in the LIO are incorporated in it, but not all, due to many circumstances in practice. These circumstances are creating problems concerning the legalisation of acquired evidence (from investigatory operations using SITs) as it is prescribed in the Criminal Procedure Code. It is complicated to use this information (acquired from investigatory operations using SITs) as evidence in court. But, by adopting the new Criminal Procedure Law, these imperfections will be solved.

Lithuania

Introduction and historical background to the problem

As in almost all post-soviet countries, Lithuania has two "stages" in criminal prosecution: the "pre-prosecution" stage that is governed by the Law on Operational Activities (LOA)[1] and the "criminal prosecution" stage that is governed by the Criminal Procedure Code (CPC). Operational activities are a complex of open and undercover methods, techniques and measures of a surveillance nature. The objectives of the operational activities are: crime prevention, detection of crimes and criminals, protection of persons from crimes, searching for absconded criminals, maintenance of state security, the protection of state secrets, counterintelligence and so on.

Up to 2003 the distinction between the LOA and the CPC was quite clear. The LOA regulated the use of special investigation techniques (SITs) and other undercover methods in crime investigation. The collected evidence could be used in criminal proceedings as material evidence or presented by witnesses. The CPC was concerned with traditional open crime investigation methods, such as interrogation of suspects and witnesses, expertise, searches and the like.

This balance has collapsed since the adoption of the new CPC (2002), which amended the soviet CPC (1961). The new CPC came into force on 1 May 2003 and now is undergoing severe examination in practice. The new CPC has made almost a revolution in pre-trial investigation. First, it brought in a new concept of pre-trial investigation, which in some way embraced the sphere of the "pre-prosecution" stage governed by the LOA. Second, the CPC incorporated a few SITs that previously were governed by the LOA – undercover agents, the criminal conduct imitation model, undercover surveillance and interception of telecommunications (the last could be used previously under the CPC of 1961 or under the LOA). Consequently, there are now questions about the position and necessity of the LOA.

There are different opinions of theorists on this issue and the questions have not been answered yet. Some of them strongly suggest that the LOA shall be repealed and all investigation methods and techniques shall be governed only by the CPC. Others are in favour of maintaining the current regulation on the operational activities.

Despite the disputes of the theorists, both laws are in force at the moment and work quite properly. There was a law adopted which had harmonised these laws, but it made only a formal distinction between them. Now all activities are separated and there are different grounds for the use of these systems. The operational activities are applied at the "operational stage" when there are no clear indications of the crime but there is information about grave, very grave or certain mediocre gravity crimes under

207

preparation, commissionned or that have been already committed. After the signs of the crime are identified, the operational activities are terminated and the criminal procedure – pre-trial investigation starts. The evidence collected under the LOA might be used in criminal proceedings as well as collected under the CPC. Most SITs are governed by the LOA; thus, those SITs that are included in the CPC are almost not applied. Another problem is that most (but not all) subjects of operational activities[2] are also pre-trial investigation subjects – and therefore they may use the regulation of the LOA or the regulation of the CPC in their activities depending on the situation. On the other hand, the Prosecutor General has adopted a recommendation according to which after the pre-trial investigation has started the operational activities may no longer be applied. This rule in some sense protects the overusing of operational activities by the LOA and obliges the investigative authorities to turn to criminal procedure as soon as appear clear indications that the crime has been committed.

It must also be noted that some SITs that are related to the fight against terrorism might be used under the law on Intelligence, the law on the State Security Department, and other such laws, but these activities are more of a preventive rather than a prosecution character; for this reason they are not discussed in these answers.

1. Please indicate the SITs used in your country, the respective legal framework governing their use and their legal definition, if any.

Law on Operational Activities

The Law on Operational Activities (2002) provides for the following SITs.

Operational interrogation

This is an operational activity, when the information is gathered using direct communication (interview). Undercover operational interrogation is when the interviewer does not expose his or her belonging to an operational activities unit. This activity is mentioned as a right of an operational activities unit and there is no supplementary regulation provided on it.

Operational inspection[3]

In this operational activity, information is gathered by overt or covert inspection of goods, documents, premises, vehicles, area, persons and so on.

This activity is also mentioned as a right of an operational activities unit for the undercover inspection of premises or vehicles, undercover temporary pick-up and inspection of samples of goods or other material.

Operational inspection is authorised by the Head of the regional court[4] or the Head of the Criminal cases division of the regional court on the basis of a reasoned request of the Prosecutor General, the commissioned Deputy Prosecutor General, the Head of the Regional Prosecutor office (Chief Prosecutor) or the commissioned deputy of the Head of the Regional Prosecutor office. The requests of these prosecutors are based on the data given by operational activities units. In all cases the Prosecutor General or the commissioned Deputy Prosecutor General must be informed.

In a matter of great urgency when there is a menace to the life, health or property of the person, or the security of society or state, such authorisation may be made by the abovementioned prosecutors. But such authorisation must within 24 hours[5] be confirmed by the abovementioned judges. If the judge does not confirm the operational inspection, such activity must be terminated and the evidence obtained immediately destroyed.

The request to the judge must include:
- the name and the position of the officer that submits the request;
- the evidence that could substantiate the necessity for operational inspection;
- the description of the premises, goods or material that will be under inspection;
- the anticipated duration of the operational inspection;
- the intended results of the operational inspection.

The authorisation may be given at most for the term of three months but it can be prolonged by the abovementioned procedure.

Operational screening

This is the operational activity when information is gathered using undercover interrogation and covert inspection.

This activity is mentioned as a right of operational activities units and there is no supplementary regulation provided on it.

Operational observation[6]

Again this is an operational activity; in this case, information is gathered using covert direct observation of the object.

This activity is mentioned as a right of operational activities units and there is no supplementary regulation provided on it.

Undercover operations[7]

This is a type of operational activity where information is gathered by gaining the confidence of suspects, using covert agents of the operational activities units. This activity is mentioned as a right of operational activities units and there is no supplementary regulation provided on it, except those that are related to other methods.

The undercover agents might be involved by written or oral agreement with the suspects of the operational activities. The undercover agents might be employees of the undercover (front store) companies and get a salary for this "work". Data on undercover agents remain a state secret.

Electronic surveillance

In this operational activity, information is gathered using electronic technologies. This activity is mentioned as a right of operational activities units and there is no supplementary regulation provided on it.

Criminal conduct imitation model[8]

This covers authorised activities that nominally appear as criminal but are used with a view to protecting the rights and liberties of persons, property, security of society and state from criminal infringements.

The criminal conduct imitation model (the Model) is authorised by the Prosecutor General, the commissioned Deputy Prosecutor General, the Head of the Regional Prosecutor's office (Chief Prosecutor) or the commissioned deputy of the Head of the Regional Prosecutor's office when the reasoned request of the Head (or the commissioned deputy of the Head) of the operational activities unit is presented. In all cases the Prosecutor General or the commissioned Deputy Prosecutor General must be informed.

The request must include:
- the name and the position of the officer that submits the request;
- the evidence that could substantiate the necessity to use the Model;
- the data on the persons towards whom this Model will be applied (if such data are possessed);
- the boundaries of the activities according to specific articles of the Criminal Code or Administrative Breaches Code;
- data on the persons that will use the Model;
- the anticipated duration of the use of the Model;
- the intended results of the use of the Model.

The authorisation may be given at most for the term of six months but it can be prolonged by the abovementioned procedure. It is forbidden to use the Model when it may menace the health or life of a person or may result in other serious consequences.

It must be stressed that on 8 May 2000 the Constitutional Court of Lithuania took a decision on the conformity of this Model with the Constitution of the Republic of Lithuania. The Court noted that the Model is not contradictory to the constitution. The Model itself does not breach the person's right to privacy. The person who is making or attempting to make crimes cannot expect privacy. The court also noted that the authorisation of the Model by the prosecutors is not contradictory to the constitution. On the other hand, the court stressed that the rights and the liberties of persons would be better protected if such authorisation were made by the court. The court decided that only the application of operational activities, including the Model, towards the President of the Republic would be contradictory to the constitution. The court did not find any contradiction if the operational activities were applied towards members of Parliament (the *Seimas*).

Controlled delivery

This covers authorised activities allowing illicit or suspect consignments of goods or other objects to move through or from the Republic of Lithuania with the knowledge and under the supervision of the operational activities unit with a view to identifying crimes and suspects. Controlled delivery may be used only under the international treaties or agreements.

The authorisation procedure for controlled delivery is similar to the abovementioned criminal conduct imitation model. The request must include:
- the name and the position of the officer that submits the request;
- the evidence that could substantiate the need to use controlled delivery;
- data on the persons suspected of delivering the controlled goods;
- the countries from or to which the goods are transported;
- the anticipated duration of the controlled delivery;
- the intended results of the use of the controlled delivery.

There are no time-limitations set for such authorisation. It is forbidden to use controlled delivery when it may menace the health or life of a person or may result in other serious consequences.

Special use of technologies[9]

This means the authorised use of technologies (technical measures) with a view to monitoring or recording the conversation of persons or other communications or activities, when no one knows about such monitoring.

The special use of technologies is authorised by the Head of the regional court[10] or the Head of the Criminal cases division of the regional court by the reasoned request of the Prosecutor General, the commissioned Deputy Prosecutor General, the Head of the Regional Prosecutor's office (Chief Prosecutor) or the commissioned deputy of the Head of the Regional Prosecutor's office. The requests of these prosecutors are based on the data given by the operational activities units. In all cases the Prosecutor General or the commissioned Deputy Prosecutor General must be informed.

In a matter of great urgency when there is a menace to the life, health or property of the person, or the security of society or state, such authorisation may be made by the abovementioned prosecutors. But such authorisation must within 24 hours[11] be confirmed by the abovementioned judges. If the judge does not confirm the special use of technologies, such use must be terminated and the gathered data immediately destroyed.

The request to the judge must include:
- the name and the position of the officer that submits the request;
- the evidence that could substantiate the need for special use of technologies;
- data on the persons towards whom this special use of the technologies will be applied;
- the phone number or other specific source that will be controlled;
- the anticipated duration of the special use of technologies;
- the intended results of the special use of technologies.

The authorisation may be given at most for the term of three months but it can be prolonged by the abovementioned procedure.

A request to render information about telecommunication events from the operators of telecommunications may be authorised by the district court[12] judge.

The authorisation is not needed when the information is gathered on application by or with the consent of the person, except when the service from the operators of telecommunications is used.

Use of an undercover company[13]

This activity is mentioned as a right of operational activities units and there is no supplementary regulation provided on it.

Undercover monitoring of post

This activity, which covers documents, consignments, remittances and their documentation,[14] is governed and authorised under the same rules as the abovementioned special use of technologies.

Use in evidence

All data gathered by the use of operational activities may be used in criminal proceedings as evidence. Such data must be laid down in, or accompanied by, a protocol that includes:
- the date and place of the protocol;
- the official that recorded the protocol;
- the names of the operational activities used;
- the persons or the objects to whom the operational activities were applied;
- the intended results of the operational activities;

- the gathered information;
- the technical characteristics of the collected data, including the place, time and content of the operational activity;
- annexes to the protocol, listing audio, video records, CDs and other material objects.

The Criminal Procedure Code

As mentioned before, the Criminal Procedure Code also provides some legal framework for the use of SITs The CPC contains these pre-trial investigation methods of an undercover nature.

Interception of telecommunications

The interception of telecommunications may be applied only for the finite list of most serious offences or when there is a danger to the victims, witnesses or other participants of the proceedings or their relatives. The authorisation is given by the pre-trial investigation judge (of the district court). In a matter of great urgency it can be used under the authorisation of the prosecutor, but within three days it must be approved by the pre-trial investigation judge. The term of authorisation is six months and it can be prolonged once by three months. At the request or with the consent of the person the authorisation is not necessary, if the service of telecommunications operators is not used. It is forbidden to monitor communications between the suspect and his or her lawyer. The interception of telecommunications must be described in the protocol. Irrelevant information must be immediately destroyed.

Undercover investigation

Undercover investigation may be applied only for the finite list of the most serious offences by the pre-trial investigation officers. The authorisation is given by the pre-trial investigation judge (of the district court) and it may be given only when there is enough evidence about the crime under investigation. When such authorisation is given officers may also use the criminal conduct imitation model. It is forbidden to instigate an offence.

Under special circumstances, where there is no other possible solution, the undercover investigation may be done by persons who are not members of a pre-trial investigation unit. All persons that have been using undercover investigation may be interrogated later as witnesses. It is possible to give them anonymity if there is a danger to their or their relatives' lives, health, or similar.

Criminal conduct imitation model

Authorisation for the criminal activity model may be given by the pre-trial investigation judge (of the district court) at the request of a prosecutor.

Permission may be given to the person who is the subject of a proposal to commit or participate in the commission of the crime.

Undercover observation

Undercover observation of a specific person or vehicle or other object may be authorised by the pre-trial investigation judge at the request of the prosecutor. If it is intended to use video cameras or audio recorders it must be indicated in the permission of the judge. Authorisation is not necessary when the observation of the object is not related to the collection of information on specific persons.

Article 145 of the CPC also provides rules for searches of premises. They are authorised by the pre-trial investigation judge (of the district court). In a matter of great urgency it can be done under the decision of the pre-trial investigation officer or prosecutor, but this decision must be approved by the judge within three days. If the judge does not approve such searches, all gathered material shall be returned and it may no longer be used in the proceedings. The searches must be done with the participation of the owner of the premises. If that is impossible, the participation of independent persons (witnesses) must be ensured.

Article 161 of the CPC states that after the use of all these activities the person must be immediately informed about it, if he or she did not know about the application of them. If the criminal investigation is terminated, all gathered information on the person's private life shall be destroyed. This rule also applies to material that is not related to the case.

2. When and under which circumstances (e.g. criminal investigation, preliminary stage, etc.) can SITs be used?

The SITs that were mentioned in the LOA may be used where:
1. There is information about the preparation, commission or already committed crime that is included in the list in Article 9 of the LOA. This list includes the most serious offences and is a little bit wider than the list under Article 154 of the CPC (interception of telecommunications);
2. There is information on the activities of another state's special services;
3. The suspect, the defendant or the convict has absconded;
4. A person is missing in action;
5. Protection from criminal impact is used;
6. The protection of state secrets is used; or
7. There is information on activities that might threaten the security of the state or other important national security interests.

The SITs that were mentioned in the CPC may be used when the pre-trial investigation of crimes has started.

3. Are there any specific features governing the use of SITs in relation to acts of terrorism? If so, please specify.

There are no specific features in the use of SITs in relation to acts of terrorism. On the other hand, acts of terrorism are very serious offences under the Lithuanian Penal Code. Also acts of terrorism threaten the life and health of citizens and the security of the state; therefore they fit into the narrow limits that are set for the application of SITs.

4. How does the legal framework governing the use of SITs guarantee respect for human rights and individual freedoms, the principles of subsidiarity and proportionality? Is the authorisation to use SITs subject to time-limits? Which bodies and procedures are in place to supervise compliance with human rights standards and with the above-mentioned principles in the use of SITs? Is supervision automatic/systematic?

Some answers to this question have already been given in the reply to the first question. The LOA and CPC stress the importance of the protection of human rights, and also the principle of proportionality. A person who thinks that the operational activities have violated his/her rights may appeal to a head of operational activities unit, a prosecutor or a court. The operational activities unit could then be obliged to compensate the harm made. It is forbidden to provoke a person to commit a crime.

There are requirements for the authorisation of independent authorities – courts (judges) or at least of prosecutors – for the most intrusive measures. The use of evidence collected not following the abovementioned rules may be appealed in court as illegal. There is a criminal responsibility set in the Penal Code for illegal intrusion into a person's private life.

There is an internal check on the use of operational activities, which is done by the heads of the operational activities units. They monitor the activities of undercover agents, the information on them and other operational activities, and documentation and tactics of operational activities.

The legality of operational activities is monitored by the Prosecutor General, the commissioned Deputy Prosecutor General, the Head of the Regional Prosecutor's office (Chief Prosecutor) or the commissioned deputy of the Head of the Regional Prosecutor's office. They authorise some operational activities, check the use of them and try the complaints of the persons over them. Complaints may also be tried in the courts. Some checking functions are also entrusted to the government and ministries.

There is a permanent parliamentary commission in charge of the supervision of operational activities units. The parliamentary commission has the right to get all necessary information on the activities of operational units, to invite the officials of operational units to the meetings of the commission and get the report from them, and so on. The members of commission have the duty to keep state secrets that may be revealed in such meetings.

Overseeing the SITs governed by the CPC is entrusted to the prosecutors and courts under the common principles of criminal procedure.

5. Which institutions are involved in the use of SITs and what is their role (e.g. law enforcement agencies, prosecutor's office, judicial authorities, etc.)? Which institutions can order and/or authorise the use of SITs? How does co-operation between these institutions work in practice?

Some answers to this question already are in the reply to the first question. The right to use operational activities (under the LOA) is within the competence of the police, Financial Crime Investigation Service, State Security Department, Special Investigation Service (which fights corruption), Customs Crime Service, the Second Department of Operational Services in the Ministry of Defence and some other institutions. There is a complete list of such institutions that is adopted by the government. The authorisation institutions for some SITs are courts (judges) and prosecutors.

The right to use SITs under the CPC is within the pre-trial investigation bodies. These are the police, prosecutors, Financial Crime Investigation Service, State Security Department, Special Investigation Service (which fights corruption), Customs Crime Service and some other institutions. It must be stressed that only some pre-trial investigation institutions have the right to use operational activities. On the other hand, not every unit of operational activities is a pre-trial investigation body.

As mentioned above, authorisation for SITs under the CPC is given by the pre-trial investigation judge (of the district court).

In both systems (under the LOA and under the CPC) the intermediary institution in the use of SITs is the prosecutors. They themselves do not have the right to use most of the SITs, but prosecutors work as co-ordinators of these activities, as proposers of the requests for authorisation of SITs to the courts (judges), and as the users of the collected evidence.

The laws quite exhaustively regulate the relations between the units of operative activities and prosecutors and other parties. On the other hand, the work in practice is not so co-ordinated among different authorities.

6. Are there any specialised counter-terrorism institutions? What is their role in the use of SITs?

The fight against terrorism is co-ordinated and governed by the State Security Department. It has the rights of pre-trial investigation and operational activities. Therefore the department may use the rights provided either in the LOA or in the CPC.

The State Security Department works to prevent terrorist actions and fights causes facilitating the spread of terrorism. The Department gathers and analyses information, and identifies persons who belong to terrorist groups, support them, or have extremist tendencies.

In fighting terrorism, the State Security Department cooperates actively with foreign services and law enforcement agencies of the Republic of Lithuania. The Department also submits proposals to the Government on how to improve the existing laws, and on how to coordinate the activities of law enforcement agencies in order to make prevention of terrorism more effective.

7. Which measures have been adopted in order to facilitate international co-operation (e.g. joint investigation teams)? Can the SITs listed in reply to question 1 be used in cross-border settings?

Article 8.3 of the LOA states that, in accordance with the international treaties and agreements of the Republic of Lithuania, operational activities units may co-operate with foreign institutions carrying out operational activities under the Lithuanian LOA.

Article 67 of the CPC enables the use of other criminal investigation methods (not regulated by the CPC) and the participation of foreign investigators (under the supervision of Lithuanian officials) when it is so stated in a Lithuanian international treaty or agreement.

8. What use can be made of SITs in the context of mutual legal assistance?

As noted in the reply to question 7, Lithuanian laws and international agreements provide a wide perspective for close international co-operation, including the use of SITs. As Lithuania acceded to the EU, mutual legal assistance became more and more cohesive.

The ratification and implementation of such international documents as the Convention on Mutual Assistance in Criminal Matters between the member states of the European Union, the Cybercrime Convention and so on shall help in forming the proper legal and institutional conditions for close-knit co-operation.

9. How can the use of SITs be improved? Please provide any comments/proposals concerning the implementation of the terms of reference of the PC-TI and in particular the use and regulation of SITs.

There are different problems relating to this topic. On the one hand, sometimes there are serious questions about constitutionality, proportionality and conformity with human rights standards. The application of SITs and their legal regulation usually is governed by instructions that are not made public, and usually SITs involve serious interference in the person's private life and other human rights and liberties. There is also the question of control of such activities and the use of gathered information on a person's private life.

On the other hand, there is a tremendous need for the improvement of intelligence, investigation and co-operation methods and techniques due to the emerging problem of worldwide terrorism. A few problems might be mentioned: the use of anonymous telephone SIM cards, which are often used in criminal activities; the authorisation of interception of telecommunications of a specific phone number, but not of the specific person (who may change phones quicker than the authorisation is possible); and there are others.

The PC-TI could have a great impact on comparative studies on the use of SITs in different countries. The PC-TI might produce some general principles and basic standards for the use of SITs and the necessary level of their authorisation. The PC-TI could single out some typical SITs and provide the essential rules for their application.

---

1. The latest Law on Operational Activities was adopted on 20 June 2002.
2. Units of operational activities are bodies that have the right to use operational activities, e.g. the police, Financial Crime Investigation Service, State Security Department, Special Investigation Service (which fights corruption), Customs Crime Service, and so on.
3. This activity might also be named "secret searches".
4. The regional court is a higher court in relation to lower (district) courts of Lithuania. There are five regional courts in Lithuania.
5. If the 24-hour term expires outside office hours, it is prolonged to the next day.
6. Operational observation is similar to the secret observation under the CPC (2002), but is applied separately. Notice that these SITs have different regulation and authorisation procedures.
7. An undercover operation is similar to the undercover investigation under the CPC (2002), but is applied separately. Notice that these SITs have different regulation and authorisation procedures.
8. This Model of criminal activity imitation is similar to the model of criminal activity imitation under the CPC (2002), but is applied separately. Notice that these SITs have different regulation and authorisation procedures.
9. This might include the interception of telecommunications, bugging, etc.
10. The regional court is a higher court in relation to lower (district) courts of Lithuania. There are five regional courts in Lithuania.
11. If the 24-hour term expires outside office hours, it is prolonged to the next day.
12. The district court is the 1st-instance court – the lowest court in the hierarchy of Lithuanian courts.
13. This SIT is without definition and is just mentioned among other rights of operational activities bodies.
14. This SIT is without definition and is just mentioned among other rights of operational activities bodies.

Luxembourg

1. Please indicate the SITs used in your country, the respective legal framework governing their use and their legal definition, if any.

The Luxembourg Criminal Investigation Code contains a section on "special surveillance measures". Judicial special surveillance measures are provided for in Articles 88-1 and 88-2 of the Criminal Investigation Code.

The Criminal Investigation Code

Article 88-1

Article 88-1 provides that the investigating judge may, exceptionally and in a decision giving particular reasons based on the facts of the case and referring to the circumstances indicated below, order the use of technical surveillance measures, and interception and inspection of all forms of communication, if:
a. the criminal proceedings concern a particularly serious offence carrying a maximum sentence of at least two years' imprisonment;
b. specific facts mean the person to be kept under surveillance is suspected either of committing the offence or taking part in it or of receiving or transmitting information to or from the accused or suspect;
c. ordinary investigation techniques prove inoperative because of the nature of the facts and the particular circumstances of the case.

The measures must be lifted as soon as they are no longer necessary. They cease automatically one month after the date of the order. They may, however, be extended, each time for a further month, the total duration not exceeding one year, by order of the investigating judge, giving reasons and with the approval of the president of the court in chambers of the Court of Appeal who rules within two days of receiving the order, after hearing the Attorney-General's opinion.

Such measures may not be ordered with respect to an accused after his or her first questioning by the investigating judge, while those ordered previously will automatically cease to have effect on that date.

Such measures may not be ordered with respect to a person bound by professional confidentiality within the meaning of Article 458 of the Criminal Code, unless he or she is personally suspected of committing or being involved in the offence.

The State Prosecutor may in all cases apply to have the investigating judge's order set aside within two days of the order. Such an application is heard by the president of the court in chambers of the Court of Appeal who

219

rules within two days of receiving the order, after hearing the Attorney-General's opinion.

Article 88-2

Article 88-2 of the Criminal Investigation Code sets out the details concerning the execution of special surveillance measures.

Where surveillance and interception of communications under Article 88-1 have produced no results, the copies and recordings, as well as all other data and information in the file, are destroyed by the investigating judge a maximum of twelve months after the order to end surveillance.

If the investigating judge considers that these copies, recordings, data or information may be useful to the continuation of the investigation, he or she may order that they be kept in the file, giving reasons based on the facts of the case.

The State Prosecutor and the person whose correspondence or telecommunications have been monitored and who has been informed under paragraph 6 of the article, may apply to have the order set aside according to the procedure set out in the last paragraph of Article 88-1. Where, following surveillance and interception of communications ordered under Article 88-1, the accused is discharged, acquitted or sentenced in final judgment, the Principal State Prosecutor or the State Prosecutor destroys copies, recordings and all other data and information within a month of the judicial decision becoming final.

Communications with persons bound by professional confidentiality who are not personally suspected of committing or being involved in an offence may not be used. Recordings and transcriptions are immediately destroyed by the investigating judge.

A person whose correspondence or telecommunications have been intercepted is informed of the measure within twelve months of its cessation.

After the first questioning session, the accused and his or her lawyer may inspect the recorded telecommunications, correspondence and all the other data and information in the file. They have the right to have the recordings reproduced in the presence of a police officer.

Article 88-3

Administrative special surveillance measures are provided for in Article 88-3 of the Criminal Investigation Code.

The head of government may, with the consent of a committee composed of the president of the High Court of Justice, the president of the Administrative Court and the president of the Audit Court, order the interception and inspection, with the aid of the appropriate technical means, of all forms of communication in order to investigate offences against the state's external security that one or more people are trying to commit, have committed or have attempted to commit, if ordinary investigation techniques prove inoperative because of the nature of the facts and the particular circumstances of the case.

In an emergency, the head of government may, on his or her own authority, order the interception and inspection referred to in the preceding paragraph, referring the matter to the committee provided for to this end, which will decide whether or not interception and inspection should be continued.

Interception and inspection must cease as soon as the information sought has been gathered and within a maximum of three months from the day they were ordered.

The head of government may, with the committee's consent, order interception and inspection for a further three-month period. His or her decision is renewable, subject to the same procedure, every three months.

Article 88-4

Article 88-4 of the Criminal Investigation Code provides in particular that the interception and inspection of telecommunications shall be effected by the Intelligence Service set up by the Act of 15 June 2004 on the protection of secrets concerning external state security.

Communications with persons bound by professional confidentiality within the meaning of Article 458 of the Criminal Code and not themselves suspected of attempting to commit, having committed or having attempted to commit the offence as principal perpetrators or accomplices may not be used. Recordings and transcriptions of them are immediately destroyed by the head of the Intelligence Service.

Correspondence is handed under seal, in return for a receipt, to the Intelligence Service. The head of the service photocopies correspondence that may be usable as evidence for the prosecution or defence and returns the written items he/she does not consider it necessary to keep to the head of posts and telecommunications, who sends them on to the addressee.

Where interception and inspection measures conducted under Article 88-3 give no results, the copies, recordings and all the other data and information obtained are destroyed by the head of the Intelligence Service.

Where these copies, recordings, data and information may be useful to the continuation of the investigation, they are destroyed at the latest on expiry of the time-limit for prosecution.

Article 67-1

Tracing of telecommunications is governed by an Act of 21 November 2002 amending the Criminal Investigation Code.

The new Article 67-1 of the code provides that where acts carrying a maximum sentence of at least six months' imprisonment have been referred to an investigating judge who considers there to be circumstances that make the tracing of telecommunications or localisation of their origin or destination necessary to the discovery of the truth, he or she may order, if necessary requesting the technical co-operation of the telecommunications operator and/or service provider, that:
1. the call data of telecommunications facilities, from or to which calls are or have been made, be traced;
2. the origin or destination of telecommunications be located.

In the cases referred to in paragraph 1, for each telecommunications facility whose call data are traced or the origin or destination of whose calls is located, the day, time, length and, if necessary, place of the telecommunication are set down in a written record.

The investigating judge indicates the de facto circumstances justifying the measure in a reasoned order transmitted to the State Prosecutor.

The length of time during which the order may be applied is given, that period not exceeding one month from the date of the order, which may be renewed. A person whose means of telecommunication have been the subject of the measure provided for in paragraph 1 is informed of it during the judicial investigation itself and in all cases within a maximum of 12 months from the date of the order.

Nevertherless, this period of 12 months does not apply when the measure has been ordered by the investigating judge for acts which were committed in the framework of, or in relation with, a criminal association or organisation in the meaning of Articles 322 to 325ter of the Criminal Code, or committed in the framework of, or in relation with, terrorism in the meaning of Articles 135-1 to 135-4 of the Criminal Code, or of Article 10, paragraph 1 of the Law of 19 February 1973 on the sale of medicinal products and the fight against drugs.

An application to have the order declared void must be lodged according to the procedure set out in Article 126 of the Criminal Investigation Code within the time-limit.

Where the tracing of telecommunications ordered by an investigating judge has produced no results, the data obtained are removed from the file and destroyed in so far as they concern persons who have not been charged.

Police provocation

As police provocation is not statutorily regulated in Luxembourg, the country's case-law, taking inspiration from Belgian case-law, has defined it as "inciting the commission of an offence or strengthening the resolve to do so of someone who will materially commit the offence".

In order to be lawful, the provocation – meaning, police intervention – must in no way have determined the offender's unlawful actions, but have had the sole consequence of enabling offences already committed to be established and preventing their continuation.

Police provocation may, therefore, be perfectly lawful and have no influence on the offender's liability or the admissibility of a prosecution, provided that:
1. the facts are sufficiently serious,
2. the police stratagem, here the infiltrating officer, has operated with the agreement and under the supervision of the prosecutor or investigating judge, and
3. the police officer has not incited a person to commit an offence or strengthened his or her resolve to do so.

There has therefore been no unlawful provocation if the person was resolved to commit an offence prior to implementation of the police stratagem.

Searches

Searches are regulated differently according to whether they are conducted in the phase where a person has been caught in the act of committing an offence or during the preliminary investigation phase (when the case has been referred to an investigating judge).

Where a person has been caught in the act and the crime is actually being committed or has just been committed, the State Prosecutor and police officers may conduct searches.

Outside the phase of capture in the act only the investigating judge, who is independent of the prosecutor's office and collects evidence both for the prosecution and the defence, may order searches.

The other SITs listed in the introduction to the questionnaire are not specifically regulated in domestic legislation (undercover operations, front store operations, informants, pseudo-purchases or pseudo-crimes).

Controlled delivery, cross-border observation and cross-border pursuit are in particular regulated by the Schengen Agreement, which Luxembourg has ratified.

2. When and under which circumstances (e.g. criminal investigation, preliminary stage, etc.) can SITs be used?

The possibility of using SITs depends, with respect to special surveillance measures, firstly on the gravity of the offences, which must carry a maximum sentence of at least two years' imprisonment.

The potential subject of surveillance must also be suspected either of having committed or having been involved in the commission of an offence, or of receiving or transmitting information to or from the accused or suspect.

Moreover, ordinary investigation techniques must be inoperative because of the nature of the facts and particular circumstances of the case (Article 88-1 of the Criminal Investigation Code).

The investigating judge may only order telephone calls to be traced if the facts concern an offence carrying a maximum sentence of at least six months' imprisonment (cf. reply to question 1).

Except in the case of capture in the act, only the investigating judge may order searches.

It should therefore be noted that the most serious measures (telephone tapping, searches and tracing of telephone calls) may only be ordered by an investigating judge in the course of an investigation.

Other SITs not involving coercive acts, such as observation and the use of informants, may be carried out by the State Prosecutor's Office during a preliminary police investigation or by an investigating judge during a preliminary judicial investigation.

3. Are there any specific features governing the use of SITs in relation to acts of terrorism? If so, please specify.

There are no specific features governing the use of SITs with respect to terrorism.

4. How does the legal framework governing the use of SITs guarantee respect for human rights and individual freedoms, the principles of subsidiarity and proportionality? Is the authorisation to use SITs subject to time-limits? Which bodies and procedures are in place to supervise compliance with human rights standards and with the above-mentioned principles in the use of SITs? Is supervision automatic/systematic?

Rights and principles

Respect for human rights and fundamental freedoms is guaranteed with respect to the use of SITs, through a strict legal framework providing for court supervision at various levels.

Special surveillance measures, including telephone tapping, may only be ordered by an investigating judge under very strict conditions (cf. reply to question 1).

The investigating judge – an independent judge – is therefore, in the initial phase, the guarantor that the measures taken will be lawful. The measures that represent the most serious infringement of individual freedoms may only be ordered by the State Prosecutor's Office, even in the case of capture in the act.

The principle of subsidiarity is respected since the most serious SITs (special surveillance measures, such as telephone tapping) require the investigating judge to state in the order that ordinary investigation techniques are inoperative because of the nature of the facts and the particular circumstances of the case.

The principle of proportionality is respected since special surveillance techniques may only be used if the investigation concerns a particularly serious offence carrying a maximum sentence of at least two years' imprisonment.

Time-limits

Authorisation to use an SIT is subject to a time-limit that varies according to the technique used.

Special surveillance measures (including telephone tapping) automatically cease one month from the date of the order. They may however be extended, for further one-month periods and for a total period of up to one year, where the investigating judge issues a reasoned order that is approved by the president of the court in chambers of the Court of Appeal who rules within two days of receiving the order, after hearing the Principal State Prosecutor's submissions.

With respect to tracing telephone calls, the investigating judge specifies the period during which it may be conducted. This period may not exceed one month, but is renewable.

Supervision

A person whose correspondence or telecommunications have been intercepted through the use of special surveillance techniques may apply to have the order set aside. The application is heard by the president of the court in the chambers of the Court of Appeal.

The courts carry out automatic supervision when cases come to trial; interested parties may also, before cases come to trial, bring an action contesting the use of SITs before the court sitting in chambers, composed of three judges (appeal also being possible).

In any case, in accordance with Article 126 of the Criminal Investigation Code, the prosecuting authorities, the accused, a party claiming damages, a party liable in civil law, as well as any third party able to prove a legitimate personal interest, may apply to the court in chambers of the district court to have the preliminary investigation or any of its acts declared void.

5. Which institutions are involved in the use of SITs and what is their role (e.g. law enforcement agencies, prosecutor's office, judicial authorities, etc.)? Which institutions can order and/or authorise the use of SITs? How does co-operation between these institutions work in practice?

The institutions involved are the State Prosecutor, the investigating judge and the police. Special surveillance techniques (including telephone tapping) and the tracing of telephone calls (obtaining lists of calls made from and received by a telephone number) are always ordered by an investigating judge.

Searches are ordered by the State Prosecutor or a police officer in the event of capture in the act; at other times a search may only be conducted on the order of an investigating judge.

Sitting in chambers, the district court may, on application, review the lawfulness of the use of SITs; the trial courts also review their lawfulness and compliance with the European Convention for the Protection of Human Rights and Fundamental Freedoms (cf. reply to question 4).

6. Are there any specialised counter-terrorism institutions? What is their role in the use of SITs?

In Luxembourg the Intelligence Service, the State Prosecutor (with the Financial Unit of the State Prosecutor's Department), the investigating judge and the police are involved in counter-terrorism.

The Financial Unit of the State Prosecutor's Department is concerned with combating money-laundering and therefore also plays an important part in combating the financing of terrorism (see previous remarks for their role).

7. Which measures have been adopted in order to facilitate international co-operation (e.g. joint investigation teams)? Can the SITs listed in reply to question 1 be used in cross-border settings?

The Convention Applying the Schengen Agreement of 19 June 1990, ratified by Luxembourg, contains provisions on international co-operation (cross-border observation, controlled delivery, etc.) common to all Schengen countries.

8. What use can be made of SITs in the context of mutual legal assistance?

In the framework of international mutual judicial assistance, the various SITs may be used if the foreign authority so requests and the necessary statutory conditions are fulfilled in the requesting and requested countries.

9. How can the use of SITs be improved? Please provide any comments/proposals concerning the implementation of the terms of reference of the PC-TI and in particular the use and regulation of SITs.

The Grand Duchy of Luxembourg has no comments or particular proposals on this subject.

Moldova

1. Please indicate the SITs used in your country, the respective legal framework governing their use and their legal definition, if any.

The special techniques of investigation in the Republic of Moldova are called operative measures of investigation. The legal ground of the operative activity of investigation is the Law of the Republic of Moldova on Operative Activity of Investigation (No. 45-XIII dated 12 April 1994).

According to Article 6 of Law No. 45-XIII/1994 the operative measures of investigation are the following:
- questioning of citizens;
- collecting information;
- visual pursuit;
- pursuit and documentation with the help of modern methods and techniques;
- collecting information (samples) for the comparative investigation;
- acquiring control and controlled delivery of goods, whether in limited or free circulation;
- examination of objects and documents;
- identification of the person;
- examination of rooms, buildings, plots of land and means of transport;
- parcels control;
- examination of convicts' mail;
- interception of telephone calls and other conversations;
- collecting information from technical channels of communication;
- discussions with the suspect using the simulated behaviour detector;
- marking with chemical substances and other special substances;
- infiltration of permanent collaborators from the operative subdivisions and of persons who collaborate confidentially with bodies that exercise the operative activity of investigation into criminal organisations;
- control of the transmission of money or other extorted goods.

Unfortunately the law does not include the definitions of the measures mentioned above; they are known from the practice of the bodies that exercise the operative activity of investigation.

2. When and under which circumstances (e.g. criminal investigation, preliminary stage, etc.) can SITs be used?

According to Article 6 of Law No. 45-XIII/1994 the operative measures of investigation are exercised only in cases when there are no other ways to achieve the following tasks:

1. to detect criminal attempts, to prevent, obstruct and discover the crimes and the persons who organise them and commit them, as well as to provide compensation for the damage caused by the crime;

2. to search for the persons who avoid the preliminary inquiry bodies, the inquest and the court, or who elude the penalty, and for those who disappear without trace;

3. to collect information about events or actions that are a danger to the ecological, economic, military and state security of the Republic of Moldova.

The reasons for concluding operative measures of investigation are (Article 7 of Law No. 45-XIII/1994):

a. indefinite circumstances concerning the sued trial;

b. information known to the bodies that carry out the operative activity of investigation:

- o regarding the action contrary to law that is being prepared, committed or was committed, as well as the persons who prepare, commit or committed it, if the facts necessary to prosecute them are not sufficient;
- o regarding persons who avoid the enquiry bodies, the preliminary inquest or the court of justice, or the persons who elude the penalty;
- o regarding persons who have disappeared without trace and regarding the detection of unidentified dead bodies;

c. the indications of the investigator, of the enquiry bodies, of the attorney or the decision of the court concerning the cases investigated by them;

d. interpellations of the bodies that perform the operative activity of investigation on the basis of the reasons mentioned in the present article;

e. interpellations of international legal organisations and of the legal institutions of the other countries in accordance with the international treaties to which the Republic of Moldova is party.

The bodies performing the operative activity of investigation have the right, within their competence, to collect information that characterises the persons:

a. regarding their access to information that represents a state secret;

b. regarding their admission to work on objects that present an increased danger to people's life and health, as well as to the environment;

c. regarding their admission to the operative activity of investigation or their access to information got during its execution;

d. regarding the establishment and maintenance of a collaborative relationship in the organisation and accomplishment of the operative measures of investigation;

e. regarding the permission given to them for the execution of the non-governmental activity of detection-protection.

The bodies that perform the operative activity of investigation, within their competence, have also the right to collect information in order to ensure their own security.

3. Are there any specific features governing the use of SITs in relation to acts of terrorism? If so, please specify.

There are no peculiarities regarding the usage of the special techniques of investigation with reference to the acts of terrorism.

4. How does the legal framework governing the use of SITs guarantee respect for human rights and individual freedoms, the principles of subsidiarity and proportionality? Is the authorisation to use SITs subject to time-limits? Which bodies and procedures are in place to supervise compliance with human rights standards and with the above-mentioned principles in the use of SITs? Is supervision automatic/systematic?

A person who considers that the actions of a body performing operative measures of investigations violates their rights can appeal against these actions to a higher hierarchical body, to the General Attorney's office or to the court. In order to ensure a thorough and multilateral examination of the complaint of the person whose rights had been violated without any motive by the operative measures of investigation, the bodies that performed these actions are obliged, at the General Attorney's request, to present all the operative documents.

Information about persons who confidentially contributed to the performance of the operative measures of investigation is presented only at the General Attorney's request. If the body (the official person) that performs the operative measures of investigation violates the legal rights and liberties of legal and natural persons, the higher hierarchical body or the General Attorney is obliged to take measures to restore these rights, to compensate for the caused damage.

At the same time, use of the operative measures of investigation that violate the rights protected by law – the secrecy of mail, telephone calls and other conversations, telegraph communications, as well as the inviolability of the home – is allowed only with a view to collecting information about persons who organise or intend to commit serious crimes, who commit or have already committed serious crimes and only with the General Attorney's sanction, on the basis of the reasoned decision of one of the chiefs of the body that performs the operative activity of investigation.

In cases that cannot be postponed and could lead to serious crimes, on the basis of the reasoned conclusion of one of the chiefs of the body that carries out the operative activity of investigation, the performance of the operative measures of investigation is allowed with the General Attorney's permission for 24 hours. If there is a danger to a person's life, health and property, at his/her request or with his/her written permission, on the basis of the decision authorised by the chief of the body that performs the operative activity of investigation with the General Attorney's permission, the interception of the telephone calls and of other types of conversation is allowed.

Control of the transmission of money or other extorted goods is performed only in cases if there is a declaration from a specific person, on the basis of the reasoned decision of one of the chiefs of the body that performs the operative activity of investigation, authorised by the General Attorney.

Supervision

Chapter 6 of Law No. 45-XIII/1994 deals with the control and supervision of the operative activity of investigation. In fact these are two types of check: parliamentary monitoring and the General Attorney's supervision.

Parliamentary monitoring of the operative activity of investigation is executed by the relevant permanent parliamentary committees (committee for national security). This type of check has a systematic character (at least once a year during the examination of the reports presented by the chiefs of the bodies that perform the operative activity of investigation), but it can also be exercised in case of any particular complaint from citizens.

Execution of laws by the bodies that perform operative activity of investigation and the legality of their decisions are supervised by the General Attorney, his assistants, city and district attorneys, anti-corruption attorneys and the chiefs of criminal prosecution.

The activity of persons who help or helped confidentially the bodies that perform the operative activity of investigation is supervised by the General Attorney or by an attorney specially authorised by the General Attorney's disposition.

The attorney's control has a systematic and automatic character if the performance of some operative measures of investigation is authorised.

5. Which institutions are involved in the use of SITs and what is their role (e.g. law enforcement agencies, prosecutor's office, judicial authorities, etc.)? Which institutions can order and/or authorise the use of SITs? How does co-operation between these institutions work in practice?

The bodies that perform the operative activity of investigation are: the Ministry of Domestic Affaires, the Ministry of Defence, the Security and Information Service of the Republic of Moldova, State Security and Protection Service, Customs Department, Penitentiary Department of the Ministry of Justice, Frontier Guard Department and the Centre for the Control of Corruption and Economic Crimes.

The General Attorney's Office supervises the execution of laws by the bodies that perform the operative activity of investigation and the legality of their decisions, authorises the performance of the operative measures of investigation that restrict the rights protected by law – the secrecy of mail, telephone calls and other types of communication, and home inviolability – as well as the control of the transmission of money or other extorted goods.

The performance of an operative measure of investigation can be ordered by the chief of the body that performs the operative activity of investigation when there are reasons for it, at the suggestions of the investigator, the criminal inquiry body, the attorney regarding the criminal cases they are responsible for, at the interpellation of other bodies that perform the operative activity of investigation, or at the interpellation of international legal organisations and the legal institutions of other states.

The bodies that perform the operative activity of investigation accomplish their tasks independently, in interaction or with citizens' support.

6. Are there any specialised counter-terrorism institutions? What is their role in the use of SITs?

The authorities of the Republic of Moldova that directly fight terrorism, within their competence, are:
- the General Attorney's Office;
- the Security and Information Service of the Republic of Moldova;
- the Ministry of Domestic Affairs;
- the Ministry of Defence;
- the Frontier Guard Department;
- the Department for Exceptional Situations;
- the State Security and Protection Service;
- the Customs Department; and
- the Information Technology Department.

There are specialised organisations to fight terrorism as part of the Security and Information Service of the Republic of Moldova, the Ministry of Domestic Affairs, State Security and Protection Service, and the Penitentiary Department of the Ministry of Justice.

The activity of the General Attorney's Office in preventing terrorism consists in ruling and performing criminal prosecution, and supervising if the law is respected during the criminal prosecution.

The Security and Information Service of the Republic of Moldova and its territorial subdivisions fight terrorism through preventing, detecting and obstructing crimes with a terrorist character, including those that have political purposes, as well as international terrorist activity. According to the legislation on criminal proceedings, the service performs criminal inquiry and preliminary inquest in criminal cases with signs of terrorism, helps to secure the institutions of the Republic of Moldova on the territories of other states, with those of its citizens employed in these institutions and their families, and collects information about international terrorist organisations.

The Ministry of Domestic Affairs fights terrorism by preventing, detecting and interrupting crimes with a terrorist character that have material purposes.

The Ministry of Defence secures the protection of armaments, ammunition, explosive substances, military objects and the air space of the country in the event of anti-terrorist actions.

The Frontier Guard Department and its territorial subdivisions fight terrorism through interrupting terrorists' attempts to cross the state border of the Republic of Moldova.

The Department for Exceptional Situations performs civil protection activities, organises rescue operations, and implements other urgent measures for removing the consequences of the terrorist acts.

The State Security and Protection Service secures natural persons and supervised objects, collects, analyses and uses information about terrorist activity with a view to preventing, detecting and interrupting terrorist attempts. The service collaborates and co-ordinates its activity with all authorities that fight terrorism, including similar services from abroad.

The Customs Department fights terrorism through preventing, detecting and interrupting attempts to take across the state border of the Republic of Moldova arms, explosives, toxic and radioactive substances, and other objects that could be used to commit crimes of a terrorist character.

The Information Technology Department guarantees information assistance to the authorities that fight terrorism, supplying them with information resources and providing specialised technical assistance, necessary for the formation of databases and information networks.

7. Which measures have been adopted in order to facilitate international co-operation (e.g. joint investigation teams)? Can the SITs listed in reply to question 1 be used in cross-border settings?

The Republic of Moldova, according to the international treaties to which it is party, co-operates in the field of fighting terrorism with the legal institutions and special services of other countries, as well as with the international organisations that deal with this subject.

The Republic of Moldova has ratified the majority of the European and international conventions dealing with the repression of terrorism, and made multilateral and bilateral agreements.

In order to guarantee the state, society and personal security, the Republic of Moldova searches on its territory for persons involved in terrorist activities,

234

including cases where the terrorist acts were organised or committed abroad, but caused damage to the country, as well as in the cases stipulated in the international agreements to which the Republic of Moldova is party.

The operative measures of investigation can be performed within a cross-border context with the agreement and together with the relevant bodies of the coterminous state.

8.   What use can be made of SITs in the context of mutual legal assistance?

As was mentioned, the operative measures of investigation can be performed at the interpellation of international legal organisations and the legal institutions of other states in accordance with the international treaties to which the Republic of Moldova is party, for example the European Convention for Legal Assistance on Criminal Matters dated 20 April 1959.

9. How can the use of SITs be improved? Please provide any comments/proposals concerning the implementation of the terms of reference of the PC-TI and in particular the use and regulation of SITs.

We consider appropriate the improvement of the usage of special techniques of investigation through improving the legislative ground in the field, the increased responsibility of the bodies authorised to use the special techniques and the growth of monitoring of their activities on the part of the relevant state structures.

According to the stipulations of the PC-TI mandate, the Republic of Moldova is interested in the exchange of information regarding the usage of special techniques of investigation in other countries that are members of the Council of Europe.

Netherlands

1. Please indicate the SITs used in your country, the respective legal framework governing their use and their legal definition, if any.

The SITs used in the Netherlands, the legal framework governing their use, and their legal definitions are as follows.

Undercover operations (including covert investigations)

Applied: yes.
Definition: infiltration to join or aid in the interests of the investigation a group of persons who can reasonably be suspected to plan or commit offences.

Legal framework

- 126h Dutch Code of Criminal Procedure (DCCP) (after commission of an offence; by NL police officers), 126h(4) (by foreign police officers);
- 126p DCCP (not necessarily after commission of an offence, but only in connection with planning or committing serious organised crime; by NL police officers), 126p(4) (by foreign police officers);
- 126w DCCP (after commission of an offence; by civilians);
- 126x DCCP (not necessarily after commission of an offence, but only in connection with planning or committing serious organised crime; by civilians).

Front store operation (e.g. undercover company)

Applied: yes.
Definition: purchase of goods from or supply of services to a suspect in the interests of the investigation.

Legal framework

- 126i DCCP (after the commission of an offence; by NL police officers), 126i(4) (by foreign police officers);
- 126q DCCP (not necessarily after the commission of an offence, but only in case of connection with planning or committing serious organised crime; by NL police officers), 126q(4) (by foreign police officers);
- 126y DCCP (after the commission of an offence; by civilians);
- 126z DCCP (not necessarily after the commission of an offence, but only in case of connection with planning or committing serious organised crime; by civilians).

Informants

Applied: yes.

Definition: a person who is not a police officer, who concludes an agreement that he or she will assist the investigation for a given duration by obtaining information in a systematic manner concerning a suspect or a person in relation to whom there is a reasonable suspicion that he or she is involved in planning or committing offences on an organised basis.

Legal framework

- 126v DCCP (order by public prosecutor to police officer, after the commission of an offence, or in case of connection with planning or committing serious organised crime).

Controlled delivery

Applied: yes.
Definition: not in Dutch law, but in 1(g) UN Drugs Convention 1988.

Legal framework

- In general: not explicitly as a method of its own, but implicit in other SITs that allow the control of a delivery; for drugs: 73 Schengen Convention + 1(g) and 11 UN Drugs Convention 1988.
- Specifically referred to in 126ff DCCP, paragraph 1 of which explicitly prohibits *laissez-passer* of prohibited or dangerous goods; confiscation may be delayed with a view to carrying it out later; paragraph 2 allows an exception to this prohibition on the basis of considerable investigative interests to be ordered in conformity with conditions specified in paragraph 3; 140a DCCP requires the order to be agreed to by the Committee of Attorneys-General, on the basis of 131(5) Judicial Organisation Act; this can only be done after consultation with the Minister of Justice.

Observation (including cross-border observation)

Applied: yes.
Definition: in the interests of the investigation, follow a person or observe his presence or behaviour on a systematic basis from a certain distance.

Legal framework

- 40 Schengen Convention;
- 126g DCCP (after the commission of an offence; by NL police officer);
- 126j DCCP ("close" observation under cover nearby; after commission of an offence; by NL police officer), 126j(4) (by foreign police officers);
- 126o DCCP (not necessarily after the commission of an offence, but only in case of connection with planning or committing serious organised crime; by NL police officers),126o(6) (by foreign police officers);

- 126qa DCCP ("close" observation under cover, from nearby; not necessarily after the commission of an offence, but only in case of connection with planning or committing serious organised crime; by NL police officers), 126qa(4) (by foreign police officers).

Electronic surveillance

Applied: yes.
Definition: use of a technical device by a police officer following a person or observing his/her presence or behaviour systematically, in the interests of the investigation, but without recording confidential communications.

Legal framework

- 126g(3) DCCP (after the commission of an offence; by NL police officers), 126g(9) (by foreign police officers);
- 126o(3) DCCP (not necessarily after the commission of an offence, but only in case of connection with planning or committing serious organised crime; by NL police officers), 126o(6) (by foreign police officers).

Bugging (private or public premises)

Applied: yes.
Definition: record confidential communication with the aid of a technical device if urgently required in the interests of the investigation; bugging of/in dwellings only for more serious offences.

Legal framework

- 126l DCCP (after the commission of an offence; entering dwellings only for offences punishable by 8 years or more; by NL police officers);
- 126s DCCP (not necessarily after commission of an offence, but only in connection with planning or committing serious organised crime; entering dwellings only for offences punishable by 6 years or more; by NL police officers).

Interception of communications

Applied: yes
Definition: communication (by telephone, fax, e-mail, mail, public and private networks) not intended for the public, via the telecommunications infrastructure or via an installation which provides a service to the public.

Legal framework

- 126m DCCP (recording telecommunications with a technical device, after the commission of an offence; by NL police officers);

- 126n DCCP (order to telecommunications provider to disclose traffic data of communications in which suspect is believed to have taken part, after the commission of an offence; by public prosecutor);
- 126t DCCP (not necessarily after the commission of an offence, but only in case of connection with planning or committing serious organised crime; by NL police officers).

Searches

Applied: yes.
Definition: entering enclosed places (including premises and objects, e.g. computers and cars, by various means including scanning), not dwellings, to secretly examine the place, secure evidence found there, place technical devices and an auxiliary measure to facilitate or enable other special investigative techniques such as observation, placing a scanner, recording confidential communications.

Legal framework

- 96b-99 DCCP and General Act on Entering: general provisions on overt searches with a view to seizure (public prosecutor may search places; dwellings and some other, specific places only with investigating judge's mandate);
- 126g(2) DCCP (to facilitate observation; after the commission of an offence; by NL police officers), 126g(9) (by foreign police officers);
- 126k DCCP (as investigating technique in its own right; after the commission of an offence; by NL police officers);
- 126l(2) DCCP (to facilitate recording confidential communications with a technical device; after the commission of an offence; by NL police officers);
- 126o(2) DCCP (to facilitate observation; not necessarily after the commission of an offence, but only in case of connection with planning or committing serious organised crime; by NL police officers), 126o(6) (by foreign police officers);
- 126r DCCP (as investigating technique in its own right; not necessarily after the commission of an offence, but only in case of connection with planning or committing serious organised crime);
- 126s(2) DCCP (to facilitate recording confidential communication with a technical device; not necessarily after the commission of an offence, but only in case of connection with planning or committing serious organised crime).

Cross-border (hot) pursuit

Applied: yes.
Definition: not in Dutch law, only in 41 Schengen Convention and 27 Benelux Extradition Convention.

Legal framework

- 41 Schengen Convention/27 Benelux Convention;
- 54(4) DCCP (foreign police officer may – after continued pursuit across Dutch border in accordance with international law – apprehend suspect after the commission of an offence in the state where the pursuit started).

Agents provocateurs

Applied: yes.
Definition: inducing a suspect or other person to commit an offence in the course of an operation involving infiltration, front store or pseudo-purchases; prohibition of inducing the commission of other offences than the ones he or she was already intending to commit.

Legal framework

- 126h(2), 126p(2), 126w(3) 126x(3) DCCP (on infiltration);
- 126i(2), 126q(2), 126y(3) and 126z(3) (on pseudo-purchases and provision of services).

For pseudo-purchases or other "pseudo-offences", see above, on front store operations and agents provocateurs.

2. When and under which circumstances (e.g. criminal investigation, preliminary stage, etc.) can SITs be used?

After the commission of an offence as in Article 67(1) DCCP (i.e. one for which pretrial detention may be allowed, most of which carry maximum penalties of 4 years or more; some SITs require more serious offences or additional criteria, e.g. regarding the nature of the offences or its organised context), in order to investigate that offence, and if SIT use is required in the interests of the investigation.

In cases of reasonable suspicion that offences as defined in Article 67(1) DCCP (some require more serious offences) are being planned or committed on an organised basis, and SIT use is urgently required in the interests of the investigation.

No SITs may be used, but exploratory investigations may be started with the aim of preparing for an investigation, if facts or circumstances give rise to indications that associations of persons are planning or committing offences as defined in Article 67(1), which in view of their nature or connection with other offences planned or committed by the same association of persons constitute a serious breach of the legal order (126gg DCCP).

In accordance with Article 132a DCCP, the use of SITs must be aimed at the taking of decisions under the Code of Criminal Procedure.

3. Are there any specific features governing the use of SITs in relation to acts of terrorism? If so, please specify.

Not as far as the use of SITs for criminal law enforcement is concerned.

4. How does the legal framework governing the use of SITs guarantee respect for human rights and individual freedoms, the principles of subsidiarity and proportionality? Is the authorisation to use SITs subject to time-limits? Which bodies and procedures are in place to supervise compliance with human rights standards and with the above-mentioned principles in the use of SITs? Is supervision automatic/systematic?

SITs may only be used if required/urgently required for investigation; the order must be terminated as soon as its conditions are no longer fulfilled.

Article 126aa obliges the public prosecutor to add to the case documents the official reports and other items, in so far as they are relevant to the investigation, and as soon as the interests of rhe investigation so allow.

Article 126bb obliges the public prosecutor to notify the person concerned in writing of the use of a SIT as soon as the interests of the investigation allow.

Article 126cc obliges the public prosecutor to destroy the official reports and other items two months after closure of the case and the last notification, unless he decides in accordance with 126dd that information obtained through the use of technical devices, the recording of confidential communications or the interception of telecommunications may be used for another criminal investigation or for storage in a serious crime file under the Data Protection (Police File) Act.

Is the authorisation to use SITs subject to time-limits?

Orders to use SITs must mention the period for which the order is valid. The validity of orders for observation and close observation may not exceed three months, but may be extended by three months at a time. The validity of orders for recording confidential communication with a technical device or the interception of telecommunication may not exceed four weeks but may be extended by four weeks at a time.

Which bodies and procedures supervise compliance with human rights and the above-mentioned principles in the use of SITs?

- In general, the public prosecutor;
- In specific cases (especially the recording of confidential communications and the interception of telecommunication, the entering of

dwellings or other specified places), the order may be given only after authorisation by a investigating judge;

- Infiltration by civilians and *laissez-passer* may be ordered only with the authorisation of the Committee of Attorneys-General after consultation with the Minister of Justice.

Is supervision automatic/systematic?

Supervision is automatic in the sense that no SIT can be used for criminal investigation without the order of a public prosecutor, and use in that context is always under the supervision and responsibility of the public prosecutor.

5. Which institutions are involved in the use of SITs and what is their role (e.g. law enforcement agencies, prosecutor's office, judicial authorities, etc.)? Which institutions can order and/or authorise the use of SITs? How does co-operation between these institutions work in practice?

SITs may be used by police officers of the regular police services, and in most cases by police officers of specialised police agencies. They may also in some situations be used by/ordered to foreign police officers, and may involve the conclusion of agreements with civilians to be used for infiltration, pseudo-offences or front store operations.

Which institutions can order and/or authorise the use of SITs?

Only the public prosecutor can order the use of SITs; in addition, in specific cases (especially: recording confidential communications and intercepting telecommunication, entering dwellings or other specified places), the order may be given only after authorisation by a investigating judge.

How does co-operation between these institutions work in practice ?

For their activities in the context of criminal investigations, police officers stand under the supervision of the public prosecutor, who may give them orders and instructions, and is responsible for their operations.

6. Are there any specialised counter-terrorism institutions? What is their role in the use of SITs?

Within the National Police Agency KLPD, there is a Unit concerned with terror and special tasks (UTBT).

What is their role in the use of SITs?

In principle, no other than the role of any other police officer involved in criminal investigations. in practice, this unit primarily collects information gathered by others and co-ordinates investigations into terrorist offences; they usually entrust operational matters to tactical KLPD units.

243

7. Which measures have been adopted in order to facilitate international co-operation (e.g. joint investigation teams)? Can the SITs listed in reply to question 1 be used in cross-border settings?

- Joint investigation teams in the sense of the EU Convention on Mutual Legal Assistance have not yet been put in place since the EU convention has not come into force yet;
- Teams in which, under the supervision of a Dutch public prosecutor, police officers from various states co-operate as one team ("joint target co-operation"), are possible already since the order for a number of SITs can be given to foreign police officers as well.

Can SITs listed in reply to question 1 be used in cross-border settings?

In principle that would be possible, especially in close co-operation as indicated in the preceding answer; in addition, for SITs like controlled delivery, a special legal framework has been created for their use in cross-border settings.

8. What use can be made of SITs in the context of mutual legal assistance?

552oa DCCP enables the use of SITs on the basis of a request from the authorities of another state; in the case of recording confidential communications with a technical device and the interception of telecommunication, the request should be based on a treaty or convention.

9. How can the use of SITs be improved? Please provide any comments/proposals concerning the implementation of the terms of reference of the PC-TI and in particular the use and regulation of SITs.

Appendix

Amendments to the Netherlands Code of Criminal Procedure

Amendments dated 27 May 1999 in connection with the regulation of certain special powers of investigation and the amendment of certain other provisions (special investigative powers):

> We, Beatrix, by the grace of God, Queen of the Netherlands, Princess of Orange-Nassau, etc.

> Greetings to all who shall see or hear this information being read! Be it known:

> That We have considered it desirable to include in the Code of Criminal Procedure certain special powers of investigation and in that connection to amend certain other provisions;

> We, therefore, having heard the Council of State, and in consultation with the States General, have approved and decreed as We hereby approve and decree:

Section I

The Code of Criminal Procedure shall be amended as follows:

A

Part Six of Title IV of Book I shall be deleted.

B

After Title IV of Book I, Titles IVa, V, Va, Vb and Vc shall be inserted, reading as follows:

Title IVA - Special powers of investigation

Part One – Surveillance

Article 126g

1.   If it is suspected that an indictable offence has been committed, the public prosecutor may, in the interests of the investigation, order an investigating officer to follow a person or to observe his presence or behaviour on a systematic basis.

2. If the suspicions relate to an offence as defined in Article 67, paragraph 1, which in view of its nature or connection with other offences committed by the suspect constitutes a serious breach of the legal order, the public prosecutor may, in the interests of the investigation, decide that in order to carry out the order referred to in paragraph 1, an enclosed place, not being a dwelling, may be entered without the permission of the title holder.

3. The public prosecutor may decide that in order to carry out the order referred to in paragraph 1, a technical device shall be used, provided it is not used to record confidential communications. No technical device shall be attached to a person without his permission.

4. The order shall be given for a period not exceeding three months and may be extended, on each occasion for a further three months.

5. A surveillance order shall be in writing and shall include:
    a.   the offence and, if known, the name or as accurate as possible a designation of the suspect;
    b.   the facts or circumstances demonstrating that the conditions set out in paragraph 1 have been fulfilled;
    c.   the name or as accurate as possible a designation of the person referred to in paragraph 1;
    d.   if paragraph 2 is applied, the facts and circumstances demonstrating that the conditions set out in that paragraph have been fulfilled, and the place to be entered;
    e.   the way in which the order is to be executed, and
    f.   the period for which the order is valid.

6. In urgent cases the order may be given verbally. In such cases, the public prosecutor shall then put the order in writing within three days.

7. As soon as the conditions set out in paragraph 1 are no longer fulfilled, the public prosecutor shall terminate the implementation of the order.

8. The order may be amended, supplemented, extended or terminated in writing, with reasons being given. In urgent cases the decision may be given verbally. In such cases, the public prosecutor shall then put his decision in writing within three days.

9. An order as referred to in paragraph 1 may also be given to a person in the public service of another State. Certain requirements may be imposed on that person by order in council. Paragraphs 2 to 8 shall apply *mutatis mutandis*.

Part Two – Infiltration

Article 126h

1.   If it is suspected that an offence has been committed as defined in Article 67, paragraph 1, which in view of its nature or connection with other offences committed by the suspect constitutes a serious breach of the legal order, the public prosecutor may, if this is urgently required in the interests of the investigation, order an investigating officer as referred to in Article 141b, to join or assist a group of persons who can reasonably be suspected of planning or committing offences.

2.   In carrying out the order referred to in paragraph 1, the investigating officer may not induce a person to commit an offence other than the one he was already intending to commit.

3.   An infiltration order shall be in writing and shall include:
  a.   the offence and, if known, the name or as accurate as possible a designation of the suspect;
  b.   a description of the group of persons;
  c.   the facts or circumstances demonstrating that the conditions set out in paragraph 1 have been fulfilled;
  d.   the way in which the order is to be executed, including any activities which constitute an offence, in so far as this is possible to foresee at the time the order is issued, and
  e.   the period for which the order is valid.

4.   An order as referred to in paragraph 1 may also be issued to:
  a.   a person in the public service of another State who complies with requirements laid down by order in council;
  b.   an investigating officer as referred to in Article 142, provided the said officer is co-operating pursuant to Section 11, subsection 2 of the 1993 Police Act with investigating officers as referred to in Article 141 (b).
Paragraphs 2 and 3 shall apply *mutatis mutandis*.

5.   Article 126g, paragraphs 7 and 8 shall apply *mutatis mutandis*, on the understanding that an infiltration order may not be extended verbally.

Part Three – Pseudo purchases and provision of services

Article 126i

1.   If it is suspected that an offence as defined in Article 67, paragraph 1 has been committed, the public prosecutor may, in the interests of the investigation, order an investigating officer to buy goods from or provide services to the suspect.

2.   In carrying out the order referred to in paragraph 1, the investigating officer may not induce the suspect to commit an offence other than the one he was already intending to commit.

3.   A pseudo-purchase or provision of services order shall be in writing and shall include:
a.   the offence and, if known, the name or as accurate as possible a designation of the suspect;
b.   the facts or circumstances demonstrating that the conditions set out in paragraph 1 have been fulfilled;
c.   the nature of the goods or services;
d.   the way in which the order is to be executed, including any activities which constitute an offence, and
e.   the date on which or the period within which the order is to be executed.

4.   An investigating officer as referred to in paragraph 1 shall also mean a person in the public service of another State who complies with requirements laid down by order in council.

5.   Article 126g, paragraphs 6 to 8 shall apply *mutatis mutandis*.

Part Four – Undercover systematic gathering of information

Article 126j

1.   If it is suspected that an indictable offence has been committed, the public prosecutor may, in the interests of the investigation, order an investigating officer as referred to in Article 141(b) systematically to gather information on the suspect without it being known that he is acting in the capacity of investigating officer.

2.   The order shall be valid for a period not exceeding three months and may be extended, on each occasion for a further three months.

3.   An order to gather information shall be in writing and shall include:
a.   the offence and, if known, the name or as accurate as possible a designation of the suspect;
b.   the facts or circumstances demonstrating that the conditions set out in paragraph 1 have been fulfilled;
c.   the way in which the order is to be executed, and
d.   the period for which the order is valid.

4.   An order as referred to in paragraph 1 may also be issued to:
a.   a person in the public service of another State who complies with requirements laid down by order in council;
b.   an investigating officer as referred to in Article 142, provided the said officer is co-operating pursuant to Section 11, subsection 2 of the

1993 Police Act with investigating officers as referred to in Article 141 (b).
Paragraphs 2 and 3 shall apply *mutatis mutandis.*

5. Article 126g, paragraphs 6 to 8 shall apply *mutatis mutandis.*

Part Five – Powers to enter enclosed places

Article 126k

1. If it is suspected that an offence as defined in Article 67, paragraph 1 has been committed, the public prosecutor may, in the interests of the investigation, order an investigating officer to enter an enclosed place, not being a dwelling, or to use a technical device, without the permission of the title holder, in order to:
    a. examine the place in question;
    b. secure evidence found there, or
    c. to place a technical device there with a view to establishing the presence or transport of a particular object.

2. An order as referred to in paragraph 1 shall be in writing and shall include:
    a. the offence and, if known, the name or as accurate as possible a designation of the suspect;
    b. the facts or circumstances demonstrating that the conditions set out in paragraph 1 have been fulfilled;
    c. the place to which the order relates;
    d. the way in which the order is to be executed, and
    e. the date on which or the period within which the order is to be executed.

3. Article 126g, paragraphs 6 to 8 shall apply *mutatis mutandis.*

Part Six – Recording confidential communications with a technical device

Article 126l

1. If it is suspected that an offence has been committed as defined in Article 67, paragraph 1, which in view of its nature or connection with other offences committed by the suspect constitutes a serious breach of the legal order, the public prosecutor may, if this is urgently required in the interests of the investigation, order an investigating officer as referred to in Article 141(b) to record a confidential communication with the aid of a technical device.

2. In the interests of the investigation, the public prosecutor may decide that an enclosed place, not being a dwelling, shall be entered without the permission of the title holder, in order to carry out the order. He can

determine, in order to carry out the order, that a dwelling shall be entered without the permission of the title holder, if the investigation urgently so requires and the suspicion involves a crime the legal description of which carries a prison sentence of eight years or more. Article 2, first paragraph, final sentence of the General Act on Entering is not applicable.

3.   An order to record a confidential communication shall be in writing and shall include:
   a.   the offence and, if known, the name or as accurate as possible a designation of the suspect;
   b.   the facts or circumstances demonstrating that the conditions set out in paragraph 1 and, in cases where the second sentence of the second paragraph are applicable, the conditions referred to in the second paragraph, have been fulfilled;
   c.   the name of at least one of the persons taking part in the communication, or, if the order relates to communication taking place in an enclosed place or vehicle, the name of one of the persons taking part in the communication or as accurate as possible a description of the place or the vehicle;
   d.   if paragraph 2 is applied, the place to be entered;
   e.   the way in which the order is to be executed, and
   f.   the period for which the order is valid.

4.   An order as referred to in paragraph 1 may be given only after written authorisation has been obtained from the examining magistrate on the application of the public prosecutor. Such authorisation shall apply to all parts of the order. If a dwelling is to be entered in executing the order, then this needs to be expressly mentioned in the authorisation.

5.   An order shall be given for a period not exceeding four weeks and may be extended, on each occasion for a further four weeks.

6.   Article 126g, paragraphs 6 to 8 shall apply *mutatis mutandis*, on the understanding that the public prosecutor requires authorisation from the examining magistrate for any change, addition or extension of the order. If the public prosecutor determines that a dwelling will be entered in executing the order, then the authorisation cannot be given verbally. As soon as the conditions referred to in the second sentence of the second paragraph are no longer fulfilled, the public prosecutor shall determine that execution of the order is terminated.

7.   In urgent cases, the authorisation of the examining magistrate referred to in paragraphs 4 and 6 may be given verbally. In such cases the examining magistrate shall then put the order in writing within three days.

8.   An official report of the recordings shall be drawn up within three days.

Part Seven – Interception of telecommunication

Article 126m

1.   If it is suspected that an offence has been committed as defined in Article 67, paragraph 1, which in view of its nature or connection with other offences committed by the suspect constitutes a serious breach of the legal order, the public prosecutor may, if this is urgently required in the interests of the investigation, order an investigating officer as referred to in Article 141(b) to record telecommunication with the aid of a technical device.

2.   In this article 'telecommunication' means communication not intended for the public which takes place via the telecommunications infrastructure or via a telecommunications installation which provides a service to the public.

3.   An order to record telecommunication shall be in writing and shall include:
   a.   the offence and, if known, the name or as accurate as possible a designation of the suspect;
   b.   the facts or circumstances demonstrating that the conditions set out in paragraph 1 have been fulfilled;
   c.   the number of the connection and the name and address of the subscriber;
   d.   the period for which the order is valid.

4.   Article 126l, paragraphs 4 to 8 shall apply *mutatis mutandis.*

Article 126n

1.   In the event of discovery *in flagrante delicto,* or suspicion that an offence as defined in Article 67, paragraph 1 has been committed, or in the case of the offence referred to in Article 138a of the Criminal Code, the public prosecutor may, in the interests of the investigation, demand disclosure of information regarding all traffic via the telecommunications infrastructure or via a telecommunications installation which provides a service to the public, in which the suspect is believed to have taken part.

2.   The demand referred to in paragraph 1 may be made to any employee of a person or company operating under the Telecommunications Act pursuant to:
   a.   a concession as defined in Section 3, subsection 1 of the said Act;
   b.   an infrastructure licence as referred to in Section 3a, subsection 1 of the said Act;

c.   a licence as referred to in Section 13a or a provisional licence as referred to in Section 13i of the said Act, and

d.   a franchise as referred to in Chapter III of the said Act, if a telecommunications installation is being used to provide a service to the public.

3.   Articles 217, 218 and 219 shall apply *mutatis mutandis*.

Title V – Special investigative powers in connection with the planning or committing of serious organised crime

Article 126o

1.   If facts or circumstances give rise to reasonable suspicion that offences as defined in Article 67, paragraph 1 are being planned or committed on an organised basis, which in view of their nature or connection with other offences planned or committed by the same organisation constitute a serious breach of the legal order, the public prosecutor may, in the interests of the investigation, order an investigating officer to follow a person or observe his presence or behaviour on a systematic basis.

2.   In the interests of the investigation, the public prosecutor may decide that an enclosed place, not being a dwelling, shall be entered without the permission of the title holder, in order to carry out the order referred to in the preceding paragraph.

3.   The public prosecutor may decide in the interests of the investigation that a technical device shall be used, provided it is not used to record confidential communications. No technical device shall be attached to a person without his permission.

4.   A surveillance order shall be in writing and shall include:
    a.   a description of the organisation;
    b.   the facts or circumstances demonstrating that the conditions set out in paragraph 1 have been fulfilled;
    c.   the name or as accurate as possible a designation of the person referred to in paragraph 1;
    d.   if paragraph 2 is applied, the place to be entered;
    e.   the way in which the order is to be executed, and
    f. the period for which the order is valid.

5.   Article 126g, paragraphs 4 and 6 to 8 shall apply *mutatis mutandis*.

6.   An order as referred to in paragraph 1 may also be given to a person in the public service of another State. Certain requirements may be imposed on that person by order in council. Paragraphs 2 to 5 shall apply *mutatis mutandis*.

Article 126p

1.   In a case as referred to in Article 126o, paragraph 1, the public prosecutor may, if this is urgently required in the interests of the investigation, order an investigating officer as referred to in Article 141(b) to join or assist the organisation in question.

2.   In carrying out the order referred to in paragraph 1, the investigating officer may not induce a person to commit an offence other than the one he was already intending to commit.

3.   An infiltration order shall be in writing and shall include:
   a.   a description of the organisation;
   b.   the facts or circumstances demonstrating that the conditions set out in paragraph 1 have been fulfilled;
   c.   the way in which the order is to be executed, including any activities which constitute an offence, in so far as this is possible to foresee at the time the order is issued, and
   d.   the period for which the order is valid.

4.   An order as referred to in paragraph 1 may also be issued to:
   a.   a person in the public service of another State who complies with requirements laid down by order in council;
   b.   an investigating officer as referred to in Article 141 (c) or Article 142, provided the said officer complies with the requirements of the order in council regarding training and co-operation with investigating officers as referred to in Article 141 (b).
Paragraphs 2 and 3 shall apply *mutatis mutandis*.

5.   Article 126g, paragraphs 7 and 8 shall apply *mutatis mutandis*, on the understanding that an infiltration order may not be extended verbally.

Article 126q

1.   In a case as referred to in Article 126o, paragraph 1, the public prosecutor may, in the interests of the investigation, order an investigating officer to buy goods from or provide services to a person concerning whom there is reasonable suspicion based on the facts or circumstances, that he is involved in planning or committing offences on an organised basis.

2.   In carrying out the order referred to in paragraph 1, the investigating officer may not induce a person to commit or plan an offence other than the one he was already intending to commit or plan.

3.   A pseudo-purchase or provision of services order shall be in writing and shall include:
   a.   a description of the organisation;

b.   the facts or circumstances demonstrating that the conditions set out in paragraph 1 have been fulfilled;
c.   the nature of the goods or services;
d.   the way in which the order is to be executed, including any activities which constitute an offence, and
e.   the date on which or the period within which the order is to be executed.

4.   An investigating officer as referred to in paragraph 1 shall also mean a person in the public service of another State who complies with requirements laid down by order in council.

5.   Article 126g, paragraphs 6 to 8 shall apply *mutatis mutandis*.

Article 126qa

1. In a case as referred to in Article 126o, paragraph 1, the public prosecutor may, in the interests of the investigation, order an investigating officer, as referred to in Article 141 (b), to systematically obtain information about a person about whom there is reasonable suspicion that they are involved in planning or committing organised crimes, without making known that he is acting as an investigating officer.

2. The order will be given for a period of a maximum of three months. The period of validity can be extended on each occasion for a period of a maximum of three months.

3. The order to obtain information shall be in writing and shall include:
   a.   a description of the organised context;
   b.   the facts or circumstances proving that the conditions referred to in the first paragraph are fulfilled;
   c.   if known, the name, or otherwise as accurate a description as possible, of the person referred to in the first paragraph;
   d.   the way in which the order will be carried out, and
   e.   the period of validity of the order.

4.   An order as referred to in the first paragraph can also be given to:
   a.   a person in the public service of a foreign country who complies with the requirements of the order in council;
   b.   an investigating officer as referred to in Article 41 (c), or Article 142, as long as this investigating officer complies with the requirements of the order in council with regard to training and co-operation with investigating officers as referred to in Article 141 (b).
The second and third paragraphs shall apply *mutatis mutandis*.

5.   Article 126g, sixth to eighth section inclusive, shall apply *mutatis mutandis*.

254

Article 126r

1.   In a case as referred to in Article 126o, paragraph 1, the public prosecutor may, in the interests of the investigation, order an investigating officer to enter an enclosed place, not being a dwelling, or use a technical device, without permission of the title holder, in order to:
   a.   examine the place in question;
   b.   secure evidence found there, or
   c.   to place a technical device there with a view to establishing the presence or transport of a particular object.

2.   An order as referred to in paragraph 1 shall be in writing and include:
   a.   a description of the organisation;
   b.   the facts or circumstances demonstrating that the conditions set out in paragraph 1 have been fulfilled;
   c.   the place to which the order relates;
   d.   the way in which the order is to be executed, and
   e.   the date on which or the period within which the order is to be executed.

3. Article 126g, paragraphs 6 to 8 shall apply *mutatis mutandis*.

Article 126s

1.   In a case as referred to in Article 126o, paragraph 1, the public prosecutor may, if this is urgently required in the interests of the investigation, order an investigating officer as referred to in Article 141(b) to record with the aid of a technical device a confidential communication one of the participants in which is the subject of reasonable suspicion, based on the facts or circumstances, that he is involved in planning or committing offences on an organised basis.

2.   In the interests of the investigation, the public prosecutor may order that an enclosed place, not being a dwelling, shall be entered without the permission of the title holder, in order to carry out the order referred to in the preceding paragraph. In carrying out an order, he can determine that a dwelling be entered without the permission of the title holder if the investigation requires this urgently and if organised crimes are being planned or committed that carry a prison sentence of six years or more. Article 2, first paragraph, last sentence of the General Act on Entering is not applicable.

3.   An order to record a confidential communication shall be in writing and shall include:
   a.   a description of the organisation;
   b.   the facts or circumstances demonstrating that the conditions set out in paragraph 1 have been fulfilled and, in cases of the application of the second sentence of the second paragraph, the conditions stated in the second paragraph have been fulfilled;

c. the name of the person referred to in paragraph 1 and, if known, other participants in the communication;
d. if paragraph 2 is applied, the place to be entered;
e. the way in which the order is to be executed, and
f. the period for which the order is valid.

4. An order as referred to in paragraph 1 may be given only after written authorisation has been obtained from the examining magistrate on the application of the public prosecutor. Such authorisation shall apply to all parts of the order. If a dwelling is to be entered in carrying out the order then this must be explicitly mentioned in the authorisation.

5. An order shall be given for a period not exceeding four weeks and may be extended, on each occasion for a further four weeks.

6. Article 126g, paragraphs 6 to 8 shall apply *mutatis mutandis,* on the understanding that the public prosecutor requires authorisation from the examining magistrate for any change, addition or extension of the order. If the public prosecutor determines that a dwelling is to be entered in carrying out the order, then the order may not be given verbally. As soon as the conditions referred to in the second sentence of the second paragraph are no longer fulfilled, the public prosecutor will determine that carrying out the order is terminated.

7. In urgent cases, the authorisation of the examining magistrate referred to in paragraphs 4 and 6 may be given verbally unless the second sentence of the second paragraph is applicable. In such cases the examining magistrate shall then put the order in writing within three days.

8. An official report of the recordings shall be drawn up within three days.

Article 126t

1. In a case as referred to in Article 126o, paragraph 1, the public prosecutor may, if this is urgently required in the interests of the investigation, order an investigating officer with the aid of a technical device to record telecommunication where one of the participants is the subject of reasonable suspicion, based on facts or circumstances, that he is involved in planning or committing offences on an organised basis.

2. In this article 'telecommunication' means communication not intended for the public which takes place via the telecommunications infrastructure or via a telecommunications installation which provides a service to the public.

3. An order to record telecommunication shall be in writing and include:
   a. a description of the organisation;

b.   the facts or circumstances demonstrating that the conditions set out in paragraph 1 have been fulfilled;

c.   the number of the connection and the name and address of the subscriber;

d.   the name of the person referred to in paragraph 1 if he is not the subscriber, and

e.   the period for which the order is valid.

4. Article 126s, paragraphs 4 to 8 shall apply *mutatis mutandis.*

Article 126u

1.   In a case as referred to in Article 126o, paragraph 1, the public prosecutor may in the interests of the investigation, demand disclosure of information regarding all traffic via the telecommunications infrastructure or via a telecommunications installation which provides a service to the public, where it is suspected that a person has taken part in that traffic who is the subject of reasonable suspicion, based on the facts or circumstances, that he is involved in planning or committing offences on an organised basis.

2.   The demand referred to in paragraph 1 may be made to any employee of a person or company operating under the Telecommunications Act pursuant to:

a.   a concession as defined in Section 3, subsection 1 of the said Act;

b.   an infrastructure licence as referred to in Section 3a, subsection 1 of the said Act;

c.   a licence as referred to in Section 13a or a provisional licence as referred to in Section 13i of the said Act, and

d.   a franchise as referred to in Chapter III of the said Act, if a telecommunications installation is being used to provide a service to the public.

3.   Articles 217, 218 and 219 shall apply *mutatis mutandis.*

Title VA – Assistance from civilians

Part One – Request to obtain information

Article 126v

1.   If it is suspected that an indictable offence has been committed, or in a case as referred to in Article 126o, paragraph 1, the public prosecutor may, in the interests of the investigation, order an investigating officer to conclude an agreement with a person who is not an investigating officer that the latter will assist the investigation for the duration of the order by obtaining information in a systematic manner concerning a suspect or a

person in relation to whom there is reasonable suspicion that he is involved in planning or committing offences on an organised basis.

2. The order referred to in paragraph 1 shall be in writing and include:
a. where commission of an offence is suspected, the offence and, if known, the suspect's name or as accurate as possible a description;
b. in a case as referred to in Article 126o, paragraph 1, a description of the organisation;
c. the facts or circumstances demonstrating that the conditions set out in paragraph 1 have been fulfilled;
d. as accurate as possible a designation of the person concerning whom information is to be obtained, and
e. the period for which the order is valid.

3. An agreement to gather information in a systematic manner shall be in writing and shall include:
a. the rights and obligations of the person assisting the investigation, and the way in which the agreement is to be implemented, and
b. the period for which the agreement is valid.

4. Article 126g, paragraphs 4 and 6 to 8 shall apply to the order *mutatis mutandis*.

Part Two – Non-police infiltration

Article 126w

1. In a case as referred to in Article 126h, paragraph 1, the public prosecutor may, if this is urgently required in the interests of the investigation, conclude an agreement with a person who is not an investigating officer that the latter will assist the investigation by joining or assisting a group of persons who can reasonably be suspected of planning or committing offences.

2. Paragraph 1 shall be applied only if the public prosecutor is of the opinion that an order as referred to in Article 126h, paragraph 1 cannot be given.

3. The person assisting the investigation pursuant to paragraph 1 may not, in providing the said assistance, induce another person to commit an offence other than the one he was already intending to commit.

4. In applying paragraph 1, the public prosecutor shall record in writing:
a. the offence and, if known, the name or as accurate as possible a designation of the suspect;
b. a description of the group of persons;
c. the facts or circumstances demonstrating that the conditions set out in paragraphs 1 and 2 have been fulfilled.

5. An infiltration agreement shall be in writing and shall include:
   a. the rights and obligations of the person assisting the investigation pursuant to paragraph 1, and the way in which the agreement is to be implemented, and
   b. the period for which the agreement is valid.

6. The person assisting the investigation pursuant to paragraph 1 may not commit any offences while so doing unless the written authorisation of the public prosecutor has been obtained in advance. In urgent cases, the authorisation may be given verbally. In such cases, the public prosecutor shall put the authorisation in writing within three days.

7. As soon as the conditions referred to in paragraph 1 are no longer fulfilled, the public prosecutor shall end implementation of the agreement.

8. The agreement may be amended, supplemented, extended or terminated in writing. The public prosecutor shall put the reasons for this in writing within three days.

Article 126x

1. In a case as referred to in Article 126o, paragraph 1, the public prosecutor may, if this is urgently required in the interests of the investigation, conclude an agreement with a person who is not an investigating officer that the latter will assist the investigation by joining or assisting the criminal organisation.

2. Paragraph 1 shall be applied only if the public prosecutor is of the opinion that an order as referred to in Article 126p, paragraph 1 cannot be given.

3. The person assisting the investigation pursuant to paragraph 1 may not, in providing the said assistance, induce another person to commit an offence other than the one he was already intending to commit.

4. Article 126w, paragraphs 4 to 8 shall apply *mutatis mutandis*.

Part Three – Non-police pseudo-purchases and provision of services

Article 126y

1. In a case as referred to in Article 126i, paragraph 1, the public prosecutor may, in the interests of the investigation, conclude an agreement with a person who is not an investigating officer that the latter will assist the investigation by buying goods from or providing services to the suspect.

2.   Paragraph 1 shall be applied only if the public prosecutor is of the opinion that an order as referred to in Article 126i, paragraph 1 cannot be given.

3.   The person assisting the investigation pursuant to paragraph 1 may not, in providing the said assistance, induce another person to commit an offence other than the one he was already intending to commit.

4.   In applying paragraph 1, the public prosecutor shall record in writing:
   a.   the offence and, if known, the name or as accurate as possible a designation of the suspect;
   b.   the facts or circumstances which demonstrate that the conditions set out in paragraphs 1 and 2 have been fulfilled;
   c.   the nature of the goods or services.

5.   A pseudo-purchase or provision of services agreement shall be in writing and shall include:
   a.   the rights and obligations of the person aiding the investigation pursuant to paragraph 1, and the way the agreement is to be implemented, including any activities that constitute an offence, and
   b.   the date on which or the period within which the agreement is to be implemented.

6.   Article 126w, paragraphs 7 and 8 shall apply *mutatis mutandis*.

Article 126z

1.   In a case as referred to in Article 126o, paragraph 1, the public prosecutor may, in the interests of the investigation, conclude an agreement with a person who is not an investigating officer that the latter will assist the investigation by buying goods from or providing services to a person who is the subject of reasonable suspicion, based on the facts or circumstances, that he is involved in planning or committing offences on an organised basis.

2.   Paragraph 1 shall be applied only if the public prosecutor is of the opinion that an order as referred to in Article 126q, paragraph 1 cannot be given.

3.   The person assisting the investigation pursuant to paragraph 1 may not, in providing the said assistance, induce another person to commit an offence other than the one he was already intending to commit.

4.   Article 126y, paragraphs 4 to 6 shall apply *mutatis mutandis*.

Title VB – General rules relating to the powers granted under Titles IVA, V, and VA

Part One – Addition to case documents

Article 126aa

1.   The public prosecutor shall add to the case documents the official reports and other items from which information may be derived that has been obtained through the exercise of one of the powers referred to in Titles IVa to Va, in so far as they are relevant to the investigation.

2.   In so far as the official reports or other items referred to in paragraph 1 contain statements made by or to a person who might be exempt pursuant to Article 218 from giving evidence if he should be asked to testify as a witness as to the content of the said statements, the official reports and other items in question shall be destroyed. Regulations regarding this shall be given by Order in Council. In so far as the official reports or other items involve different statements than those referred to in the first sentence made by or to persons referred to in the first sentence, they will not be added to the case documents without obtaining prior permission from the examining magistrate.

3.   The said official reports or other items shall be added to the case documents as soon as the interests of the investigation so allow.

4.   If no official report of the exercise of one of the powers referred to in Titles IVa to Va is added to the case documents, the latter documents shall make reference to the fact that the said power has been exercised.

5.   A suspect or his counsel may request the public prosecutor in writing to add certain official reports or other items specified by him to the case documents.

Part Two – Notification of person concerned

Article 126bb

1.   The public prosecutor shall notify the person concerned in writing of the exercise of one of the powers referred to in Titles IVa to Va as soon as the interests of the investigation so allow. Notification will not take place if it is not reasonably possible to do so.

2.   A person concerned within the meaning of paragraph 1 shall be:
a.   a person in respect of whom one of the powers referred to in Titles IVa, V or Va has been exercised;
b.   a user of telecommunication or the technical aids to telecommunication as referred to in Articles 126m, paragraph 3(c), and 126t, paragraph 3(c);

c.   a title holder in respect of an enclosed place as referred to in Articles 126g, paragraph 2, 126k, 126l, paragraph 2, 126o, paragraph 2, 126r and 126s, paragraph 2.

3.   If the person concerned is the suspect, he need not be notified provided he is informed of the exercise of powers pursuant to Article 126aa, paragraph 1 or 4.

Part Three – Storage and destruction of official reports and other items and use of information for other purposes

Article 126cc

1.   As long as the case has not been concluded, the public prosecutor shall keep the official reports and other items from which information may be derived that has been obtained through surveillance using a technical device that records signals, through the recording of confidential communications, or the investigation of telecommunication, in so far as these have not been added to the case documents, and shall make them available for the purposes of the investigation.

2.   Two months after the case has been concluded and the last notification as referred to in Article 126bb has been made, the public prosecutor shall have the official reports and other items referred to in paragraph 1 destroyed in his presence. An official report shall be drawn up regarding their destruction.

3.   For the purposes of paragraph 2, a preliminary investigation which cannot reasonably be expected to lead to criminal proceedings shall be equated with a case that has been concluded.

4.   Regulations shall be laid down by order in council governing the manner in which the official reports and other items referred to in paragraph 1 shall be stored and destroyed.

Article 126dd

1.   The public prosecutor may decide that information obtained through surveillance using a technical device which records signals, through the recording of confidential communications, or the investigation of telecommunication may be used for:
a.   a criminal investigation other than the one in which the power was exercised;
b.   storage in the serious crime file, if the information in question concerns a person as referred to in Section 13a, subsection 1 (a-c) of the Data Protection (Police Files) Act.

2.   If paragraph 1(a) is applied, the information need not be destroyed, Article 126cc, paragraph 2 notwithstanding, until the other investigation

has been concluded. If paragraph 1(b) is applied, the information need not be destroyed until such time as the Data Protection (Police Files) Act no longer permits the storage of information.

Part Four – Technical devices

Article 126ee

Rules shall be laid down by order in council governing:
    a.   the storage and issue of technical devices as referred to in Articles 126g, paragraph 3, 126l, paragraph 1, 126o, paragraph 3 and 126s, paragraph 1;
    b.   the technical requirements to be met by the devices, notably with a view to the integrity of the observations recorded;
    c.   monitoring compliance with the requirements referred to under b.;
    d.   the agencies responsible for the technical processing of the recorded signals;
    e.   the way in which processing as referred to under d. takes place, in connection with *ex post* control, or the safeguards attached to processing and the opportunities for a counter-inquiry.

Part Five – Ban on *laissez-passer*

Article 126ff

1.   The investigating officer who is carrying out an order as described in titles IVa to V inclusive, is under an obligation to make use of his powers of confiscation if whilst carrying out the order he comes to know the place in which objects can be found, the presence or possession of which are forbidden by law due to their harmfulness to public health or their danger to safety. Confiscation may only be delayed in the interests of the investigation with a view to carrying it out at a later date.

2.   The obligation to confiscate referred to in the first paragraph is not valid in a case where the public prosecutor orders otherwise on the basis of considerable investigative interests.

3.   An order as described in the second paragraph shall be in writing and shall include:
    a.   the items involved,
    b.   the considerable investigative interests, and
    c.   the period of time during which the obligation to confiscate is invalid.

Title VC – Exploratory investigations

Article 126gg

If facts or circumstances give rise to indications that associations of persons are planning or committing offences as defined in Article 67, paragraph 1, which in view of their nature or connection with other offences planned or committed by the same association of persons constitute a serious breach of the legal order, the public prosecutor may order investigating officers to make inquiries into the said association with the aim of preparing for an investigation.

C

The following article shall be inserted after Article 132.

Article 132a

The investigation shall mean an investigation led by the public prosecutor with the aim of taking decisions under the Code of Criminal Procedure and prompted by reasonable suspicion that an offence as defined in Article 67, paragraph 1 has been committed or that such offences are being planned or committed by a criminal organisation, which in view of their nature or connection with other offences planned or committed by the same organisation constitute a serious breach of the legal order.

D

After Article 140, Article 140a will be added, which reads as follows:

Article 140a

The Committee of Attorneys-General shall agree in advance and in writing with an order referred to in Article 126ff, or an agreement such as that referred to in the second part of Title Va of Book I or an alteration or extension in same, respectively.

E

Article 187 shall be amended as follows.

a. The second sentence of paragraph 2 shall be deleted and the following sentence added: He may decide that the suspect and his counsel may not be present at the hearing of the witness in so far as this is strictly necessary in view of the interests referred to in Article 187d, paragraph 1. In the latter case, the public prosecutor is not entitled to be present either.

b.   A third paragraph shall be added, reading:

3.   If the witness or expert is heard in their absence, the public prosecutor, the suspect and his counsel shall be informed as soon as possible of the statements made by the said witness or expert, in so far as this is compatible with the interests referred to in Article 187d, paragraph 1.

F

Article 187b shall be amended as follows.

a.   The number 1. shall be placed at the beginning of the existing text.

b.   A second paragraph shall be added, reading:

2.   The official report of the interrogation shall mention the fact that the examining magistrate prevented an answer being given to a particular question.

G

After Article 187c, the following article shall be inserted:

Article 187d

1.   The examining magistrate may, *ex proprio motu*, on the application of the public prosecutor or at the request of the suspect, his counsel or a witness, prevent the answers to questions relating to specific information becoming known to the public prosecutor, the suspect or his counsel, if there are grounds for suspecting that making such information known will:
    a.   cause severe difficulties for the witness or hamper the exercise of his office or profession;
    b.   be highly prejudicial to the interests of the investigation.

2.   The examining magistrate shall state the grounds for applying paragraph 1 in his official report.

3.   The examining magistrate shall take any measures which may reasonably be deemed necessary to prevent information as referred to in paragraph 1 being disclosed. To this end he is empowered to refrain from including information in the case documents.

4.   If the examining magistrate prevents an answer to a question becoming known to the public prosecutor, the suspect or his counsel, he shall state in the official report that the relevant question was answered.

5. There shall be no possibility of appeal or appeal in cassation against a decision taken pursuant to paragraph 1.

Article 219a shall read as follows.

Article 219a

A witness who by virtue of his office or profession is involved in the hearing of a threatened witness or a hearing whereby Article 187d is applied, or a hearing preceding such a hearing, may be exempted from answering a question put to him, in so far as this is necessary to protect the interests referred to in Article 187d, paragraph 1 or Article 226a, paragraph 1.

I

After the words "coercive measures" in Article 552i, paragraph 2 the following shall be inserted: "or the powers regulated in Articles 126g to 126z and Article 126gg".

J

Article 552n, paragraph 1, shall be amended as follows:

a. Point c shall read:

c. if it is necessary in view of the desired result to impound items of evidence.

b. Point d shall be deleted.

K

Article 552o shall be amended as follows:

a. In paragraph 1a the words "and the tapping or recording of data traffic not intended for the public which is transmitted via the telecommunications infrastructure or via a telecommunications installation which provides a service to the public" shall be replaced by "and the investigation of data in automated systems."

b. Paragraph 3 shall read as follows:
3. Unless the relevant treaty or convention states otherwise, coercive measures may not be employed in order to comply with a request for legal assistance except in accordance with the preceding paragraphs.

c. Paragraph 4 shall be deleted.

L

The following article shall be inserted after Article 552o.

Article 552oa

1.   The powers defined in Articles 126l, 126m, 126s and 126t may be exercised if an admissible request to that end, based on a treaty or convention, is received from the authorities of another State.

2.   Other powers, as defined in Titles IVa, V, Va and Vc of Book 1, may be exercised if an admissible request for legal assistance so requires.

3.   Unless the relevant treaty or convention states otherwise, the powers defined in Titles IVa, V, Va and Vc of Book 1 may not be exercised in order to comply with a request for legal assistance other than in accordance with the preceding paragraphs.

4.   Official reports and other items obtained through the application of one of the powers defined in Articles 126l, 126m, 126s and 126t may be handed over to foreign authorities by the public prosecutor provided the court has given permission taking into account the relevant treaty or convention.

5.   Articles 126aa, paragraph 2 and 126bb to 126dd shall apply *mutatis mutandis*. Article 126cc shall apply only if the relevant official reports and other items have not been handed over to the foreign authorities. The public prosecutor shall ensure that at some point the person concerned may see the official reports and other items relating to him.

M

Article 552p shall be amended as follows:

a. In paragraph 2, the words "data carriers" shall be followed by: "in his charge".

b. Paragraph 5 shall be deleted.

Section II

The Data Protection (Police Files) Act shall be amended as follows:

In Section 1, point j after the word "case", the following words shall be inserted: "or as part of an exploratory investigation as referred to in Article 126gg of the Code of Criminal Procedure".

Section III

To the Judicial Organisation Act will be added Article 131, fifth paragraph: , this shall include in any case decisions referred to in Article 140a of the Code of Criminal Procedure.

Section IV

This Act shall come into force on a date to be determined by Royal Decree, a date which may vary for the different part of articles of the Act.

Section V

1. Orders and agreements issued or concluded before the date on which this Act comes into force shall be equated with orders and agreements within the meaning of Articles 126g to 126z and Articles 126ff and 126gg, if they comply with the requirements laid down in the relevant article.

2. In cases where before the date on which this Act came into force orders for the tapping and recording of data traffic were given or demands for the disclosure of information regarding data traffic were made, Articles 125f, 125g and 125h of the Code of Criminal Procedure shall remain in force as they read before this Act entered into effect.

We order and command that this Act shall be published in the Bulletin of Acts and Decrees (*Staatsblad*) and that all ministries, authorities, bodies and officials whom it may concern shall diligently implement it.

Norway

1. Please indicate the SITs used in your country, the respective legal framework governing their use and their legal definition, if any.

Norwegian case-law has adopted some restrictions for using undercover police work, infiltration and provocation. In addition, the Norwegian Criminal Procedure Act establishes and regulates three different special investigation techniques. The latter are discussed further below.

Communication control – Section 216 a

According to 216 a, the police may be permitted to monitor communications: listening in to conversations or other communications to or from telephones, computers or other apparatus for telecommunication or data communication (communication apparatus) that the suspect possesses or, it may be assumed, will use. Such permission may be given regardless of who owns or supplies the network or service used for the conversation or communication. The police may order the owner or supplier of the network or service to provide such help as is necessary for effecting the listening-in.

Covert video surveillance and technological tracking – Section 202 c

According to Section 202 c the police may be permitted:
   a) to place a technological direction-finder in clothes or objects that the suspect wears or carries,
   b) to place a technological direction-finder in a bag or other hand baggage that the suspect carries, or
   c) to effect a break-in in order to place a technological direction-finder as specified in this provision or in Section 202 b.

Search without notifying the suspect or other persons – Section 200 a

According to Section 200 a, the police may be permitted to search without notifying the suspect or other persons.

2. When and under which circumstances (e.g. criminal investigation, preliminary stage, etc.) can SITs be used?

Communication control – Section 216 a

According to Section 216 a, the court may make an order permitting the police to listen in to communications when any person is with just cause suspected of an act or attempt at an act
   a) that is punishable pursuant to statute by imprisonment for a term of 10 years or more, or
   b) that is contrary to Chapter 8 or 9 of the Penal Code etc.

(Chapter 8 and 9 of the Penal Code establish provisions, which concern felonies against the independence and safety of the State, and felonies against the constitution of Norway and the head of state.)

Covert video surveillance and technological tracking – Section 202 c

According to Section 202 c, the court may by order permit the police to conduct concealed video surveillance and technological tracking when any person is with just cause suspected of an act or attempt at an act punishable pursuant to statute by imprisonment for a term of 10 years or more, or that is contrary to Section 5 of the Act relating to control of the export of strategic goods, services and technology etc.

Furthermore, permission pursuant to Section 202 c may only be granted if it must be assumed that technological tracking will be of essential significance for clarifying the case, and that such clarification will otherwise be impeded to a considerable degree.

Permission to effect a break-in in order to place the direction-finder may moreover only be granted if it is strictly necessary.

Search without notifying the suspect or other persons – Section 200 a

According to Section 200 a, the court may by order decide that a search may be instituted without notifying the suspect or other persons if any person is with just cause suspected of an act or attempt at an act that is punishable pursuant to statute by imprisonment for a term of 10 years or more, or that contravenes Chapter 8 or 9.

Furthermore, permission pursuant to Section 200 a may only be given if it must be assumed that it will be of essential significance for the clarification of the case, and such clarification will otherwise be impeded to a considerable degree. The court may by order decide that notification of a search and the result thereof may also subsequently be postponed if it is strictly necessary for the investigation of the case that notification shall not be given.

3. Are there any specific features governing the use of SITs in relation to acts of terrorism? If so, please specify.

The abovementioned special investigation techniques also apply to investigations regarding terrorist acts.

4. How does the legal framework governing the use of SITs guarantee respect for human rights and individual freedoms, the principles of subsidiarity and proportionality? Is the authorisation to use SITs subject to time-limits? Which bodies and procedures are in place to supervise compliance with human rights standards and with the above-mentioned principles in the use of SITs? Is supervision automatic/systematic?

According to Section 4 of the Criminal Procedure Act, the provisions of this Act shall apply subject to such limitations as are recognised in international law or which derive from any agreement made with a foreign state. This reservation applies to any convention concerning human rights and individual freedoms.

The principles of subsidiarity and proportionality are secured through Section 170 a; coercive measures may be used only when there is sufficient reason for doing so. Coercive measures may not be used when that would be a disproportionate intervention in view of the nature of the case and other circumstances.

These provisions apply to the police who carry out the special investigation techniques and to the court, which permit such measures. There are time-limits for the use of special investigation techniques:

Communication control – Section 216 a

According to Section 216 f, permission for communication control shall be given for a specific period of time, which must not be longer than is strictly necessary. Such permission may not be given for more than four weeks at a time. If the suspicion relates to a contravention of Chapter 8 or 9 of the Penal Code, such permission may, however, be given for up to eight weeks at a time if the nature of the investigation or other special circumstances indicate that a review after four weeks would be pointless.

The communication control shall be stopped before the expiry of the time-limit fixed in the court order if the conditions for such control are no longer deemed to exist or if such control is no longer considered to be appropriate.

Covert video surveillance and technological tracking – Section 202 c

According to Section 202 c, fourth paragraph, the court's permission shall be granted for a specific period of time which may not exceed what is strictly necessary. Such permission must not be granted for more than four weeks at a time. Section 216 f, second paragraph, see above, shall apply correspondingly.

Search without notifying the suspect or other persons – Section 200 a

According to Section 200 a, third paragraph, a decision to postpone notification for up to eight weeks at a time may be made, and notification shall be given not later than when an indictment is preferred. In cases concerning a contravention of Chapter 8 or 9 of the Penal Code the court may decide that notification may be postponed for up to six months at a time

271

or completely omitted. Section 216 f second paragraph, see above, shall apply correspondingly.

5. Which institutions are involved in the use of SITs and what is their role (e.g. law enforcement agencies, prosecutor's office, judicial authorities, etc.)? Which institutions can order and/or authorise the use of SITs? How does co-operation between these institutions work in practice?

According to Section 216 d, when the police make decisions or request the court's consent in regard to telephone control, the decision shall be made by the chief of police or deputy chief of police. In the absence of the chief of police his or her permanent deputy may make the decision. The chief of police may, with the written consent of the senior public prosecutor, decide that other officials of the prosecuting authority in leading positions shall also have the same power as the permanent deputy of the chief of police.

These provisions also apply to search without notifying the suspect or other persons according to Section 200 a, and concealed video surveillance and technological tracking according to Section 202 c.

The chief of police is instructed to report the use of special investigation techniques to the Director of Public Prosecution. Such a report shall be submitted four times a year. These reports shall be examined by the Director of Public Prosecution, and afterwards be sent (but remaining anonymous) to the Ministry of Justice.

6. Are there any specialised counter-terrorism institutions? What is their role in the use of SITs?

The Norwegian authorities established shortly after the terrorist attacks on the United States on 11 September 2001 an advisory group on anti-terrorism under the auspices of the Ministry of Justice to closely monitor international measures taken to combat terrorist acts. The group is entrusted with examining the legal steps and law enforcement initiatives, including those concerning financial aspects, that are being taken by other states and that should also be considered by Norway.

However, the police are still responsible for investigation and use of coercive measures during investigation of terrorism acts.

7. Which measures have been adopted in order to facilitate international co-operation (e.g. joint investigation teams)? Can the SITs listed in reply to question 1 be used in cross-border settings?

Norway has established an advisory group, as mentioned above in the answer to question 6. The purpose of the advisory group is to co-ordinate the police and the prosecution authorities in the implementation of counter-terrorist measures, exchange of information and co-operation between Norwegian and foreign authorities.

In the field of police co-operation, Norway is working to strengthen existing mechanisms for exchanging information with the services of other states and is forging new links and patterns of co-operation, in particular with regard to ciphered communications.

Norway is a party to the European Convention on Mutual Legal Assistance of 20 April 1959 and the Schengen Co-operation Agreement with the European Union of 18 May 1999. Being a party to the Schengen co-operation agreement, Norway also takes part in judicial co-operation within the scope of the Schengen legislation, facilitating simplified procedures for exchanging letters rogatory and other requests for legal assistance between judicial authorities. Norway has also signalled its readiness to co-operate with the European Union on further measures against international terrorism.

Norway is a member of the ICPO-Interpol and the Schengen Co-operation and recently signed a co-operation agreement with the European Police Office (EUROPOL). Due to recent events EUROPOL has been given new tasks in the fight against terrorism. Norway is in the process of establishing a liaison officer in EUROPOL headquarters in The Hague in order to accelerate the exchange of information and assist in operational investigations.

In addition to this, the Nordic Police and Customs Co-operation operates a common pool of liaison officers stationed in different countries around the world, facilitating the rapid exchange of information between law enforcement authorities.

8. What use can be made of SITs in the context of mutual legal assistance?

When using special investigation techniques within Norwegian territory, the investigation must be in compliance with Norwegian law. However, foreign police may on request assist Norwegian police during the investigation. In principle, Norwegian police may also on request assist foreign police using special investigation techniques on foreign territory.

As mention above in question 7, Norway has taken part in the judicial co-operation within the scope of the Schengen legislation, facilitating simplified procedures for exchanging letters rogatory and other requests for legal assistance between judicial authorities.

9. How can the use of SITs be improved? Please provide any comments/proposals concerning the implementation of the terms of reference of the PC-TI and in particular the use and regulation of SITs.

In order to elaborate further needs for special investigation techniques, the Ministry of Justice has set up two committees. The terms of reference of the two committees are, among other things, to consider new provisions concerning special investigation techniques.

In order to strengthen the suspect's interests in cases involving special investigation techniques, Norway has introduced a system where the court shall immediately appoint an official defence counsel for the suspected person. According to Section 100 a of the Criminal Procedure Act, the defence counsel shall protect the interests of the suspected person in connection with the court's hearing of the application. Defence counsel shall be informed of the application and the grounds for it, and shall be entitled to notice of court meetings for dealing with the application and to comment thereon before the court makes its decision. Defence counsel may bring an interlocutory appeal against the court's order. Defence counsel must not communicate with the suspected person. Defence counsel shall preserve secrecy about the application and the decision concerning coercive measures and about information obtained by the use of coercive measures.

Poland

1. Please indicate the SITs used in your country, the respective legal framework governing their use and their legal definition, if any.

Polish law allows for use of the following special investigative techniques:
- operations audit, which includes:
  - correspondence checks,
  - delivery checks,
  - use of technical means to obtain information and evidence secretly and to record it, in particular telephone calls and other information conveyed by means of telecommunications networks;

- "controlled transaction" – a secret purchase, sale or taking over of objects from crime, objects subject to forfeiture or ones whose manufacture, possession, transport or sale is illegal, and also the acceptance or giving of financial profits;
- "controlled delivery";
- "undercover operations";
- use of informants:
  - agents,
  - informers,
  - others; consultants;
- observation;
- search.

Use of SITs is regulated in the Police Act (see Appendix 2, at the end of this section), Act of Border Guard (see Appendix 3), Act of Internal Security Agency and Intelligence Agency and Act of Revenue Control. Provisions of the Acts mentioned are applicable only in so far as provisions of the Code of Criminal Procedure (see Appendix 1) are not.

When obtained information includes crime suspicion, trial activities (operational) are used to check if there is the reasonable suspicion, as well to identify offenders and obtain and secure evidence. In this case activities (including SITs) are regulated by the abovementioned acts.

In case of confirmation that crime was committed, criminal proceedings are initiated and regulated in the Code of Criminal Procedure, trial activities are took up (if needed SITs also).

Regulations of the minister appropriate for internal affairs or Minister of Justice include detailed information about technical use of SITs.

2. When and under which circumstances (e.g. criminal investigation, preliminary stage, etc.) can SITs be used?

SITs regulated in the Code of Criminal Procedure (search, surveillance and recording conversations) can be used only within the framework of criminal proceedings and during criminal proceedings.

SITs regulated in the abovementioned acts can be used before, during and after criminal proceeding, when suspect is unknown.

In every case the decision to use SITs is connected to the most serious crime and is made in the following conditions: when there is reasonable suspicion of crime being committed, when other measures have proved ineffective or there is every likelihood that they will be ineffective or useless.

3. Are there any specific features governing the use of SITs in relation to acts of terrorism? If so, please specify.

No, there are not. All rules connected to the use of SITs are regulated in the abovementioned acts. Acts of terrorism are treated on the same level as the most serious crimes.

4. How does the legal framework governing the use of SITs guarantee respect for human rights and individual freedoms, the principles of subsidiarity and proportionality? Is the authorisation to use SITs subject to time-limits? Which bodies and procedures are in place to supervise compliance with human rights standards and with the above-mentioned principles in the use of SITs? Is supervision automatic/systematic?

Guaranteed respect for human rights and individual freedoms was considering during the creation of acts of law, especially the Code of Criminal Procedure. On 26 November 1991 Poland signed, and on 19 January 1993 ratified, the ECHR.

It should be remembered that all laws are regulated in the constitution, in connection with which Acts have to be drafted in accordance with the constitution. This accordance is guaranteed by the Constitutional Court and Ombudsman.

Some uses of SITs are time-limited in the way they can be used, which is regulated in the abovementioned acts. For example: operations audit in the form of tapping can be used for a period no longer than 3 months and can be extended just once for another 3 months, when reasons for using operations audit are still current. In reasonable case, after 6 months, when new circumstances significant for the prevention and detection of crime or finding offenders and obtaining evidence of crime appear, operations audit can be extended for a fixed period of time.

Use of SITs is under strict supervision and control by the public prosecution office and the court. The abovementioned institutions have to be informed about the obtaining of information and results of the operation, and they have sight of collected data.

A proposal for an order or extension of an operations audit (including phone tapping), after a written permit has been received from a district attorney, is submitted to the appropriate district court, which may order an operations audit and determine its operating range, period of use, person, means, etc., or refuse to order or extend the operational audit and give reasons for that.

It is important to note that, in the case of a proposal to extend operations audit, the appropriate district court, before it makes a decision, can have sight of collected data that give reasons for extending the operations audit.

In cases of urgency, where any delay could result in the loss of information or the obliteration or destruction of the evidence of a crime, an entitled body having received a written permission from the appropriate attorney, may institute an operations audit while at the same time applying to the appropriate district court for an order on that matter. In the event that the court fails to grant such permission 5 days after the initiation of the operations audit, the instituting body shall stop the operations audit and destroy the evidence collected thus far in the presence of a committee, to be evidenced by a report.

Experience shows that these procedures guarantee the proper use of law and observance of law and order.

According to Article 19 of the Police Act, the Attorney General shall present an annual report to the Sejm and Senate about the activities in connection with operational audit. So far two such reports have been prepared and the abovementioned bodies had no objections.

Supervision is formally and systematically under the control of the bodies of the public prosecution office and the court.

5.   Which institutions are involved in the use of SITs and what is their role (e.g. law enforcement agencies, prosecutor's office, judicial authorities, etc.)? Which institutions can order and/or authorise the use of SITs? How does co-operation between these institutions work in practice?

All entitled authorities mentioned in point 1 use SITs (Police, Border Guard, Internal Security Agency, Intelligence Agency, Revenue Intelligence, as well as the public prosecution office and the court).

All the abovementioned bodies are entitled to take decisions about using SITs within the operating range determined in acts of law. For example, law enforcement can independently take decisions about co-operation with informants, observation and "undercover operations".

In case of urgency, where any delay could result in the loss of information or the obliteration or destruction of the evidence of a crime, entitled law enforcement bodies can take decisions about search and operational audit, and then these activities shall be confirmed by the appropriate bodies (prosecutor for search, judge for operational audit).

Co-operation between the abovementioned bodies is carried out correctly and present law regulations are very useful in practice.

6. Are there any specialised counter-terrorism institutions? What is their role in the use of SITs?

There is no special body designed to combat terrorism. All competent authorities within the framework of their duties in combating and finding crime take up terrorism too.

7. Which measures have been adopted in order to facilitate international co-operation (e.g. joint investigation teams)? Can the SITs listed in reply to question 1 be used in cross-border settings?

and

8. What use can be made of SITs in the context of mutual legal assistance?

Poland has accepted and ratified many conventions allowed combating organised crime within the framework of international co-operation. In connection with that, bilateral agreements have been signed on co-operation in combating organised crime, and on co-operation between police and other law enforcement bodies. The model example of co-operation is the co-operation between the Polish police and Border Guard and the German authorities, where, based on bilateral agreements, it is possible to create common investigating groups.

Poland has attempted to ratify the European Convention on Mutual Legal Assistance in Criminal Matters and the Second Additional Protocol to the Convention, which is very important for international co-operation and makes it easy.

International co-operation is also possible within the framework of Eurojust and Europol.

Significant institutions in connection with information exchange are the liaison officers of police, border guard and customs.

9.   How can the use of SITs be improved? Please provide any comments/proposals concerning the implementation of the terms of reference of the PC-TI and in particular the use and regulation of SITs.

The use of SITs can be improved by the intensification of international co-operation, organising international training and conferences. In this matter, also important are legislation work and the creation of new law, which will allow the use of SITs in other countries, for example of phone tapping.

Appendix 1

Provisions of the Code of Criminal Procedure

Act of 6 June 1997
Code of Criminal Procedure

Chapter 25

Seizure of objects. Search

Article 217. § 1. Objects which may serve as evidence in a case, or be subject to seizure in order to secure penalties regarding property, penal measures involving property or claims to redress damage, should be surrendered when so required by the court, the state prosecutor, and in cases not amenable to delay, by the Police or other authorised agency.

§ 2. A person holding the objects subject to surrender shall be called upon to release them voluntarily.

§ 3. In the event of seizure of an object, provisions of Article 228 shall be applied accordingly. The record of seizure may not necessarily be prepared when the object is attached to the files of the case.

§ 4. If the surrender is demanded by the Police or other authorised agency operating within the scope of its own activities, the person who surrendered the object shall have the right to lodge a motion for an order of the court or of the state prosecutor confirming the seizure; the person concerned should be instructed of this right. The service shall be effected within fourteen days of the seizure of the objects.

§ 5. In the event of refusal to release an object voluntarily, a seizure may be carried out. The provisions of Article 220 § 3 and Article 229 shall be applied accordingly.

Article 218. § 1. Offices, institutions and entities operating in the fields of post and telecommunication activities, customs offices, and transport institutions and companies, shall be obligated to surrender to the court or state prosecutor upon demand included in their order, any correspondence or mail as well as listings of connection through telecommunication system, with dates and time and other information relevant to the connection, which is not the contents of the telephone conversation, when the above are significant to the pending proceedings. Only the court and a state prosecutor shall be entitled to inspect them or to order their inspection.

§ 2. The order referred to in § 1 shall be served on the addressees of the correspondence and the subscriber of the telephone whose listing of connections was released. The service of the order may be adjourned for a prescribed period, necessary to promote the proper conduct of the case.

§ 3. Correspondence and mail irrelevant to the criminal proceedings should be returned to the appropriate offices, institutions or companies as set forth in § 1, without delay.

Article 219. § 1. A search may be made of premises and other places in order to detect or arrest a person or to ensure his compulsory appearance, as well as to locate objects which might serve as evidence in criminal proceedings, if there is good reason to suppose that the suspected person or the objects sought are to be located there.

§ 2. A search of a person, his clothing and objects at hand, may also be carried out in order to find the objects referred to in § 1, under the conditions set forth in the provision.

Article 220. § 1. A search may be conducted by the state prosecutor or, when the court or state prosecutor so orders, by the Police, and – in cases specified in law – also by another agency.

§ 2. The person on whose premises the search is to be conducted should be presented with a order issued by a court or state prosecutor.

§ 3. In cases not amenable to delay, if the court's or state prosecutor's order cannot be issued, the agency conducting the search shall produce a warrant from the chief of the unit or an official identity card, and then apply without delay to the court or the state prosecutor for approval of the search. The person on whose premises the search was conducted should be served, within seven days of the date of the action, upon a demand from such person made for the record, an order of the court or the state prosecutor authorising the action. The person should be instructed about his right to make such a demand.

Article 221. § 1. Searches of occupied premises shall be conducted at night only in cases not amenable to delay; "night" shall be the period from 10 p.m. to 6 a.m.

§ 2. A search commenced by day may be continued into the night.

§ 3. A night search may be conducted on premises that are at the time open to an unspecified number of people, or used for the storage of goods.

Article 222. § 1. If a search is to be made of the premises or a closed place of a state or local government institution, the head of such

281

an institution or his deputy, or the agency superior to the institution shall be notified and permitted to attend the search.

§ 2. A search of military premises shall be conducted only in the presence of the commanding officer or a person designated by him.

Article 223. Searches of person and clothing are to be conducted, as far as possible, by a person of the same sex as the person searched.

Article 224. § 1. A person on whose premises the search is to be conducted, shall be notified before the commencement of the search of its objective and summoned to surrender the objects sought.

§ 2. A person referred to in § 1 has the right to be present at the search, in addition to the person designated for that purpose by the person conducting the search. Furthermore, the search may be attended by a person designated, by the occupant of the premises searched, provided that this will not seriously obstruct the search, or render it impossible.

§ 3. In the event that the search is made in the absence of the owner of the premises, at least one adult member of the household or a neighbour shall be called in to attend the search.

Article 225. § 1. If the head of a state or local government institution subject to search or the person from whom objects have been seized, or whose premises are searched, declares that a piece of writing or other document surrendered or discovered during the search, contains information relating to state, official, professional or other secrets protected by law, or that this information is of a personal nature, those conducting the search shall immediately transmit such written material or other document without prior reading, to the state prosecutor or the court, in a sealed package.

§ 2. The procedure described in § 1 shall not apply to written material and other documents relating to official, professional or other secrets protected by law, if they are in the possession of a person suspected of an offence, nor to written material and other documents of a personal nature of which such person is an owner, author or addressee.

§ 3. If a defence counsel or other person of whom surrender of objects is demanded, or whose premises are searched, declares that writings or other documents discovered in the course of a search, relate to facts connected with the performance of the function of the defence counsel, the agency conducting the actions shall leave these documents with such a person, without ascertaining their contents or appearance. When the declaration of a person not being a defence counsel gives rise to doubts, the agency conducting the actions shall transmit the documents in accordance with the requirements set forth in § 1 to the court which, having acquainted itself with the documents, shall return them all or in part, in accordance with requirements set forth in § 1, to the person from whom they were taken, or issue an order for their seizure for the purposes of the proceedings.

§ 4. A psychiatric dossier released, seized or found during a search shall be transmitted by the agency conducting the search, in accordance with requirements set forth in § 1, to the court or state prosecutor.

Article 226. In matters regarding the use of documents containing state, official or professional secrets as evidence in criminal proceedings, the prohibitions and limitations set forth in Articles 178-181 shall apply accordingly. During the preparatory proceedings, however, a decision on using as evidence, documents containing a physician's confidential information, should be made by the state prosecutor.

Article 227. Searching or seizing objects shall be conducted in accordance with the objective of the action, with moderation and respect for the dignity of the persons to whom the action relates, and without unnecessary damage or hardship.

Article 228. § 1. Material objects surrendered or discovered during a search, after being viewed and recorded, shall be seized or deposited with a trustworthy person who shall be notified of his duty to present them whenever so required, by the agency conducting the proceedings.

§ 2. Similar action should be taken concerning objects discovered during a search which may constitute evidence of some other offence, or are subject to forfeiture, or the possession of which is prohibited by law.

§ 3. Persons concerned shall be given without delay a receipt specifying the objects seized, and the identity of the persons performing the seizure;

Article 229. The record of objects seized or of the search should include, apart from the requirements set forth in Article 148, the designation of the case with which the objects seized or the search have been connected, and should specify the precise time of the beginning and the end of the action, a detailed list of the objects seized and, when needed, their description, and also an indication of the order of the court or state prosecutor. If the order has not been issued before the action, the record shall contain a note advising a person in whose premises the action has been conducted, that, upon a motion from him, an order regarding the approval of action will be served.

Article 230. § 1. If the seizure of objects or search was without a prior order issued by the court or state prosecutor, and no order

283

approving the action has been issued, the objects seized shall be returned to the authorised person, unless the release has been made voluntarily and the person concerned has not lodged a motion referred to in Article 217 § 4.

§ 2. Material objects, as soon as they are deemed unnecessary for the purposes of the criminal proceedings shall be returned to the authorised person. If there is a dispute as to the right of the possession of the objects, and no grounds for immediate solution can be found, the interested parties will be referred to the process under civil law.

§ 3. The objects, possession of which is prohibited, should be transmitted to the appropriate bureau or institution.

Article 231. § 1. If the person to whom a given material object seized should be released cannot be ascertained, such an object shall be deposited with the court or with a trustworthy person until the right to the possession thereof has been clarified. Provisions on the escheat of deposits and unclaimed objects shall be applied accordingly.

§ 2. Material objects of artistic or historic value shall be deposited with an appropriate institution.

Article 232. § 1. Material objects that are perishable, or the storage of which would entail unreasonable expense or excessive hardship or would significantly impair the value of the object, may be sold without an auction, by means of an appropriate trading unit, in compliance with the provisions applicable to sales resulting from the execution against chattels.

§ 2. The pecuniary proceeds of such a sale shall be deposited with the court.

§ 3. All persons concerned including the accused should be notified, if possible, of the time and circumstances of such a sale.

Article 232a. § 1 Objects and materials presenting a hazard to health or life, and in particular weapons, ammunition, explosives or flammable materials, radioactive materials, toxic, suffocating or blistering agents, narcotic drugs, psychotropic substances or precursors, shall be stored in a place and in a manner ensuring their proper security.

§ 2. If the storage of objects or substances referred to in § 1 would entail unreasonable expense or excessive hardship or would impose a threat to public security, the court having jurisdiction to examine the case may, upon a motion from the state prosecutor, order their destruction in whole or in part.

§ 3. If needed, an opinion of an expert shall be sought prior to the issuance of the order.

§ 4. The Minister of Justice, in consultation with the Minister of National Defence, and the minister responsible for internal affairs, shall set forth, by ordinance, the detailed principles and place for storing the objects and substances referred to in § 1, as well as the conditions and methods for destroying them, with a view as to the necessity to ensure an effective course of proceedings, and of costs thereof.

Article 233. When depositing Polish or foreign currency, the depositing agency shall indicate the nature of the deposit and the manner in which it should be disposed.

Article 234. Dispositions of the material object after it has been seized or secured shall be without effect on the State Treasury.

Article 235. During the court proceedings, the determinations and actions shall be undertaken by the court, or in the preparatory proceedings by the state prosecutor, unless provided otherwise by law.

Article 236. Orders regarding search and seizure shall be subject to interlocutory appeal by a person whose rights have been violated.

Article 236a. The provisions of this Part shall be applied accordingly, to those exercising control over or using information technology (IT) systems with respect to data stored in this system or on a storage medium being at his disposal or being used, including correspondence send by electronic mail.

Chapter 26

Surveillance and recording conversations

Article 237. § 1. After the proceedings have started, the court, upon a motion from the state prosecutor, may order the surveillance and recording of the content of telephone conversations, in order to detect and obtain evidence for the pending proceedings or to prevent a new offence from being committed.

§ 2. In cases not amenable to delay, the surveillance and recording of conversations may be ordered by the state prosecutor who is obligated to seek an approval for the order from the court within 3 days. The court decides on the motion within 5 days, on a session without participation of the parties.

§ 3. The surveillance and recording of the content of telephone conversations is allowed only when proceedings are pending or a justified concern exists about possible committing of a new offence of:

(1) homicide,

(2) being a danger to the public or causing a catastrophe,

(3) trade in humans or white slavery,

(4) the abduction of a person,

(5) the demanding of a ransom,

(6) the hijacking of an aircraft or a ship,

(7) robbery, robbery with violence, or extortion with violence.

(8) an attempt against the sovereignty or independence of the state,

(9) an attempt against the constitutional order of the state or on its supreme agencies, or against a unit of the Armed Forces of the Republic of Poland,

(10) spying or disclosing a state secret,

(11) amassing weapons, explosives or radioactive materials,

(12) the forging of money, or effecting of transactions involving counterfeit money, including the means or instruments of payment, or transferable documents that entitle one to obtain an amount of money, goods, consignment or a material object, or such documents containing the obligation to pay in capital, interest or a share in profits, or that contain a declaration of participation in profit,

(13) producing, processing or effecting transactions in, or smuggling, narcotic drugs, substitutes thereof or psychotropic substances,

(14) an organised crime group,

(15) property of significant value,

(16) the use of violence or unlawful threats in connection with criminal proceedings,

(17) bribery and influence-trading,

(18) pandering or obtaining profits from facilitating and protecting prostitution.

§ 4. Surveillance and recording of the contents of telephone conversations shall be permitted with regard to a suspected person, the accused, and with regard to the injured person or other person whom the accused may contact or who might be connected with the perpetrator or with a threatening offence.

§ 5. Offices, institutions and entities operating in the fields of post and telecommunication activities shall be obligated to facilitate the execution of an order from the court or state prosecutor regarding the surveillance of telephone conversations, and to ensure that the conducting of such a surveillance is registered.

§ 6. Only the court and a state prosecutor shall be entitled to play the recordings, and, in cases not amenable to delay, the Police with the approval of the court or state prosecutor.

§ 7. Only the court shall have the right to acquaint itself with the register of telephone conversation surveillance, and, in the course of proceedings, the state prosecutor.

Article 238. § 1. The surveillance and recording of telephone conversations may be conducted for a period not exceeding 3 months, with a possibility to extend, in particularly justified cases, for a period not exceeding a further 3 months.

§ 2. The surveillance should be ended without delay after the reasons listed in Article 237 § 1 through 3 have ceased to exist, and no later, than with the expiration of the period for which it was introduced.

§ 3. After the surveillance has been completed, the court orders the destruction of the recordings when they have no relevance to the criminal proceedings; the destruction of the recordings shall also take place when the court has not approved the order by the state prosecutor referred to in Article 237 § 2.

Article 239. The announcement of the order to conduct surveillance and recording of telephone conversations to the person concerned may be adjourned for a period necessary to promote the proper conduct of the case but not beyond the valid conclusion of the case.

Article 240. The order for surveillance and recording of telephone conversations shall be subject to interlocutory appeal. The person whom the order regards may demand in the interlocutory appeal that the grounds and legality of surveillance and recording of telephone conversations be examined. The appeal against the order of the state prosecutor is considered by the court.

Article 241. The provisions of this chapter shall apply respectively to surveillance and recording by technical means, of the content of other conversations or information transmissions, including correspondence transmitted by electronic mail.

Article 242. The Minister of Justice in consultation with the Minister responsible for posts and telecommunications, the Minister of National Defence, and the minister responsible for internal affairs shall set forth, by ordinance, the method for the technical preparation of the networks serving the purpose of information transmission, surveillance of telephone conversations or of other information transmissions effected with the use of these networks, as well as the method for making, registering, storing, playing and destroying recordings of the telephone conversations recorded, including the correspondence transmitted by electronic mail, with a view to properly secure the recordings made, against loss, distortion or unauthorised disclosure.

Appendix 2

Provisions of the Police Act of 6 April 1990

Article 19[1]

1. In the course of preliminary investigation carried out by Police in order to prevent, detect, identify perpetrators and obtain and secure evidence of intended crimes, prosecuted by a public prosecutor,

1) against life as specified in Article 148-150 of the Criminal Code; as specified in Article 134, Article 135 Section 1, Article 136 Section 1, Article 156 Section 1 and 3, Article 163 Section 1 and 3, Article 164 Section 1, Article 165 Section 1 and 3, Article 166, 167, 173 Section 1 and 3, Article 189, 204 Section 4, Article 223, 228, 229, 232, 245, 246, 252 Section 1-3, Article 253, 258, 269, 280-282, 285 Section 1, Article 286, 296, 299 Section 1-6 and in Article 310 Section 1, 2 and 4 of the Criminal Code;

2) causing serious bodily injury or severe breakdown of health;

3) economic crimes specified in Articles 297-306 of the Criminal Code which cause damage to property if the damage is in excess of the multiple of fifty minimum wages, as specified in separate regulations;

4) fiscal crimes if the crime value or amount of public law proceeds reduction is in excess of the multiple of fifty minimum wages, as specified in separate regulations

5) illegal production, possession and trade in firearms, ammunition, explosives, narcotics or psychotropic agents or their precursors as well as nuclear and radioactive materials;

6) those specified in Article 8 of the 6 June 1997 Act – Regulations introducing the Criminal Code (Journal of Laws No. 88, item 554, No. 160 item 1083 and of 1998 No. 113 item 715)

7) those specified in Article 20 of the 26 October 1995 Cells, Tissues and Organs Act (Journal of Laws No. 138 item 682, of 1997, No. 88 item 554 and No. 104 item 661 and of 2000 No. 120 item 1268);

8) prosecuted under international agreements and treaties;

when other measures have proved ineffective or there is every likelihood that they will be ineffective or useless, a district court, at the written request of the Chief Police Commander made after having received a prior written permit of Attorney General or at the written request of the voivodeship police commander, made after having received a prior written permit of the appropriate district attorney, may order an operations audit.

2.   The provision specified in Section 1 shall be issued by the District Court whose location is appropriate for the police body submitting the request.

3.   In cases of urgency, where any delay could result in the loss of information or the obliteration or destruction of the evidence of a crime, the Chief Police Commander or Voivodeship Police Commander having received a written permission from the appropriate attorney as specified in Section 1, may institute an operations audit while at the same time applying to the appropriate district court for an order on that matter. In the event that the court fails to grant such permission 5 days after the initiation of the operations audit, the instituting body shall stop the operations audit and destroy the evidence collected thus far in the presence of a committee to be evidenced by a report.

4.   The district court may, at the written request of the Chief Police Commander or Voivodeship Police Commander made after having received a written permission from the appropriate attorney, decide to allow the Police to keep the evidence, specified in Section 3, if it constitutes a proof or indicates the intention to commit a crime the detection of which under the statutory regulations allows an operations audit or preliminary investigation.

5.   Where an operations audit is deemed necessary in relation to a suspect or person charged, the request for an operations audit made by the Police body specified in Section 1, shall include information about the institution of proceedings in relation to such person.

6.   An operations audit shall be performed secretly and shall involve:
   1. correspondence checks;
   2. deliveries checks;
   3. use of technical means to obtain information and evidence secretly and to record it, in particular telephone calls and other information conveyed by means of telecommunications networks;

7.   The request specified in Section 1 made by Police applying to the district court for an operations audit permission, shall include, in particular:
   1. case number and cryptonym, if applicable;
   2. description of the crime and its legal qualification, whenever possible;
   3. the circumstances to justify the need for an operations audit, including information about the ineffectiveness or uselessness of other measures, real or probable;

4. personal data of the person to be subjected to an operations audit, indicating the location and manner of the audit;
5. the purpose, duration and type of the operations audit as specified in Section 6.

8. An operations audit may not last longer than 3 months. The district court may, at the written request of the Chief Police Commander or Voivodeship Police Commander made after having received a written permission from the appropriate attorney, allow a single extension of the audit for not longer than 3 months, if the causes of the audit still persist.

9. Where, in the course of an operations audit, reasonably justified by the appearance of new circumstances that are critical for the prevention or detection of a crime or identification of perpetrators and securing evidence, the district court, at the request of the Chief Police Commander made after having received a written permission of the Attorney General, may allow an extension of the operations audit, even when the periods specified in Section 8 have elapsed.

10. The requests specified in Sections 3, 4, 8 and 9 are subject to Section 7. The court, prior to the issuance of the order specified in Sections 3, 4, 8 and 9 may wish to see the materials collected during the relevant operations audit that support the request.

11. The requests specified in Sections 1, 3-5, 8 and 9 shall be reviewed by the district court represented by a single person, but the activities involved in the reviewing of the requests shall comply with the regulations on passing, storing and giving qualified information and the regulations pursuant to Article 118 Section 2 of the Criminal Proceedings Code. The court sitting may only be attended by the prosecutor and representative of the police body making the operations audit request.

12. Operators of public telecommunications networks and postal service providers shall, at their own cost, provide such technical and organisational measures so as to allow the Police to conduct an operations audit.

13. An operations audit should be completed immediately when the causes of its institution no longer exist, at the latest, however, upon the expiry date.

14. The police body specified in Section 1 shall inform the appropriate prosecutor of the results of the operations audit upon its completion, and when so requested, about its course.

15. Where evidence is obtained that justifies the institution of criminal proceedings or has a bearing on pending criminal proceedings, the Chief Police Commander or Voivodeship Police Commander shall pass on to the appropriate prosecutor all the materials collected in the course of the

operations audit, and, if applicable, with a request to initiate criminal proceedings. Court proceedings in relation to these materials shall be subject to Article 393 Section 1, sentence one of the Criminal Proceedings Code.

16. The materials collected in the course of an operations audit shall not be made available to the person subjected to that audit. This provision is not in violation of the rights under Article 321 of the Criminal Proceedings Code.

17. Any materials obtained in the course of an operations audit that do not justify the institution of criminal proceedings shall be stored for 2 months following the completion of the audit. They shall then be destroyed in the presence of a committee and the process evidenced in a report. The destruction of the materials shall be ordered by the police body which made the request for the operations audit.

18. The procedures specified in Section 1-11 shall not apply where the operations audit is conducted at the written permission of the person sending or receiving the information.

19. In cases specified in Section 18, the operations audit shall be instituted by the police body appropriate for preliminary investigation of the case.

20. Complaints may be filed against operations audit court orders specified in Sections 1, 3, 8 and 9 and court orders on keeping the evidence collected during the operations audit as specified in Section 4 by the police body requesting such orders. The complaint shall be subject to the Criminal Proceedings Code.

21. The minister appropriate for internal affairs in agreement with the Minister of Justice and the minister appropriate for communications, shall, by way of a regulation, determine how operations audits shall be documented, requests and orders given, and how evidence obtained in the course of the operations audit shall be stored, given, processed and destroyed, giving due regard to the secrecy of these activities and materials, as well as specimen of forms and records to be used.

22. The Attorney General shall present an annual report to the Sejm and Senate about the activities specified in Section 1-12, including information and data specified in Article 20 Section 3.

Article 19a^2

1. In the case of crimes specified in Article 19 Section 1, preliminary investigations to verify credible information about the crime and identify the perpetrators and obtain evidence of the crime may involve a secret purchase, sale or taking over of objects from crime, objects subject to

forfeiture or ones whose manufacture, possession, transport or sale is illegal, and also the acceptance or giving of financial profits.

2.   Preliminary investigations specified in Section 1 may also involve a proposal to buy, sell or take over objects from crime, that are subject to forfeiture or ones whose manufacture, possession, transport or sale is illegal, and also the acceptance or giving of financial profits

3.   The Chief Police Commander or Voivodeship Police Commander may institute, for a specified period of time, the activities specified in Section 1, after having received a written permission of the appropriate district attorney who shall be kept to date about the results of the activities. The attorney may stop the activities at any time.

4.   The activities specified in Section 1 shall be instituted for not longer than 3 months. The Chief Police Commander or Voivodeship Police Commander may, after having received a written permission of the appropriate attorney, order a onetime renewal of the activities for a period not longer than 3 months, if the causes still persist.

5.   Where, in the course of activities specified in Section 1, reasonably justified by the appearance of new circumstances that are critical for the examination of credible information about a crime and the detection of perpetrators and securing evidence, the Chief Police Commander or Voivodeship Police Commander may after having received a written permission of the appropriate prosecutor allow an extension of the operations audit, even when the periods specified in Section 4 have elapsed.

6.   The activities specified in Section 1 may be secretly recorded using image or sound recording devices.

7.   Where evidence is obtained that justifies the institution of criminal proceedings or has a bearing on pending criminal proceedings, the Chief Police Commander or Voivodeship Police Commander shall pass on to the appropriate district prosecutor all the materials collected in the course of the activities specified in Section 1, and, if applicable, with a request to initiate criminal proceedings. Court proceedings in relation to these materials shall be subject to Article 393 Section 1, sentence one of the Criminal Proceedings Code.

8.   Any materials obtained in the course of the activities specified in Section 1 and 2 that do not justify the institution of criminal proceedings shall be stored for 2 months following the completion of the audit. They shall then be destroyed in the presence of a committee and the process evidenced in a report. The destruction of the materials shall be ordered by the police body which made the request for the operations audit

9. The minister appropriate for internal affairs in agreement with the Minister of Justice, shall, by way of a regulation, determine how the activities specified in Section 1 shall be documented, and how evidence obtained in the course of the activities shall be given, processed and destroyed, giving due regard to the secrecy of these activities and materials, as well as specimen of forms and records to be used.

Article 19b[3]

1. To document crimes specified in Article 19 Section 1 or establish the identity of those involved in the crimes or take over the objects of crime, the Chief Police Commander or Voivodeship Police Commander may institute secret surveillance of the manufacture, transporting, storing and sale of crime objects, provided this does not involve a threat to human life or health.

2. The prosecutor appropriate for the seat of the Police body in charge of the activities specified in Section 1 shall be promptly notified of such institution of surveillance. The prosecutor may order the cessation of the activities at any time.

3. The Police body specified in Section 1 shall keep the prosecutor informed about the results of the activities.

4. In accordance with the institution specified in Section 1, public bodies and institutions and entrepreneurs shall allow the shipment of a delivery containing crime objects in the original condition or, if removed or replaced, in whole or in part.

5. Where evidence is obtained that justifies the institution of criminal proceedings or has a bearing on pending criminal proceedings, the Chief Police Commander or Voivodeship Police Commander shall pass on to the district prosecutor all the materials collected in the course of the activities specified in Section 1, and, if applicable, with a request to initiate criminal proceedings. Court proceedings in relation to these materials shall be subject to Article 393 Section 1, sentence one of the Criminal Proceedings Code.

6. The minister appropriate for internal affairs in agreement with the Minister of Justice, shall, by way of a regulation, determine how the activities specified in Section 1 shall be conducted and documented, giving due regard to the secrecy of these activities and materials, as well as specimen of forms and records to be used.

Article 20

1. The Police may obtain information, including secret and confidential information, as well as collect, verify and process them, subject to restrictions under Article 19.[4]

2. For the purposes of detection and identification, the Police may collect, process and use information, including personal information about persons suspected of committing crimes prosecuted by the public prosecutor, minors committing illegal acts prohibited under the Act as crimes prosecuted by the public prosecutor, persons of unknown identity or those seeking to conceal their identity and persons wanted, without their knowledge of the fact or permission, in particular:

1. personal data specified in Article 27 Section 1 of the 29 August 1997 Personal Data Act (Journal of Laws No. 133 item 883, of 2000 No. 12 item 136, No. 50 item 580 and No. 116 item 1216 and of 2001 No. 42 item 474 and No. 49 item 509), except that genetic code data shall be solely about non-coding regions of the genome;

2. fingerprints;

3. photographs and descriptions of appearance;

4. special features and marks, nicknames;

5. information about:
    a) place of residence;
    b) education, profession, place of work and position;
    c) identity documents they use;
    d) how the perpetrator behaves, their environment and contacts;
    e) perpetrators' attitude to persons affected.[5]

3. Where rendered necessary to effectively prevent crimes specified in Article 19 Section 1 or detect crimes or identify the perpetrators and secure evidence, the Police may use information from contracts of insurance, in particular those processed by insuring agencies of the entities involved, including persons who have signed a contract of insurance, as well as information processed by data banks that are a bank secret.[6]

4. The information and data specified in Section 3 and information involved in the passing of the information and data shall be protected under qualified information regulations and may be made available solely to police officers involved in the case and their superiors that have authority to oversee preliminary investigations. Files containing the information and data shall be made available to courts and prosecutors solely for the purpose of prosecution.[7]

5. The information and data specified in Section 3 shall be made available pursuant to an order issued at the written request of the Chief Police Commander or Voivodeship Police Commander by a district court whose seat is appropriate for the seat of the body making the request.[8]

6. The request specified in Section 5 shall include:
    1) case number and cryptonym, if applicable;
    2) description of the crime and its legal qualification, whenever possible;
    3) the circumstances to justify the need for information and data;

4) the entity the information and data of whom is involved;

5) the entity responsible for making the information and data available.

6) the type and scope of information and data.[9]

7. Having examined the request, the court, by way of an order, shall give permission to make available the information and data about the entity, their type and scope, the entity responsible for making them available and the police body authorised to request such information and data, or shall refuse permission to make the information and data available. Article 19 Section 11 shall apply.[10]

8. Complaints may be filed against Court orders specified in Section 7 by the Police body requesting the order.[11]

9. In exercising the power conferred by the court, the police body shall inform the entity responsible for making available information and data about the type and scope of such information and data as may be required, about the entity affected and the police officer authorised to collect these.[12]

10. Within 90 days from receipt of information and data specified in Section 3, the Police, subject to Sections 11 and 12, shall inform the entity specified in Section 6 point 4 about the court order allowing access to information and data.[13]

11. The court issuing the order about access to information and data, at the request of the Chief Police Commander made after having received a written permission of Attorney General, may suspend, by way of an order, for a specified duration and possible renewal, the requirement specified in Section 10, if reasonably demonstrated that informing the entity specified in Section 6 point 4, may impair the preliminary investigation. Article 19 Section 11 shall apply.[14]

12. If within the period specified in Sections 10 or 11 preliminary proceedings were instituted, the entity specified in Section 6 point 4 shall be notified by the prosecutor, or at this request, by the Police, about the court's order to grant access to information and data, prior to the closure of the preliminary proceedings or promptly after their cessation.[15]

13. If the information and data specified in Section 3 fail to deliver evidence to initiate preliminary proceedings, the body requesting the order shall inform the entity of that, giving the information and data in a written statement.[16]

14. The State Treasury shall be liable for damage caused by violating the provisions of Section 4 as provided for in the Civil Code.[17]

15. To prevent or detect crimes and identify persons, the Police may obtain, store and process information, including personal data from records held under separate regulations by bodies of official authority, in particular the National Criminal Register and the Electronic System of Population Records. Administrators of data held in these registers shall make the information available free of charge.[18]

16. Bodies of official authority that run registers specified in Section 15 may, by way of an order, agree to make the information available using telecommunications devices to Police organisational entities, without the need to submit written requests, if the entities:
    1. dispose of devices that can record in a system who used the data, when, for what purpose and the data involved;
    2. dispose of technical and organisational means that will prevent an illegal use of the data;
    3. use the information to fulfil their duties and for the purpose of their line of business.[19]

17. Personal data collected to detect a crime shall be stored for as long as they are needed for the fulfilment of the Police's statutory duties. Police bodies shall verify the data at least every 10 years from information receipt date and remove obsolete data.[20]

18. Personal data that disclose the race or ethnicity, political views, religious or philosophical attitudes, religion, party or trade union membership, data about health, addictions or sexual relations of persons suspected of a crime prosecuted by a public prosecutor that have not been convicted for those crimes, shall be destroyed promptly after a relevant ruling takes effect. The data shall be destroyed in the presence of a committee and the process evidenced in a report.[21]

19. The Chief Police Commander after consultation with the Inspector General for Personal Data Protection shall determine, by way of a regulation, the manner and procedures for collecting, processing and using information specified in Section 2, establishing and running information databases, the types of police prevention forces allowed to utilise the databanks, the superiors appropriate for the case and specimen of documents used to process data, giving due regard to qualified information protection regulations.[22]

Article 20a

1. In connection with the performance of tasks referred to in Article 1, Section 2, the Police shall ensure the protection of the forms and methods of realisation of tasks, information and its own facilities and the particulars of those police officers.

2. During the performance of preliminary investigation activities, police officers may use documents which make it impossible to establish the

particulars of a police officer, and the measures applied by them when performing official duties.

3.   In special cases, the provisions of Section 2 may apply accordingly to persons mentioned in Article 22, Section 1.

3a. A person shall not be guilty of a crime, if they:
   1.   order the documents specified in Sections 2 and 3 to be made or oversee the making of such documents;
   2.   make the documents specified in Sections 2 and 3;
   3.   assist in the making of documents specified in Sections 2 and 3;
   4.   are a police officer or a person specified in Section 3 and use the documents specified in Sections 2 and 3 for the purpose of preliminary investigation.[23]

3b. Government administration bodies and local government bodies in their respective powers shall assist the Police in issuing and securing documents specified in Sections 2 and 3.[24]

4.   The minister appropriate for internal affairs shall, by way of a regulation, determine detailed rules and procedures for issuing, using and storing documents specified in Sections 2 and 3, giving due regard to the types of documents and their purpose, the bodies and persons authorised to issue, use and store the documents, the validity of the documents, activities to ensure protection of the documents and rules of storing and recording the documents.[25]

Article 20b

The disclosure of information about the detailed forms, terms and organisation of preliminary investigation activities as well as pending actions and applied measures and methods of their implementation may only take place in case of reasonable suspicion that a crime, subject to prosecution by a general prosecutor, was committed in connection with the performance of such activities. In such a case, relevant information shall be disclosed in the manner laid down in Article 9 of the 21 June 1996 Act on the powers of the minister of interior affairs staff and the powers of officers and staff supervised by the minister (Journal of Laws No. 106 item 491, of 1997 No. 70 item 443 and No. 141 item 943 and of 1998 No. 131 item 860).[26]

Article 20c

1.   Data that identify a telecommunications network subscriber or network termination points between which a connection was established, data about completed or attempted connections between specific network termination points and the circumstances and type of the

connection may be disclosed to the Police and processed by the Police – solely for the purpose of crime prevention or detection.

2.   The data specified in Section 1 may be disclosed:
   1.   at a written request of the Chief Police Commander or Voivodeship Police Commander;
   2.   verbal request made by a police officer who has authorisation in writing from persons specified in point 1).

3.   Where data are disclosed under Section 2 point 2, the telecommunications network operator shall inform of that the appropriate Voivodeship Police Commander.

4.   Telecommunications network operators shall make available the data specified in Section 1 to police officers designated in the request of the Police body.

5.   The data specified in Section 1 may be disclosed using a telecommunications network.

6.   Materials obtained as a result of activities under Section 2 which contain information critical for criminal proceedings shall be passed on by Police to the appropriate prosecutor.

7.   Materials obtained as a result of activities under Section 2 which do not contain information critical for criminal proceedings shall be promptly destroyed in the presence of a committee and the process evidenced in a report.

Article 21

1.   The disclosure of personal information obtained in the course of preliminary investigation activities and in accordance with the procedure referred to in Article 14, Section 4, may be possible only at the request of the court or prosecutor and the Head of the National Criminal Information Centre, and such information may be solely used for the purpose of criminal prosecution.[27]

2.   The prohibition laid down in Section 1 shall not apply if the Act provides for an obligation to disclose such information to a specified body or if such an obligation results from international agreements or treaties, and also in cases when failure to disclose would pose a threat to life or health of other persons.

Article 22

1.   During the performance of its duties, the Police may avail themselves of the assistance of people other than police officers. It is

prohibited to disclose the particulars of persons assisting the Police in preliminary investigation activities.

1a. The particulars of the person referred to in Section 1 may only be disclosed in cases and in the manner laid down in Article 9 of the Act specified in Article 20b.[28]

1b. The particulars of the person referred to in Section 1 may be disclosed at the request of the prosecutor, in case of reasonable suspicion that a crime, subject to prosecution by a general prosecutor, was committed in connection with the performance of such activities. In such a case such particulars shall be disclosed in the manner laid down in Article 9 of the Act specified in Article 20b.[29]

2. Non-police officers may be remunerated for the assistance referred to in Section 1.[30]

2a. The costs incurred during preliminary investigations of the Police where because of the protection specified in Article 20a Sections 1-3 the regulations on public finance and accounting may not apply, and the remuneration of persons specified in Section 1, shall be covered from a special operations fund.[31]

3. The minister appropriate for internal affairs shall by way of a regulation determine the principles of how an operations fund shall be created and managed.[32]

4. Where persons specified in Section 1 lost their life, or their health or property suffered in the course of and in connection with the Police using their assistance, they are eligible for damages as specified in a resolution of the minister appropriate for internal affairs.

Appendix 3

Provisions of the Border Guard Act
of 12 October 1990 (final text)

Chapter 3

Scope of powers of the Border Guard

Article 9. 1. In order to spot, prevent and detect crimes and offences according to the scope discussed under Article 1, Section 2, paragraph 4, and under Section 2a, the officers of the Border Guard shall proceed with their service, border activities, operating-investigation activities and administrative-organisational activities, and shall also proceed with the preparatory proceedings in accordance with regulations of Code of Penal Proceedings, as well as with proceedings ordered by court and public prosecutor office and other competent state agencies, according to the scope stipulated by separate regulations.

1a. In order to perform its statutory duties the Border Guard shall be free to use information about a physical person, including personal data, obtained by duly empowered state agencies, departments and institutions resulting from operating-investigation activities or operating control, as well as to process the said information, as construed by the Personal Data Protection Act of 29 August 1997 (Journal of Law, 2002 – No 101, paragraph 926 and No 153, paragraph 1271), without the knowledge and consent of the person involved.

1b. The administrator of data discussed under Section 1a shall be obliged to make available the said data, taking into account reservations formulated under Section 1d, according to an individual warrant issued by Chief Commanding Officer of the Border Guard, the Commanding Officer of the Border Guard regional unit or a duly empowered authorised officer, presented by an officer together with his or her service ID. The fact that the said data shall be made available shall be protected according to the Act on Protection of Non-Public Data, dated 22 January 1999 (Journal of Law, 1999 – No 11, paragraph 95, of 2000 – No 12, paragraph 136 and No 39, paragraph 462, of 2001 No 22, paragraph 247 and No 27, paragraph 298, No 56, paragraph 580, No 110, paragraph 1189, No 123, paragraph 1353 and No 154, and 1800, and of 2002 – No 74, paragraph 676, No 89, paragraph 804 and No 153, paragraph 1271).

1c. The Prime Minister shall issue an ordinance to present a sample form of the warrant that shall be discussed under Section 1b, taking into account the necessary data of the authorised officer, and the possibility of issuing such warrants to officers on behalf of the Chief Commanding

Officer of the Border Guard or the Commanding Officer of the Border Guard regional unit.

1d. The Prime Minister shall issue an ordinance to decide the scope, governing conditions and procedure applicable to delivery of the data about a physical person to the Border Guard, as acquired as a result of performance of the operating-investigation or operational control activities by duly authorised state agencies, service departments and institutions, taking into account the scope of information needed for performance of the statutory tasks of the Border Guard, the purpose, the system of data delivery and the method of their documenting.

1e. The Border Guard shall be free to use the criminal information collected at the National Centre of Criminal Information, as required in the context of performance of its statutory tasks.

2. (abated)

3. (abated)

4. (abated)

5. In the course of their performance of official duties, officers shall be required to respect the dignity of the person, and observe freedom, human and citizen rights.

6. In context of performing the duties, which are discussed under Article 1, Section 2, it shall be allowed to appoint the officers of the Border Guard as the border agents. The function of the main border agent shall be performed by the Chief Commanding Officer of the Border Guard.

7. The Chief Commanding Officer of the Border Guard shall decide:
   1. methods and forms in ways of performance of tasks connected with protection of the state borders according to the scope which is not covered by other regulations issued on the grounds of the Act;
   2. way of performing the border service and conducting border activities;
   3. detailed procedure applicable to issuing of state border crossing permits, including visas, by Commanding Officers of border checkpoints of the Border Guard;
   4. detailed procedure applicable to conduct of activities by border checkpoints of the Border Guard, as ordered by the competent state agencies according to Section 1;
   5. method and procedure of collection and processing of information concerning state border protection and border traffic control;
   6. scope of management of the property that remains under management of the Border Guard;
   6a. scope and detailed methods of training officers and employees of the Border Guard;

7. detailed rules to govern training of officers who work with the animals used in performance of duties of the Border Guard, and also the animal feeding standards;

8. detailed conditions of safety and hygiene of the service.

Executive provisions

Article 9a. 1. Giving information about a physical person, acquired by way of operation-investigation activities and according to the procedure that is discussed under Article 9, Section 1a), shall be allowed only on demand of the court or prosecutor, while use of such information shall be allowed to take place exclusively in the line of prosecution of the offender.

1. Giving information about a physical person, acquired by way of operation-investigation activities and according to the procedure that is discussed under Article 9, Section 1a), shall be allowed only on demand of the court or prosecutor, and also on the demand of the Head of the National Centre of Criminal Information, while use of such information shall be allowed only in the line of prosecution of the offender.

2. The ban discussed under Section 1 shall not apply if an Act imposes an obligation to give such information to given agency, or if such an obligation results from international treaties or agreements, and also in cases when refusal to give such an information would result in a threat to health or life of other people.

Article 9b. 1. Performing its duties the Border Guard shall be free to use the assistance of people who are not its officers. Disclosing of any data about a person who renders assistance to the Border Guard in the line of the operation-investigation activities shall not be allowed.

2. Disclosing of information about the person discussed under Section 1 shall be allowed to take place only possible in cases stipulated under Article 9, Section 2, of the Act of 22 June 1996 on Some Powers of Employees of the Office that Serves the Minister of the Internal Affairs Competence, and of Officers and Employees of the Offices that are Supervised by That Minister (Journal of Law, 1996, No. 106, paragraph 491, of 1997 – No. 70, paragraph 443 and No. 141, paragraph 943, and of 1998 – No. 131, paragraph 860).

3. Disclosing of data of the person discussed under Section 1 shall be allowed to demand of the prosecutor, and also when it shall be reasonable suspected that said person may have committed a publicly prosecuted crime in connection with performance of the operation-investigation activities; disclosure of said data shall take place according to the procedure discussed under art 9, Section 2, of the Act of 22 June 1996 on Some Powers of Employees of the Office that Serves the Minister of the Internal Affairs Competence, and of Officers and

Employees of the Offices that are Supervised by That Minister (Journal of Law, 1996, No. 106, paragraph 491; 1997 – No. 70, paragraph 443 and No. 141, paragraph 943; and 1998 – No. 131, paragraph 860).

4. Offering of remuneration for assistance, to the persons discussed under Section 1, shall be allowed.

4a. The costs of operation-investigation activities and remuneration of persons discussed under Section 1 shall be covered, in that part, which by reason of protection stipulated under Article 9c, Section 1, is not governed by regulations on public finance and accounting, from an operational fund.

5. The minister of the internal affairs competence shall issue an ordinance to decide the rules of establishment and management of the operational fund, while said rules shall constitute a state secret.

6. (abated).

Article 9c. 1. In connection with performing duties mentioned under Article 1, Section 2, the Border Guard shall institute protection of the form and method of performance of tasks, protection of information, and protection of its own facilities and data that identify officers.

2. Proceeding with the operation-investigation activities, officers shall be free to use documents that prevent identification of the officer of the Border Guard and the means that he or she uses in the performance of their duties.

2a. The central and local government administration agencies shall be obliged to render assistance to the Border Guard according to the scope of their competence, in the province of issuing and protection of documents that are discussed under Section 2.

3. The minister of the internal affairs competence shall issue an ordinance to decide the procedure to be applied in issuing of the documents discussed under Section 2, and how they are used and kept, taking into account the types of documents and their purpose, and the agencies and persons authorised to issue, use and keep them, the period the documents are issued for, the activities meant to facilitate their protection, and the system of their keeping and recording.

Executive provisions

Article 9d. Giving of information about detailed forms, rules and organisation, and also on operation-investigation proceedings, and applied means and methods, shall be allowed to take place exclusively on the grounds of reasonable suspicion that a publicly prosecuted crime is committed in connection with the said proceedings. In such a case the disclosure of data shall take place according to the procedure stipulated under Article 9, Section 2, of the Act of 22 June 1996 on Some Powers of Employees of the Office that Serves the Minister of the Internal Affairs Competence, and of Officers and Employees of the Offices that are Supervised by That Minister (Journal of Law, 1996, No. 106, paragraph 491; 1997 – No. 70, paragraph 443 and No. 141, paragraph 943; and 1998 – No. 131, paragraph 860).

Article 9e. 1. If in the implementation of operation-investigation proceedings by the Border Guard to prevent, detect, identify perpetrators, as well as to collect and secure evidence related to deliberate, publicly prosecuted offences:

1)   discussed under Article 264 of the Penal Code;

2)   concerning documents that allow crossing of the state border, as defined under Articles 270-275 of the Penal Code;

3)   of the fiscal type, discussed under Article133, § 1, paragraph 1, of the Fiscal Penal Code, if the value of the relevant object of offence or value of reduction of public dues exceeds fifty times the value of the lowest monthly salary, as defined by separate regulations;

4)   connected with crossing of the state border or transportation through the state border of goods or objects subject to regulations on marking of goods with excise stamps, regulations on weapons, ammunition and explosives, as well as regulations on prevention of drug addiction;

5)   as defined under Article 103 of the Foreign Citizens Act of 25 June 1997;

6)   committed by officers or employees of the Border Guard in reference o their performance of duties, as defined under Articles 228, 229 and 231 of the Penal Code;

7)   persecuted by virtue of international agreements,

when all other means have proven to be insufficient or if there is a high probability that they will be ineffective or unproductive, a regional court, responding to a written request of the Chief Commanding Officer of the Border Guard, approved in writing by the General Public Prosecutor, or responding to a written request of the commanding officer of the Border Guard regional unit, approved by the Chief Commanding Officer of the Border Guard and the competent regional prosecutor, shall be free to issue a decision that requests conduct of an operational control.

2. The written approval for the commanding officer discussed under Section 1 shall be granted by the regional prosecutor whose competence is decided according to the location of the regional unit.

3. A decision discussed under Section 1 shall be issued by the regional court of a competence determined according to location of the Border Guard regional unit, which files the request.

4. In urgent cases, where delay may cause loss of information or obliteration or destruction of evidence of the offence:

    1. the Chief Commanding Officer of the Border Guard, having been granted a written approval of the General Public Prosecutor,

    2. the Commanding officer of the Border Guard regional unit, having informed the Chief Commanding Officer of the Border Guard and having been granted a written approval of the prosecutor discussed under Section 2,

shall be free to order operational control, simultaneously filing a request at the competent court asking for the relevant decision. If the court does not grant approval within 5 days after the control is ordered, the body that ordered control shall discontinue the same and proceed with recorded destruction by a committee of all materials collected during the control.

5. A regional court shall be free to respond to a written request by the Chief Commanding Officer of the Border Guard or by the commanding officer of the Border Guard regional unit, approved in writing by the competent prosecutor, and order abandonment of the destruction of the collected material discussed under Section 4, if the material constitutes evidence of-, or suggests a will to commit, a type of offence that according to the regulations of the Act may be investigated by means of an operational control or other operation-investigation proceedings.

6. If the ordered operational control involves a suspect or a defendant, the written request of the Border Guard regional unit shall include information about proceedings taking place against that person.

7. Operational control shall not be conducted openly and shall consist in:

    1.   control of correspondence;

    2.   control of content of parcels;

    3.   use of technical measures allowing secret collection and recording of information and evidence, particularly images, telephone conversations and other information transmitted via telecommunication networks.

8. A request of the Border Guard regional unit discussed under Section 1, requesting that the court issues an order of the operational control, should contain in particular:

    1.   the case number and its code name;

    2.   description of the offence complete with its legal qualification;

    3.   circumstances which justify the order of an operational control, including the determined or probable ineffectiveness or unproductively of other means;

    4.   personal data of the person against whom the operational control will be conducted, including location and means of conducting the same;

5) purpose, time and category of operational control discussed under Section 7.

9. An order for the operational control shall be allowed for a period not exceeding 3 months. If the reasons for the control have not ceased to exist, the regional court shall be free to respond to the written request by the Chief Commanding Officer of the Border Guard or the commanding officer of the Border Guard regional unit, approved in writing by the Commanding Officer of the Border Guard and the competent prosecutor, and decide a single extension of the control period by no more than three months.

10. In particularly justified cases, if new, important facts shall be revealed in the process of control, while said facts are important for prevention or detection of an offence, or identification of perpetrators and collection of evidence, the regional court of a competence determined according to the location of the Border Guard regional unit, responding to a written request by the Chief Commanding Officer of the Border Guard or the commanding officer of the Border Guard regional unit, approved in writing by the Chief Commanding Officer of the Border Guard and the competent prosecutor, shall be free to decide conducting of the operational control also after the period of time defined stipulated under Section 9, for a specified period of time.

11. Stipulations found under Section 8 shall be applied accordingly to requests discussed under Sections 4, 5, 9 and 10. Before taking the decision discussed under Sections 9 or 10 the court shall be free to examine materials that support the request, collected in the process of operational control that was ordered in that case.

12. The requests discussed under Sections 1, 4, 5, 9 and 10 shall be examined and decided upon at a session of the regional court held in a bench of one person. The court proceedings shall be conducted in conditions stipulated for delivery, keeping and making available non-public information, combined with application of regulations, which result from Article 181 § of the Code of Penal Proceedings. It is only the prosecutor and a representative of the Border Guard regional unit who requests the order for the operational control that is allowed to take part in the court session.

13. Businessmen who proceed with telecommunication business in public networks and business entities that render postal services shall be obliged to facilitate at their own cost the organisational and technical conditions that make it possible for the Border Guard to conduct operational controls.

14. Operational control should be discontinued immediately after its reasons cease to exist, no later than with lapse of the period for which it has been ordered.

15. The Border Guard regional unit discussed under Section 1 shall inform the competent prosecutor about results of the operational control at its completion, and to his or her request also about the course of the control.

16. If evidence allowing starting of penal proceedings or evidence of importance for conducted proceedings is revealed, the Chief Commanding Officer of the Border Guard or the commanding officer of the Border Guard regional unit shall pass all the collected materials to the competent prosecutor, together with a request to start penal proceedings. The regulation found in the first sentence of Article 393, § 2, of the Code of Penal Proceedings shall be applied accordingly to said materials in the court proceedings.

17. Materials collected in the process of operational control shall not be made available to the person against whom the control has been ordered. This regulation does not violate rights resulting from Article 321 of the Penal Proceedings Code.

18. Materials collected in the process of operational control, which do not contain evidence allowing the start of penal proceedings or are unimportant for the conducted proceedings, shall be kept for 2 months after the end of control. After that period of time the recorded destruction of the aforementioned materials by the committee shall be ordered. Destruction of the materials shall be ordered by the Border Guard regional unit that requested conduct of the operational control.

19. The Border Guard regional unit that requested the order of operational control shall hold the right to appeal against the court decision on operational control, discussed under Sections 1, 4, 9 and 10. and also the right to appeal against court decision issued according to Section 5. Regulations of the Code of Penal Proceedings shall be applied accordingly to the appeals.

20. The minister of internal affairs competence, acting in agreement with the Minister of Justice and the minister for telecommunication issues competence shall decide in the form of an ordinance the methods of operational control documentation, and the methods of filing and keeping requests and decisions, as well as the methods of keeping, handing over, processing and destroying materials collected during controls. The non-open character of proceedings and collected materials shall be taken into account, and specimen forms and registers shall be prepared.

Executive provisions

Draft Acts

Article 9f. 1. In cases concerning criminal offences identified under:
1. Articles 228 and 229 of the Penal Code, committed by officers and employees of the Border Guard in connection with their performance of duties,
2. Article 264 § 3 of the Penal Code,

the operation-investigation proceedings meant to verify credibility of earlier obtained information about the crime, identify offenders and obtain evidence shall be allowed to consist in a non-open purchase, sale or taking-over of objects connected with the crime, subject to confiscation, or objects whose production, possession, transport or sale is banned, or to consist in acceptance or offering of a material gain.

2. The operation-investigation proceedings discussed under Section 1 shall be allowed also to consist in offering a purchase, sale or taking-over of objects derived from crime, items that are subject to confiscation, or objects whose production, possession, transport or sale is banned, or to consist in acceptance or offering of a material gain.

3. The Chief Commanding Officer of the Border Guard in criminal cases discussed under Section 1, paragraphs 1 and 2, or the commanding officer of the Border Guard regional unit in criminal cases discussed under Section 1, paragraph 2, shall be allowed to order for an unspecified period of time the conduct of activities discussed under Sections 1 and 2, after having been granted a written approval of the competent prosecutor who is regularly informed about the results of performed activities. The prosecutor shall be free to decide at any moment to stop said activities.

4. Activities discussed under Sections 1 and 2 shall be ordered for a period of no more than 3 months. The Chief Commanding Officer of the Border Guard or the commanding officer of the Border Guard regional unit shall be allowed to decide a single prolongation of relevant activities for a period of maximum 3 months, after having been granted a written approval of the competent prosecutor, if the causes of their ordering continue to be the case.

5. The use of technical means shall be allowed in conducting the activities discussed under Sections 1 and 2, facilitating collection of information and recording of its contents, including picture and sound.

6. If evidence is obtained, allowing starting of penal proceedings or being of importance for the conducted proceedings, the Chief Commanding Officer of the Border Guard or commanding officer of the Border Guard regional unit shall deliver to the regional prosecutor all the

collected materials resulting from activities discussed under Sections 1 and 2, together with a request to start penal proceedings. In court proceedings, the regulation found under Article 393, § 1, first sentence of the Penal Code, shall be applied to said materials.

7. The minister of internal affairs competence, acting in agreement with the Minister of Justice, shall decide by way of an ordinance the method of conducting and evidencing the activities discussed under Sections 1 and 2, taking into account the need of facilitation of a non-open character of said activities and the materials obtained that way, and also the sample forms of applied forms and registers.

Executive acts

Article 9g. 1. In operational-evidence activities conducted to find evidence of crimes, as discussed under Article 9e, Section 1, or conducted to identify people who take part in the crimes, or to take over the objects of crime, the Chief Commanding Officer of the Border Guard or the commanding officer of the Border Guard regional unit shall be free to order non-open monitoring of production, transport, storage and sale of the objects of crime, if this does not create a threat to human life or health.

2. He or she shall immediately notify about the order discussed under Section 1 the local prosecutor whose competence is determined according to the seat of the notifying body, while the said prosecutor shall be free to order at any moment stopping of the activities.

3. The body of the Border Guard discussed under Section 1 shall regularly inform the regional prosecutor, discussed under Section 2, about the results of conducted activities.

4. The use of technical means shall be allowed in conducting the activities discussed under Section 1, facilitating collection of information and recording of its contents, including picture and sound.

5. According to the order discussed under Section 1, public agencies and institutions, and businessmen shall be obliged to enable further transport of the consignment that contains intact objects of crime, or after their complete or partial removal or replacement.

6. If evidence is obtained, allowing starting of penal proceedings or being of importance for the conducted proceedings, the Chief Commanding Officer of the Border Guard or commanding officer of the Border Guard regional unit acting according to the consent of the Chief Commanding Officer of the Boarder Guard shall deliver to the regional prosecutor all the collected materials resulting from activities discussed under Section 1, if required together with a request to start penal proceedings. In court proceedings, the regulation found under

Article 393, § 1, first sentence of the Penal Code, shall be applied to said materials.

7. The minister of internal affairs competence, acting in agreement with the Minister of Justice, shall decide by way of an ordinance the method of conducting and evidencing of the activities discussed under Section 1, taking into account the need of facilitation of a non-open character of said activities and the materials obtained that way, and also the sample forms of applied forms and registers.

Executive acts

Article 10. Commanding Officers of the border checkpoints of the Border Guard shall co-ordinate the work of the agencies and institutions functioning at the border crossings, according to the scope defined under Article 9, Section 1.

Article 10a. 1. In line with its scope of competence and in compliance with restrictions that results from stipulations found under Article 9e the Border Guard shall be allowed to obtain, keep, verify and process information, including non-open information.

2. The Border Guard shall be allowed collect, gather and use for identification and detecting purposes the fingerprints, photographs and personal data, including data revealing ethnic origin, religion and health condition, of persons suspected of having committed a crime prosecuted by the state, and of persons whose identity is unknown or who try to conceal their identity, without their knowledge and agreement.

3. Personal data discussed under Section 2, save for the data revealing ethnic origin and religion, shall be kept, with reservations found under Sections 4 and 5 taken into account, for a period of time required by the Border Guard to comply with their statutory duties. Bodies of the Border Guard shall verify said data at least once every 10 years from after the date when said information is obtained.

4. Restrictions specified under Section 3 shall not apply to keeping data revealing ethnic origin and the religion of persons sentenced for having committed a crime prosecuted by the state.

5. Personal data revealing ethnic origin and religion of persons who were suspected of having committed a crime prosecuted by the state but who were not sentenced for committing the said crimes shall be subject to recorded destruction by a committee immediately after the relevant judgment comes into force.

6. According to its competence the Border Guard shall be free to obtain and process information found in the data records kept by the public authorities. Administrators of data kept in said records shall be obliged to

make them available free of charge to officers who hold relevant document of authorisation, as discussed under Article 9, Section 1b.

7. Authorities discussed under Section 6 shall be free to decide their written consent to facilitation of access of the organisational units of Border Guard for collection of data through telecommunication equipment, without filing a written request, provided said units meet the following conditions:
1. They have facilities that enable the system to record who obtained the data, what kind of data was obtained, when was it obtained and for what purpose;
2. They have technical and organisational protections to prevent making use of the data for a different purpose than it was obtained for;
3. It is justified by the specificity or the scope of the duties or activities.

Article 10b. 1. Data identifying the user of the telecommunication network or terminals of the network between which the connection is made, and data concerning connection or attempted connection between specified terminals of the network, as well as the circumstances and type of the realised connection, shall be allowed to be revealed to the Border Guard and processed by the Border Guard only in order to prevent or detect crimes.

2. Data specified under Section 1 shall be revealed:
1. on written request of the Chief Commanding Officer of the Border Guard or of the Commanding Officer of the Border Guard regional unit;
2. on verbal request of the Border Guard officer who holds authorisation of the bodies specified under paragraph No. 1;
3. automatically, via electronic devices, to officers who use remote IT systems that support collection of alarm notices from citizens.

3. Businessmen engaged in a telecommunications business in public networks must reveal, at their own expense, data specified under Section 1 to officers identified in the request of a competent body of the Border Guard, or to officers discussed under Section 2, paragraphs 2 and 3.

4. Revealing to the Border Guard data specified under Section 1 shall be allowed to take place via telecommunication networks, without a written request, if:
1. The networks are equipped with:
   a. devices for storing information about who obtains the data, when it takes place and what kinds of data are obtained;

311

        b.   technical   and   organisational   protections preventing unauthorised persons from making use of the data when said data are being revealed through the teletransmission devices;

2. This is justified by the specificity or scope of duties or activities performed by the structural bodies of the Border Guard.

5. Materials obtained from activities undertaken in accordance with Section 1, containing information of importance for penal proceedings, shall be delivered by the Border Guard to a competent public prosecutor.

6. Materials obtained from activities undertaken in accordance with Section 1, containing information of importance for penal proceedings, shall be subject to an immediate recorded destruction by the committee.

---

1. Article 19 changed by Article 1 point 11 of the 27 July 2001 Act (Journal of Laws 01.100.1084), which changed this Act as of 19 March 2002.
2. Article 19a changed by Article 1 point 11 of the 27 July 2001 Act (Journal of Laws 01.100.1084), which changed this Act as of 19 March 2002.
3. Article 19b changed by Article 1 point 11 of the 27 July 2001 Act (Journal of Laws 01.100.1084), which changed this Act as of 19 March 2002.
4. Article 20 Section 1 changed by Article 1 point 12 of the 27 July 2001 Act (Journal of Laws 01.100.1084), which changed this Act as of 19 March 2002.
5. Article 20 Section 2 changed by Article 1 point 12 of the 27 July 2001 Act (Journal of Laws 01.100.1084), which changed this Act as of 19 March 2002.
6. Article 20 Section 3 changed by Article 1 point 12 of the 27 July 2001 Act (Journal of Laws 01.100.1084), which changed this Act as of 19 March 2002.
7. Article 20 Section 4 added by Article 1 point 12 of the 27 July 2001 Act (Journal of Laws 01.100.1084), which changed this Act as of 19 March 2002.
8. Article 20 Section 5 added by Article 1 point 12 of the 27 July 2001 Act (Journal of Laws 01.100.1084), which changed this Act as of 19 March 2002.
9. Article 20 Section 6 added by Article 1 point 12 of the 27 July 2001 Act (Journal of Laws 01.100.1084), which changed this Act as of 19 March 2002.
10. Article 20 Section 7 added by Article 1 point 12 of the 27 July 2001 Act (Journal of Laws 01.100.1084), which changed this Act as of 19 March 2002.
11. Article 20 Section 8 added by Article 1 point 12 of the 27 July 2001 Act (Journal of Laws 01.100.1084), which changed this Act as of 19 March 2002.
12. Article 20 Section 9 added by Article 1 point 12 of the 27 July 2001 Act (Journal of Laws 01.100.1084), which changed this Act as of 19 March 2002.
13. Article 20 Section 10 added by Article 1 point 12 of the 27 July 2001 Act (Journal of Laws 01.100.1084), which changed this Act as of 19 March 2002.
14. Article 20 Section 11 added by Article 1 point 12 of the 27 July 2001 Act (Journal of Laws 01.100.1084), which changed this Act as of 19 March 2002.
15. Article 20 Section 12 added by Article 1 point 12 of the 27 July 2001 Act (Journal of Laws 01.100.1084), which changed this Act as of 19 March 2002.
16. Article 20 Section 13 added by Article 1 point 12 of the 27 July 2001 Act (Journal of Laws 01.100.1084), which changed this Act as of 19 March 2002.
17. Article 20 Section 14 added by Article 1 point 12 of the 27 July 2001 Act (Journal of Laws 01.100.1084), which changed this Act as of 19 March 2002.
18. Article 20 Section 15 added by Article 1 point 12 of the 27 July 2001 Act (Journal of Laws 01.100.1084), which changed this Act as of 19 October 2001.
19. Article 20 Section 16 added by Article 1 point 12 of the 27 July 2001 Act (Journal of Laws 01.100.1084), which changed this Act as of 19 October 2001.

20. Article 20 Section 17 added by Article 1 point 12 of the 27 July 2001 Act (Journal of Laws 01.100.1084), which changed this Act as of 19 October 2001.
21. Article 20 Section 18 added by Article 1 point 12 of the 27 July 2001 Act (Journal of Laws 01.100.1084), which changed this Act as of 19 October 2001.
22. Article 20 Section 19 added by Article 1 point 12 of the 27 July 2001 Act (Journal of Laws 01.100.1084), which changed this Act as of 19 October 2001.
23. Article 20a Section 3a added by Article 1 point 13 letter a) of the 27 July 2001 Act (Journal of Laws 01.100.1084), which changed this Act as of 19 October 2001.
24. Article 20a Section 3b added by Article 1 point 13 letter a) of the 27 July 2001 Act (Journal of Laws 01.100.1084), which changed this Act as of 19 October 2001.
25. Article 20a Section 4 changed by Article 1 point 13 letter b) of the 27 July 2001 Act (Journal of Laws 01.100.1084), which changed this Act as of 19 October 2001.
26. Article 20b changed by Article 1 point 14 of the 27 July 2001 Act (Journal of Laws 01.100.1084), which changed this Act as of 19 October 2001.
27. Article 21 Section 1 changed by Article 52 point 3 of the 6 July 2001 Criminal Information Collection, Processing and Transfer Act (Journal of Laws 01.110.1189) as of 6 April 2002.
28. Article 22 Section 1a changed by Article 1 point 15 letter a) of the 27 July 2001 Act (Journal of Laws 01.100.1084), which changed this Act as of 19 October 2001.
29. Article 22 Section 1b changed by Article 1 point 15 letter a) of the 27 July 2001 Act (Journal of Laws 01.100.1084), which changed this Act as of 19 October 2001.
30. Article 22 Section 2 changed by Article 1 point 15 letter b) of the 27 July 2001 Act (Journal of Laws 01.100.1084), which changed this Act as of 19 October 2001.
31. Article 22 Section 2a added by Article 1 point 15 letter c) of the 27 July 2001 Act (Journal of Laws 01.100.1084), which changed this Act as of 19 October 2001.
32. Article 22 Section 3 changed by Article 1 point 15 letter d) of the 27 July 2001 Act (Journal of Laws 01.100.1084), which changed this Act as of 19 October 2001.

Portugal

1. Please indicate the SITs used in your country, the respective legal framework governing their use and their legal definition, if any.

Generally speaking, the Portuguese legal system provides for special investigation techniques as techniques strictly necessary for the effective prevention and combating of objectively serious crimes that have highly damaging consequences, undermining as they do the foundations of an open, democratic society, and whose investigation is normally difficult, such as terrorism, organised crime and drug-trafficking.

The legal framework governing SITs in Portugal is contained in the Code of Criminal Procedure (CCP) and a number of Acts not inserted in the Code.

The CCP covers investigation, search, seizure and interception of communications; Act 101/2001 of 25 August regulates infiltration operations for the purposes of the prevention and investigation of crime; controlled delivery is governed by Act 144/99 of 31 August; international mutual assistance in criminal matters; and the legal framework governing drug trafficking and use is provided by legislative decree 15/93 of 22 January.

Code of Criminal Procedure (CCP)

Samples may be taken from persons, places and objects in order to analyse evidence at the scene of a crime as well as all clues as to the way and place in which an offence has been committed and to its perpetrators and victims.

Searches

Under Article 174 ff of the CCP, searches are authorised by the relevant judicial authority, which as far as possible directs execution of the measure. This means that, depending on whether a measure is carried out during the investigation or the preliminary investigation, it is ordered by the public prosecutor or the investigating judge and then carried out by the police.

The police may, nonetheless, conduct searches without the authorisation of a judicial authority where there is legitimate reason to believe and strong evidence to suggest the imminent commission of an offence endangering a person's life or physical integrity:

- in the case of terrorism, violent crime and highly organised crime, but, in order for it to be valid, the police must inform the investigating judge of the measure immediately;
- where the potential victim gives his or her express consent;
- where a person has been caught in the act of committing an offence carrying a prison sentence;

House searches are void unless ordered by an investigating judge and carried out between 7 a.m. and 9 p.m. With respect to terrorist acts, violent crime and highly organised crime, the public prosecutor and the police may, with the express consent of the potential victim, order or carry out this type of measure, but must immediately inform the investigating judge (Articles 174, paragraph 5, and 177 of the CCP).

Searches of a lawyer's or doctor's office conducted in this context must be carried out under the personal supervision of an investigating judge and in the presence of a member of the Bar Association or Medical Association.

Interception of communications

Only an investigating judge may order the interception, recording and transcription of such communications if the offence carries a prison sentence of at least three years or in the case of offences connected with the trafficking of drugs, arms or explosives, smuggling, and insults, threats, invasion of privacy and disturbing the peace, where they are committed by telephone – Articles 187 and 188 of the CCP.

There are no restrictions on private lines, except for the interception and recording of communications between a person who is being investigated or has been indicted and his or her lawyer, unless the judge has good reason to believe that the latter is the victim or means of an offence – Article 187, paragraph 3, of the CCP.

Controlled delivery

Controlled delivery is only provided for in the legislation on drugs – Article 61 of legislative decree 15/99, 22 January. It may be authorised by the public prosecutor who is directing the investigation in order to take part, in collaboration with the countries of destination and other countries of destination and transit, in the identification and prosecution of as many as possible of those involved in various trafficking and distribution operations, but without prejudice to criminal actions for offences to which Portuguese law is applicable.

Similarly, Article 160 of Act 144/99 of 31 August provides for the use of this type of SIT when a foreign state so requests in the framework of a cross-border investigation.

Undercover operations

This type of SIT is provided for in Act 101/2001 of 23 August and consists of actions by a criminal investigation officer or any person who, acting under police supervision, conceals his or her occupation and identity in order to further the prevention or prosecution of the offences referred to in the law.

Prior authorisation of the public prosecutor, who must inform the investigating judge, is required.

Where an undercover operation takes place in the framework of crime prevention, the powers of initiative and decision-making lie, respectively, with the public prosecutor of the Central Investigation and Criminal Action Department, and the Central Criminal Investigation Court.

Observation

This includes cross-border observation and electronic surveillance. The police may use various techniques in their information-gathering work, including observation, informers and front store operations, provided they are not prohibited under Article 126, paragraph 2 of the CCP. As for cross-border observation, Portugal has only one land border, with Spain.

There is a special agreement with the Kingdom of Spain, Decree 48/99 of 9 November on cross-border pursuits, which is in the spirit of the Schengen Agreement. Pursuit is limited to a distance of 50 km from the border.

2. When and under which circumstances (e.g. criminal investigation, preliminary stage, etc.) can SITs be used?

The Constitution of the Republic establishes a principle of separation and interdependence of powers. Under the constitution, the prosecuting authorities constitute an autonomous body with its own status, which is part of the court system. Therefore the organisation of the prosecuting authorities is similar to that of an independent legal service in two ways: firstly, the political authorities may not interfere in the practical exercise of prosecution powers and, secondly, the prosecution authorities constitute a specific legal service that is separate from and operates in parallel to the judiciary.

The prosecuting authorities are organically and functionally autonomous. Their powers include prosecuting and directing the investigation of offences.

Criminal investigation consists of two phases in the Portuguese criminal justice system: investigation and preliminary investigation, directed, respectively, by the prosecuting authorities and the investigating judge, who are assisted by the police – Articles 263, paragraph 1, and 288, paragraph 1, of the CCP.

SITs may be used in the framework of a criminal investigation only during the investigation and preliminary investigation phases. During the investigation the police work under the direct orders of the prosecuting authorities and come under their authority. The criminal investigation police are the only police body that investigates terrorist offences.

3. Are there any specific features governing the use of SITs in relation to acts of terrorism? If so, please specify.

In the event of terrorism, the prosecuting authorities may order house searches and the police may carry out this type of measure, but the former must immediately inform the investigating judge (Articles 177, paragraph 2, and 174, paragraph 5, of the CCP).

Prior authorisation for interception of communications may be requested from the investigating judge of the district where the conversation or communication may take place – Article 187, paragraph 2, of the CCP.

4. How does the legal framework governing the use of SITs guarantee respect for human rights and individual freedoms, the principles of subsidiarity and proportionality? Is the authorisation to use SITs subject to time-limits? Which bodies and procedures are in place to supervise compliance with human rights standards and with the above-mentioned principles in the use of SITs? Is supervision automatic/systematic?

As indicated in the reply to question 1, in Portugal the use of SITs is supervised by the relevant judicial authority and, in the case of searches likely to infringe fundamental rights and freedoms, house searches and interception of communications, by an investigating judge.

The judicial authority sets the time-limit on a SIT; the same authority may amend it by an order giving reasons. It is set for a period of time considered adequate for the purposes of the investigation and the means of executing the SIT.

SITs are under the supervision of the prosecuting authorities and investigating judge. The procedures in place to supervise compliance with human rights standards and the principles of subsidiarity and proportionality are nullity of the action and appeal against the decision.

5. Which institutions are involved in the use of SITs and what is their role (e.g. law enforcement agencies, prosecutor's office, judicial authorities, etc.)? Which institutions can order and/or authorise the use of SITs? How does co-operation between these institutions work in practice?

See replies to questions 1 and 4.

6. Are there any specialised counter-terrorism institutions? What is their role in the use of SITs?

The Principal State Counsel's Office is the highest tier of the prosecuting authorities and includes the Central Investigation and Criminal Action Department (CICAD) which comes directly under the Principal State Counsel, and the Investigation and Criminal Action Departments (ICADs).

CICAD is responsible for directing the investigation and prosecution of the offences referred to in Section 47 of Act 60/98 of 27 August, such as terrorist organisation and terrorism, provided the criminal activity takes place in more than one judicial district or if, on the Principal State Counsel's decision, it is determined that, in relation to manifestly serious or particularly complex offences or if the criminal activity is geographically dispersed, centralised direction of the investigation is truly justified.

The ICADs are responsible for directing the investigation and prosecution of the offences referred to in the Criminal Code, including terrorism.

The prosecution and investigation of terrorist offences is the responsibility of these two prosecution departments, depending on the context of the criminal activity.

The police conduct the investigation. There is a special police unit responsible for this type of offence – the Central Department to Combat Crime (CDCC).

In the case of terrorism, the investigating judge of the Central Court for Criminal Investigation and all investigating judges may order and/or authorise the use of all SITs, as can the prosecuting authorities, but with the restrictions mentioned in the reply to question 1.

7. Which measures have been adopted in order to facilitate international co-operation (e.g. joint investigation teams)? Can the SITs listed in reply to question 1 be used in cross-border settings?

Under the terms of the Schengen Agreement, they are permitted within the geographical limits set by the authorities of the country pursued into, and it is possible to act in joint teams.

8. What use can be made of SITs in the context of mutual legal assistance?

Provided a SIT is permitted under Portuguese law, it may be used at the request of another country and in the context of mutual legal assistance.

9. How can the use of SITs be improved? Please provide any comments/proposals concerning the implementation of the terms of reference of the PC-TI and in particular the use and regulation of SITs.

Use of SITs would be improved if countries were able to harmonise procedures in criminal matters and simplify co-operation in criminal investigations. Co-operation and co-ordination between countries need to be improved, through the Eurojust judges, by enabling direct contact between the judges directing the case and those requesting action.

Information exchange, especially on terrorism and organised crime, is essential to the functioning of a co-ordinating structure. Joint investigation teams also need to be organised.

Romania

Within the Romanian law system, the means of investigation of terrorist acts are not regulated by a "special corpus" of judicial acts. The investigation of terrorist acts is done with common methods also used in other cases (narcotic smuggling, organised crime and money laundering).

The main direction that is followed, where terrorist acts are concerned, is the prevention of these acts, through miscellaneous organisational measures aimed at discovering the preparation activities that precede them and the control of the conditions that can favour their perpetration.

Romania demonstrated a special sensibility and had a prompt reaction to the concerns that were shown on the international level regarding the prevention and countering of terrorism. But this fact did not mean the toughening of the investigation methods or the setting-up of some special proceedings applicable to terrorist acts only.

The adopted measures were mainly realised in:
1. The establishment of a multi-institutional/national system of preventing and countering terrorism, with the following main tasks:
   a. Guarding, protection activities and other special methods to discourage attempts, to ensure the security/guarding of Romanian and foreign personalities and objectives (on the national territory) forming potential targets of terrorist activities;
   b. Activities against the influx of specific means of action, human, financial, logistics and informational resources directed towards terrorist organisations;
   c. Activities preparing for intervention in civil emergency situations generated by terrorist actions in order to limit or counter their effects;
   d. International co-operation activities;
   e. The continual improvement of the legal framework.
2. Specific legal regulations were adopted in the field of combating terrorism, between 2001 and 2002, consisting of:
   a. incrimination by law of terrorist acts;
   b. legal regulations on preventing and countering the utilisation of the financial banking system for financing terrorist actions;
   c. ratification of the International Convention on the repression of the financing of terrorism.

At the same time, there have been regulated the means of using undercover agents for investigating offences regarding organised crime and narcotic smuggling. This method will be included in the Code of Criminal Procedure and it can be used in the investigation of real terrorist actions.

Certain modifications and amendments to the Code of Criminal Procedure have been initiated and discussed in Parliament. Among these there are specific provisions for:

- a ruling by a judge, for urgent and completely justified causes, on measures regarding: house search, retaining and delivering mail and the objects, audio and/or video interception or recording for the actions of preparing or committing offences.
- witness protection when the disclosure of their real identity could endanger their life, physical integrity or health.
- undercover agents – for investigating certain facts when it is difficult to gather evidence through regular means (narcotic smuggling and weapons traffic, traffic of individuals, terrorist acts, money laundering).

In accordance with the current legal regulations (applicable in the field of investigation of narcotic smuggling and organised crime), undercover agents are members of the Ministry of Interior.

The law on the modification and annotation of the Code of Criminal Procedure extends the use of this method to the investigation of real terrorist actions. It also provides for the possibility of using as undercover agents members of the intelligence services.

The current regulations as well as those in the project stage specify that this method can be used:

- based on the authorisation issued by the judge
- only for a limited period of time and under the permanent supervision of the judge.

Finally, we can make the following specifications regarding the Romanian concept and juridical system of preventing and countering terrorism:

- Investigating techniques or procedures derogating from the common law are not used only for the investigation of terrorist actions.
- Only strongly law-regulated action methods are used, and these are, mostly, supervised by a judge;
- There is a preoccupation concerning improvement of the criminal procedure regulations that will be applied also in the investigation of terrorist actions.

The means and techniques of investigation that are used are in accordance with the provisions of the international treaties and conventions in the field of human rights, and the preventing and countering of terrorism.

1. Please indicate the SITs used in your country, the respective legal framework governing their use and their legal definition, if any.

The main special investigation techniques used in Romania are as follows.

Undercover operations:

The current legal framework consists of the following.

Law No. 14/1990 concerning the organisation and functioning of the Romanian Intelligence Service

Article 28

The operative personnel of the Romanian Intelligence Service operate openly or undercover, based on national security requirements.

The Romanian Intelligence Service will ensure the protection of operative personnel whose activity is disclosed under circumstances that do not involve it and will transfer them to other units or departments.

Law No. 143/2000 concerning the suppression of drugs trafficking and use

h) Undercover investigators – police officers especially designated to investigate cases – with the attorney's authorisation – for gathering intelligence concerning the existence of a crime and for identifying the perpetrators as well as the preparatory activities, using another identity than their real one, assumed for a period of time.

Article 21

(1) The attorney can authorise the use of undercover investigators for uncovering the facts, identifying the perpetrators and gathering conclusive evidence for cases where there are reliable indications that an offence specified in this law has been perpetrated or is being planned.

Law No. 678/2001 concerning the prevention and suppression of human smuggling

Article 22

In accordance with the provisions of the law, undercover investigators can be used for gathering the necessary data for instituting legal proceedings.

Government Emergency Ordinance No. 43/2002 concerning the National Anti-corruption General Attorney's Office

Article 17

(1) If there are reliable indications that one of the offences – specified by this law as being under the jurisdiction of the National Anti-corruption

General Attorney's Office – has been perpetrated or is being planned and the usual methods cannot lead to the identification of the perpetrators or to the uncovering of the plan, undercover investigators can be used in accordance with the law for gathering intelligence concerning the existence of the offence and the identity of the suspected persons.

(2) The persons referred to at sub-paragraph (1) are police officers working with the Ministry of Interior, especially appointed for this purpose and can make investigations only with the reasoned authorisation of the Head of the National Anti-corruption General Attorney's Office.

Law No. 218/2002 concerning the organisation and functioning of the Romanian Police

Article 33

(1) In order to prevent and suppress corruption, transnational crime, human smuggling, terrorism, drugs trafficking, money laundering, cybernetic offences and organised crime, at the proposal of the Head of the Romanian Police's General Inspectorate, with the approval of the Minister of Interior and with the authorisation of the attorney designated by the Head of the General Attorney's Office belonging to the Court of Appeals, the Romanian Police can use informants and undercover police officers for gathering intelligence to be used as evidence during the court trial.

Law No. 39/2003 concerning the prevention and suppression of organised crime

Article 17

If there are reliable indications that a serious crime has been perpetrated or is being planned by one or several members of an organised-crime group and the usual methods cannot lead to the identification of the perpetrators or the uncovering of the plan, undercover police officers working with the specialised structures of the Ministry of Interior can be used for gathering data on the crime and the identity of the perpetrators.

Article 23

An undercover police officer and an informant; as well as their relatives, can enjoy the specific measures designed for witnesses' protection in accordance with the law.

De lege ferenda

Draft law concerning the aspects to be changed and added in the Criminal Procedure Code

Article 224₁

If there are reliable and concrete indications that one of the offences against national security – included in the Penal Code and in the special laws – has been perpetrated or is being planned, as well as for cases of drugs and weapons trafficking, human smuggling, terrorism, money laundering, money and securities forging; or for other offences stipulated by Law No. 78/2000 for preventing, uncovering and punishing acts of corruption (with the subsequent changes and additional provisions); or for other serious crime in which the usual methods cannot lead to the identification of the suspected persons or the uncovering of the plan, investigators having another identity than their real one can be used.

The undercover investigators are operative officers working with the Ministry of Interior or other governmental bodies who – in accordance with the law – carry out intelligence activities for ensuring national security, are especially designated for this purpose and can be used for an established period of time, pursuant to Articles 224₂ and 224₃.

Based on the authorisation issued in accordance with the provisions of Article 224₂, the undercover investigator gathers data and intelligence and provides them to the judicial authorities.

Article 224₄

The real identity of the undercover investigators cannot be disclosed during the operation or after its conclusion.

The attorney that authorises the use of an undercover investigator has the right to know his real identity and has to obey the law concerning the professional secret.

Draft law concerning the national security of Romania

Article 14

(1) For ensuring national security, the intelligence services and departments use intelligence officers who operate openly or under cover.
(2) ...
(3) The intelligence activities carried out for ensuring national security, including identification data and the status of undercover intelligence officers, represent state secrets."

Informants/sources

The current legal framework:

Law No. 39/2003 concerning the prevention and suppression of organised crime

Article 2

For the purposes of this law, the term "informant" has the following meaning:

d) Informant – a person that has knowledge of a criminal organised group and provides the judicial authorities with relevant intelligence and data for preventing, uncovering and punishing the perpetration of serious crimes by one or several members of this group.

Article 21

In exceptional cases, if there are reliable indications that one or several members of a criminal organised group has/have perpetrated or is/are planning the perpetration of a serious crime in which the usual methods cannot lead to the identification of the perpetrators or the uncovering of the plan, informants can be used for gathering data on the crime and for identifying the perpetrators.

Article 22

Informants can enjoy financial rewards in accordance with the order of the Minister of Interior and the Head of the General Attorney's Office belonging to the Supreme Court of Justice.

Article 23

An undercover police officer and an informant, as well as their relatives, can enjoy the specific measures designed for witnesses' protection in accordance with the law.

Law No. 218/2002 concerning the organisation and functioning of the Romanian Police

Article 33

(1) In order to prevent and suppress corruption, transnational crime, human smuggling, terrorism, drugs trafficking, money laundering, cybernetic offences and organised crime, at the proposal of the Head of the Romanian Police's General Inspectorate, with the approval of the Minister of Interior and with the authorisation of the attorney designated by the Head of the General Attorney's Office belonging to the Court of

Appeals, the Romanian Police can use informants and undercover police officers for gathering intelligence to be used as evidence during the court trial.

Law No. 682/2002 concerning witnesses' protection

Article 2

For the purposes of this law, the terms and phrases below have the following meaning:

a. The witness is a person that fits one of the following conditions:
1.   He/she has the status of witness, in accordance with the Criminal Procedure Code, and by his/her statements provides intelligence and data that have crucial importance for establishing the truth concerning serious crimes and contributes to the prevention/recovering losses resulting from such crimes;
2.   Without playing a role in the trial, by providing intelligence and data, he/she contributes to the establishing of the truth in cases concerning serious crime or in preventing/recovering important losses that might result from such crimes;

h) A serious crime is an offence that belongs to one of the following categories: crimes against peace and mankind, crimes against the state or national security, terrorism, murder in the first degree, murder in the second degree, drugs trafficking, human smuggling, money laundering, money or securities forging, violations of the law concerning weapons and ammunitions, as well as the law on the nuclear and radioactive materials, corruption, crimes against the state patrimony that resulted in particular serious losses, as well as any other offence for which the law stipulates at least a ten-year imprisonment.

De lege ferenda

Draft law concerning the national security of Romania

Article 15

(1) Intelligence that is relevant for the national security is gathered by using secret human sources, technical sources and specific methods of intelligence activity.

(2) The secret human sources that operate for ensuring national security enjoy the protection of the law.

Controlled delivery

The current legal framework consists of the following.

Law No. 143/2000 concerning the suppression of drugs trafficking and use

j) Controlled delivery is a method used by the specialised legal institutions or bodies, with the authorisation and under the control of an attorney, that consists in allowing drugs or illegal precursors or other substances replacing drugs and precursors to pass/circulate through our country's territory, with the aim of uncovering the criminal activities and identify the persons involved in them;

Article 20

At the request of the specialised legal institutions or bodies, the General Attorney's Office belonging to the Supreme Court of Justice can authorise controlled deliveries with/without the complete substitution of the drugs or precursors.

Law No. 218/2002 concerning the organisation and functioning of the Romanian Police

Article 32

(1) For suppressing crimes perpetrated by organised crime, or in the interest of the legal proceedings, the Police can use the method of controlled delivery.

(2) Controlled delivery represents the method used by the specialised legal institutions or bodies, with the authorisation and under the control of an attorney, that consists in allowing drugs or precursors or assets resulted from criminal activities or other materials whose possession and trading are prohibited by the law, with the aim of uncovering criminal activities and identifying the persons involved in them.

Electronic surveillance

This is not explicitly stipulated by any law, but it can be used. The current legal framework consists of the following.

Law No. 51/1991 concerning the national security of Romania

Article 13

In documented cases and in accordance with the provisions of the Criminal Procedure Code, the situations referred to at Article 3 represent the legal grounds for requesting the attorney's authorisation to adopt intelligence measures such as: interception of communications, access to a place or thing, opening of this thing to seek intelligence, documents or handwritten notes; getting/replacing an object or document with the aim of examining it for intelligence purposes, use of various methods for recording, copying or obtaining excerpts from documents; installing objects, ensuring their maintenance and recovering them.

Law No. 14/1992 concerning the organisation and functioning of the Romanian Intelligence Service

Article 8

The Romanian Intelligence Service is authorised to possess and use appropriate means for obtaining, checking, processing and storing intelligence on national security, in accordance with legal provisions.

De lege ferenda

Draft law concerning the national security of Romania

Article 15

(1) Intelligence relevant to national security is gathered by secret human and technical sources and specific methods of the intelligence type.

Article 16

The intelligence services and departments referred to at Article 13 are authorised to create, purchase, possess and use means and methods for obtaining, checking, storing, processing, protecting, exploiting and transmitting the intelligence and data that are needed for ensuring national security, in accordance with the tasks assigned to them by law.

Communication listening and interception

The current legal framework consists of the following.

Criminal Procedure Code

Tapping of calls

Article 91^1

Tape recordings of some conversations, with reasoned authorisation of the prosecuting attorney assigned by the first Prosecutor of the Appeal Court, in the legally allowed situations and circumstances, if there are data or specific indications of the preparation or committing of a crime for which penal prosecution is done ex-officio, and tapping can reveal the truth, may be used in evidence if by the content of the recordings facts or circumstances result that are useful in establishing the truth.

Law No. 51/1991 on the national security of Romania

Article 13

The situations mentioned in Article 3 are legally bases to apply for the prosecutor, in vindicable cases, obeying the Code of Penal Prosecution, to authorise acts in order to gather intelligence, consisting in: interception of communication, searches of some data, documents, written papers for which it is necessary to enter a place, to obtain an artefact or to open a res; taking or installing of an artefact or a document, its examination, recovering the data they contain or recording, copying or obtaining some excerpts by any means; installing res, maintaining or taking res from the place they were placed.

Law No. 14/1992 concerning the organisation and functioning of the Romanian Intelligence Service

Article 8

The Romanian Intelligence Service is authorised to possess appropriate means to obtain, verify, analyse and store intelligence on national security, in accordance with the law.

Law No. 676/2001 concerning personal-data processing and the protection of private life in the communication sector

Article 4

The confidentiality of communications undertaken in a public communication network or by the help of a public communication service is guaranteed.

Listening, recording, storing in any means of interception or surveillance of communications is forbidden, except in the following cases:
- If it is carried out by the users concerned in the communication referred to;
- The users agreed to the interception, in writing
- The act is carried out as an act of public authority, obeying the law.

A user or a subscriber has the duty to inform the interlocutor or another subscriber when, during a conversation, equipment is used that allows the conversation to be listened to, recorded or stored by other persons.

Law No. 678/2001 concerning the prevention or suppression of trafficking in human beings

Article 23

(1) When there are solid data or indications that a person is preparing a crime mentioned in the current law, or that they have committed such kind of offence, using communication and computer systems, the prosecution authority can, with the authorisation of the attorney, have access in a particular period of time to those systems and survey them.

Governmental Regulation No. 43/2002 concerning the National Anti-corruption Magistracy

Article 16

When there are indications concerning the undertaking of crimes mentioned in the current regulation as being in the competence of the National Anti-corruption Magistracy, to collect evidence or to identify the perpetrator, the prosecutors of the National Anti-corruption Magistracy can approve for a maximum of 30 days:
a) monitoring bank accounts and assimilated accounts;
b) interception of phone communication lines;
c) access to the computer systems.

De lege ferenda

Draft law concerning the modification and completion of the Code of Penal Prosecution

Article 911

Wire-tapping and tape recording, or any other recording of a conversation or communication, will operate under court authorisation, at the prosecutor's request, obeying the law, if there are serious data or indications concerning the preparation or committing of a crime through which the penal prosecution is done ex-officio, and the intercepting and recording are necessary for establishing the truth. The authorisation is issued by the appropriate court president who will judge the case in the first phase, in the council chamber. The interception and recording of conversations help in establishing the truth, in cases when the real situation or identification of the perpetrator cannot be achieved by other evidence.

The interception and recording of conversation or communication can be authorised in the case of crimes against national security, mentioned in the Penal Code and other special laws, and in the smuggling of drugs/weapons/human beings, terrorist acts, money laundering, forging currency or other valuables, in cases of the Law No. 78/2000 for preventing, discovering and punishing corruption or other serious crimes that cannot be discovered or whose perpetrators can not be identified by other means or in the case of crimes carried out with the help of phone communication or other telecommunication means.

Draft law concerning the national security of Romania

Article 64

When there are the legal conditions, in the interest of national security, to eliminate a danger threatening the rule of law, democracy, economy, liberty and security of Romania, the services can be authorised to carry out operations collecting intelligence by acts that imply temporary restriction of some human rights.

The operations mentioned at item 1 are:
- interception of communications;
- mail control;
- secret audio/video recording of conversations or activities taking place in public or private places;
- covert penetration in premises where technical audio/video recording means are installed, maintained or collected, or secretly studied some res with operational importance.

There is a reason for the authorisation: preventing or discovering serious crimes, such as those against national security, life and private property, against the country's defence capacity or against peace and humanity.

Draft law concerning the protection of human rights in activities for achieving national security and national defence

Article 10

The operation of collecting intelligence through the acts that imply the temporarily restriction of some human rights to the Romanian citizens:
- surveillance and communication interception;
- mail control;
- secret audio/video recording of conversations or activities taking place in public or private places;
- covert penetration in premises where technical audio/video recording means are installed, maintained or collected, or secretly studied some res with operational importance or copied/collected intelligence through the technical operations.

Searching

The current legal framework for authorised searches is as follows.

The Code of Criminal Prosecution

Searching

Article 100

When a person who has been asked to deliver over an res or a document of those kinds mentioned in Article 98, if the individual covers up the existence or possession of those things, whenever it is necessary for discovering or collecting evidence, the criminal authority or the court can order a search.

The search can be a body search or a residence search.

Article 103

Seizing the res or documents and residence searching can be carried out between 6 a.m. and 8 p.m., and at other times only if the crime is flagrant or the search is to be carried out on public premises, by the criminal authority. A search started between 6 a.m. and 8 p.m. can be continued during the night. The prosecutor can undertake to seize res or documents and search a residence during the night also. "

Law No. 143/2000 concerning the suppression of drug trafficking and addiction

Article 24

A search can be carried out in locations where there are indications that a crime has taken place or that specific acts for committing a crime punishable by the law have been carried out, in accordance with the Code of Penal Prosecution.

Law No. 161/2003 concerning measures to ensure transparency in carrying out high public duties, public positions and business affairs, to prevent and punish corruption

Article 56

Whenever it is necessary to study a computer system or recorded material, to gain evidence, the qualified authority can order a search.

De lege ferenda

Article 100

A search can be a body search or a residence search.

When a person who has been asked to give up a res or a document of the kinds indicated in Article 98 denies possession, or when there are strong indications that a search is needed to find or collect evidence, the court, at the prosecutor's request, in a court investigation or ex officio during the prosecution, can issue a written order to make a search.

In emergency cases and where it is completely justified, during the criminal prosecution, the attorney can issue a written order for a search, being obliged to inform, as soon as possible, the court.

The search can be ordered only after criminal prosecution has started, aside from cases *in flagrante* and whenever the law mentions otherwise.

The search can be ordered before the criminal law process has started, only with the approval of the incriminated person.

Surveillance of computerised systems

Law No. 143/2000 concerning the suppression of illegal drug trafficking and consumption

Article 23

When there are indications that a person is preparing to commit a crime of those punishable by the current law or has committed such a crime, and is using communication and computerised systems, the proper authority with the prosecutor's permission will have access, for a specified period of time, to those systems and to monitor them.

Stipulations of the Code of Penal Prosecution, Articles 91_1-91_5, have to be applied in a suitable way.

Law No. 161/2003 concerning measures to ensure transparency in carrying out high public duties, public positions and business affairs, to prevent and punish corruption

Article 54

In emergency and in justified cases, if there are indications concerning the preparing or committing a crime by the help of computerised systems, a decision can be taken to collect evidence or identify the perpetrator, with the immediate preservation of computer data or other data referring to computerised traffic that are in danger of being destroyed or altered.

Article 57

Access to a computerised system and the recording or tapping of the communication in the computerised system are undertaken when they are of help in establishing the truth and for the correct identification of the existing situation or of the perpetrator, and these can not be carried out by means of other evidence.

So-called purchase and other so-called crimes

Law No. 143/2000 on illegal drug trafficking and consumption

Article 22

The policemen in the specialised structures acting as covert investigators, and their co-workers, can obtain drugs, chemical substances, pure or precursors, authorised by the prosecutor, in order to discover illegal activities and the persons involved in such activities.

The documents issued by the policemen and their co-workers, mentioned in the first item can be considered as evidence.

2. When and under which circumstances (e.g. criminal investigation, preliminary stage, etc.) can SITs be used?

As a general rule, as shown by the text presented under item I, SITs can be used, in the cases mentioned by law, if there are data or solid indications about preparing or committing a crime.

The concept of "solid indications", mentioned in the special law, is also used in the Code of Penal Prosecution and has the meaning of an action, circumstances or situation that is part of a system of closely connected indications, along with existing evidence that helps to discover the truth.

To complete these dispositions, the special laws establish, taking into account the subject to be regulated, cases and circumstances in which the public authorities can use special investigation techniques.

Thus, SITs can be used to collect information when the deed/crime cannot be discovered or the perpetrator/perpetrators cannot be identified by other means, or with a motive of prevention, or to be used as evidence during a process in court or in the criminal investigation.

The preventive reason they are used is emphasised by the Law No. 51/1991 on the national security of Romania. It mentions: "the existence of threats to national security represents a legal reason for the prosecutor to apply, in justified cases, in obedience to the Code of Penal Prosecution, for authorisation to undertake acts to collect information. As follows – communication interception, searching for information, documents or written papers obtaining which implies the need for access to a location or opening an object; taking or replacing a res or a document, the examination of the res and collecting the information it contains and the tapping, copying or gaining some excerpts by any means; installing the res, maintaining and taking those from the places where they were fixed.

In exceptional cases, to avoid imminent jeopardising of national security, these activities can be undertake with no authorisation, and permission may be obtained within a maximum of 48 hours from the moment they started.

3. Are there any specific features governing the use of SITs in relation to acts of terrorism? If so, please specify.

Acts of terrorism are included in the class of serious crime; in accordance with Law No. 218/2002 on the organisation and functioning of the Romanian police, to prevent and combat such acts, informants or cover policemen can be used.

In the same context, as is stressed in Law No. 51/1991 concerning the national security of Romania, terrorism as a threat to national security is one of the main directions of action of the intelligence services.

To prevent and combat such a phenomenon, the Romanian Intelligence Service, having the role of technical co-ordinator of the National System for prevention and countering of terrorism, is authorised to possess and use proper means to obtain, verify, analyse and store intelligence concerning national security, obeying the law (Law No. 14/1992 concerning the organisation and functioning of the Romanian Intelligence Service.)

4. How does the legal framework governing the use of SITs guarantee respect for human rights and individual freedoms, the principles of complementarity and proportionality? Is the authorisation to use SITs subject to time-limits? Which bodies and procedures are in place to supervise compliance with human rights standards and with the above-mentioned principles in the use of SITs? Is supervision automatic/systematic?

According to the effective legal regulations, the use of the techniques for gathering intelligence necessary for preventing and combating offences should not injure or impede in any way people's human rights and fundamental freedoms, their private life, honour and reputation.

The law protects all persons against such trespassing and violations. Persons guilty of illegally initiating, transmitting or carrying on such measures should be the subjects of a civil, administrative or penal lawsuit.

Thus, the necessary requirement for authorising the use of SITs is the existence of credible indications that a person has committed, is committing or is about to commit an offence, on the one hand, or that some specific papers or evidence related to this offence could be obtained using SITs.

According to the Penal Code, the prosecutor's authorisation lasts for the whole period necessary for recording (no longer than 30 days), except for cases where the law stipulates other provisions. When based on well-founded reasons, the authorisation can be extended under the same conditions for subsequent periods no longer than 30 days.

As an exception to this rule, Law No. 51/1991 concerning Romanian national security stipulates in Article 13 that "the mandate's period of validity cannot exceed 6 months. By request, based on well-founded reasons, the prosecutor is able to prolong the term of the mandate for periods no longer than 3 months each."

At the same time, Law No. 218/2002 concerning the establishment and co-ordination of the Romanian Police stipulates in Article 33 that "the prosecutor's authorisation will be issued in writing for a period of time no longer than 60 days and can be prolonged under the same conditions for other periods of 30 days each."

Any person considering that their rights and individual freedoms have been violated by the use of SITs can freely bring suit.

In cases of using SITs for activities aimed at ensuring national security, as a guarantee for respecting rights and fundamental freedoms, the Law concerning national security stipulates that "the citizen considering that their rights and fundamental freedoms have been violated by the use of the means written in paragraph 1 can inform any of the permanent defence and law enforcement committees belonging to the two chambers of the Parliament."

De lege ferenda, the Draft Law concerning Romanian national security allows every person considering that their rights have been violated to notify the People's Lawyer, an institution that acts to protect the rights and individual freedoms of citizens in their relations with the public authorities. According to Law No. 35/1997 concerning the establishment and organisation of the People's Lawyer institution, the public authorities have the legal obligation to inform or (if necessary) to submit the intelligence, papers or documents they have concerning requests received by the People's Lawyer and to ensure the necessary support for accomplishing its duties.

Moreover, the declared goal of the Draft Law concerning the preservation of rights and individual freedoms related to activities for ensuring national safety, defence and security is "to protect the individual freedoms of Romanian citizens related to their privilege of safe residence, of confidential communications, of intimate, family and private life as well as to regulate those procedures by which, based on the Constitution, the exercise of some rights and constitutional freedoms could be temporarily limited".

5. Which institutions are involved in the use of SITs and what is their role (e.g. law enforcement agencies, prosecutor's office, judicial authorities, etc.)? Which institutions can order and/or authorise the use of SITs? How does co-operation between these institutions work in practice?

The institutions involved in the use of SITs are as follows:
- The Romanian Police by its judicial authorities;
- The Romanian Police belongs to the Ministry of Interior and is the state's specialised institution that is in charge of the protection of people's rights and fundamental freedoms, of private and public property as well as the prevention and identification of criminal offences and the protection of public order and peace.
- The state's structures in charge of the protection of national security: the Romanian Secret Service, External Intelligence Service, Guard and Protection Service as well as the internal specialised structures belonging to the National Defence Ministry, Ministry of Interior and Ministry of Justice.
- The prosecutor, for those offences under his jurisdiction.
- The National Anti-Corruption General Attorney's Office – a self-ruling structure within the Ministry of Interior in charge of the prosecution of offences stipulated in Law No. 78/2000 concerning the prevention, identification and proscription of acts of corruption.

De lege lata, the authorisation of SITs is issued by the prosecutor.

The law regulating the use of SITs is the Penal Code: Article 91_1 of the Penal Code stipulates that the person issuing the authorisation is the prosecutor appointed by the prime prosecutor of the General Attorney's Office belonging to the Appeal Court.

The authorisation document is issued by the prosecutors specially appointed by the General Prosecutor of Romania (currently they are prosecutors of the General Attorney's Office belonging to the Appeal Court), at the request of the structures in charge of the national security's preservation.

The authority in charge of crimes of corruption is the National Anti-Corruption General Attorney's Office.

De lege ferenda, the Draft Law concerning the change and completion of the Penal Code, the projected Law concerning the Romanian national security and the projected Law concerning the protection of rights and fundamental freedoms within activities for the fulfilment of national safety, defence and security specify that corruption-related crimes are to become the responsibility of the judge.

As for the criminal law, the authorisation is to be issued by the president of the court that is to judge the case in the trial court (the council's chamber).

The authorisation by court orders in cases of the threats against the national safety, defence and security will be issued by the judges specially appointed by the Supreme Court of Justice.

6. Are there any specialised counter-terrorism institutions? What is their role in the use of SITs?

In order to achieve the goals of the National Strategy for Preventing and Countering Terrorism, there was established a mechanism (National System for Preventing and Countering Terrorism) for ensuring, organising and carrying out, in an integrated manner, co-operation between institutions aimed at the optimal fulfilment of all tasks subsumed in the counter-terrorism national efforts.

The National System for Preventing and Countering Terrorism includes the following institutions:
- the Supreme Council for National Defence, strategic co-ordination role;
- the Romanian Secret Service, the national authority in the field of preventing and combating terrorism – technical co-ordination role;
- some ministries;
- the External Intelligence Service, the Guard and Protection Service, the Special Telecommunication Service;
- the General Attorney's Office belonging to the Appeal Court – in charge of co-ordination and monitoring of the proceedings (carried out by the prosecutors specially appointed) for identifying and punishing the perpetrators of any crime consisting in terrorist acts or any other action facilitating or supporting the perpetration of such acts;
- the National Bank of Romania;
- national authorities.

For a continuous and optimal accomplishment of their tasks, the institutions belonging to the National System for Preventing and Countering Terrorism decide the nature of their consultative, co-operative and current partnership relations with other institutions and bodies in Romania and abroad.

In accordance with their legal responsibilities, the institutions organise and carry out activities for collecting terrorism-related data and intelligence from the national soil and abroad in order to prevent, counter and suppress the terrorist threats against the Romanian national security.

In this respect, the institutions are allowed to have and use the means and methods for obtaining, checking, storing, protecting, exploiting and transmitting the necessary intelligence in accordance with their legal duties.

7. Which measures have been adopted in order to facilitate international co-operation (e.g. joint investigation teams)? Can the SITs listed in reply to question 1 be used in cross-border settings?

The institutions in charge of preventing and countering crimes have established (based on the co-operation fields) liaison structures that ensure permanent consultative discussions with the foreign liaison structures dealing with the same offences and with the specialised organisations.

According to Law No. 704/2001 concerning international judicial assistance in the penal domain, at another country's request, Romania gives full assistance in any proceedings concerning offences that, by the time of the request, enter under the jurisdiction of the respective state's legal authorities.

International judicial assistance in the penal domain covers the following:
- notifying the procedural documents necessary in a penal trial;
- establishing the rogatory committees;
- the presence in the soliciting state of the witnesses, experts and defendants;
- the criminal record;
- measures concerning the postponement of the verdict or suspension of the sentence, release on parole, postponement of the sentence or cessation of the sentence;
- the official request for the lawsuit;
- other forms of co-operation, including those deriving from the international agreements concerning the prevention and countering of terrorism.

The requests of judicial assistance received by the Romanian authorities are resolved based on the Romanian internal legal system.

The international rogatory committee in the penal domain is a form of international judicial assistance consisting in entrusting power by some state's judicial authority to another similar authority in another state for carrying out, in its name, some judicial activities concerning a certain penal case.

The subjects of the request for the rogatory committee are as follows:
a. Accomplishing the lawsuit-related activities, such as: locating and identifying the persons and objects; interviewing the defendant; hearing the plaintiff, the other sides, the witnesses and experts as well as confrontation; searches, acts of sequestration and asset confiscation as well as the preservation of the assets of the plaintiffs; local investigations, expert evaluations; submitting the intelligence resulted from communications monitoring, audio/video surveillance, temporarily suspending privacy protected by law (concerning bank accounts, commercial transactions, personal correspondence, etc.), analysing archived documents and special files, and other forms of the legal suit.
b. Transmitting the evidence;
c. Transmitting the documents and files.

Law No. 39/2003 concerning the prevention and countering of organised crime stipulates that "at the request of the Romanian or other countries' authorities, Romania can be the host of some joint inquiries aimed at preventing and combating the transnational crimes committed by criminal organised groups." The Romanian authorities' representatives can attend joint inquiries held on other states' soil, in accordance with their legislation.

Based on Law No. 161/2003 concerning the measures for ensuring transparency in the performance of public responsibilities and duties and in the business environment and for preventing and punishing acts of corruption "the Romanian judicial authorities directly co-operate (in accordance with the law and obeying the obligations resulted from the international judicial tools that Romania is a party to) with the institutions abroad in charge with similar responsibilities". At the request of the Romanian competent authorities or those belonging to other states, Romania can be the host of some joint inquiries aimed at preventing and combating the cybernetic crimes.

Within the framework of international co-operation, the foreign competent authorities can request the Service for combating cybernetic crimes to immediately preserve the computerised data or those data concerning computer-operated traffic existing in an computer system in Romania on which the foreign authority is to submit an international judicial assistance request.

Russian Federation

1. Please indicate the SITs used in your country, the respective legal framework governing their use and their legal definition, if any.

The following special investigation techniques, mentioned in the questionnaire, are being used in Russian Federation:
- undercover operations (including covert investigations),
- front store operation (e.g. undercover company),
- informants,
- controlled delivery,
- observation (including cross-border observation),
- electronic surveillance,
- bugging (private or public premises),
- interception of communications (telephone, fax, e-mait, mail, public and private networks),
- searches (including of premises, of objects, e.g. computers, cars, by various means including scanning),
- cross-border (hot) pursuit, and
- pseudo-purchases or other "pseudo-offences".

There is no legal basis provided by Russian legislation for the activities of *agents provocateurs*.

Special Investigation Techniques and legal framework

The legal framework governing the use of special investigation techniques (operational-search measures) is the Federal Law On the Operational-Search Activity adopted on 12 August 1995, the Code of Criminal Procedure of the Russian Federation and other legislative acts.

According to the Russian legislation, while performing an operational-search activity, the following special investigation techniques may be carried out:
- interviewing citizens,
- making inquiries,
- collection of samples for comparative study,
- controlled purchase,
- examination of objects and documents,
- surveillance,
- identification of persons,
- examination of premises, buildings, structures and sites, and of means of transport,
- exerting control over mail, telegraph and other kinds of communications,
- wiretapping of telephone conversations (bugging),
- taking information off technical communications channels,

- operational implanting,
- controlled delivery, and
- operational experiment.

In the course of carrying out operational-search measures, use shall be made of information systems, audio and video recordings, cinema films and photographs, as well as other kinds of technical and suchlike means, which do not cause damage to the life and health of people and do not inflict any harm upon the natural environment.

Operational-search measures, involved in controlling mail, telegraph and other kinds of communications, wiretapping of telephone conversations with link-up to station apparatus of enterprises, institutions and organisations, regardless of their forms of ownership, as well as of the natural and legal persons who render services and provide the means of communication, with taking information off technical communications channels, shall be carried out using the operational-technical forces and the means of the federal security bodies and of the internal affairs bodies in conformity with the procedure, defined by the inter-departmental normative acts or by agreements, signed between the bodies engaged in the operational-search activity.

The officials of the bodies engaged in the operational-search activity shall fulfil its tasks by personally taking part in organising and in carrying out the operational-search measures, while drawing on the assistance of official persons and of specialists possessing scientific, technical and other kinds of specific knowledge, as well as of certain citizens with their consent, on both the open and the covert principle.

2. When and under which circumstances (e.g. criminal investigation, preliminary stage, etc.) can SITs be used?

The grounds for launching operational-search measures shall be:

1. The existence of an instituted criminal case.

2. Information that has become known to the bodies engaged in the operational-search activity:
    1) from indications that an unlawful act is being prepared or committed, or has been perpetrated, as well as on the persons who are preparing or committing it or have perpetrated it, if the information is insufficient to resolve the question of instituting a criminal case;
    2) on the events or the actions, creating a threat to the state, military, economic or ecological security of the Russian Federation;
    3) on persons fleeing from the bodies of inquest and of investigation, and from the court, or on those avoiding the criminal punishment;
    4) on missing persons and on finding unidentified corpses.

3.   Orders from the investigator or from the inquiry body, instructions from the prosecutor or the ruling of the court on criminal cases in the process of examination.

4.   The inquiries of other bodies performing the operational-search activity, on the grounds, indicated in the-present Article.

5.   A decision on applying the measures, aimed at ensuring the security of protected persons, implemented by the specially authorised state bodies, in conformity with the procedure envisaged by the legislation of the Russian Federation.

6.   The inquiries of international law enforcement organisations and of the law enforcement bodies of foreign states in conformity with the international treaties of the Russian Federation.

The bodies carrying out the operational-search activity shall also have the right to collect information, necessary for passing decisions, within the scope of their jurisdiction:

1.   On giving access to the information, which is a state secret;

2.   On the admittance to different kinds of work, connected with the exploitation of objects presenting a heightened threat to the life and health of the people, as well as to the environment.

3.   On the admittance to participation in the operational-search activity or on access to the materials, obtained as a result of its performance.

4.   On establishing or on maintaining co-operative relations with a person when preparing and carrying out the operational-search measures.

5.   On providing security for the bodies engaged in the operational-search activity.

6.   On issuing permits for private detectives and guarding activity.

The citizenship, nationality and sex, the place of residence, the property, the official and social position, affiliation to non-government associations, the attitude towards religion and the political views of individual persons shall not be an obstacle to launching with respect to them operational-search measures on the territory of the Russian Federation.

The carrying out of operational-search measures that restrict the constitutional rights of citizens to privacy of correspondence, telephone conversations, mail, telegraph and other communications, passed through electric communication system and through the mails, as well as the right to inviolability of the home, shall be admitted on the grounds of a court decision and if there is information:

1. On indications of an unlawful action being prepared or committed, or already perpetrated, by which it is necessary to carry out a preliminary investigation.

2. On persons who are preparing or committing, or have perpetrated, an unlawful action, by which it is necessary to carry out a preliminary investigation.

3. On events or actions creating a threat to the state, military, economic or ecological security of the Russian Federation.

In cases that cannot be procrastinated and which may lead to perpetrating a grave crime, and also if there is information on events and actions creating a threat to the state, military, economic or ecological security of the Russian Federation, the carrying out of operational-search measures, envisaged in the second part of the present Article, shall be admitted on the ground of a reasoned decision of one of the heads of the body engaged in the operational-search activity, with an obligatory notification within 24 hours of the court (the judge). In the course of 48 hours from the moment of starting the operational-search measure, the body carrying it out shall be obliged to obtain a court decision on carrying out such an operational-search measure, or to cease its carrying out.

If a threat to life, health and property of individual persons arises, it shall be admitted upon their application or with their consent in written form, to wiretap conversations held by their telephones, on the grounds of the decision, approved by the head of the body, engaged in the operational-search activity, with an obligatory notification within 48 hours of the corresponding court (the judge).

Controlled purchase or controlled delivery of things, substances and products, whose free realisation is forbidden or whose circulation is restricted, as well as operational experiment or operational implanting of official persons of the bodies engaged in the operational-search activity, as well as of persons who render them assistance, shall be effected on the grounds of the decision approved by the head of the body engaged in the operational-search the activity.

Carrying out an operational-search experiment shall be allowed only for the purposes of exposing, preventing, suppressing and revealing a grave crime, as well as for the purposes of exposing and identifying the persons who are preparing, committing or have perpetrated crimes.

3.   Are there any specific features governing the use of SITs in relation to acts of terrorism? If so, please specify.

The use of results of operational-search activity

The results of operational-search activity may be used to prepare and to implement investigatory and judicial actions, to carry out operational-search measures involved in exposure prevention, suppression and revelation of crimes, in the exposure and identification of persons preparing and committing them or who have perpetrated them, and also to search for persons who have fled from the inquiry bodies, from the investigation and the trial, are avoiding execution of punishment or are missing.

The results of operational-search activity may serve as a pretext and the ground for instituting a criminal case, may be presented to the inquiry body, to the prosecutor or to the court that has instituted proceedings on the criminal case, and may also be used to prove criminal cases in conformity with the provisions of the criminal-procedural legislation of the Russian Federation, regulating the collection, checking and appraisal of proofs.

The results of operational-search activity shall be presented to the inquiry body, to the prosecutor or to the court on the grounds of the decision of the head of the body engaged in the operational-search activity, in conformity with the procedure stipulated by the departmental normative acts.

4. How does the legal framework governing the use of SITs guarantee respect for human rights and individual freedoms, the principles of subsidiarity and proportionality? Is the authorisation to use SITs subject to time-limits? Which bodies and procedures are in place to supervise compliance with human rights standards and with the above-mentioned principles in the use of SITs? Is supervision automatic/systematic?

Observation of the rights and freedoms of man and the citizen, while performing operational-search activity

The performance of operational-search activity to achieve goals and to fulfill tasks, not stipulated by the Law, shall not be admitted.

The person, who believes that the actions of bodies, engaged in operational-search activity, have violated his rights and freedoms, shall have the right to appeal against these actions with the higher placed body, engaged in the operational-search activity, with the Prosecutor or with the court.

The person whose guilt in the perpetration of the crime was not proved in conformity with law-established procedure, i.e. the institution of court proceedings against whom was refused, or the court proceedings on the criminal case against whom were terminated in connection with the absence of the criminal event or the absence of the corpus delicti, and who puts forward facts proving that operational-search measures were launched against him, and believes that in doing this his rights were violated, has the right to demand that the body that performed the operational-search activity provide to him data on the information that it has collected on him, within limits compatible with the requirements of clandestinity and excluding the possibility of divulging any state secret. If the provision of the claimed data is refused, or if the said person believes that the data have not been supplied to him in full, he has the right to appeal against this to the court. In the course of the case being examined in the court, the duty to prove that the refusal to supply the data to this person, including in full, is well-grounded, shall lie with the corresponding body engaged in the operational-search activity.

To ensure an exhaustive and comprehensive examination of the case, the body performing the operational-search activity shall be obliged to supply to the judge, upon his demand, the operational-official documents containing information on the persons planted into organised criminal groups, as well as on the persons, rendering them assistance on the confidential principle, the supply of which was refused to the plaintiff.

If the decision of the body engaged in the operational-search activity, on the refusal to provide the necessary information to the plaintiff, is recognised as ungrounded, the judge may oblige the said body to supply to the plaintiff the information, stipulated in the third part of the present Article.

The materials concerning the persons, whose guilt in perpetrating the crime is not proved in the law-established procedure, obtained as a result of carrying out the operational-search measures, shall be kept for one year, after which they shall be destroyed, unless otherwise required by official interests or by justice. Three months prior to the date fixed for the destruction of the materials, reflecting the results of the operational-search measures, carried out on the grounds of the court decision, the corresponding judge shall be informed about this.

The bodies (official persons) engaged in the operational-search activity shall be forbidden:
- to carry out operational-search measures in the interest of a certain political party, a non-governmental or religious association;
- to covertly participate in the work of federal state power bodies, of state power bodies of subjects of the Russian Federation and of local self-government bodies, as well as in the activity of political parties, or public and religious associations, registered in conformity with established procedure and not banned, in order to exert an impact on the nature of their activity;
- to divulge information that infringes the inviolability of private life, personal and family secrets, the honour and good name of citizens, and which has become known in the course of carrying out operational-search measures, without the citizens' consent, with the exception of those cases stipulated by federal laws.

If the body (the official person), engaged in the operational-search activity, violates the rights and legitimate interests of the natural and of legal persons, the higher placed body, Prosecutor or judge shall be obliged to take measures, in conformity with the legislation of the Russian Federation, for the re-institution of these rights and legitimate interests, and for making good the harm thus done.

Violations of the present Federal Law, committed in performing an operational-search activity, shall entail responsibility, as stipulated by the legislation of the Russian Federation.

5. Which institutions are involved in the use of SITs and what is their role (e.g. law enforcement agencies, prosecutor's office, judicial authorities, etc.)? Which institutions can order and/or authorise the use of SITs? How does co-operation between these institutions work in practice ?

6. Are there any specialised counter-terrorism institutions? What is their role in the use of SITs?

Control over operational-search activity

Control over operational-search activity shall be exerted by the President of the Russian Federation, by the Federal Assembly of the Russian Federation and by the Government of the Russian Federation, within the scope of the jurisdiction defined by the Constitution of the Russian Federation, the federal constitutional laws and the federal laws.

Prosecutor's supervision of operational-search activity

Execution of the laws of the Russian Federation by bodies engaged in operational-search activity shall be supervised by the Prosecutor-General of the Russian Federation and by the prosecutors, authorised by him.

On the inquiry of the authorised prosecutor in connection with the materials, information and appeals of citizens on the violation of laws in carrying out operational-search measures, which have come in to the Prosecutor's Office, and also when checking the established order of carrying out operational-search measures and the legality of decisions passed in doing this, the heads of the body engaged in operational-search activity, shall present to the said prosecutor the operational-official documents that have served as the ground for launching these measures.

Information on persons planted in organised criminal groups, and on the undercover officers of the bodies engaged in operational-search activity, as well as on those persons who are rendering or were rendering assistance to these bodies on the confidential principle, shall be presented to the prosecutor only with written consent of the said persons, with the exception of cases when they shall be brought to criminal responsibility. Information on the organisation, on tactics, methods and means of performing operational-search activity shall not be subject to the prosecutor's supervision.

The heads of the Prosecutor's Office bodies create the conditions that would ensure protection of the information contained in operational-official documents, presented to the prosecutor.

Departmental control

The heads of those bodies engaged in operational-search activity bear personal responsibility for the observation of legality, while organising and carrying out operational-search measures.

Bodies engaged in operational-search activity

The right to engage in operational-search activity on the territory of the Russian Federation shall be granted to the operational sub-units:
- of the internal affairs bodies of the Russian Federation (MVD),
- of the Federal Security Service bodies (FSB),
- of the Federal Tax Police bodies,
- of the federal bodies of the Federal Protection Service,
- of the bodies of the Frontier Guards Service of the Russian Federation,
- of the customs service bodies of the Russian Federation,
- of the intelligence service bodies of the Russian Federation,
- of the Ministry of Justice of the Russian Federation.

The operational sub-units of the intelligence service body of the Ministry of Defence of the Russian Federation and of the intelligence service body of the Federal Agency for Governmental Communications and Information, shall carry out operational-search measures only for the purpose of ensuring the security of the said intelligence service bodies and if the carrying out of these measures does not infringe upon the jurisdiction of the bodies, pointed out in Items 1-8.

While fulfilling the tasks of operational-search activity, the bodies authorised to perform it shall be obliged:

1. To launch, within the scope of their jurisdiction, all the necessary measures to protect the constitutional rights and freedoms of man and the citizen, as well as property, and also to provide for the security of society and of the state.

2. To execute, within the scope of their jurisdiction, the written orders of the inquiry body and of the investigator, the instructions of the prosecutor and the decisions of the court on carrying out operational-search measures in the criminal cases they have accepted for examination.

3. To answer, on the grounds of and in conformity with the procedure stipulated by the international treaties of the Russian Federation, the

inquiries of the corresponding international law-enforcement organisations, of the law-enforcement bodies and of the special services of foreign states.

4. To inform the other bodies engaged in operational-search activity on the territory of the Russian Federation about the facts of unlawful activity, which have become known to them and which are referred to the jurisdiction of these bodies, and to render the necessary assistance to these bodies.

5. To observe the rules of clandestine behaviour, while performing operational-search activity.

6. To assist in providing, in conformity with the procedure established by the legislation of the Russian Federation for the security and for the maintenance of the property of its officers, of persons rendering assistance to the bodies engaged in the operational-search activity, of the participants in criminal court proceedings, as well as of the family members and close relatives of the said persons from criminal attempts.

7. Which measures have been adopted in order to facilitate international co-operation (e.g. joint investigation teams)? Can the SITs listed in reply to question 1 be used in cross-border settings?

8. What use can be made of SIT in the context of mutual legal assistance?

9. How can the use of SITs be improved? Please provide any comments/proposals concerning the implementation of the terms of reference of the PC-TI and in particular the use and regulation of SITs.

Mutual legal assistance

While fulfilling the tasks of the operational-search activity, defined by the present Federal Law, the bodies authorised to perform it are obliged to answer, on the grounds of and in conformity with the procedure stipulated by the international treaties of the Russian Federation, the inquiries of the corresponding international law-enforcement organisations, of the law-enforcement bodies and of the special services of foreign states.

The provisions of mutual legal assistance in criminal matters are based on the Constitution of the Russian Federation, European Convention on Extradition of 1957 with Protocols Additional to it of 1975 and 1978, European Convention on Mutual Assistance in Criminal Matters of 1959 with Protocol Additional to it of 1978, Code of Criminal Procedure of the Russian Federation of 2001, and so on.

The Russian Federation, guided by the interests of ensuring the security of person, society and state, on its territory carries out the criminal prosecution of persons involved in terrorist activities, including cases where acts of terrorism were planned or carried out outside its borders, but damaging the Russian Federation, and in other cases provided for by international agreements of the Russian Federation.

The activities of the provision of mutual legal assistance in criminal matters are based on the commonly accepted principles and norms of international law, constitutional principles of law, respect and observance of human and civil rights and freedoms, as well as on the respective agreements of the Russian Federation.

In accordance with the Russian legislation in force, extradition issues are within the competence of the General Prosecutor's Office of the Russian Federation.

The following authorities are competent in providing mutual legal assistance in criminal matters:
- The Supreme Court of the Russian Federation – in issues of judicial activities of the Supreme Court of the Russian Federation; and Ministry of Justice of the Russian Federation – issues of activities of other courts;
- Ministry of the Interior (MVD), Federal Security Service (FSB) and Federal Tax Police Service (FSNP) of Russia – relating to requests requiring no sanction of prosecutor or a judge and connected with conducting an inquiry and a preliminary investigation on the cases within their competence;
- The General Prosecutor's Office of the Russian Federation – in all other cases of conducting an inquiry and a preliminary investigation.

In practice the General Prosecutor's Office of the Russian Federation deals practically with all requests on mutual legal assistance in criminal matters. Permission for the movement in transit of a person placed under detention also shall be requested at the General Prosecutor's Office of the Russian Federation.

Requests for legal assistance sent to the Russian Federation with attached materials should be accompanied by translations into Russian.

Slovak Republic

1.   Please indicate the SITs used in your country, the respective legal framework governing their use and their legal definition, if any.

The general legal framework for the SITs used in the Slovak Republic is given in two legal instruments:
- Code of Criminal Procedure – Act No. 141/1961 Coll. as amended;
- Act No. 171/1993 Coll. on Police Force as amended (hereinafter referred as "Act on the Police Force").

Some details concerning the SITs are specified within the orders of the Minister of the Interior (e.g. telephone interception, observation, preparation, training and use of special undercover agents).

Please see Appendix 1, at end of this section.

2.   When and under which circumstances (e.g. criminal investigation, preliminary stage, etc.) can SITs be used?

At the stage of verification of information and/or criminal police investigation, the provisions of the Act on the Police Force are used. If necessary, non-repetitive activity and/or no-delay (urgent) activity are used, under the relevant provisions of the Code of Criminal Procedure.

3.   Are there any specific features governing the use of SITs in relation to acts of terrorism? If so, please specify.

There are no specific features governing the use of SITs in relation to acts of terrorism in Slovak legislation. General rules on SITs apply also in such cases.

4.   How does the legal framework governing the use of SITs guarantee respect for human rights and individual freedoms, the principles of subsidiarity and proportionality? Is the authorisation to use SITs subject to time-limits? Which bodies and procedures are in place to supervise compliance with human rights standards and with the above-mentioned principles in the use of SITs? Is supervision automatic/systematic?

The Constitution of the Slovak Republic as well as the relevant international agreements in the field of human rights and individual freedoms are considered as the general provisions for the protection of human rights. Any intervention into human rights shall be regulated only by law, which cannot be contrary to the regulation given in the constitution and international treaties binding on the Slovak Republic (see Appendix 2).

The authorisation to use SITs is subject to time-limits. Supervision depends on the nature of the SIT being used and on the stage of the procedure, but the judicial authorities (alongside other bodies) are the supervision and ordering bodies in most cases. Evidence shall be obtained in a lawful way; otherwise it will be refused.

According to Section 12, paragraph 2 of the Code of Criminal Procedure:
> (2) The term "police bodies" means the competent bodies of the Police Force. The competent bodies of the Military Police shall have the same status in proceedings held against members of the armed forces, the competent bodies of the Prison Force and Judicial Guard of the Slovak Republic shall have the same status in proceedings against members of that Force and persons serving imprisonment sentences or held in custodial detention, the competent bodies of the Railway Police of the Slovak Republic shall have the same status in proceedings against members of that Force and persons who committed crimes within the bounds of railway tracks and sidings, customs authorities shall have the same competence for offences involving the violation of customs regulations, and the captains of long-distance vessels shall have the same competence for criminal offences committed on their ships.

Supervision is automatic.

5. Which institutions are involved in the use of SITs and what is their role (e.g. law enforcement agencies, prosecutor's office, judicial authorities, etc.)? Which institutions can order and/or authorise the use of SITs? How does co-operation between these institutions work in practice?

Please see answers under 1 and 4 c.

6. Are there any specialised counter-terrorism institutions? What is their role in the use of SITs?

The specialised counter-terrorism institutions are as follows:
- Counter-Terrorism Department, Bureau of Combat against Organised Crime, Criminal and Financial Police Administration, Presidium of the Police Force;
- Slovak Intelligence Service (information gathering).

7. Which measures have been adopted in order to facilitate international co-operation (e.g. joint investigation teams)? Can the SITs listed in reply to question 1 be used in cross-border settings?

Measures to facilitate international co-operation

On international co-operation, the amendment to the Act on the Police Force introduced new provisions (Sections 77a–77c) as follows:

Section 77a

(1) The Police Force co-operate with police of other states, with international police organisations, international bodies and bodies with official status on the territories of other states, particularly by exchanging information, exchanging liaison officers, and eventually by other forms.

(2) The Police Force can also perform the tasks of a police force outside the territory of the Slovak Republic, if so stated in the international treaties to which the Slovak Republic is bound, or by agreement of the parties concerned. Delegation of the police officers to operate abroad on state service is within the competence of the minister.

(3) The ministry for performance of the tasks of the Police Force can also delegate police officers to go outside the territory of the Slovak Republic to the international police organisations, other states' police forces, international peace missions, international operations of civil crisis management, or by agreement concluded with the Ministry of Foreign Affairs of the Slovak Republic to diplomatic missions of the Slovak Republic or to international organisations.

Section 77b

(1) A Police Officer is authorised to operate also on the territory of other state according to conditions, in the scope and by the means stated in the international treaty to which the Slovak Republic is bound,
a) on the ground of a decision of the Government of the Slovak Republic on participation in a peace operation according to the decision of a international organisation of which the Slovak Republic is a member and on which the Slovak Republic has concluded relevant agreements,
b) if the officer was delegated for performance of the tasks on the ground of a decision of the Minister and with the approval of an appropriate body of the foreign state or at the request of an appropriate body of another state.

(2) In the course of the delegation of the police officer to go abroad, according to paragraph 1, is being preceded according to special Act.

Section 77c

(1) A police officer of another state can, according to conditions, in the scope and by the means stated in an international treaty to which the Slovak Republic is bound, carry out the authority and duties of a police officer of the Slovak Republic.

(2) If no international treaties have been concluded, to which the Slovak Republic is bound, and if it is necessary for performance of tasks of the Police Force, it is possible, with approval of the minister or a delegated

person and with the approval of an appropriate body of the foreign state, to utilise within the scope stated by this act a police officer of another state:

    a)   as a legalised person or agent,
    b)   for carrying out a simulated transfer of things,
    c)   for the surveillance of persons or things, or
    d)   for use of information and technical means.

(3) A police officer manages an activity of the police officer of another state in accordance with paragraph 2.

(4) In case of compensation for damage in connection with carrying out tasks, this is in accordance with paragraph 2, Section 78 and any special Act.

SITs in cross-border operations

Bi- or multi-lateral agreement is in such cases required, and can be used only in a frame of such agreement.

8.   What use can be made of SITs in the context of mutual legal assistance?

Any use to the extent allowed by international agreements or arrangements based on reciprocity.

9. How can the use of SITs be improved? Please provide any comments/proposals concerning the implementation of the terms of reference of the PC-TI and in particular the use and regulation of SITs.

The existing legal framework is sufficient. No improvement is necessary at the moment.

Appendix 1

Selected provisions of the Code of Criminal Procedure of the Slovak Republic
regarding special investigation techniques in relation to acts of terrorism

Title Three
Surrender and Seizure of a Thing

Section 78
Duty to Surrender a Thing

(1) Whoever is in the possession of a thing relevant for criminal proceedings shall have the duty to hand it over, when requested, to the court, prosecutor, investigator or police authority; if the purpose of criminal proceedings requires it, he shall have the duty to surrender, when requested, such thing to these bodies.

(2) The duty under paragraph 1 shall not apply to a written document whose content deals with questions barred from interrogation unless the confidentiality or non-disclosure obligation has been lifted (Section 99).

(3) The authority to request that a thing be surrendered shall be vested with the presiding judge of a panel or, in pre-trial proceedings, a prosecutor, an investigator or a police body.

Section 79
Seizure of a Thing

(1) If a thing relevant for criminal proceedings is not surrendered upon request by the person who has it in his possession, it may be seized upon an order issued by the presiding judge of a panel or, in pre-trial proceedings, by a prosecutor, investigator or police authority. An investigator or a police body shall issue such order only upon a prior authorisation by a prosecutor.

(2) If the body having issued the seizure order does not seize the object concerned itself, the seizure shall be effected by the police on the basis of an order.

(3) Without a prior authorisation under paragraph 1 an investigator or a police body may issue an order only if such prior authorisation cannot be obtained and if the matter is urgent.

(4) Whenever possible, a person who is not involved in the case shall be present during the seizure of a thing.

(5) The report on the surrender and seizure of a thing shall give also an accurate description of the thing surrendered or seized which is sufficient to identify such thing.

(6) The person who surrendered or had seized from them a thing shall be immediately issued a certificate on the taking of the thing or a copy of the report.

Section 79c
Placing an Account on Hold

(1) If money held in a bank account is relevant for criminal proceedings held in respect of crimes specified under separate legislation, the presiding judge of a panel or, in pre-trial proceedings, a prosecutor may issue an order to place the account on hold.

(2) In cases of emergency, a prosecutor may also issue an order pursuant to paragraph 1 outside pre-trial proceedings. Unless such order is confirmed within at most three days by a judge, it becomes null and void.

(3) The order pursuant to paragraphs 1 and 2 shall be issued in writing and shall give the justification. It shall always specify the financial amount placed on hold and its currency. As regards orders issued under paragraphs 1 and 2 and unless the presiding judge of a panel or prosecutor decides otherwise the financial amount placed on hold shall be barred from any disposition orders.

(4) If it is no longer necessary to keep the account on hold for the purposes of criminal proceedings, the order is withdrawn. If the surety is lower than the originally specified amount, the amount placed on hold shall be reduced. The ruling on canceling or reducing the surety shall be made by the presiding judge of a panel or, in pre-trial proceedings, by a prosecutor.

(5) An order under paragraph 1 and 2 shall always be delivered to the bank concerned. It shall be served on the owner of the account only if the presiding judge or the prosecutor has issued a ruling to this effect.

Section 79d
Attachment of registered securities

(1) Where the registered securities are materially relevant for criminal proceedings, the presiding judge of a panel and the prosecutor during formal investigation may issue an order requesting registration of the suspension of the right of disposal with the securities.

(2) Where the attachment of registered securities is no longer required for the purposes of criminal proceedings, the presiding judge of a panel and the prosecutor during formal investigation shall forthwith issue an order requesting registration of the withdrawal of the suspension of the right of disposal with the securities.

(3) The order pursuant to paragraphs 1 and 2 shall be issued in writing and duly justified.

Section 80
Restituting the Thing

(1) If the thing surrendered under Section 78 or seized under Section 79 is no longer needed for the purpose of the proceedings and if its forfeiture or confiscation is not considered, it shall be restored to the person who surrendered it or from whom it has been seized. If it is claimed by another person, it shall be restored to that person whose title to the thing is uncontested. When in doubt, the thing is deposited at the court and the person claiming the title to the thing shall be notified to lodge its claim through civil action. If the person having an unquestionable right to the thing fails to reclaim it when requested to do so, the thing shall be sold and the amount obtained shall be deposited at the court. The sale shall abide, as applicable, by the rules on the judicial sale of movable things obtained by execution.

(2) If a thing that cannot be restored or surrendered under paragraph 1 is perishable and there is a danger of spoilage, it shall be sold and the amount received shall be deposited at the court. As applicable, the sale shall be governed by the rules on judicial sale of movable things obtained by execution.

(3) Rulings made under paragraphs 1 and 2 shall be made by the presiding judge of a panel or, in pre-trial proceedings, by a prosecutor, an investigator or a police authority. The ruling on the restitution and surrendering of a thing and on its safekeeping shall be liable for complaint having a suspensive effect.

Section 81

(1) If the accused surrendered or had seized from them a thing obtained or probably obtained by means of crime and if the owner of the thing is not known or if the whereabouts of the injured party are not known, the description of the thing shall be publicly announced. The announcement shall be made in the manner that is most likely to lead to reaching the injured party and shall ask the injured party to claim the object within six months from the announcement.

(2) If a different party than the accused claims the thing within the time-limit under paragraph 1, then Section 80 paragraph 1 shall apply. If no

other party has claimed the thing, then the thing itself or the amount obtained for the sale of a perishable thing shall be surrendered to the accused on his request, unless he gained possession of the thing through crime. If the thing was obtained through crime or if the accused did not claim it, the thing shall be handed over to the body competent under separate prescriptions that will proceed with its sale. This shall not prejudice the right of the owner to claim the amount received for the sale of the thing.

(3) If the thing is worthless, it can be destroyed and, if it has a trifling value, it may be handed over to the body competent under separate legislation for sale; in either case, no previous announcement of its description shall be required.

(4) The measures and rulings under paragraphs 1 to 3 shall be made by the presiding judge of a panel or, in pre-trial proceedings, by a prosecutor, an investigator or a police body. The ruling on surrendering a thing, on handing a thing over to the body competent under separate legislation for the sale or for the destruction of the thing shall be liable for complaint having a suspensive effect.

Title Four
House search and search of a person, search of other premises and property, right of entering a dwelling, other premises and property

Section 82
The grounds for conducting the search of a house and of a person, search of other premises and property

(1) House search may be conducted if there are reasonable grounds to believe that a thing relevant for criminal proceedings may be found or a person suspected of crime is hiding in that house or other places used for residential purposes or premises attached to them (dwellings).

(2) In there are grounds under paragraph 1 it shall be possible to search also premises that do not serve residential purposes (other premises) and property that is not open to the public.

(3) Search of a person may be conducted if there are reasonable grounds to believe that the person concerned has on him a thing relevant for criminal proceedings.

(4) A detained person, an arrested person or a person being taken into custody may also be searched if there are reasonable grounds to believe that he carries a weapon or other thing which constitutes a threat to the life or health of that or another person.

Section 83
House Search Warrant

(1) A house search warrant shall be issued by the presiding judge of a panel or, in pre-trial proceedings, by a judge on application by a prosecutor. In cases of emergency, such a warrant may be issued by the presiding judge of a panel or a judge of the court in whose district the search is to be conducted rather than the competent presiding judge of a panel or a judge (Section 18). The house search warrant shall be in writing and contain the justification. It shall be served on the person whose home is to be searched at the time of the search and, if this is not possible, not later than 24 hours after the impediment that prevented the service was lifted.

(2) House search ordered by the presiding judge of a panel or a judge shall be conducted by a police body or, in pre-trial proceedings; it may also be conducted by an investigator.

Section 83a
Warrant for Searching Other Premises and Property

(1) A warrant for searching other premises or property shall be issued by a judge or the presiding judge of a panel or, in pre-trial proceedings, by a prosecutor, investigator or a police body. An investigator or a police body shall need a prior authorisation by a prosecutor. The warrant shall be issued in writing and shall contain the justification. It shall be served on the owner or the user of premises or property, or an employee thereof, at the time of the search and, if this is not possible, immediately after the impediment that prevented the service was lifted.

(2) The search of other premises or property shall be conducted by the body which issued the warrant or, at its order, by a police body.

(3) In the absence of a warrant or authorisation pursuant to paragraph 1, an investigator or a police body may conduct the search of other premises or property only if such warrant or authorisation could not be secured in advance and in cases of emergency, or if it involves a person caught in the act of committing a crime or a person in respect of which an arrest warrant was issued. Such procedure shall, however, be immediately reported to the body authorised to issue the warrant or to grant the authorisation pursuant to paragraph 1.

Section 83b
Warrant for the Search of a Person

(1) The warrant to conduct the search of a person shall be issued by a judge or the presiding judge of a panel or, in pre-trial proceedings, by a prosecutor; upon the authorisation by the latter it may be issued by an investigator or a police body.

(2) The search of a person shall not be conducted by the body that issued the warrant; on its order, it shall be carried out by a police body.

(3) The search of a person shall always be conducted by a person of the same sex.

(4) In the absence of a warrant or authorisation pursuant to paragraph 1, an investigator or a police body may conduct the search of a person only if such warrant or authorisation could not be secured in advance and in cases of emergency, or if it involves a person caught in the act of committing a crime or a person in respect of which an arrest warrant has been issued. The search of a person may also be conducted without a warrant or authorisation in cases set out in Section 82 paragraph 4.

Section 83c
Entry to a Dwelling, Other Premises and Property

(1) An investigator or a police body may enter a dwelling, other premises or property only in cases of emergency when the entry is necessary to protect the life or health of persons or to safeguard other rights and freedoms, or to avert serious threat to public safety and, in particular, if the dwelling, other premises or property belong to a person caught committing a crime.

(2) They may enter the places set out in paragraph 1 also if an arrest warrant was issued in respect of a person who stays there, if an order was issued to bring such a person in to serve a prison sentence or if an accused who stays in such places is to be brought in.

(3) Upon entering the places set out in paragraph 1 it shall only be possible to conduct the procedures that cannot be delayed and that are necessary for bringing a person in.

Section 84
Previous Summons

House search, search of a person or search of other premises or property shall be undertaken only if a previous summons addressed to the person whose house or person is to be searched did not result in a voluntary surrender of the thing being sought or in the elimination of any other reason for the search.

Section 85
Conduct of the Search and Entry to a Dwelling, Other Premises and Property

(1) The body conducting a search of a house or person, or a search of other premises or property, shall enable the person whose dwelling is

searched or an adult member of the household thereof, or an employee if other premises are being searched, to be present at the search. It shall advise such persons of the right to be present at the search.

(2) An uninvolved person shall be invited to be present at the house search or search of a person. The body conducting the search shall show its authorisation.

(3) The search record shall state also whether the provisions concerning prior interrogation had been observed and, if not, give the reasons. If the search results in the surrender or seizure of a thing, the record shall include also the data set out in Section 79 paragraph 5.

(4) The body that conducted the search shall issue the person subjected to the search a written protocol on the result of the search and on the receipt of the things that were surrendered or seized, or a copy of the record; it shall do it either immediately or, if this is not possible, not later than within 24 hours after the search.

(5) The provisions of paragraphs 1 to 4 shall apply, as appropriate, to the entry to a dwelling, other premises and property. The presence of persons under paragraph 1 and of the person under paragraph 2 may, however, be waived if it could constitute a threat to their life or health.

Section 85a

(1) The person whose house, other premises and property are to be searched, who is to be subjected to the search of a person or whose home is to be entered, shall have the duty to endure such procedures.

(2) If the person in respect of whom a procedure under paragraph 1 is to be conducted does not make it possible, the bodies conducting such procedure shall have the right, after a previous unproductive summons, to overcome the resistance of such person or the impediment he created. Such action shall be noted down in the record (Section 85 paragraph 3).

Section 85b
Securing Evidence in a Home, Dwelling, Other Premises and on the Property

(1) The provisions of Sections 83, 83a, 84, 85 and 85a shall also apply if the inspection of the scene, reconstruction, recognition or investigation are to be conducted in the places set out in them and if such procedures cannot, in view of their nature, be conducted elsewhere and the person concerned did not give his consent.

Title Five
Intercepting Mail Consignments

Section 86
Intercepting and Opening Mail Consignments

(1) If the clarification of facts relevant for criminal proceedings makes it necessary to ascertain the content of undelivered telegrams, letters or other private communications dispatched by or addressed to the accused, the presiding judge of a panel or, in pre-trial proceedings, a prosecutor or an investigator shall issue an order to the post office or the mail delivery organisation to surrender such private communications; the investigator may do so upon a prior authorisation by a prosecutor.

(2) In criminal proceedings carried out in respect of criminal offences set out in Chapter One of a separate section of the Criminal Code and other serious criminal offences, corruption and criminal offence under the Section 158 of the Criminal Code, a prosecutor or an investigator, upon a prior authorisation by a prosecutor, may order the post office or the mail delivery organisation to surrender the mail consignment in respect of which there are reasonable grounds to believe that it was used to commit a criminal offence or is related to a criminal offence, and that the clarification of facts in criminal proceedings requires the determination of the content thereof.

(3) The delivery of a mail consignment may be withheld on the order of an investigator or a police body even in the absence of the order pursuant to paragraphs 1 and 2, but only if such order cannot be obtained in advance, and in cases of emergency. If, in such a case, the post office or the mail delivery organisation does not receive within three days an order from the presiding judge of a panel, a prosecutor or an investigator to surrender the mail consignment, the post office or the mail delivery organisation shall not withhold the delivery of the communication any longer.

Section 87
Opening Mail Consignments

(1) Mail consignments surrendered under Section 86 paragraphs 1 or 2 may be opened only by the presiding judge of a panel or, in pre-trial proceedings, by a prosecutor, an investigator or a police body; the investigator or the police body shall have to obtain a prior authorisation by a prosecutor.

(2) The opened mail consignment shall be delivered to the addressee or, if his whereabouts are unknown, to a person close to him. If, however, there is reason to believe that delivery of a mail consignment could prejudice the proceedings, the mail consignment shall be attached to the files if its size and character make this possible; otherwise it shall

be placed in safe-keeping. If appropriate, the addressee shall be informed of the contents of a letter or a telegram. If his whereabouts are unknown, a person close to him shall be notified of the contents thereof.

(3) The mail consignment that was not deemed necessary to open shall be handed over to the addressee without any further delay or returned to the post office or organisation having surrendered it.

Section 87a
Substituting the Content of Consignments

To identify the persons involved in the handling of a consignment that contains narcotics, psychotropic substances, poisons, nuclear or similar radioactive materials, counterfeit money and public papers, firearms or mass destruction weapons, ammunition and explosives, a prosecutor or an investigator with a prior authorisation by a prosecutor may order that the content of such consignment be surrendered pursuant to Section 86 paragraphs 1 and 2, that a different content be substituted and that the altered consignment be released for the delivery. The substitution shall be done by a police body that shall draw up a protocol and secure the safekeeping of the supplanted items or materials.

Title Six
Interception and Recording of Private Communications

Section 88

(1) If the criminal proceedings are held in respect of an intentional and exceptionally serious criminal offence, corruption and crime offences under Section 158 of Criminal Code or an intentional criminal offence the prosecution of which is mandatory under a promulgated international treaty, or a criminal offence set out in a separate legislation, the presiding judge of a panel or, in pre-trial proceedings, a prosecutor or an investigator may order the wiretapping of telephone lines and the recording of private communications if there are reasonable grounds to believe that important facts for criminal proceedings may thus be revealed. It shall not be allowed to intercept and record private communications between the counsel and the accused.

(2) The order to intercept and record private communications shall be issued in writing and shall contain a justification. The order shall also specify the time-limit for intercepting and recording telecommunication messages. The time-limit for intercepting and recording shall not exceed six months. The presiding judge of a panel or, in pre-trial proceedings, a prosecutor may extend this time-limit by another six months. The order is considered to be as secret data. Interception and recording of private communications shall be conducted by a police body.

(3) In criminal proceedings held in respect of other offences than those listed in paragraph 1, the body active in criminal proceedings shall issue an order to intercept and record private communications or carry it out itself only with the consent of the telephone subscriber concerned.

...

(5) If the interception and recording did not produce any facts relevant for criminal proceedings, the body active in criminal proceedings shall have to destroy the obtained records pursuant to the shredding regulations applicable to the body active in criminal proceedings.

Title Seven
Controlled Delivery

Section 88a

(1) A controlled delivery means that a consignment being imported, exported, or transported is subjected to surveillance, if there are reasonable grounds to believe that it is an illegal consignment containing narcotics, psychotropic substances, poisons, nuclear and other similar radioactive materials, counterfeit money and public papers, firearms or mass destruction weapons, ammunition and explosives, in order to identify the persons who took part in the handling of such consignment.

(2) The order to proceed pursuant to paragraph 1 shall be issued by the presiding judge of a panel or, in pre-trial proceedings, by a prosecutor.

(3) In cases of emergency, a prosecutor may also issue an order pursuant to paragraph 2 outside pre-trial proceedings. Such order shall be confirmed by a judge within at most three days; otherwise it shall become void.

(4) The surveillance of a consignment shall be conducted by the competent bodies of the Police Force in conjunction with the Customs Administration bodies, which shall be given advance notice of any such procedure.

(5) When proceeding pursuant to paragraph 1 it shall be possible to use, under conditions set out in separate prescriptions, information technology and operational and searching devices and to duly record the procedure also in other ways (Section 55, Code of Criminal Procedure).

Title Eight
Agents

Section 88b

(1) In the course of disclosure, detection and conviction of those committing especially serious criminal offences, corruption and criminal offences set out under Section 158 of the Criminal Code, it shall be possible to use an agent. The use of an agent shall only be admissible if the disclosure detection and conviction of offenders in the abovementioned criminal offences and identification of their perpetrators would otherwise be much more difficult and the acquired information justifies the suspicion that the crime has been committed or an intention of the offender to commit such crime .

(2) An unacceptable act of an agent is, if on his own initiative, acting with the aim of acquiring a gain or other advantage to himself or to another person, or in order that another person could have a loss, he passes or plants a drug, money or other thing on another person, who is unwilling, as evidence of their criminal behaviour.

(3) An agent operates under a temporary or a permanent cover story or without a cover story. The cover story of an agent shall consist of a set of cover personal data, in particular data on his identity, family status, education and employment. Data cannot be used as cover personal data, where using such data as cover data is forbidden by special law.

(4) If the construction or preservation of the cover story makes it necessary, cover documents may be produced, altered and used in keeping with the provisions of separate legislation.

(5) Before the start of the pre-trial proceeding and during this proceeding, the order to use an agent shall be issued by the presiding judge of a panel on application by a prosecutor; the order can also be issued by the presiding judge of the panel without this application, when the case is before court.

(6) In cases of emergency, and if the use of an agent does not involve entering the home of another person, the order under paragraph 5 may be issued also outside pre-trial proceedings and during pre-trial proceedings. Such order shall be confirmed by a judge within three days at most; otherwise it shall become void.

(7) The warrant issued under paragraphs 5 and 6 shall be in writing and shall specify the time period during which the agent will be deployed. The warrant is to be considered as secret data.

(8) Written materials obtained in connection with the use of an agent shall be included in the file only after a prosecutor has made a motion in

the indictment that the evidence be taken on the basis of facts ascertained by the agent.

(9) When acting under a cover story, an agent may enter a home with the consent of an entitled person. Such consent, however, may not be obtained on the basis of pretending to have the right of entry.

(10) The true identity of an agent shall have to remain secret even after the termination of his deployment. Upon request, the true identity of an agent shall be disclosed to the presiding judge of a panel, a prosecutor and a judge competent to decide pursuant to paragraphs 5 and 6 and to the presiding judge of a panel in judicial proceedings.

(11) In pre-trial proceedings, the prosecutor shall make examination of an agent on the facts that are important for the criminal proceedings, while adequately keeping to Section 101b paragraph 3 of the Code of Criminal Procedure to ensure that the true identity of the agent shall not be disclosed.

The agent shall be examined in the courtroom only with adequate use of Section 105 paragraph 5, Section 101b paragraph 3 and Section 209 of the Code of Criminal Procedure by such means that the true identity of the agent shall not be disclosed. The summons to the agent to appear at the main hearing shall be served by a Police Force officer appointed by the President of the Police Force.

(12) The facts related to criminal offences that are not linked to the case to which the agent was assigned may be used as evidence in other proceedings only if such proceedings are held in respect of especially serious criminal offences, corruption and criminal offences set out under Section 158 of the Criminal Code.

Selected provisions of Act No. 171/1993 Coll. on the Police Force of the Slovak Republic

Block III
Information and technical means, and means of investigative operational activities

Section 35

For the purposes of the present Act the information and technical means are understood to be particularly electro-technical, radio engineering, photo-technical, optical, mechanical and other technical means and equipment or sets used under cover while detecting, disclosing and investigating consignments conveyed and their assessment with the help of investigative methods, interception, recording, storing information and data learning by means of the telecommunication, radio-communication, computer and other technique, making audio, visual or other types of records.

Section 36

(1) The Police Force is authorised to use information and technical means while performing tasks connected with the combat against terrorism, legalisation of income from criminal activities, disclosure of international organised crimes and organised criminal activities related to illicit manufacturing, possession and spread of narcotic and psychotropic substances and poisons, precursors and nuclear material, to smuggling, fraud and counterfeiting of money, stamps or bonds, the disclosure of other extremely serious criminal acts, offering protection and help to a threatened witness or a protected witness referred to in special law, operative control of legalised persons and agents, disclosure of tax evasions and illicit financial transactions, disclosure of deliberate criminal offences referred to in the second and third chapters of the Criminal Code which are liable to imprisonment not exceeding 2 years, or other deliberate criminal offences, which are prosecuted pursuant to an international agreement binding on the Slovak Republic, and while detecting their perpetrators and conducting an investigation, the Police Force is authorised to use information and technical means. The provision of the preceding sentence shall not apply during the time when the accused is contacting his defence counsel.

(2) The Police Force is authorised to use information and technical means also while disclosing another deliberate criminal activity referred to in paragraph 1 herein if agreed by the person whose rights and freedoms are going to be affected.

Conditions for the use of information and technical means

Section 37

(1) The Police Force may use information and technical means only in cases when the disclosure of criminal acts referred to in Section 36, detection of their perpetrators and gathering of necessary evidence would be otherwise ineffective or considerably more difficult.

(2) Information and technical means can be used only on the basis of previous written consent of the judge, and only for such time as is unavoidably necessary, but not exceeding the period of six months from the day the consent was issued.

(3) The judge who has issued a consent for the use of information and technical means can prolong the term of their use upon a new request, but not for more than six months each time.

(4) In exceptional cases, if the case cannot be delayed and written consent of the judge cannot be obtained in advance, the information and technical means can be used without this consent. The Police Force is obliged, however, to request the written consent of the judge afterwards. If the Police Force does not receive the additional written consent of the judge within 24 hours from the time the information and technical means were applied, or if the judge denies issuing such consent, the Police Force is obliged to stop the use of information and technical means. The information thus obtained must not be used by the Police Force and must be destroyed in the presence of the judge who would have been otherwise authorised to issue the additional consent.

(5) The request for the use of information and technical means is submitted in writing by the Police Force to the court; it must contain data about the person concerned with the use of information and technical means, the type of information and technical means, place, time, length and reasons for their use.

(6) The judge who has issued consent for the use of information and technical means is obliged to continually examine the validity of the reasons for their further use; if the reasons cease, he is obliged to immediately terminate their use.

(7) The Police Force can use information and technical means also without previous written consent of the judge referred to in paragraphs 2 and 3, if agreed in written form by the person whose rights and freedoms are being affected. The person having given the consent shall be notified about ending of the use of information and technical means. Also, if the person cancels the consent given by him/her, the Police Force is obliged to immediately stop the use of information and technical means.

Section 38

(1) While using information and technical means, the Police Force are obliged to continually monitor if the reasons for their use remain valid. If these reasons have ceased to exist, the Police Force is obliged to terminate the use of the information and technical means.

(2) The Police Force is obliged to inform the judge who has issued the consent about the termination of use of the information and technical means pursuant to paragraph 1.

(3) Information obtained by information and technical means can be used only with a view to achieve the goals referred to in Section 36.

(4) The use of information and technical means is allowed to the extent necessary to affect the privacy of the dwelling place, secrecy of mail and the secrecy of conveyed messages.

(5) The information obtained by information and technical means can only exceptionally be used as evidence in criminal proceedings in cases of criminal offences referred to in Section 36, when such evidence cannot be obtained by any other means. In such a case, the record produced shall be supplemented with a protocol specifying the reason, place, time, means and content of the record.

Section 38a
Investigative Operational Activity

(1) Investigative operational activity is a system of secret, intelligence measures, as a rule carried out by the Police Force for the purposes of prevention, prohibition, disclosing and registering of criminal activity and investigating perpetrators, assuring protection to persons affected and premises watched, technical surveillance of premises, assuring and offering protection and help to a threatened witness who is a protected witness, protection of the state border and searching for persons and things.

(2) Designated services of the Police Force authorised for this purpose to use service dogs for tracking may carry out investigative operational activities.

Section 39
Means of Investigative Operational Activities

(1) For the purposes of the present Act, by the means of investigative operational activities is meant surveillance of persons and things, controlled delivery, criminal intelligence, the use of undercover documents, trap and alarm systems and the use of persons collaborating with the Police Force, premises and places used under a cover story and disguised transfer of an object.

(2) The Police Force is authorised to use means of investigative operational activities to disclose wilful criminal acts and to investigate for perpetrators, protect legalised persons and agents, protect watched premises, protect the state border and in cases referred to in Section 36; the Police Force is authorised to use means of investigative operational activities to carry out a security check referred to in a special act.

Section 39a
Criminal Intelligence, Legalised Person and Agent

(1) For the purposes of the present Act, by criminal intelligence is meant activity focused on obtaining, gathering and evaluating information on criminal offences and their perpetrators, and creating the conditions for an agent to be used.

(2) To carry out a task in the field of criminal intelligence it is possible to use a police officer as a legalised person whose activity is under permanent cover story or limited cover story.

(3) A police officer operating under a permanent or limited cover story can be used as an agent, when he is entitled to perform the tasks of criminal intelligence, under conditions referred to in a special law.

(4) The Police Force is authorised for criminal intelligence to use information and technical means to carry out security checks referred to in a special act.

Section 39b
Protection of a Police Officer

If necessary in the course of performance of the tasks of criminal intelligence and for an agent to be used for the protection of a police officer, a cover story can be created with a view to concealing his action, and in this connection all necessary data can be recorded and selected in information systems of the police Force (Section 69), information systems of state bodies and information systems of bodies of self-government; the use of special means is allowed for elaboration of the statement of the state budget utilisation, including the management of foreign currency utilisation, tax returns, statements of general health insurance, of social security insurance and dues to unemployment insurance.

Section 39c
Special Funds

(1) Special funds mean finances that have been singled out of the budget of the Ministry of Interior of the Slovak Republic and used by the Police Force to cover expenses in the performance of investigative operational activities, criminal intelligence services, the use of an agent and witness protection.

(2) The utilisation and control of special funds is regulated by the Minister of the Interior of the Slovak Republic.

Section 40
Undercover Documents

(1) For the purposes of the present Act, by undercover documents are meant documents and objects serving to conceal the real identity of the police officer, witness, protected witness, agent and persons collaborating with the Police Force (Section 41). To conceal the operation of a police officer, witness, protected witness and agent, a cover story can be created, and in this connection all necessary data can be recorded and selected in the information systems of the Police

Force (Section 69), information systems of state bodies, information systems of public institutions and information systems of self-government bodies. For this purpose state bodies, organs of public institutions and self-government bodies are obliged provide to the Police Force uncompleted blanks issued under its authority, other documents and parts for their finalisation.

(2) As an undercover document, the following must not be used:
- o   ID of a member of the National Council of the Slovak Republic,
- o   ID of a member of the government,
- o   official ID of a judge,
- o   official ID of a prosecutor,
- o   diplomatic passport.

(3) Undercover documents are issued by the Police Force on the basis of the minister's decision or his nominee. The Police Force issues these documents also for other state bodies if these are allowed to use them, in accordance with special acts.

(4) The Police Force maintains a register of undercover documents.

Section 41
Persons Collaborating with the Police Force

(1) For the purposes of the present Act, a person collaborating with the Police Force is understood to be a private person that willingly, in a secret manner, provides information and services for the Police Force when disclosing criminal activities.

(2) The Police Force can maintain a register of persons collaborating with the Police Force only in the course of fulfilling each individual task.

Section 41a
Disguised Transfer of a Thing

For the purposes of the present Act, by the disguised transfer of a thing is meant a simulation of purchase, sale or other kind of transfer of a thing the possession of which requires a special permit, or is prohibited.

Appendix 2

Selected provisions of the Constitution of the Slovak Republic
regarding special investigation techniques in relation to acts of terrorism

Chapter Two
Basic rights and freedoms

Part One
General Provisions

Article 11

Revoked.

Article 12

(1) People are free and equal in dignity and their rights. Basic rights and freedoms are inviolable, inalienable, secured by law, and unchallengeable.

(2) Basic rights and freedoms on the territory of the Slovak Republic are guaranteed to everyone regardless of sex, race, colour of skin, language, creed and religion, political or other beliefs, national or social origin, affiliation to a nation or ethnic group, property, descent, or any other status. No one must be harmed, preferred, or discriminated against on these grounds.

(3) Everyone has the right to freely decide on his nationality. Any influence on this decision and any form of pressure aimed at assimilation are forbidden.

(4) No one must be restricted in his rights because he upholds his basic rights and freedoms.

Article 13

(1) Duties can be imposed
a) by law or on the basis of a law, within its limits, and while complying with basic rights and freedoms,
b) by international treaty pursuant to Article 7 paragraph 4 which directly establishes rights and obligations of natural persons or juridical persons, or
c) by government decree pursuant to Article 120 paragraph 2.

(2) Limits to basic rights and freedoms can be set only by law, under conditions laid down in this constitution.

(3) Legal restrictions of constitutional rights and freedoms must apply equally to all cases that meet the set conditions.

(4) When restricting constitutional rights and freedoms, attention must be paid to their essence and meaning. These restrictions must not be used for any other than the set purpose.

Part Two
Basic Human Rights and Freedoms

Article 14

Everyone is worthy of having rights.

Article 15

(1) Everyone has the right to life. Human life is worthy of protection prior to birth.

(2) No one must be deprived of life.

(3) Capital punishment is not permitted.

(4) If someone was deprived of life as a result of an action that does not represent a criminal act under the law, this does not constitute a violation of rights according to this article.

Article 16

(1) The inviolability of the person and its privacy is guaranteed. It can be limited only in cases defined by law.

(2) No one must be tortured or subjected to cruel, inhuman, or humiliating treatment or punishment.

Article 17

(1) Personal freedom is guaranteed.

(2) No one must be prosecuted or deprived of freedom other than for reasons and in a manner defined by law. No one must be deprived of freedom solely because of his inability to comply with a contractual obligation.

(3) A person accused or suspected of a criminal act can be detained only in cases defined by law. The detained person must be immediately informed of the reasons for their detainment, interrogated, and either released or brought before the court within 48 hours at the latest. The judge must question the detained within 48 hours, and in particularly

serious crimes within 72 hours, of taking over the case and decide on his or her custody or release.

(4) An accused person may be arrested only on the basis of a written, substantiated court warrant. The arrested person must be brought before the court within 24 hours. The judge must question the detained within 48 hours, and in particularly serious crimes within 72 hours, of taking over the case and decide on his or her custody or release.

(5) A person can be taken into custody only for reasons and for a period defined by law and on the basis of a court ruling.

(6) The law will specify in which cases a person can be admitted to, or kept in, institutional health care without his or her consent. Such a measure must be reported within 24 hours to the court, which will then decide on this placement within five days.

(7) The mental state of a person accused of criminal activity can be examined only on the basis of the court's written order.

Article 18

(1) No one must be subjected to forced labour or services.

(2) The provision of paragraph 1 does not apply to
a) work assigned according to the Act to persons serving a prison term or some other punishment substituting for a prison term,
b) military service or some other service assigned by law in lieu of compulsory military service,
c) services required on the basis of the Act in the event of natural catastrophes, accidents, or other dangers posing a threat to life, health, or property of great value,
d) activities laid down by law to protect life, health or rights of others,
e) small community services pursuant to the law.

Article 19

(1) Everyone has the right to the preservation of his human dignity and personal honour, and the protection of his good name.

(2) Everyone has the right to protection against unwarranted interference in his private and family life.

(3) Everyone has the right to protection against the unwarranted collection, publication or other illicit use of his personal data.

Article 20

(1) Everyone has the right to own property. The ownership right of all owners has the same legal content and deserves the same protection. Inheritance of property is guaranteed.

(2) The law will specify which property other than property listed in Article 4 that is essential to meet the needs of society, the development of the national economy and the public interest can be owned only by the state, municipality or designated juridical persons. The law can also specify that certain property can be owned only by citizens or juridical persons resident in the Slovak Republic.

(3) Ownership is binding. It must not be misused to the detriment of others or at variance with general interests protected by law. By exercising ownership, no harm must be done to human health, nature, cultural monuments, and the environment beyond limits set by law.

(4) Expropriation or enforced restriction of the ownership right is admissible only to the extent that it is unavoidable and in the public interest, on the basis of law, and in return for adequate compensation.

Article 21

(1) A person's home is inviolable. It must not be entered without the resident's consent.

(2) A house search is admissible only in connection with criminal proceedings and only on the basis of the judge's written and substantiated order. The method of carrying out a house search will be set out in a law.

(3) Other infringements upon the inviolability of one's home can be permitted by law only if this is inevitable in a democratic society in order to protect people's lives, health, or property, to protect the rights and freedoms of others, or to ward off a serious threat to public order. If the home is used also for business or to perform some other economic activity, such infringements can be permitted by law also when this is unavoidable in meeting the tasks of public administration.

Article 22

(1) The privacy of correspondence and secrecy of mailed messages and other written documents and the protection of personal data are guaranteed.

(2) No one must violate the privacy of correspondence and the secrecy of other written documents and records, whether they are kept in privacy or sent by mail or in another way, with the exception of cases to be set

out in a law. Equally guaranteed is the secrecy of messages conveyed by telephone, telegraph, or other similar means.

Article 23

(1) Freedom of movement and of abode is guaranteed.

(2) Everyone who is rightfully staying on the territory of the Slovak Republic has the right to freely leave this territory.

(3) Freedoms according to Sections 1 and 2 can be restricted by law if it is unavoidable for the security of the state, to maintain public order, protect the health and the rights and freedoms of others, and, in designated areas, also for reasons of environmental protection.

(4) Every citizen has the right to freely enter the territory of the Slovak Republic. A citizen must not be forced to leave his homeland and may not be deported.

(5) A foreign national can be deported only in cases specified by law.

Article 24

(1) The freedoms of thought, conscience, religion, and faith are guaranteed. This right also comprises the possibility to change one's religious belief or faith. Everyone has the right to be without religious belief. Everyone has the right to publicly express his opinion.

(2) Everyone has the right to freely express his religion or faith on his own or together with others, privately or publicly, by means of divine and religious services, by observing religious rites, or by participating in the teaching of religion.

(3) Churches and religious communities administer their own affairs. In particular, they constitute their own bodies, inaugurate their clergymen, organise the teaching of religion, and establish religious orders and other church institutions independently of state bodies.

(4) Conditions for exercising rights according to sections 1 to 3 can be limited by law only if such a measure is unavoidable in a democratic society to protect public order, health, morality, or the rights and freedoms of others.

Article 25

(1) The defence of the Slovak Republic is a duty and a matter of honour for each citizen. The law shall determine the scope of compulsory military service.

(2) No one must be forced to perform military service if this runs counter to his conscience or religious belief. Details will be set out in a law.

Slovenia

1.   Please indicate the SITs used in your country, the respective legal framework governing their use and their legal definition, if any.

SITs are regulated in the Criminal Procedure Act, Chapter Fifteen – "Pre-Trial Procedure". All the SITs, listed below, may be used in the pre-trial procedure, as well as in the investigation procedure.

A. If there are well-founded grounds for suspecting that a particular person has committed, is committing or is preparing or organising the committing of any of the criminal offences listed below, and if there exists a well-founded suspicion that such a person is using for communications in connection with this criminal offence a particular means of communication or computer system or that such means or system will be used, wherein it is possible to reasonably conclude that other measures will not permit the gathering of data or that the gathering of data could endanger the lives or health of people, the following may be ordered against such a person: monitoring of telecommunications through bugging and recording, control of letters and other parcels, control of the computer systems of banks or other legal entities that perform financial or other commercial activities, bugging and recording of conversations with the permission of at least one person participating in the conversation, control of messages conveyed by electronic mail system and other forms of information technology.

The criminal offences, in connection with which these measures may be ordered, are:
- o   criminal offences against the security of the Republic of Slovenia and its constitutional order, and crimes against humanity and international Act for which the law prescribes a prison sentence of five or more years;
- o   the criminal offence of kidnapping under Article 144, illegal production of and trade in drugs under Article 196, enabling the taking of drugs under Article 197, blackmail under Article 218, unauthorised acceptance of gifts under Article 247, unauthorised giving of gifts under Article 248, money laundering under Article 252, smuggling under Article 255, accepting of a bribe under Article 267, giving of a bribe under Article 268, undue influence under Article 269, criminal association under Article 297, unauthorised production of and trade in arms or explosives under Article 310, and causing danger with nuclear substances under Article 319 of the Penal Code of the Republic of Slovenia;
- o   other criminal offences for which the law prescribes a prison sentence of eight or more years.

B. If there exist well-founded reasons to suspect that a particular person has committed, is committing, or is preparing or organising the committing of any of the criminal offences listed below, wherein it is possible to reasonably conclude that it will be possible in a precisely defined place to obtain evidence which more lenient measures, including the measures listed under item A., would not be able to obtain or the gathering of which could endanger the lives of people, exceptionally bugging and surveillance in another person's home or in other areas with the use of technical means for documentation and where necessary secret entrance into the aforementioned home or area may be ordered against such a person.

These measures may be ordered in connection with all criminal offences listed in the first clause of the third paragraph of item A., criminal offences from the second clause of the same item, except for the criminal offence of kidnapping under Article 144, enabling the taking of drugs under Article 197, blackmail under Article 218, money laundering under the first, second, third and fifth paragraphs of Article 252 and smuggling under Article 255 of the Penal Code, and in connection with other criminal offences from the third clause of the same item for which the law prescribes a prison sentence of eight or more years only if there exists a real danger to the lives of people.

Measures listed under items A. and B. are ordered by a written order by the investigating judge following the state prosecutor's written proposal. By way of exception, if a written order cannot be obtained in due time and when there is danger in deferment, the investigating judge may, following an oral proposal by the public prosecutor, order the execution of the measures by means of an oral order. A written order must be issued no later than twelve hours after the issuing of the oral order.

The implementation of the above-listed SITs may last no longer than one month, but the duration may be extended for one month at a time for well-founded reasons; however measures listed under item A. may last for a maximum total of six months, and measures listed under item B. may last for a maximum total of three months. The implementation of these measures shall be halted as soon as the reasons for which they were ordered cease to apply.

The Police implement orders for SITs. Companies that perform the transfer of information are obliged to enable the Police to implement the order.

C. If it is possible to justifiably conclude that a particular person is involved in criminal activities relating to the above-listed criminal offences, the state prosecutor may, pursuant to a reasoned proposal from the Police, by written order permit measures of feigned purchase, feigned acceptance or giving of gifts or feigned acceptance or giving of bribes. The proposal and order shall become constituent parts of the criminal record. The order from the public prosecutor may only refer to one-off measures. Proposals for each further measure against the same person must contain the reasons that justify their use.

In the implementation of these measures, the Police and their staff may not incite criminal activities. In determining whether the criminal activity was incited, primary consideration must be given to whether the measure as implemented led to the committing of a criminal offence by a person who would otherwise not have been prepared to commit this type of criminal offence. If the criminal activity was incited, this shall be a circumstance that excludes the initiation of criminal proceedings for criminal offences committed in connection with the measures from the first paragraph of this Article.

D. If justified grounds exist for the suspicion that a particular person has committed a criminal offence which is prosecuted ex officio, the investigating judge may, based on a reasoned proposal by the state prosecutor, order banks, savings banks or savings-credit services to report confidential data on deposits, account balances and transactions or any other dealings of this person and of other persons of whom it is possible to reasonably conclude that they are participants in the financial transactions or other deals of the suspect or accused person, if these data could represent evidence in the criminal procedure or if they are needed for the seizure of possessions or the securing of a request for a deprivation of pecuniary advantage or of possessions to the value of the pecuniary advantage. A bank, savings bank or savings-credit service must provide the requested data and documentation specified in the preceding paragraph to the investigating judge without delay. A bank, savings bank or savings-credit service must not reveal to its client or a third party that it has or will send the data and documentation to the investigating judge.

The quoted article allows the investigating judge only to order a "production order", but not a "monitoring order". With the last amendments to the Criminal Procedure Act, which were passed by the Parliament on 29 May 2003, the ordering of a monitoring order will also be possible. The law on amendments has not yet been published in the Official Gazette of the Republic of Slovenia, so it is not yet in force.

2.   When and under which circumstances (e.g. criminal investigation, preliminary stage, etc.) can SITs be used?

Please see answer under item 1.

3.   Are there any specific features governing the use of SITs in relation to acts of terrorism? If so, please specify.

No. The punishments determined in the Penal Code for acts of terrorism are sufficiently high that SITs may be used for those kind of criminal offences as well.

4.   How does the legal framework governing the use of SITs guarantee respect for human rights and individual freedoms, the principles of subsidiarity and proportionality? Is the authorisation to use SITs subject to time-limits? Which bodies and procedures are in place to supervise compliance with human rights standards and with the above-mentioned principles in the use of SITs? Is supervision automatic/systematic?

The Criminal Procedure Act determines conditions, which must be fulfilled, for the use of SITs. Under normal circumstances there must be a written proposal from the state prosecutor, and the investigative judge must order the use of SITs with a written order. The proposal, as well as the order, must explain: data of any person against whom the measure is proposed or ordered; justification or determination of the grounds for suspicion of the committing, preparation or organisation of the criminal offences stipulated in articles that govern the use of SITs; the measure being proposed or ordered, the method of implementation of the measure, the scope and duration of the measure, precise specification of the area or place in which the measure will be implemented, the means of communication or telecommunication and other important circumstances that require the use of an individual measure; the justification or determination of the unavoidable necessity of the use of individual measures in relation to the collection of evidence in another manner and the use of less severe measures.

A. The Criminal Procedure Act determines that the monitoring of telecommunications through bugging and recording, control of letters and other parcels, control of the computer systems of banks or other legal entities which perform financial or other commercial activities, bugging and recording of conversations with the permission of at least one person participating in the conversation, control of messages conveyed by electronic mail system and other forms of information technology may be used wherein it is possible to reasonably conclude that other measures will not permit the gathering of data or that the gathering of data could endanger the lives or health of people.

B. Exceptionally bugging and surveillance in another person's home or in other areas with the use of technical means for documentation and where necessary secret entrance into the aforementioned home or area may be ordered where it is possible to reasonably conclude that it will be possible in a precisely defined place to obtain evidence where more lenient measures, including the abovementioned SITs, will not permit the gathering of data or where the gathering of data could endanger the lives or health of people.

The SITs under items A. and B. may be ordered only for one month, with possible prolongations for one month by one order. The SITs under A. may last for six months at the longest and the SITs under B. may last for three months at the longest.

C. Feigned purchase, feigned acceptance or giving of gifts or feigned acceptance or giving of bribes may be ordered by the state prosecutor. The state prosecutor's order may refer to only one SIT of this kind.

If any of the SITs has been used without the order of the competent person, or if the oral order, where possible, was not followed by the written order within 12 hours, or if the SIT was used contrary to written order, the court may not base its ruling on data, messages, recordings or evidence so obtained.

5.   Which institutions are involved in the use of SITs and what is their role (e.g. law enforcement agencies, prosecutor's office, judicial authorities, etc.)? Which institutions can order and/or authorise the use of SITs? How does co-operation between these institutions work in practice?

Please see answer under item 1.

6.   Are there any specialised counter-terrorism institutions? What is their role in the use of SITs?

In the framework of the Police organisation there is also a branch of the criminal police that deals with organised crime. One of the groups within the sector against organised crime is also the group working against extreme violence and terrorism. They can use SITs under same conditions as described above.

7.   Which measures have been adopted in order to facilitate international co-operation (e.g. joint investigation teams)? Can the SITs listed in reply to question 1 be used in cross-border settings?

The Criminal Procedure Act gives the legal basis for direct co-operation:

If reciprocity applies or if so determined by an international treaty, international criminal-legal help may be exchanged directly between the Slovene and foreign bodies that participate in pre-criminal and criminal proceedings, wherein modern technical assets, in particular computer networks and aids for the transmission of pictures, speech and electronic impulses may be used.

In emergency cases and on condition of reciprocity, requests for legal assistance may be sent also through the Ministry of Internal Affairs, or in instances of criminal offences of money laundering or criminal offences connected to the criminal offence of money laundering, also to the body responsible for the prevention of money laundering.

Under the provisions of the Criminal Procedure Act and the Police Act, the Police may make an agreement with the foreign police for the joint investigation team in a specific case. In those cases also, SITs may be used under the same conditions as explained above.

8.   *What use can be made of SIT in the context of mutual legal assistance?*

When in the context of mutual legal assistance there is a request for the SIT to be carried out in Slovenia, the procedure and the conditions are the same as described above.

Spain

1.   Please indicate the SITs used in your country, the respective legal framework governing their use and their legal definition, if any.
and
2.   When and under which circumstances (e.g. criminal investigation, preliminary stage, etc.) can SITs be used?

The following are the main SITs that are regulated in Spanish legislation.

Infiltrated officers

Infiltrated officers can be deployed against organised crime, which includes terrorism. Section 282 of the Criminal Procedure Act defines them as

> criminal investigation officers, who by substantiated ruling and having due regard for the purposes of the investigation, are authorised to act under an assumed identity and to purchase and transport objects, effects and instruments of the offence and delay the seizure thereof. Such officers shall have lawful authority to act in all circumstances relating to the investigation in question and to engage in judicial and social relations under that identity.

Authorisation is granted by the investigating judge or the Public Prosecutor's Office (which shall immediately inform the judge) and the assumed identity is supplied by the Minister of the Interior for renewable periods of six months.

Controlled delivery

Section 263 bis of the Criminal Procedure Act grants judges, the Public Prosecutor's Office and the heads of organisational units of the criminal investigation police the power to authorise the controlled delivery or movement of toxic drugs, narcotic or psychotropic substances and other prohibited substances. The Act states that

> Controlled delivery or movement shall be understood to mean the technique whereby illicit or suspicious consignments of toxic drugs, psychotropic substances or other prohibited substances shall be allowed to travel across, leave or enter Spanish territory under the surveillance of the authority or its agents without any restrictive interference by them for the purpose of discovering or identifying the persons involved in the commission of any offence connected with such items and of furnishing assistance to foreign authorities for those same purposes.

Although this was originally intended for use in investigating drug trafficking, provision was made to extend it to other forms of organised crime, whether or not related to such trafficking. Paragraph 2, for example, states it shall also be possible to authorise the controlled delivery or movement of equipment, materials and substances referred to in Article 371 of the Criminal Code, of property and proceeds referred to in Article 301 of the Criminal Code, in all the cases provided for therein, and of property, materials, objects and animal and plant species referred to in Articles 332, 334, 386, 566, 568 and 569 of the Criminal Code.

Accordingly, the scope of paragraph 2 of Section 263 includes the controlled delivery of money carried out in application of Section 301, that is, in relation to crimes involving money laundering.

Joint investigation teams

The use of joint investigation teams is provided for under EU legislation. Such teams are regulated by Law No. 11/2003 of 21 May and are defined as

teams set up with the agreement of the competent authorities of two or more European Union member states to carry out criminal investigations in one or all of their countries, requiring co-ordinated action for a specific purpose and for a specified duration.

Freezing of accounts, balances, financial positions, transactions and movements of capital

Such matters are regulated by Law No. 12/2003 of 21 May. Freezing or blocking is defined as the means to prevent

any movement, transfer, conversion, use or transaction of capital or financial assets which results or could result in a change of volume, amount, location, ownership, possession, nature or destination of the said capital or assets and any other change which could facilitate their use, including the management of a securities account.

3. Are there any specific features governing the use of SITs in relation to acts of terrorism? If so, please specify.

In the terrorism field, special investigation techniques can include blocking the financial transactions of individuals or entities where the transaction or movement has been made for the purposes of, or in the course of, the perpetration of terrorist activities, or to contribute to the aims pursued by terrorist groups or organisations. Similarly, it is possible to prevent the opening of accounts in financial entities or their subsidiaries operating in Spain, owned or controlled by such individuals or for which they are designated representatives. These measures were introduced by Law No. 12/2003 of 31 May on the prevention and freezing of the financing of terrorism, drafted in application of United Nations Security Council Resolution 1373 (2001).

4.   How does the legal framework governing the use of SITs guarantee respect for human rights and individual freedoms, the principles of subsidiarity and proportionality? Is the authorisation to use SITs subject to time-limits? Which bodies and procedures are in place to supervise compliance with human rights standards and with the above-mentioned principles in the use of SITs? Is supervision automatic/systematic?

The use of special investigation techniques is based on the lawfulness principle, given that their use and regulations are provided for in a text having the force of law. At the same time however, they uphold fundamental human rights.

Accordingly, when special investigation techniques affect fundamental rights, infiltrated officers must obtain from the competent judicial body the authorisations laid down by the Constitution and the Law and must also comply with other applicable legislative provisions (Section 282.3 of the Criminal Procedure Act). Their activities must be commensurate with the purpose of the investigation; where this is not the case, they may be held criminally liable (Section 282.5).

In addition, all information obtained by infiltrated officers "shall be made fully available to the trial and be evaluated by the competent judicial body at its discretion" (Section 282 bis).

With regard to controlled delivery, the relevant texts provide that "the use of controlled delivery shall be made on a case-by-case basis and, at international level, shall be in accordance with the provisions contained in international treaties".

For joint investigation teams, Implementing Act No. 3/2003 of 21 May provides that, in the exercise of their activities, members of the teams are subject to the same criminal liability regime as the Spanish public authorities and their officers and staff.

In order to comply with the principle of proportionality as regards the freezing of transactions, such measures cannot be decided without a hearing of the person concerned, unless such would seriously compromise the effectiveness of the measure or be contrary to the public interest. In general terms, such measures may not last longer than six months, and this period may be extended only by a court order if the reasons behind the original decision continue to be valid; in this case there must be a hearing of the person concerned. In any event, it is provided that the Supervisory Committee shall order the cessation of the measure when the investigations carried out have failed to show that the assets in question bear any relationship to the financing of terrorist activity. All decisions by the Supervisory Committee may be appealed against directly via the courts, and such appeals must be given priority. Where there are criminal proceedings ongoing simultaneously, it is for the courts to take a decision on the measure to freeze accounts.

5.   Which institutions are involved in the use of SITs and what is their role (e.g. law enforcement agencies, prosecutor's office, judicial authorities, etc.)? Which institutions can order and/or authorise the use of SITs? How does co-operation between these institutions work in practice?

As regards the competent authorities for authorising such techniques, notwithstanding what has been stated above, in the case of joint investigation teams, the competent authority is, depending on the nature of the case, either the Ministry of Justice or the Ministry of the Interior, except in certain matters, such as terrorism, for which the competent body is the *Audiencia Nacional*.

6.   Are there any specialised counter-terrorism institutions? What is their role in the use of SITs?

From a judicial point of view, the *Audiencia Nacional* is the institution with responsibility for dealing with acts of terrorism. The preliminary enquiries, investigations and indictment proceedings are assigned to different bodies: the central investigation courts, the central criminal courts or the criminal division of the *Audiencia Nacional*. It is for the central investigation courts, on their own motion or upon application, to order, in the course of criminal proceedings, special investigation techniques in relation to acts of terrorism.

The *Audiencia Nacional* also has a public prosecution department, headed by a chief prosecutor, responsible, amongst other things, for initiating the necessary criminal or civil proceedings in response to offences or crimes, and to take action in criminal cases by asking the courts to adopt appropriate preventive measures and to carry out procedural acts to elucidate the facts. He may order the police to carry out any other measures he deems appropriate (Law No. 50/81 of 30 December on the Statute of the Public Prosecution Service).

With regard to joint investigation teams, the *Audiencia Nacional* is once again the competent authority in Spain in cases of terrorism (Section 3 of Law No. 11/2003 of 21 May). In such cases, it is for the *Audiencia Nacional* to set up a joint investigation team when operating in Spain, or to ask for such a team to be set up when it will be operating outside Spain (Sections 4 and 12 of Law No. 11/2003 of 21 May).

From an administrative point of view, the Supervisory Committee on Activities relating to the Financing of Terrorism was set up under Law No. 12/2003 of 21 May on the prevention and freezing of the financing of terrorism.The acts of this committee may be appealed against before the courts, including the *Audiencia Nacional* (Section 66 of the Judiciary Act, in accordance with the wording appearing in Implementing Act No. 4/2003 of 21 May).

7.   Which measures have been adopted in order to facilitate international co-operation (e.g. joint investigation teams)? Can the SITs listed in reply to question 1 be used in cross-border settings?

Spain has adopted several measures to facilitate international co-operation in this field. Legislation includes the abovementioned Law No. 11/2003 of 21 May governing joint investigation teams within the context of the European Union and Law No. 12 /2003 of 21 May on the prevention and freezing of the financing of terrorism. With regard to controlled delivery, there are explicit provisions (Section 263 bis. 3 of the Criminal Procedure Act) whereby "the use of controlled delivery shall be ... in accordance with the provisions contained in international treaties." Spain is also party to relevant international conventions of the United Nations and European Union.

8.   What use can be made of SIT in the context of mutual legal assistance?

International co-operation in this field could be improved, particularly through joint investigation teams, as a means of co-ordinating investigations into organised crime-related offences, especially in connection with terrorism.

Secondly, agreements on the freezing of movements of capital, ordered in a member state, could be extended as part of international co-operation in the fight against organised crime, to other countries wishing to co-operate in this sphere.

9.   How can the use of SITs be improved? Please provide any comments/proposals concerning the implementation of the terms of reference of the PC-TI and in particular the use and regulation of SITs.

Possible improvements in this field could include enhanced co-operation between operational units and a study into the ways and means of making international recommendations on the fight against the financing of terrorism more effective.

Sweden

1. Please indicate the SITs used in your country, the respective legal framework governing their use and their legal definition, if any.

Secret wiretapping and secret tele-surveillance is regulated in the Code of Judicial Procedure (Chapter 27). Secret wiretapping is the covert monitoring or recording by technical means of telecommunications, conveyed to or from a telephone number, a code or other telecommunications address, for reproduction of the content of the message.

Secret tele-surveillance means the covert reporting of telecommunications conveyed to or from certain telecommunications to or from a certain telecommunications address or that such a message is prevented from reaching its destination.

Search of premises is also regulated in the Code of Judicial Procedure (Chapter 28).

Secret camera surveillance is regulated in a separate law (1995:1506).

Cross-border (hot) pursuits are regulated in the Act (2002:343) on International Police Co-operation.

Bugging is not permitted in Sweden.

Currently, Swedish legislation does not contain any stipulations concerning the other SiTs listed in the questionnaire. Some of them – for example, undercover operations (not allowing for new identities), controlled delivery and pseudo-purchases – are to some extent used by the police. The need for legislation explicitly allowing for SiTs is being discussed in a drafting committee on the development of the judicial system.

2. When and under which circumstances (e.g. criminal investigation, preliminary stage, etc.) can SITs be used?

Surveillance

Secret wiretapping, secret tele-surveillance and secret camera surveillance are allowed only within the framework of a preliminary investigation.

Secret wiretapping and secret tele-surveillance require that someone is reasonably suspected of a crime and that the measure is of utter importance to the investigation. It may only used on a telephone that the suspect is likely to use or contact.

Secret wiretapping may be used in preliminary investigations (1) concerning crimes punishable by imprisonment for at least two years, (2) attempt, preparation or conspiracy to commit such a crime or (3) another offence, if it can be assumed in view of the circumstances that the offence will carry a penalty of more than two years' imprisonment.

Secret tele-surveillance may be used in preliminary investigations concerning (1) crimes punishable by imprisonment for at least six months, (2) breach of data secrecy, child pornography crimes and certain drug offences, or (3) attempt, preparation or conspiracy to commit crimes that are punishable according to (1) or (2).

Secret camera surveillance may be used in preliminary investigations (1) concerning crimes punishable by imprisonment for at least two years, (2) attempt, preparation or conspiracy to commit such a crime or (3) another offence, if it can be assumed in view of the circumstances that the offence will carry a penalty of more than two years' imprisonment.

The measures may only be imposed if the reasons for the measure outweigh the consequent intrusion or other detriment to the suspect or to another adverse interest.

Search of premises

If there is reason to believe that an offence punishable by imprisonment has been committed, any house, room, or closed place of storage, may be searched in order to uncover any object that is subject to seizure, or otherwise to detect any circumstance that may be of importance to the investigation of the offence.

The premises of a person, other than one reasonably suspected of having committed the offence, may not be searched unless the offence was committed there, the suspect was apprehended there, or extraordinary reason indicates that the search will reveal an object liable to seizure or other information concerning the offence.

Cross-border (hot) pursuits

In the case of an on-going investigation in another state (that is, EU member states, Norway and Iceland) concerning a crime that could lead to extradition, foreign officers may continue the surveillance of a suspect, initiated on their own territory, on Swedish territory, if a Swedish competent authority has given its authorisation. Surveillance may be conducted without preceding authorisation, if the matter is of such urgency that authorisation cannot be acquired in advance and if it concerns crimes referred to under Article 40.7 of the Schengen Convention.

Supervision

All Swedish authorities are supervised by the Parliamentary Ombudsman, (*Riksdagens ombudsmän JO*), the Chancellor of Justice (*Justitiekanslern JK*) and the National Board of Auditors (*RiksrevisionDCCPerket RRV*).

3. Are there any specific features governing the use of SITs in relation to acts of terrorism? If so, please specify.

The Act (1952: 98) with special regulations on coercive measures in certain cases (e.g. crimes against national security and terrorism), contains supplementary and exceptional stipulations for urgent cases. According to this law, interception of communications and secret camera surveillance may be used for some crimes that do not meet the requirements of the Code of Judicial Procedure. According to the Act of 1952, the prosecutor may also decide in urgent cases (instead of the court). The decision must, without delay, be reported to the court, which speedily shall review the matter.

According to the Act (1991: 572) concerning special control in respect of aliens, the court may grant the police permission to examine letters or use interception of telephone conversation and telecommunication surveillance. Such measures may only be imposed in order to find out if a foreigner, or an organisation he belongs to, is planning acts of terrorism.

4. How does the legal framework governing the use of SITs guarantee respect for human rights and individual freedoms, the principles of subsidiarity and proportionality? Is the authorisation to use SITs subject to time-limits? Which bodies and procedures are in place to supervise compliance with human rights standards and with the above-mentioned principles in the use of SITs? Is supervision automatic/systematic?

The court decides on interception of communications. The decision shall specify the duration, which may not be longer than necessary and not exceed one month. The decision can be prolonged. According to the Code of Judicial Procedure, the measure may only be imposed if the reasons for the measure outweigh the consequent intrusion or other detriment to the suspect or to another adverse interest. The same condition applies to searches.

A public representative shall watch over the interests of individuals' integrity in cases concerning secret wiretapping, secret tele-surveillance and secret camera surveillance that come before a court. A public representative has the right to receive all information in the case, the right to speak in the case and the right to appeal against the decision of the court.

The principle of proportionality is laid down in the Police Act.

In addition to this, the following general principles, discussed in the bill proposing the Police Act, are considered to apply for the use of SITs:

- The police must never commit a criminal act in order to investigate or detect a crime.
- The police must never provoke or induce a person to initiate a criminal act.
- The police must never for surveillance reasons neglect to take the measures laid down by law against crime or against a person suspected of crime (although an intervention may be postponed).
- Decisions on SITs shall be made by a prosecutor or a police officer holding the position of police commissioner, and must always be documented.

5. Which institutions are involved in the use of SITs and what is their role (e.g. law enforcement agencies, prosecutor's office, judicial authorities, etc.)? Which institutions can order and/or authorise the use of SITs? How does co-operation between these institutions work in practice?

A preliminary investigation is initiated either by the police or by the prosecutor. If it is initiated by the police and the matter is not of a simple nature, the prosecutor shall take over its conduct as soon as someone can be reasonably suspected of the offence. The prosecutor shall also take over the conduct of the investigation if special reasons so require.

When there is need to use interception of communications in a preliminary investigation, the police contact the public prosecutor. The prosecutor can then apply to the court for a decision. If the court allows interception, the police execute the measure.

Orders for the search of premises are issued by the investigating authority, the prosecutor or the court. If delay entails risk, a policeman may conduct a search of premises without a search order.

6. Are there any specialised counter-terrorism institutions? What is their role in the use of SITs?

The Security Service is responsible for counter-terrorism. The Security Service is part of the police, and is subject to the same legislation.

7. Which measures have been adopted in order to facilitate international co-operation (e.g joint investigation teams)? Can the SITs listed in reply to question 1 be used in cross-border settings?

New legislation on joint investigation teams came into force on 1 January 2004, namely the Act (2003: 1171) on Joint Investigation Teams for Criminal Investigations and Ordinance (2003: 1176) on Joint Investigation Teams for Criminal Investigations, in order to implement the Framework Decision on Joint Investigation Teams.

8. What use can be made of SITs in the context of mutual legal assistance?

The general principle in the Act (2000: 562) on International Legal Assistance in Criminal Matters is that every measure, including SITs (e.g. searches, interception of telecommunications and secret camera surveillance), that is available to the Swedish authorities in domestic investigations and proceedings is available for a foreign authority under the same conditions as in domestic cases.

Switzerland

Introductory remarks

While the substance of criminal law in Switzerland falls within the competence of the Confederation (central government), criminal procedure still remains within that of the cantons (federal states). We therefore have 26 different cantonal codes of procedure, in addition to a Federal Code of Criminal Procedure (covering offences within the competence of the Confederation, which include espionage, organised crime, money laundering, corruption, etc.), a Military Code of Criminal Procedure (covering offences under the Military Criminal Code) and an administrative criminal procedure.

On 12 March 2000, the Swiss people adopted an amendment to the federal constitution transferring criminal procedure from the competence of the cantons to the Confederation. The Swiss Federal Department of Justice is therefore now working on a draft unified Code of Criminal Procedure. It is planned to submit it to Parliament by the end of 2004.

It should be pointed out that, despite the existence of a plethora of codes of procedure, the case-law of the Federal Court has a harmonising effect with respect to the fundamental rights protected by the constitution and the European Convention on Human Rights. The same is true of the case-law of the Strasbourg Court of Human Rights, which is also directly applicable in Swiss law.

The replies that follow refer essentially to the Federal Code of Criminal Procedure (FCCP).

1.   Please indicate the SITs used in your country, the respective legal framework governing their use and their legal definition, if any.

Undercover operations

Undercover operations are used in Switzerland at federal level in the framework of police investigations (FCCP Article 100 ff). The Federal Act on Secret Investigations (FASI, RO 2004, 1409), which regulates investigation techniques for federal and cantonal authorities, will enter into force on 1 January 2005. The use of secret investigations is confined to a restricted list of offences (Article 4, paragraph 2 FASI).

Front store operations

These are not used in Switzerland. First experiences with the FASI will assist, in particular, in deciding if this technique should be used in the future.

Informants

Although they have no formal legal basis, informants are used in Switzerland. They are regarded as tactical police instruments. As there is no formal legal basis, there is no strict legal definition.

Controlled delivery

No formal legal standard in Swiss law, but used in Switzerland. Controlled delivery is possible in the framework of police investigations. This investigation technique is, however, regulated by the German-Swiss agreement on police matters (Article 19), as well as in the agreement between the Swiss Confederation, the Republic of Austria and the Principality of Liechtenstein on cross-border co-operation by the relevant authorities on security and customs matters (Article 12).

Observation

This is used in Switzerland. At federal level, observation is referred to in the Federal Act on the Central Criminal Police Offices of the Confederation (Article 3(f)), but no formal legal standard provides for it. It is a tactical police instrument. Cross-border observation is regulated by Article 14 of the German-Swiss agreement on police matters, Article 10 of the agreement between the Swiss Confederation, the Republic of Austria and the Principality of Liechtenstein on cross-border co-operation by the relevant authorities on security and customs matters, and Article 7 of the agreement between the Swiss Federal Council and the French Republic on cross-border co-operation on judicial, police and customs matters. In the absence of a formal legal basis at federal level, there is no strict legal definition.

Electronic surveillance

This is used in Switzerland. The term electronic surveillance covers the use of GPS transmitters and video surveillance. The use of GPS transmitters is not regulated by any formal legislative norm.

Video surveillance is a tactical police instrument used only in the public domain (violations are punishable under Article 179quater of the Criminal Code). However in the framework of a police investigation it may also be used in the private sphere of a particular individual.

Bugging

This is used in Switzerland. Only the federal police have bugging equipment that may be used inside buildings.

Interception of communications

Interception of communications is used in Switzerland. It is regulated by the Federal Act of 6 October 2000 on surveillance of post and telecommunications correspondence.

Taking into account current technical means, the Act regulates surveillance of postal correspondence and interception of telephone conversations (mobile and land lines), faxes and e-mails.

Searches

Provided for in the FCCP (Article 67 ff and 73bis) and all the cantonal codes. Searches are used in Switzerland. The circumstances in which they may be conducted are set out in law.

Cross-border pursuits

Cross-border pursuits are used. They are regulated by Article 11 of the agreement between the Swiss Confederation, the Republic of Austria and the Principality of Liechtenstein on cross-border co-operation by the relevant authorities on security and customs matters, Article 16 of the German-Swiss agreement on police matters, and Article 5, ch. 2, and Article 8 of the agreement between the Swiss Federal Council and the Government of the French Republic on cross-border co-operation on judicial, police and customs matters.

Agents provocateurs

The case-law of the Federal Court prohibits the use of *agents provocateurs*. Consequently, no evidence gathered in this way may be used in court.

Pseudo-purchases or other "pseudo-offences"

Once the FASI has entered into force, it will be possible to conclude fictitious deals in connection with the offences that appear in the restricted list of offences mentioned above (Article 20 FASI; "necessary amounts to make fictitious deals").

2.   When and under which circumstances (e.g. criminal investigation, preliminary stage, etc.) can SITs be used?

Undercover operations

These may be used only where there is sufficient reason to presume that offences falling within the jurisdiction of the federal court have been committed.

Informants

They are used to establish a presumption of guilt and provide evidence that will enable a suspect to be charged. They are therefore used in the framework of both police investigations and preliminary inquiries.

Observation

It is used to establish a presumption of guilt and provide evidence that will enable a suspect to be charged. It is therefore used in the framework of both police investigations and preliminary inquiries.

Electronic surveillance

It is used to establish a presumption of guilt and provide evidence that will enable a suspect to be charged.

Bugging

Since it is a coercive measure, it may be used only in the framework of a criminal investigation that has been formally opened or where there are sufficient grounds for suspicion.

Interception of communications

Since it is a coercive measure, it may be used only in the framework of a criminal investigation that has been formally opened into the offences listed in Article 3, paragraphs 2 and 3, of the Federal Act of 6 October 2000 on surveillance of post and telecommunications correspondence.

Searches

Since they are a coercive measure, they may be used only in the framework of a criminal investigation that has been formally opened or where there are sufficient grounds for suspicion.

Cross-border pursuits

They are used to establish a presumption of guilt and provide evidence that will enable a suspect to be charged.

3. Are there any specific features governing the use of SITs in relation to acts of terrorism? If so, please specify.

Generally speaking, the measures referred to here are applied according to the gravity of offences and taking into account the ease or, on the contrary, the difficulty, of gathering evidence in the various areas of crime. In other words, they are not restricted to the case of terrorism. Furthermore, no investigation technique is confined to cases of terrorism in Switzerland.

With respect to interception of communications, although terrorism is not mentioned as a distinct offence in the Swiss Criminal Code, all terrorism-related offences are included in the list of offences for which this SIT may be implemented.

4.   How does the legal framework governing the use of SITs guarantee respect for human rights and individual freedoms, the principles of subsidiarity and proportionality? Is the authorisation to use SITs subject to time-limits? Which bodies and procedures are in place to supervise compliance with human rights standards and with the above-mentioned principles in the use of SITs? Is supervision automatic/systematic?

Since they flow from the values underlying constitutional law and administrative law, the authorities must comply with the principles of proportionality and subsidiarity in every measure they take, whether or not that measure has a formal legal basis.

Coercive measures are always ordered by the prosecuting authorities and may never be implemented on police initiative.

Action taken by the federal police may be disputed before the Principal State Counsel of the Confederation (FCCP Article 105bis, paragraph 1); as for operations and omissions of the Principal State Counsel, a complaint may be lodged with the Indictments Chamber of the Federal Court (FCCP Article 105bis, paragraph 2).

5.   Which institutions are involved in the use of SITs and what is their role (e.g. law enforcement agencies, prosecutor's Office, judicial authorities, etc)? Which institutions can order and/or authorise the use of SITs? How does co-operation between these institutions work in practice?

In general, the authorities concerned with the implementation of SITs are the prosecuting authorities and the police. The latter may use SITs on their own initiative, provided they do not constitute interference with private life. If they do, these are coercive measures and must either be authorised by the prosecuting authorities or, depending on the particular SIT (interception of communications, searches and undercover operations), a court.

Undercover operations

Such operations must be authorised by the federal prosecuting authorities. A contact person supervises the undercover agent and makes contact with the authority in charge of the procedure (Article 11 FASI). This SIT is used by special federal police units in all areas of crime within the competence of the federal court, provided that it is in connection with an offence that appears in the restricted list of offences mentioned above (Article 4, paragraph 2 FASI).

Informants

The use of such persons is not in practice subject to authorisation by the prosecuting authorities. However, where informants are used in connection with police investigations, those authorities are generally informed.

Controlled delivery

Controlled delivery is subject to authorisation by the relevant prosecuting authorities (those of a canton or of the Confederation).

Observation

In practice, this investigation technique is not subject to authorisation by the prosecuting authorities. However, in order to avoid its taking on the character of a coercive measure, it has been restricted to the public domain.

Electronic surveillance

In practice, the prosecuting authorities (in co-operation with the police) make a distinction according to whether or not the use of a GPS transmitter constitutes interference in private life (interference exists where the mechanism is installed inside a vehicle; there is no interference where it is simply placed outside the vehicle). Where the use of a GPS transmitter (in the context of police investigations) constitutes interference in private life, it is subject to authorisation by the prosecuting authorities; where, on the other hand, it does not interfere with private life, it is considered a tactical police instrument which, as such, may be used without authorisation from the prosecuting authorities, as well as in the framework of preliminary inquiries seeking to establish a presumption of guilt.

Where video surveillance is conducted only in the public domain, it is not subject to authorisation by the prosecuting authorities. However, it may also be used in the private sphere of a particular person in the framework of a police investigation (cf FCCP Article 170octies), provided it has been ordered by the prosecuting authorities and that order has been approved by the Complaints Chamber of the Federal Criminal Court (Article 28 FA on the Federal Criminal Court).

Bugging

Like video surveillance, bugging is a coercive measure that the federal police may use on the order of the prosecuting authorities and with the approval of the Complaints Chamber of the Federal Criminal Court.

Interception of communications

Interception of communications is subject to the principles of subsidiarity and proportionality. It may only be used in a police investigation on the order of the prosecuting authorities and with the approval of the Complaints Chamber of the Federal Criminal Court.

Searches

The prosecuting authorities may order them in the context of police investigations (FCP Article 71).

Cross-border pursuits

These are a tactical police instrument and are not subject to authorisation by the prosecuting authorities.

6.   Are there any specialised counter-terrorism institutions? What is their role in the use of SITs?

No.

7.   Which measures have been adopted in order to facilitate international co-operation (e.g. joint investigation teams)? Can the SITs listed in reply to question 1 be used in cross-border settings?

International police co-operation is governed by the generally applicable provisions of the Federal Act on international mutual assistance in criminal matters. Agreements have also been concluded with Germany, France, Austria and Liechtenstein (see above), to which should be added the agreement between the Swiss Confederation and the Italian Republic on co-operation between police and customs authorities.

International co-operation on secret investigations is not only possible but indispensable in some cases in view of the limited size of Swiss territory. However, it is only regulated in the German-Swiss agreement on police matters (Article 17) and not in the other three police co-operation agreements Switzerland has concluded with its neighbours.

8.   What use can be made of SITs in the context of mutual legal assistance?

Where appropriate, the measures mentioned above may be applied in the framework of requests for mutual legal assistance made by foreign authorities.

9.   How can the use of SITs be improved? Please provide any comments/proposals concerning the implementation of the terms of reference of the PC-TI and in particular the use and regulation of SITs.

This question is very political. There are two opposing camps, one in favour of extending the use of SITs in order better to protect society from crime, the other in favour of restricting (and strictly supervising) their use in order better to protect citizens from police interference in their private lives.

"The former Yugoslav Republic of Macedonia"

According to our present Constitution, SITs are not allowed. Namely, Article 17 says: The freedom and confidentiality of correspondence and other forms of communication is guaranteed. Only a court decision may authorise non–application of the principle of the inviolability of confidentiality of correspondence and other forms of communication, in cases where it is indispensable to a criminal investigation or required in the interest of defence of the Republic.

However, now in the procedure there are new changes to our criminal legislation, which release the constitution for Article 17 and a new Code of Criminal Procedure. In order to obtain data and evidence necessary for successful conduct of criminal procedure, that cannot be obtained in another way, or their obtaining would be in circumstances of disproportionate difficulties, against a person for whom there is a ground for suspicion that he/she has perpetrated a criminal offence mentioned in this law, the undertaking of special measures can be ordered, from within the following:

- Monitoring and recording telephone conversations and other types of communication by electronic and other technical devices and monitoring and recording in rooms with technical means;
- Access (insight) into a computer system of a bank or another legal entity that performs financial activities;
- Ostensible (simulated) purchase of goods and ostensible (simulated) giving of a bribe and ostensible taking of a bribe;
- Controlled delivery of goods and persons;
- Opening of an ostensible (simulated) banking account, where funds originating from a criminal offence could be deposited;
- Use of persons with undercover identity;
- Secret surveillance, monitoring and recording of people and objects by use of technical devices.

The measures mentioned in the bullet points above are ordered by the president of the competent appellate court or the judge appointed by him/her with the annual schedule, under the circumstances and in a procedure determined by law. These measures can be ordered also for persons for whom there are grounds for suspicion that they will exchange messages regarding the act with the perpetrator of the offences mentioned in an article of this law, and also in cases where the perpetrator is using their telephone, telex, telefax, computer connections or similar devices.

Some of the measures mentioned above are ordered by the investigative judge, by his/her written order, upon a proposal (with a rationale) of the public prosecutor. In case of disagreements between the public prosecutor and the investigative judge, the council takes the decision.

In a court order on measures from the bullet points above, the data on the person against whom the measures will be applied must be noted, as well as the grounds for suspicion regarding the criminal offence concerned, the manner, extent and the duration of such measures.

The implementation of measures can last up to 30 days and for justified reasons the duration of the measures can be extended, but up to the maximum of two instances of 30 days each. In exceptionally complex cases of organised forms of severe criminal offences perpetrated by many persons, in a large area, in several states, or when there is a well-founded danger that with severe criminal and subversive activities the safety and the defence of the state are jeopardised, the court can extend the time period for permanent monitoring of communications up to one year.

After the termination of implementation of these measures, the Ministry of the Interior has the duty to communicate to the court a report and to submit all the reports and objects obtained by their implementation. The court determines whether the Ministry of the Interior acted according to its order and invites the public prosecutor to familiarise themself with the materials obtained with the implementation of the measures. If the public prosecutor, after becoming familiar with the objects and the information from the measures undertaken, states that he/she will not initiate a criminal procedure, the materials will be destroyed under the supervision of the court, on which a minute will be prepared.

Some of the measures mentioned in paragraph 1, items 4, 5, 6 and 7 of this article are undertaken on the basis of an approval by the public prosecutor. After the termination of the implementation of these measures, the Ministry of the Interior has the obligation to communicate a report to the public prosecutor.

The measures from paragraph 1 of this article are implemented by the Ministry of the Interior. The implementation of the measures is terminated immediately after the termination of reasons due to which the measures were ordered.

The undertaking of the measures mentioned in this article must not inspire perpetration of a criminal offence. Also there is a gradation in what kind of measure should be taken for what kind of criminal offence.

Turkey

1. Please indicate the SITs used in your country, the respective legal framework governing their use and their legal definition, if any.

Having had to cope with terrorism for more than two decades, Turkey is well equipped with internal legal instruments required for the struggle against terrorism. It is also party to a number of bilateral and multilateral agreements on co-operation in the prevention of terrorism and in connection with this, organised crime and drugs trafficking. According to the new Turkish Code on Criminal Proceeding, which is going to come into effect after 1 April 2005, SITs can be also applied to serious offences such as human trafficking, migrant smuggling and murder.

Turkey has various legislation that contains provisions that may apply to the prevention and suppression of both terrorism and the financing of it. The basic legal instruments prohibiting and penalising terrorist acts are:
- The Law on the Fight Against Terrorism,
- The Penal Code,
- The Law on the Prevention of Money Laundering,
- The Law on Combating Benefit-Orientated Criminal Organisations.

Undercover operations, informants, controlled delivery, observation (including cross-border observation), electronic surveillance, bugging, interception of communications, searches and pseudo-purchases are the techniques commonly used in Turkey during investigations.

Undercover operations and informants are used in order to gather information before the committing of terrorist acts. Law enforcement bodies take advantage of information given by informants before both the perpetration and planning of the act.

Controlled delivery is governed under the Law on the Prevention of Money Laundering, Law No. 4208. Article 10 of the said Law stipulates the following conditions to apply controlled delivery:

a. Existence of a very seriously organised smuggling activity that falls within the scope of controlled delivery,

b. Absence of other means to expose organisers, capital owners and members of the organisation and to find out all the evidence pertaining to them,

c. Securing the supervision of the smuggled goods or funds till they reach the final destination without any interruption,

d. Existence of a required period of time for controlled delivery,

e. Additionally, for goods and funds prepared in Turkey for smuggling in order to be taken abroad or transported in transit through Turkey, the following conditions must be met:

1. Assurance of the requesting state for the uninterrupted continuance of controlled delivery and prosecution and investigation of perpetrators,

2. Commitment for the extradition of Turkish nationals and repatriation of substances and funds, together with the vehicles used for their transport, by the state where the controlled delivery has come to an end and the Turkish nationals have been captured.

Implementation of controlled delivery shall be decided by the Chief Public Prosecutor of the State Security Court of Ankara, provided that the conditions stated in Article 10 exist. In case the follow-up and surveillance operations are in danger or if the possibility of loss of evidence or escape of the accused arises when controlled deliveries are carried on, controlled delivery shall, without a decision, be terminated immediately. The jurisdictional power with respect to controlled delivery belongs to the court where the operation terminates. Controlled delivery shall not abolish the jurisdictional power of the Turkish courts.

The Law on Combating Benefit-Orientated Criminal Organisations empowered the law enforcement authorities with several new investigative techniques, yet with full respect for human rights, such as telephone tapping or intercepting telecommunications, clandestine surveillance, employing secret agents. Intercepting or recording communications, secret surveillance, reviewing records and data, and using secret agents.

Signals, writings, pictures, images or sounds and other type of information received or sent by means of cable or non-cable or any other electromagnetic devices like telephone, facsimile and computer or one-way systems by the persons suspected of committing or participating the offences stated in this Act or abetting or acting as intermediaries or harbouring the offenders in any way after the offence has been committed, may be intercepted or recorded, The records shall be minuted by means of sealing by competent authorities.

The decisions on carrying out interception or recording can only be made upon the existence of strong criminal indications.

When it is possible to detect and to catch the offender or to obtain the evidences of the offence by means of another measure, no decision shall be made on intercepting or recording.

The provisions mentioned above shall also apply to the records which are kept by any official or private communication organisations except for the content of the record pertaining to that communication.

The judges shall decide whether to conduct interception or recording or examining the records. Public Prosecutors shall also have the power on these matters in cases where delay might cause problems. It is required to have a judge's decision within 24 hours for this sort of activities where carried out without a judge's decision. In cases where this period finishes, or where the judge makes a decision against these activities, this provisional measure shall be lifted by the Public Prosecutor immediately.

The decisions on intercepting and recording may be for maximum period of three months. Such periods may be extended twice at most, provided that each extension shall be three months.

If the suspicion regarding commission of the offences disappears during interception or recording then the provisional measure shall be lifted by the Public Prosecutor. In that case, data obtained as a result of conducting such provisional measures shall be deleted immediately and within a maximum of 10 days under control of the Public Prosecutor and this situation shall be minuted.

When the Public Prosecutor or the law enforcement officer assigned by the Public Prosecutor requests those who are the officers in communication organisations or those who have the authority to carry out such services, to perform interception and recording processes and to install devices for this purpose, this request shall be immediately met and starting and finishing dates and hours pertaining to this activity shall be minuted.

Article 3 of the Act mentioned provides that: "Any activities of those who are suspected of committing the offences stated in this Act in their residences, business places or public places may be observed, monitored or recorded secretly by means of audio visual devices."

Except for the ones requiring to be kept secret in respect of national security of the state, any official or private records or computer data pertaining to the persons exhibiting attitudes or behaviour suggesting the commission of the offences at their locations, institutions, environs and establishments may be examined in order to uncover offences stated in this Act or evidences related to these offences.

Agents provocateurs are not available in Turkish law. Only agents can be used, but not with the intention of provocation. Cross-border (hot) pursuits, are preventive law enforcement measures and do not fall into our ministry's scope of responsibility.

2. When and under which circumstances (e.g. criminal investigation, preliminary stage, etc.) can SITs be used?

Special investigative techniques can be used in both criminal investigations and preliminary stages.

3.   Are there any specific features governing the use of SITs in relation to acts of terrorism? If so, please specify.

Specific features are as mentioned in the answer to the first question.

4.   How does the legal framework governing the use of SITs guarantee respect for human rights and individual freedoms, the principles of subsidiarity and proportionality? Is the authorisation to use SITs subject to time-limits? Which bodies and procedures are in place to supervise compliance with human rights standards and with the above-mentioned principles in the use of SITs? Is supervision automatic/systematic?

Personal liberty and security, privacy of individual life, inviolability of the home and freedom of communication are not only guaranteed but also limited by constitutional provisions, as explained below.

Individuals against whom there is strong evidence of having committed an offence can be arrested by decision of a judge solely for the purposes of preventing escape, or preventing the destruction or alteration of evidence as well as in similar other circumstances which necessitate detention and are prescribed by law. Apprehension of a person without a decision by a judge shall be resorted to only in cases when a person is caught in the act of committing an offence or in cases where delay is likely to thwart the course of justice; the conditions for such acts shall be defined by law.

Individuals arrested or detained shall be promptly notified, and in all cases in writing, or orally, when the former is not possible, of the grounds for their arrest or detention and the charges against them; in cases of offences committed collectively this notification shall be made, at the latest, before the individual is brought before a judge.

The person arrested or detained shall be brought before a judge within at latest 48 hours and in the case of offences committed collectively within at most four days, excluding the time taken to send the individual to the court nearest to the place of arrest. No one can be deprived of his or her liberty without the decision of a judge after the expiry of the above-specified periods. These periods may be extended during a state of emergency, under martial law or in time of war.

The arrest or detention of a person shall be notified to next of kin immediately.

Unless there exists a decision duly passed by a judge on one or several of the grounds of national security, public order, prevention of crime commitment, protection of public health and public morals, or protection of the rights and freedoms of others, or unless there exists a written order of an agency authorised by law in cases where delay is prejudicial, again on the abovementioned grounds, neither the person nor the private papers, nor belongings, of an individual shall be searched nor shall they be seized and no dwelling may be entered or searched or the property therein seized. The decision of the authorised agency shall be submitted for the approval of the judge having jurisdiction within 24 hours. The judge shall announce his decision within 48 hours from the time of seizure; otherwise, seizure shall automatically be lifted.

Secrecy of communication is fundamental, unless there exists a decision duly passed by a judge on one or several of the grounds of national security, public order, prevention of crime commitment, protection of public health and public morals, or protection of the rights and freedoms of others, or unless there exists a written order of an agency authorised by law in cases where delay is prejudicial, again on the abovementioned grounds, communication shall not be impeded nor its secrecy be violated. The decision of the authorised agency shall be submitted for the approval of the judge having jurisdiction within 24 hours. The judge shall announce his decision within 48 hours from the time of seizure; otherwise, seizure shall automatically be lifted. Public establishments or institutions where exceptions to the above may be applied are defined by law.

As understood from the abovementioned constitutional provisions, implementation of any kind of special investigative technique is subject to the approval of a judge; in other words in every stage of the implementation judicial review is obligatory.

5.   Which institutions are involved in the use of SITs and what is their role (e.g. law enforcement agencies, prosecutor's office, judicial authorities, etc.)? Which institutions can order and/or authorise the use of SITs? How does co-operation between these institutions work in practice?

In criminal investigations and in the preliminary stage, law enforcement agencies are involved in the use of SITs under the supervision of the Public Prosecutor's office and a judge. Law enforcement agencies request permission for the use of SITs; in urgent circumstances the Public Prosecutor gives permission first, afterwards submitting it to the judge's approval. In ordinary circumstances, law enforcement agencies request permission and the Public Prosecutor forwards it to the judge with his/her opinion added, and the judge makes a decision whether it is convenient and necessary to use SITs.

6.   Are there any specialised counter-terrorism institutions? What is their role in the use of SITs?

Specialised counter-terrorism institutions are outside the scope of the Ministry of Justice. Since it is deemed to be a kind of preventive law enforcement agency, it is at the discretion of the Ministry of the Interior.

7. Which measures have been adopted in order to facilitate international co-operation (e.g. joint investigation teams)? Can the SITs listed in reply to question 1 be used in cross-border settings?

In order to combat terrorism, many countries are inclined to enact special legislation or incorporate special articles into their criminal codes and codes of criminal procedure. Their acts are defined in terms of their targets, their nature and their effects. On this basis, they establish penalties equivalent to those applicable to similar criminal offences. Such kinds of legislation are important from the standpoint of effectiveness and respect for human and public liberties, and facilities for international co-operation, in particular regarding extradition.

Even though acts of terrorism often take place in one country, terrorism is an international phenomenon in that terrorists receive outside help, take refuge in other countries and commit their acts from places located abroad.

Terrorist acts should be regarded as serious offences, indeed as crimes. States should consider criminal acts among the offences subject to extradition under their criminal laws, they should prosecute anyone who has helped to organise, prepare or commit terrorist acts, and they should make terrorism an offence under their national legislation.

Turkey, being a country that has suffered from systematic campaigns of terrorism for many years, is determined to continue its struggle against terrorism. We therefore fully support all efforts aiming at combating terrorism.

As we experience it now, terrorism is not solely the problem of any single country but that of the whole international community; it is obvious that an appropriate solution can only be found through international effective co-operation. As we all know, criminals often flee the country where the crime was committed and find safe havens in other countries. Therefore their extradition is an effective measure for international co-operation in combating crime, but particularly terror crimes. Maintaining an effective fight against terrorism requires national legislation and efforts to be supported by international co-operation.

The greatest difficulty encountered in the implementation of international conventions is the frequent refusal to extradite perpetrators of terrorist acts. The same situation applies also to rogatory letters emanating from courts, which remain unprocessed. It is certain that the United Nations Model Agreements on Extradition and Mutual Assistance, as well as the European Convention on Extradition, provide for the exclusion of political offences from the scope of these agreements. However, a careful distinction must be made between a political offence and a terrorist crime.

According to the standards and norms set by these agreements, a terrorist crime shall not be deemed to be a political offence. The European Convention on the Suppression of Terrorism, to which Turkey is a state

414

party, stipulates in its Article 1, paragraph (e) that "an offence involving the use of a bomb, grenade, rocket, automatic firearm or letter or parcel bomb, if this use endangers persons;" shall not be regarded "as a political offence or as an offence connected with a political offence or as an offence inspired by political motives".

Similarly, Article 7 imposes the obligation on a contracting state in whose territory a person suspected to have committed a terrorist offence was found, and which refuses to extradite that person, to submit the case to its competent authorities for the purpose of prosecution.

Article 8 of the same convention stipulates that the "Contracting States shall afford one another the widest measure of mutual assistance in criminal matters in connection with proceedings brought in respect of those offences as mentioned in Article 1 or 2." Although the convention does not contain a definition of a political offence, it does clearly define and delineate acts of terrorism.

The said convention has, by ruling out political motives, made a big contribution to the fight against terrorism. Conversely, misuse of the right to asylum and the existence of reservations entered by states at the time of ratification are a hindrance to co-operation.

Article 13 of the convention provides that any state may declare that it reserves the right to refuse extradition in respect of any offence mentioned in Article 1 that it considers to be a political offence, an offence connected with a political offence or an offence inspired by political motives. The convention has altered extradition practices and assistance arrangements between the Council of Europe's member states.

However, there is a growing tendency to regard terrorist acts as political offences and this obstructs the extradition of their perpetrators. Moreover, states seem to grant terrorists refugee status easily. This is another obstacle to extradition, which should nevertheless over-ride requests for asylum. Although the 1959 European Convention on Mutual Assistance in Criminal Matters includes a similar provision, some contracting states regard acts of terrorism as political offences and reject requests for judicial co-operation; that effectly prevents terrorists from being prosecuted in their territories.

Article 3 of the 1957 European Convention on Extradition enables extradition to be refused in the case of a political offence. However international law, leaving it to each state's national legislation, does not make a definition of a political offence. Referring to the right of asylum, most countries give precedence to the spirit of Article 3 of the Geneva Convention; a request for asylum suspends extradition.

Furthermore, UN General Assembly Resolution 48/122, dated 20 December 1993, on "Human rights and terrorism" underlines, with reference to the UN Charter, the Universal Declaration of Human Rights and the Vienna

Declaration and Programme of Action, adopted by the World Conference on Human Rights, held in Vienna from 14 to 25 June 1993, "that the most essential and basic human right is the right to life", expresses serious concern "at the gross violation of human rights perpetrated by terrorist groups", profoundly deplores "the increasing number of innocent persons, including women, children and the elderly, killed, massacred and maimed by terrorists in indiscriminate and random acts of violence and terror, which cannot be justified under any circumstances", notes with great concern "the growing connection between the terrorist groups and the illegal traffic in arms and drugs", and,

> Mindful of the need to protect human rights of and guarantees for the individual in accordance with the relevant international human rights principles and instruments, particularly the right to life,

> Unequivocally condemns all acts, methods and practices of terrorism in all its forms and manifestations,…

> Calls upon States, in accordance with international standards of human rights, to take all necessary and effective measures to prevent, combat and eliminate terrorism,…

The Annex "Declaration of Measures to Eliminate International Terrorism" to UN General Assembly Resolution 49/60, adopted on 9 December 1994, on "Measures to Eliminate International Terrorism", expresses concern "at the growing and dangerous links between terrorist groups, drug traffickers and their paramilitary gangs", and "Solemnly declares" that (paragraph 3): "criminal acts intended or calculated to provoke a state of terror in the general public, a group of persons or particular persons for political purposes are in any circumstance unjustifiable, whatever the considerations of a political, philosophical, ideological, racial, ethnic, religious or any other nature that may be invoked to justify them;"

And, with reference to their contractual international obligations, it calls on states in its paragraph 5:

> (a) To refrain from organising, instigating, facilitating, financing, encouraging or tolerating terrorist activities and to take appropriate practical measures to ensure that their respective territories are not used for terrorist installations or training camps, or for the preparation or organisation of terrorists acts intended to be committed against other States or their citizens;

> (b) To ensure the apprehension and prosecution or extradition of perpetrators of terrorist acts, in accordance with the relevant provisions of their national law;…

and:

416

(f) To take appropriate measures, before granting asylum, for the purpose of ensuring that the asylum-seeker has not engaged in terrorist activities and, after granting asylum, for the purpose of ensuring that the refugee status is not used in a manner contrary to the provisions set out in subparagraph (a) above;

UN General Assembly Resolutions 50/53, 51/210, 52/165, 53/108 and 54/110 have reconfirmed the previous UN Resolutions on the subject, classifying "all acts, methods and practices of terrorim as criminal and unjustifiable, wherever and by whomsoever committeed" and called upon all states to adopt further measures to prevent terrorism and to strengthen international co-operation in combating terrorism.

Moreover, the UN Security Council, in its Resolution 1269 adopted on 18 October 1999, underlines – with reference to all relevant Resolutions of the General Assembly, including the above-mentioned Resolution 49/60 – the importance of effective co-operation between states and the full implementation of relevant international anti-terrorist conventions, and calls upon all states to:
- deny those who plan, finance or commit terrorist acts, safe havens by ensuring their apprehension and prosecution or extradition;
- take appropriate measures in conformity with the relevant provisions of national and international law, including international standards of human rights, before granting refugee status, for the purpose of ensuring that the asylum-seeker has not participated in terrorist acts;

Being the last stage, the UN Security Council, in its Resolution 1373 adopted on 28 September 2001, outlines, with reference to all relevant Resolutions of the General Assembly, in Article 3, paragraph (f) and (g) and calls upon all states to:

(f) Take appropriate measures in conformity with the relevant provisions of national and international law, including international standards of human rights before granting refugee status, for the purpose of ensuring that the asylum-seeker has not planned, facilitated or participated in the commission of terrorist acts;

(g) Ensure, in conformity with international law, that refugee status is not abused by the perpetrators,organisers or facilitators of terrorist acts and that claims of political motivation are not recognised as grounds for refusing requests for the extradition of alleged terrorists.

Against this background, suffice it to say that the refusal to extradite terrorists, despite the existence of a whole series of international conventions and resolutions on the issue, constitutes in itself a denial of justice, an obstacle to the implementation of international law and thus, to the prevention and suppression of crime.

Bearing in mind the international conventions and resolutions and in particular Article 33/2 of the Geneva Convention related to the Status of Refugees, all states should be sensitive before granting refugee status.

8. *What use can be made of SIT in the context of mutual legal assistance?*

The main catalyst for an adequate response to the challenge posed by the globalisation of terrorist crimes can only be a strengthening of international co-operation against it. Turkey has always advocated better-co-ordinated international co-operation in the prevention and prosecution of crime, including an effective system of bilateral and multilateral collaboration in the fields of law-enforcement and legal assistance in criminal matters.

For an effective, reliable and speedy exchange of information on terrorist activity, liaison officers are being reciprocally appointed with a number of countries (USA, Germany, Belgium, Denmark, France, Netherlands, UK, Spain, Italy and Saudi Arabia). There are also Turkish contact persons at expert level in Germany, Austria, Holland, Italy and Romania. Furthermore, within a well established co-operation and information-exchange mechanism, all information regarding persons for whom there are grounds to believe that they have been or will be involved in terrorist activities is immediately conveyed by the Turkish Ministry of the Interior to its counterparts.

The existing exchange of operational intelligence with regard the activities of terrorist groups within the co-operation between the relevant security authorities of Turkey and their foreign counterparts greatly intensified after the terrorist attacks of 11 September 2001.

Relevant bodies exchange intelligence and co-operate on administrative and judicial matters with their foreign counterparts with a view to preventing terrorist activities.

The Committee of Ministers, taking into consideration the lists of terrorist organisations, persons and entities attached to the UNSC Resolutions 1267/1999, 1333/2000 and 1373/2001, decided to freeze all the funds, financial assets, economic resources, rights and claims, including the contents of safe deposit boxes, of these terrorist organisations, persons and entities, in banks or non-bank institutions, and other real or corporate bodies. Also, according to the said decision, all transactions in relation to these assets are subject to the permission of the Ministry of Finance.

With a circular dated 25 October 2001, the Ministry of Justice has forwarded UNSC Resolution 1373 (2001) to all public prosecutors, with the instruction that the resolution be meticulously implemented and be taken into consideration with respect to requests for judicial assistance received in accordance with agreements to which Turkey is party. In addition to its multilateral commitments, Turkey is also party to bilateral agreements with some 40 countries on co-operation in combating terrorism, organised crime and drugs trafficking.

Turkey has ratified twelve UN Conventions relating to terrorism. Turkey has signed and ratified the 1977 European Convention on the Suppression of Terrorism. The fact that the Convention is far from being satisfactory with regard to current needs in the field has become evident over time. The very concept of "political crimes" contained in the text and the possibility of making reservations in matters of extradition have seriously flawed the mechanism stipulated by the convention. Turkey has long been stressing the need to update and if necessary revise the instrument.

9.   *How can the use of SITs be improved? Please provide any comments/proposals concerning the implementation of the terms of reference of the PC-TI and in particular the use and regulation of SITs.*

As mentioned through the whole text, it is important to make effective use of existing SITs. Bearing in mind the transnational feature of terrorist crimes, international co-operation among law enforcement authorities and judicial authorities on a broader scope is mandatory. Customary diplomatic channels for ensuring assistance between the law enforcement and judicial authorities of one state and another remain insufficient in cases of terror crimes.

Ukraine

1.   Please indicate the SITs used in your country, the respective legal framework governing their use and their legal definition, if any.

There is no specific definition of "special investigation techniques" (SIT) in Ukrainian law. Therefore, for the purposes of this document, this concept will be regarded in accordance with Article 4 of the European Convention on Laundering, Search, Seizure and Confiscation of Proceeds from Crime, which was ratified by Ukraine, using the definition of a SIT contained in documents PC-S CO(2000)3 and PC-TI (2003)Misc.2bil.rev. 1 recommended by the Expert Committee. There a SIT is defined as a way of gathering information systematically in such a way as not to alert the target person(s), applied by law enforcement officials for the purpose of detecting and investigating crimes and suspects.

It should be noted that the basic legislative Act that regulates the procedure and the immediate mechanism of obtaining such information in Ukraine is the Law of Ukraine on Operative Investigation Activities dated 18 February 1992. According to Article 1 of the Law, operative investigation activities represent a. system of open and secret search, and intelligence and counter-intelligence measures conducted by specially designated authorities that use operative and operative/technical means of searching for and determining factual data about the illegal activities of individuals and groups, responsibility for which is established by the Criminal Code of Ukraine, aimed at the prevention of offences or conducted in the interests of legal criminal proceedings, as well as obtaining information in the interests of the security of citizens, society and the state.

The norms of Ukraine's Constitution, its Criminal and Customs Codes, the Laws on the Security Service of Ukraine, on Combating Terrorism and on Counter-intelligence Activities, and other regulations are applied in the said sphere.

According to those laws, the following SITs are used in Ukraine in accordance with the procedure established by law.

Undercover operations (including covert investigations)

As used in Ukraine, these take the form of infiltration into a criminal group of an undercover officer of an operative unit of a competent authority into or of a person co-operating with the former, while their true identity remains secret (Article 8(8) of the Law of Ukraine on Operative Investigation Activities).

Front store operation (e.g. undercover company)

In Ukraine this is used in the form of permission granted to competent authorities to create, for the purposes of conspiracy, enterprises or organisations, and to use documents that disguise the identity or affiliation of individuals, premises and vehicles of operative units (Article 8(16) of the Law of Ukraine on Operative Investigation Activities).

Informants

Used in accordance with Articles 12-14 of the Law of Ukraine on Operative Investigation Activities, this enables special competent authorities to have open and secret permanent and non-permanent staff; to establish voluntary confidential co-operation with individuals; and to obtain from legal bodies and individuals, free of charge or for a fee, information about crimes being plotted or already committed, or about threats to the security of society or the state.

Controlled delivery

In the context of relevant international documents, including the Second Additional Protocol to the European Convention on Mutual Assistance in Criminal Matters (ETS 182), they are included in the Customs Code of Ukraine and relevant bilateral agreements on customs co-operation as a permission to Ukrainian customs authorities, on a case-by-case basis, subject to arrangement with the customs and other authorities of foreign states or on the basis of international agreements of Ukraine, to allow, under their control, the import, export or transit through Ukraine of drugs or psychotropic substances engaged in illegal trafficking.

Article 55 of the new Customs Code entering into force from 1 January 2004 only indicates the right of customs authorities to use controlled delivery of the said articles; detailed definitions shall be contained in a special interagency regulation.

At the same time, Article 318 of the code provides for a method of investigation new to Ukrainian law, which is the movement of goods under secret control – in order to detect and prosecute individuals involved into smuggling, as well as to seize goods that are being illegally transferred through Ukraine's border. Such movement of goods may be performed under the control and operative surveillance of law enforcement authorities.

Observation (including cross-border observation)

Electronic surveillance

This is used in the form of an authorisation granted to special authorised agencies to conduct visual surveillance in public places with the use of photography, cine and video filming, optical and radio devices (Article 8(11) of the Law of Ukraine on Operative Investigation Activities).

Bugging (private or public premises)

Permission can be granted to authorised agencies to use technical means of data acquisition, including the bugging of private (subject to court decision) or public premises (Article 8(9) of the Law of Ukraine on Operative Investigation Activities).

Interception of communications

This covers telephone, fax, e-mail and mail, through public or private networks. According to Ukraine's laws, this may be used in both procedural and non-procedural form:

1.   the non-procedural form is defined in Article 8(9) and (10) of the Law of Ukraine on Operative Investigation Activities as the right of authorised units to intercept information from communication channels and use other technical means of data acquisition, as well as monitor mail and telegrams in accordance with selection by certain indications;

2.   the procedural form is regulated by Article 187 of the Code of Criminal Procedure of Ukraine in the form of permission given to an investigator or investigatory authority to make decisions regarding seizure of correspondence and interception of information from communication channels, *inter alia*, for the purposes of prevention of crime and before the launch of a criminal case.

Searches

This includes searching of premises as well as objects, such as computers or cars, by various means including scanning. As a type of SIT, it is provided in the form of permission given to officers of authorised agencies to secretly detect and secure traces of a grave crime, documents and other items that may represent evidence of preparation or perpetration of such a crime, or to obtain intelligence information, including by means of penetration of an operative into premises, vehicles and land plots (Article 8(7) of the Law of Ukraine on Operative Investigation Activities).

Within criminal proceedings, such actions may be performed only openly, in the presence of the owner of the object of search, or his representatives, or other persons. In any case, such actions may be performed only on the basis of a court decision with regard to objects located within the grounds of a private estate.

Pseudo-purchases

Pseudo-purchases or other "pseudo-offences" are determined as the right of authorised agencies to conduct controlled and operative purchase and supply of goods, including those it is prohibited to sell, to individuals and legal bodies irrespective of ownership, in order to detect and secure illegal actions. The procedure of controlled and operative purchase and supply is established by regulations of the Ministry of Internal Affairs of Ukraine, the Tax Police and the Security Service of Ukraine. It must be approved by the Office of Prosecutor-General of Ukraine and registered by the Ministry of Justice of Ukraine (Article 8(2) of the Law of Ukraine on Operative Investigation Activities).

Cross-border (hot) pursuit

In the form of continued pursuit of a criminal by foreign law enforcement units within Ukrainian territory, this is presently not used. Pursuit of a criminal, who has committed a crime in another state, within the territory of Ukraine may be carried out by its authorised agencies after the procedure of transfer of criminal prosecution according to international agreements to which Ukraine is a party.

Agents provocateurs

Agents provocateurs are illegal as a method of investigation within the territory of Ukraine, if understood as individuals who, on the instructions of an authorised agency, provoke other individuals to commit or prepare a crime.

Article 10 of the Law of Ukraine on Operative Investigation Activities and Article 65(2) of the Code of Criminal Procedure of Ukraine establish the possibility and form of the use of information, obtained as a result of a SIT, as a source of evidence in the course of criminal proceedings.

2.   When and under which circumstances (e.g. criminal investigation, preliminary stage, etc.) can SITs be used?

The grounds for the use of SITs may be divided into those pertaining to open criminal investigatory activity of investigatory authorities and those required in case of non-procedural use of SITs during secret investigations.

In the first case, the grounds are established by the Code of Criminal Procedure of Ukraine; they fall in two categories:

1. the fact of a criminal case, if there is sufficient information to indicate a crime; it should be noted that according to Article 16 of the Criminal Code of Ukraine, criminal responsibility exists for preparations for crime (except for minor offences), therefore, indications of preparations for crime lead to the same consequences;

2. the need to investigate reports about crime before a criminal case is initiated, over a period of ten days, by means of operative investigation activities (use of some SITs).

In other cases (secret investigations), the ground for operative investigation, and accordingly, for the use of SITs, in the context of issues covered by this document, is that sufficient information be obtained according to the procedure established by the law, if such information needs examination with the use of operative investigation measures and techniques and if such information is related to:
- crimes being prepared or committed by unidentified individuals;
- individuals who prepare or have committed a crime;
- individuals who escape investigation authorities or court or escape from criminal punishment;
- a real threat to the life, health, residence or property of the personnel of courts or law enforcement agencies (or to these of their relatives), related to their duties.

If there are no grounds provided for in Article 6 of the Law of Ukraine on Operative Investigation Activities, operative investigation activities and SITs may not be used.

3.   Are there any specific features governing the use of SITs in relation to acts of terrorism? If so, please specify.

An act of terrorism, according to Ukrainian criminal law, is a grave or (depending on consequences) especially grave crime (see Articles 12 and 258 of the Criminal Code of Ukraine); therefore, investigation of its preparation or perpetration is fully covered by the norms that regulate use of SITs with regard to any grave crime. At present, there are no special provisions that regulate the use of SITs with regard to acts of terrorism in Ukraine.

Nevertheless, Ukraine's law provides for the possibility to use SITs in the fight against terrorism, as established in Article 3 of the relevant Law of Ukraine on Combating Terrorism, in the form of the principle of combination of open and secret methods of combating terrorism.

4.   How does the legal framework governing the use of SITs guarantee respect for human rights and individual freedoms, the principles of subsidiarity and proportionality? Is the authorisation to use SITs subject to time-limits? Which bodies and procedures are in place to supervise compliance with human rights standards and with the above-mentioned principles in the use of SITs? Is supervision automatic/systematic?

In Articles 21 and 22 of the Ukrainian Constitution it is stated that human rights and freedoms are inalienable and inviolable and that constitutional rights and freedoms are guaranteed and may not be cancelled.

Article 64 of the Constitution envisages that furthermore constitutional human and civil rights and freedoms may not be restricted except in cases provided for in the Constitution of Ukraine.

The constitution guarantees to each person inviolability of habitation. It is not allowed to penetrate the dwelling or other property of a person, carry out an examination or search in them, except in the case of a substantiated court decision (Article 30).

Privacy of letters, telephone conversations, telegraph and other correspondence is guaranteed to each person. Any exceptions may be determined only by a court in cases envisaged by the law for the purpose of preventing a crime or establishing the truth during an investigation into a criminal case, if it is impossible to obtain the information by any other means (Article 31).

It is not allowed to collect, keep, use and disseminate confidential information about a person without his/her consent, except in cases envisaged by the law and only in the interests of national security, economic well-being and human rights (Article 32).

The principles mentioned, as regards ensuring the mechanism of SITs' use, are detailed in relevant legislative provisions, in particular:

1. Article 8 of the Law of Ukraine on Operative Investigation Activities determines that secret penetration into a dwelling or other property of a person, taking of information from communication channels, control over correspondence, and use of any other techniques of obtaining information are carried out according to a court decision. Additional guarantees of observing lawfulness in the course of using SITs (including secret ones) are contained in Article 9 of that Law;

2. Article 187 of the Code of Criminal Procedure of Ukraine points out that in case of necessity of seizing correspondence and taking information from communication channels, an investigator shall address the head of a court of appeal with a petition previously agreed with a prosecutor. The head of the court or his/her deputy shall consider the petition, examine the case papers, if necessary hear the prosecutor's opinion and after this he/she shall make a decision to seize the correspondence or take information from communication channels or to refuse it, depending on the grounds for a corresponding decision.

The principle of proportionality is, particularly, provided for in Article 9(7) of the Law of Ukraine on Operative Investigation Activities in the form of an obligation on operational staff using SITs to take into account their correspondence with a level of public danger of criminal assaults and with a threat to the interests of society and state.

The principle of subsidiarity is also defined in the same Law as recognition of the fact that secret penetration into a dwelling or other property of a person, taking of information from communication channels, control over letters, telephone conversations, telegraph and other correspondence, and the use of other techniques to obtain information shall be carried out exclusively with the purpose of preventing a crime or establishing the truth in the course of an investigation into a criminal case, if it is impossible to obtain the information by any other means. Similar provisions are contained in Article 187 of the Code of Criminal Procedure of Ukraine in respect of the seizure of correspondence or taking of information from communication channels.

The authorisation to use SITs, according to Article 9(1) of the Law of Ukraine on Operative Investigation Activities, is subject to time-limits on the period for which SITs are allowed to be carried on and is also subject to legislative requirements related to determination by courts, in the course of granting permission to carry out certain SITs that temporarily restrict human rights, of a certain time-limit within which they may be used.

In conformity with Article 121 of the Constitution of Ukraine, the prosecutor's offices are charged with supervising the observation of laws by the authorities carrying out operational search and investigation activities, inquest and pre-trial investigation.

The rules that ensure the human rights and individual freedoms of citizens established in the Ukrainian Constitution in the course of the use of SITs are stipulated in Article 14 of the Law of Ukraine on Operative Investigation Activities, which states that supervision of the observing of laws during operational search and investigation activities is carried out by the Prosecutor General of Ukraine and prosecutors subordinate to him/her; and this article contains the list of powers of these prosecutors, which are aimed to facilitate them in the mentioned activities.

5.   *Which institutions are involved in the use of SITs and what is their role (e.g. law enforcement agencies, prosecutor's Office, judicial authorities, etc)? Which institutions can order and/or authorise the use of SITs? How does co-operation between these institutions work in practice?*

The right to directly use SITs within the framework of search and investigation activities is granted only to the operational sub-units (of seven state authorities) specially designated and listed in Article 5 of the Law of Ukraine on Operative Investigation Activities. A decision concerning the necessity of using certain SITs is taken by the heads of these sub-units or their deputies.

Some SITs, which explicitly or implicitly provide for temporary violations of human rights or freedoms, are used according to a special procedure. The essence of this procedure lies in the following: secret penetration of a dwelling or other property of a person, taking of information from a communication channel, control over letters, telephone conversations, telegraph or other correspondence, and the use of other techniques are carried out only under a court decision taken following an application by the chief of the respective operational sub-unit or his/her deputy. The prosecutor of corresponding level is informed of the obtaining of such permission or a refusal to grant it by the chief of the relevant operational sub-units or his/her deputies within 24 hours (Article 8(2) of the Law of Ukraine on Operative Investigation Activities).

Currently, within the framework of criminal process in Ukraine, only such SITs as seizure of correspondence and taking of information from communication channels may be used.

6. Are there any specialised counter-terrorism institutions? What is their role in the use of SITs?

The list of institutions that are to combat terrorism is contained in Article 4 and their tasks and powers are determined in Articles 5-7 of the Law of Ukraine on Combating Terrorism of 20 March 2003.

The Cabinet of Ministers of Ukraine, within its competence, arranges the struggle against terrorism and the necessary resources and means for it.

The central executive authorities participate in combating terrorism within their competence, as defined in laws and statutory Acts adopted on their basis. The bodies directly involved in combating terrorism within their competence are the following:
- The Security Service of Ukraine, which is the main authority in the state system for combating terrorism;
- The Ministry of Internal Affairs: the Ministry of Defence; the Ministry for Emergencies and Affairs of Population Protection from the Consequences of the Chornobyl Disaster; the State Committee for Border Protection; the State Department for Execution of Punishments; the State Guard Department. The powers of these authorities in respect of combating terrorism are determined in Article 5 of the Law of Ukraine on Combating Terrorism of 20 March 2003.
- If necessary, the following authorities are also involved in carrying out measures relating to prevention, detection and termination of terrorist activities: the Ministry of Foreign Affairs; the Ministry of Health Protection; the Ministry for Fuel and Energy; the Ministry of Industrial Policy; the Ministry of Transport; the Ministry of Finance; the Ministry for Ecology and Natural Resources; the Ministry of Agrarian Policy; the State Customs Service; and the State Tax Administration of Ukraine.

- If the leadership of counter-terror operations so decide, other central and local executive authorities, local self-government authorities, enterprises, institutions and organisations irrespective of their subordination and ownership, with their officials, as well as citizens (with their consent), may participate in counter-terrorism operations.
- The Counter-terrorism Centre under the Security Service of Ukraine co-ordinates the activities of bodies involved in combating terrorism.

Besides, according to the Law of Ukraine of 4 October 2001 on Ratification of Decisions on the Creation and Activities of the Counter-terrorism Centre of the member states of the Commonwealth of Independent States, Ukraine is a member of the Counter-terrorism Centre of the member states of the Commonwealth of Independent States. The aforementioned centre is a permanently operating specialised body of the Commonwealth of Independent States (hereinafter referred to as "the CIS") and has the task of ensuring co-ordination of interaction between the competent authorities of the CIS member states in the field of combating international terrorism and other manifestations of extremism.

It follows from the above that special investigation techniques in relation to terrorism may be initiated and used by the respective subdivisions of the Security Service of Ukraine, the Ministry of Internal Affairs of Ukraine, the State Border Service of Ukraine, the State Guard Department, bodies of the state tax service, authorities and institutions of the State Department of Ukraine for Execution of Punishments, and any intelligence body of the Ministry of Defence of Ukraine.

7.   Which measures have been adopted in order to facilitate international co-operation (e.g. joint investigation teams)? Can the SITs listed in reply to question 1 be used in cross-border settings?

At present, carrying out criminal investigations in Ukrainian territory by joint international teams (in particular, in the context of Article 20 of the Second Additional Protocol to the European Convention on Mutual Assistance in Criminal Matters) is not envisaged legislatively and is not used, since the aforementioned Protocol has not been ratified to date.

A new draft Criminal Procedural Code of Ukraine envisages such forms of co-operation. The issue of special investigation techniques in cross-border settings is tackled in paragraph 8 of this Questionnaire.

8.   What use can be made of SITs in the context of mutual legal assistance?

International co-operation of Ukraine's authorised agencies with relevant foreign authorities in the sphere of using SITs is conducted on the basis of international conventions and agreements in force, their binding character being approved by the *Verkhovna Rada* of Ukraine, in compliance with the

Constitution of Ukraine (Article 9). They become an integral part of national legislation, and in addition it is defined in the internal legislation that:

1. the legal basis of special investigation techniques in Ukraine is provided for, in particular, in international legal agreements and treaties, to which Ukraine is party (Article 3 of the Law of Ukraine on Operative Investigation Activities);

2. grounds for using special investigation techniques (SITs) may be found in the requests of investigation units of international law enforcement bodies and organisations of other states (Article 6 of the Law of Ukraine on Operative Investigation Activities);

3. responding to the requests of relevant international law enforcement bodies and organisations of other states, on the basis of treaties and agreements, is among the responsibilities of those units authorised to use SITs (Article 7(3) of the Law of Ukraine on Operative Investigation Activities).

As to international co-operation of Ukraine in terms of counteracting terrorism, it should be noted that – according to Article 3 of the Law of Ukraine On Combating Terrorism – co-operation in this area with foreign states, their law enforcement authorities and special services, as well as with international organisations fighting against terrorism, is one of the principles that combating terrorism is based on.

Ukraine is a party to the European Convention on Mutual Legal Assistance in Criminal Matters of 1959 and the Additional Protocol to it. The Second Additional Protocol of 2001 to this Convention is now being prepared for ratification. Besides, Ukraine is party to the Convention on Legal Assistance and Legal Relations in Civil, Family and Criminal Matters, concluded within the framework of the Commonwealth of Independent States of 22 January 1993, as well as to a number of bilateral agreements on legal assistance in criminal matters.

Ukraine has ratified the European Convention on the Fight against Terrorism, the International Convention on Fight the against Terrorism Financing, and the Convention on Legalisation, Search, Arrest and Seizure of Proceeds from Crime. Ukraine has joined the International Convention on the Fight against Bomb Terrorism.

9. How can the use of SITs be improved? Please provide any comments/proposals concerning the implementation of the terms of reference of the PC-TI and in particular the use and regulation of SITs.

Ukraine has taken measures aimed at enhancing international co-operation efficiency in the sphere of the fight against crime, in particular, terrorism.

As to measures aimed at improvement of the legislation governing application of SITs to acts of terrorism in Ukraine, the following provisions were proposed and introduced in a number of draft laws, which are now at different preparation stages:

1. The new draft Code of Criminal Procedure, submitted for consideration to the Parliament of Ukraine, contains provisions aimed at fixing in the basic procedural law, regulating legal procedure in criminal cases, rules of international co-operation in criminal cases, rendering legal assistance, including use of such SITs as establishment and operation of special investigating groups, controlled delivery, cross-border pursuit, applying SITs in the interests of our states.

2. The Second Additional Protocol to the European Convention on Mutual Assistance in Criminal Matters is being agreed now by the state authorities concerned. If the *Verkhovna Rada* of Ukraine authorises its binding character, it will determine for Ukraine, at the law level, the order of use of such SITs as controlled delivery, international pursuit, establishing special investigating groups, and covert investigations (Articles 17-20 of the Protocol drawn up by the Council of Europe).

Appendix 1

Constitution – the Fundamental Law of Ukraine

Chapter II
Human and citizens' rights, freedoms and duties

Article 21

All people are free and equal in their dignity and rights.

Human rights and freedoms are inalienable and inviolable.

Article 22

Human and citizens' rights and freedoms affirmed by this constitution are not exhaustive.

Constitutional rights and freedoms are guaranteed and shall not be abolished.

The content and scope of existing rights and freedoms shall not be diminished in the adoption of new laws or in the amendment of laws that are in force.

Article 30

Everyone is guaranteed the inviolability of his or her dwelling place.

Entry into a dwelling place or other possessions of a person, and the examination or search thereof, shall not be permitted, other than pursuant to a substantiated court decision.

In urgent cases related to the preservation of human life and property, or to the direct pursuit of persons suspected of committing a crime, another procedure established by law is possible for entry into a dwelling place or other possessions of a person, and for the examination and search thereof.

Article 31

Everyone is guaranteed privacy of mail, telephone conversations, telegraph and other correspondence. Exceptions shall be established only by a court in cases envisaged by the law, with the purpose of preventing crime or ascertaining the truth in the course of the investigation of a criminal case, if it is not possible to obtain the information by other means.

Article 32

No one shall be subject to interference in his or her personal and family life, except in cases envisaged by the Constitution of Ukraine.

The collection, storage, use and dissemination of confidential information about a person without his or her consent shall not be permitted, except in cases determined by law, and only in the interests of national security, economic welfare and human rights.

Every citizen has the right to examine information about himself or herself, that is not a state secret or other secret protected by law, at the bodies of state power, bodies of local self-government, institutions and organisations.

Everyone is guaranteed judicial protection of the right to rectify incorrect information about himself or herself and members of his or her family, and of the right to demand that any type of information be expunged, and also the right to compensation for material and moral damages inflicted by the collection, storage, use and dissemination of such incorrect information.

Article 62

A person is presumed innocent of committing a crime and shall not be subjected to criminal punishment until his or her guilt is proved through legal procedure and established by a court verdict of guilty.

No one is obliged to prove his or her innocence of committing a crime.

An accusation shall not be based on illegally obtained evidence or on assumptions. All doubts in regard to proof of the guilt of a person are interpreted in his or her favour.

In the event that a court verdict is revoked as unjust, the state compensates the material and moral damages inflicted by the groundless conviction.

Article 63

A person shall not bear responsibility for refusing to testify or to explain anything about himself or herself, members of his or her family or close relatives in the degree determined by law.

A suspect, an accused or a defendant has the right to a defence.

A convicted person enjoys all human and citizens' rights, with the exception of restrictions determined by law and established by a court verdict.

Article 64

Constitutional human and citizens' rights and freedoms shall not be restricted, except in cases envisaged by the Constitution of Ukraine.

Under conditions of martial law or a state of emergency, specific restrictions on rights and freedoms may be established with indication of the period of effectiveness of these restrictions. The rights and freedoms envisaged in Articles 24, 25, 27, 28, 29, 40, 47, 51, 52, 55, 56, 57, 58, 59, 60, 61, 62 and 63 of this constitution shall not be restricted.

Chapter VII
Procuracy

Article 121

The Procuracy of Ukraine constitutes a unified system that is entrusted with:

1)   prosecution in court on behalf of the state;

2)   representation of the interests of a citizen or of the state in court in cases determined by law;

3)   supervision of the observance of laws by bodies that conduct detective and search activity, inquiry and pre-trial investigation;

4)   supervision of the observance of laws in the execution of judicial decisions in criminal cases, and also in the application of other measures of coercion related to the restraint of personal liberty of citizens.

Appendix 2

Criminal Code of Ukraine

Chapter III
Crime, its types and stages

Article 11
Definition of a crime

1. A crime shall mean a socially dangerous culpable act (action or inaction) prescribed by this code and committed by an offender (a perpetrator of a crime).

2. An action or inaction that formally may have elements of any act under this code shall not be considered as a crime if, due to its insignificance, it is not a social danger, that is, it neither did nor could cause considerable harm to any natural or legal person, society or the state.

Article 12
Classification of crimes

1. Depending on the degree of gravity, crimes shall be classified as of minor gravity, of medium gravity, grave, or of special gravity.

2. A crime of minor gravity shall mean a crime punished by imprisonment for a term up to two years or a more lenient penalty.

3. A crime of medium gravity shall mean a crime punished by imprisonment for a term up to five years.

4. A grave crime shall mean a crime punished by imprisonment for a term up to ten years.

5. A crime of special gravity shall mean a crime punished by more than ten years' imprisonment or a life sentence.

Article 13
Consummated and unconsummated crimes

1. An consummated crime shall mean a crime which comprises all formal elements of a crime as prescribed by the relevant article of the Special Part of this code.

2. An unconsummated crime shall mean preparation for crime and criminal attempt.

Article 14
Preparation for crime

1.   Preparation for crime shall mean the finding or adapting of means and tools, or looking for accomplices to, or conspiring for commission of a crime, removing obstacles to a crime, or otherwise intended to prepare conditions for the commission of a crime.

2.   Preparation to commit a crime of minor gravity shall not give rise to criminal liability.

Article 15
Criminal attempt

1.   A criminal attempt shall mean a directly intended act (action or inaction) made by a person and aimed directly at the commission of a crime, prescribed by the relevant article of the Special Part of this code, where this crime has not been consummated for reasons beyond that person's control.

2.   A criminal attempt shall be consummated where a person has completed all such acts as he/she deemed necessary for the consummation of a crime, but the crime was not completed for reasons beyond that person's control.

3.   A criminal attempt shall be unconsummated where a person has not completed all such acts that he/she deemed necessary for the consummation of a crime, for reasons beyond that person's control.

Article 16
Criminal liability for an unconsummated crime

Criminal liability for the preparation for crime and a criminal attempt shall arise under Articles 14 or 15 and that article of the Special Part of this code that prescribes liability for the consummated crime.

Article 258
Act of terrorism

1.   An act of terrorism, that is, the use of weapons, explosions, fire or any other actions that exposed human life or health to danger or caused significant pecuniary damage or any other grave consequences, where such actions were performed with a view to violating public security, intimidating the population, provoking armed conflict or international tension, or exerting influence on decisions made or actions taken or not taken by government agencies or local government authorities, officials and officers of such bodies, associations of citizens and legal bodies, or with a view to attracting the attention of the public to certain political,

religious or any other convictions of the culprit (the terrorist), and also a threat to commit any such acts for the same purposes.

- o shall be punished by deprivation of freedom for a term of five to ten years.

2. The same acts, committed repeatedly or by a group of persons upon their prior conspiracy, or where these actions have caused significant property damage or other grave consequences,

- o shall be punished by deprivation of freedom for a term of seven to twelve years.

3. Acts provided for by paragraphs 1 or 2 of this article, where they have caused death of people,

- o shall be punished by deprivation of freedom for a term of ten to fifteen years or life deprivation of freedom.

4. Establishing, leading or participating in a terrorist group or terrorist organisation, and also providing logistical, organisational or any other assistance in order to facilitate the establishment or operation of a terrorist group or terrorist organisation,

- o shall be punished by deprivation of freedom for a term of eight to fifteen years.

5. Any person, other than an organiser or leader, shall be discharged from criminal responsibility for any acts provided for in paragraph 4 of this article, if he (she) has voluntarily reported it to a law enforcement authority and assisted in terminating the existence or operations of such terrorist group or organisation, or in uncovering crimes related to the creation or operation of such terrorist group or organisation, unless his (her) actions contain elements of another offence.

Appendix 3

Law of Ukraine on the Fight against Terrorism

In order to protect the individual, the state and society from terrorism, and to detect and eliminate the causes and conditions that breed terrorism, this Law establishes the legal and organisational principles governing the fight against this dangerous phenomenon, the powers and duties of organs of executive power, associations of citizens and organisations, officials and individual citizens in this sphere, the procedure for co-ordinating their activity, and guarantees of the legal and social protection of citizens in connection with their participation in the fight against terrorism.

The provisions of this Law may not serve as grounds for persecuting citizens who, acting within the law, act to defend their constitutional rights and freedoms.

Section I
General Provisions

Article 1
Definition of Key Terms

For the purposes of this Law, the terms below are defined as follows:

Terrorism – a socially dangerous activity consisting in the intentional and deliberate use of violence in the form of the taking of hostages, arson, murder, torture and intimidation of the population or government bodies, or other attempts on the life and health of innocent people, or threats to commit criminal acts for criminal purposes;

Terrorist act – a criminal act in the form of using weapons, detonating explosions, setting fires, or other actions punishable under Article 258 of the Criminal Code of Ukraine. If the terrorist activity is accompanied by the commission of crimes punishable under Articles 112, 147, 258-260, 443 and 444, as well as other articles of the Criminal Code of Ukraine, legal responsibility for the commission of such crimes ensues in accordance with the Criminal Code of Ukraine;

Technological terrorism – crimes committed for terrorist purposes using nuclear, chemical, bacteriological (biological) and other weapons of mass destruction or their components, other substances harmful to the health of people, electromagnetic devices, computer systems and communication networks, including the seizure, disablement and destruction of potentially dangerous facilities, which cause or threaten to cause an emergency situation and pose a danger to personnel, the population and the environment; and crimes which create conditions for accidents and catastrophes of a technogenic nature;

Terrorist activity – activity that includes the planning, organisation, preparation and perpetration of terrorist acts; incitement to commit terrorist acts, violence against natural persons or organisations, and the destruction of physical objects for the purposes of terrorism; the organisation of illegal armed units, criminal groups (criminal organisations) or organised criminal groups to commit terrorist acts, as well as participation in such acts; recruiting, arming, training and using terrorists; propaganda and dissemination of the ideology of terrorism; financing of known terrorist groups (organisations) or other forms of support thereof;

International terrorism – the perpetration on a world or regional scale by terrorist organisations or groups, including perpetration with the support of state organs of individual states, for the purpose of achieving certain goals, of socially dangerous acts of violence involving the kidnapping, capture or killing of innocent people or a threat to their life and health; the destruction or threat of destruction of important national economic facilities, essential services or communication systems; the use or threat to use nuclear, chemical, biological and other weapons of mass destruction;

Terrorist – a person who takes part in terrorist activity;

Terrorist group – a group of two or more persons that have joined together to commit terrorist acts;

Terrorist organisation – a stable association of three or more persons created for the purpose of committing terrorist acts, with assigned functions and certain rules of conduct binding on all members during the preparation and commission of terrorist acts. An organisation is designated as a terrorist body if even one of its structural elements engages in terrorist activity with the knowledge of even one of the leaders (leading organs) of the entire organisation;

Fight against terrorism [combating terrorism] – activity to prevent, detect, suppress and minimise the effects of terrorist activity;

Anti-terrorist operation – a complex of co-ordinated special measures aimed at forestalling, preventing and suppressing criminal acts committed for terrorist purposes, the freeing of hostages, rendering harmless terrorists, and minimising the effects of a terrorist act or other crime committed for terrorist purposes;

Zone of an anti-terrorist operation – areas of ground or water designated by the authority in charge of an anti-terrorist operation, means of transport, buildings, structures, premises and territories or waters adjacent to them within the borders of which the anti-terrorist operation is being conducted;

Regime in the zone of an anti-terrorist operation – a special regime that may be established in the zone of an anti-terrorist operation during the conduct of such an operation and may entail granting the bodies designated to combat terrorism special powers, defined by this Law, that are needed to free hostages, ensure the safety and health of citizens located in the zone of the anti-terrorist operation and the normal functioning of state government organs, local self-government bodies, enterprises, institutions and organisations;

Hostage – a natural person who has been captured and (or) is being held for the purpose of compelling a state organ, enterprise, institution or organisation, or individual persons, to carry out or refrain from carrying out some act as a condition for the release of the captured and (or) held person.

Article 2
The legal basis of the fight against terrorism

The legal basis for the fight against terrorism consists in the Constitution of Ukraine (254k/96-VR), the Criminal Code of Ukraine (2341-14), this Law, other laws of Ukraine, the European Convention on the Suppression of Terrorism (994_331 of 1977), the International Convention for the Suppression of Terrorist Bombings (995_374 of 1997), the International Convention for the Suppression of the Financing of Terrorism (995_518 of 1999), other international treaties to which Ukraine is a party, which have been approved as binding by the Supreme Council of Ukraine, the edicts and directives of the President of Ukraine, the decrees and directives of the Cabinet of Ministers of Ukraine, as well as other normative-legal acts approved for the purpose of implementing the laws of Ukraine.

Article 3
The basic principles of the fight against terrorism

The fight against terrorism is founded on the principles of:
- legality and the strict observance of the rights and freedoms of individuals and citizens;
- the comprehensive use for this purpose of legal, political, socio-economic, informational and propaganda, and other means;
- the primacy of preventive measures;
- the inevitability of punishment for participating in terrorist activity;
- the primacy of protecting the life and rights of persons exposed to danger as a result of terrorist activity;
- the use of a combination of overt and covert methods in combating terrorism;

- confidentiality regarding information about the technical means and the tactics of conducting anti-terrorist operations, as well as regarding the membership of participants in such operations;
- unity of command over the forces and means used to conduct anti-terrorist operations;
- co-operation in the sphere of combating terrorism with foreign states, their law enforcement agencies and special services, as well as with international organisations that combat terrorism.

Section II
Organisational principles of the fight against terrorism

Article 4
Bodies responsible for combating terrorism

The body responsible for the organisation of the fight against terrorism in Ukraine and the provision of the necessary forces, means and resources for this fight shall be the Cabinet of Ministers within the limits of its jurisdiction.

The central organs of executive power shall take part in the fight against terrorism within the limits of their jurisdiction as defined by existing laws and other normative-legal acts issued on their basis.

The bodies directly responsible for combating terrorism within the limits of their jurisdiction are:
- The Security Service of Ukraine, which is the principal agency in the national system of the fight against terrorist activity;
- Ministry of Internal Affairs;
- Ministry of Defence;
- Ministry for Emergency Situations and for the Protection of the Population From the Aftermath of the Chornobyl Catastrophe;
- State Committee for the Protection of the State Border;
- State Department of Correction;
- State Security Administration.

If necessary, the following shall also be engaged to participate in taking measures to prevent, detect and suppress terrorist activity:
- Ministry of Foreign Affairs;
- Ministry of Health;
- Ministry of Fuel and Energy;
- Ministry of Industrial Policy;
- Ministry of Transport;
- Ministry of Finance;
- Ministry of Ecology and Natural Resources;
- Ministry of Agrarian Policy;
- State Customs Service;

o State Tax Administration.

If any central organs of executive power listed in this article are reorganised or renamed, their functions in the sphere of combating terrorism may be passed on to their legal heirs pursuant to an edict of the President of Ukraine to that effect.

By a decision of the authority in charge of conducting an anti-terrorist operation, other central and local executive power organs, local self-government bodies, enterprises, institutions and organisations, irrespective of subordination or form of ownership, as well as citizens, with their consent, may also be engaged to participate in anti-terrorist operations in compliance with the provisions of this Law.

The activity of all bodies engaged in the fight against terrorism shall be co-ordinated by the Anti-terrorism Centre of the Security Service of Ukraine.

Article 5
Powers of bodies directly responsible for combating terrorism

The Security Service of Ukraine shall conduct the fight against terrorism by means of operational-investigative measures aimed at preventing, detecting and suppressing terrorist activities, including international terrorist activities; shall gather information about the activity of foreign and international terrorist organisations; shall conduct operational-technical measures within the limits of its jurisdiction in telecommunication systems and channels that could be used by terrorists solely for the purpose of obtaining pre-emptive information in case of a threat of the commission of a terrorist act or when conducting an anti-terrorist operation; shall ensure through the Anti-terrorism Centre of the Security Service of Ukraine the organisation and conduct of anti-terrorist measures, and the co-ordination of the activities of the bodies responsible for combating terrorism in accordance with the authority granted it by the legislation of Ukraine; shall conduct pre-trial investigations in cases involving terrorist activity; and shall provide protection against terrorist attempts attacking the institutions of Ukraine outside the borders of her territory, their employees and the members of their families.

The Ministry of Internal Affairs shall conduct the fight against terrorism by means of preventing, detecting and suppressing crimes committed for terrorist purposes, the investigation of which has been placed under the jurisdiction of internal affairs organs by the legislation of Ukraine; shall provide the Anti-terrorism Centre of the Security Service of Ukraine with the necessary forces and means; and shall ensure their effective use during the conduct of anti-terrorist operations.

The Ministry of Defence of Ukraine, military administrative organs, formations, combined units, and units of the Armed Forces of Ukraine shall protect against terrorist attempts on facilities of the Armed Forces of Ukraine, weapons of mass destruction, missiles and firearms, ammunition, and explosive and toxic substances possessed by military units or stored in designated places; shall organise the training and use of forces and means of the Ground Forces, Air Force and Air Defence Forces, and Naval Forces of the Armed Forces of Ukraine in case of a terrorist act committed in the airspace or territorial waters of Ukraine; and shall take part in conducting anti-terrorist operations at military facilities and if terrorist threats arise to the security of the state from outside Ukraine.

The Ministry of Ukraine for Emergency Situations and the Protection of the Population from the Aftermath of the Chornobyl Catastrophe, civil defence administrative organs and special units under its jurisdiction, and civil defence troops shall take measures to protect the population and territories in case of a threat of – or occurrence of – emergency situations connected with manifestations of technological terrorism and other forms of terrorism; shall participate in taking measures to minimise and eradicate the effects of such situations during the conduct of anti-terrorist operations; and shall conduct educational and practical training measures in order to prepare the public to act in conditions in which a terrorist act has occurred.

The State Committee for the Protection of the State Border of Ukraine, regional administrative bodies and the frontier security organs of the Border Troops of Ukraine shall conduct the fight against terrorism by means of preventing, detecting and suppressing attempts by terrorists to cross the state border of Ukraine, or to illegally transport across the state border of Ukraine weapons, explosives, toxic and radioactive substances, and other items that can be used as means to commit terrorist acts; shall ensure the safety of maritime shipping in the territorial waters and the exclusive (maritime) economic zone of Ukraine during the conduct of anti-terrorist operations; and shall provide the Anti-terrorism Centre of the Security Service of Ukraine with the necessary forces and means during the conduct of anti-terrorist operations on the border crossings of Ukraine and other objects located on the state border or in the border zone.

The State Department of Correction of Ukraine shall take measures to prevent and suppress crimes of a terrorist kind at correctional facilities.

The State Security Administration of Ukraine shall take part in operations to prevent terrorist acts aimed against officials and facilities, which the units of this administration have been assigned to protect.

Article 6
Powers of other bodies that may be engaged to combat terrorism

Bodies engaged to combat terrorism shall, within the limits of their jurisdiction, take measures to prevent, detect and suppress terrorist acts and crimes of a terrorist nature; shall develop and carry out preventive, systemic, organisational, educational and other measures; shall provide the conditions needed to conduct anti-terrorist operations at facilities under their jurisdiction; and shall provide units conducting such operations with material, technical and financial means, transport and communications, medical equipment, medicines and other means, as well as the information needed to execute the tasks to combat terrorism.

Article 7
The Anti-terrorism Centre of the Security Service of Ukraine

The Anti-terrorism Centre of the Security Service of Ukraine shall be responsible for:
- developing the conceptual principles and programmes for the fight against terrorism, recommendations aimed at enhancing the effectiveness of the means used to detect and eliminate the conditions that promote the commission of terrorist acts and other crimes committed for terrorist purposes;
- gathering in accordance with prescribed procedure, generalising, analysing and assessing information about the state of and trends in the spread of terrorism in Ukraine and outside her borders;
- organising and conducting anti-terrorist operations and co-ordinating the activity of the bodies that conduct the fight against terrorism or are engaged to take part in specific anti-terrorist operations;
- organising and conducting command-headquarters and special tactical exercises and training;
- participating in preparing drafts of international treaties of Ukraine, preparing and submitting according to prescribed procedure proposals for improving the legislation of Ukraine in the sphere of the fight against terrorism, financing the conduct of anti-terrorist operations by bodies that conduct the fight against terrorism, taking measures to prevent, detect and suppress terrorist activity;
- co-operating with the special services and law enforcement agencies of foreign states and international organisations on matters pertaining to combating terrorism.

The Anti-terrorism Centre of the Security Service of Ukraine shall consist of the Interdepartmental Co-ordinating Commission and Headquarters as well as the co-ordinating groups and their headquarters created in the regional offices of the Security Service of Ukraine.

The Interdepartmental Co-ordinating Commission of the Anti-terrorism Centre of the Security Service of Ukraine shall consist of the head of the Anti-terrorism Centre and his deputies; the deputy state secretaries of the Ministry of Internal Affairs of Ukraine and the Ministry for Emergency Situations and the Protection of the Population from the Aftermath of the Chornobyl Catastrophe; the deputy chief of the General Staff of the Armed Forces of Ukraine; the deputy heads of the State Committee for the Protection of the State Border of Ukraine, the State Security Administration of Ukraine and the State Correction Department of Ukraine; the state secretary of the Ministry of Internal Affairs of Ukraine and the head of the Main Administration of the Ministry of Internal Affairs of Ukraine in the city of Kyiv; the commander of the internal troops of the Ministry of Internal Affairs of Ukraine; the head of the Administration of the Security Service of Ukraine in the city of Kyiv, the deputy chairman of the Kyiv City State Administration; and the deputy heads of other central executive power organs.

The Statute on the Anti-terrorism Centre of the Security Service of Ukraine and the members of the Interdepartmental Co-ordinating Commission shall be approved by the President of Ukraine on the submission of the Cabinet of Ministers of Ukraine. The head of the Anti-terrorism Centre of the Security Service of Ukraine shall be appointed by the President of Ukraine.

The routine work in carrying out the tasks assigned to the Anti-terrorism Centre of the Security Service of Ukraine shall be organised by its staff.

The co-ordinating groups in the regional offices of the Security Service of Ukraine shall consist of the heads of the regional offices of the Security Service of Ukraine, the main administration of the Ministry of Internal Affairs of Ukraine in the Autonomous Republic of Crimea, the main administrations of the Ministry of Internal Affairs of Ukraine in each *oblast* and in the cities of Kyiv and Sevastopol, the relevant organs responsible for emergency situations and civil defence in the Autonomous Republic of Crimea, the *oblast* state administrations, and the Kyiv and Sevastopol city state administrations, in regions where units of the Border Troops of Ukraine are deployed, the State Security Administration – their commanders and heads, as well as representatives of other local executive branch bodies, enterprises, institutions and organisations.

The co-ordinating groups in the regional offices of the Security Service of Ukraine shall be headed, respectively, by the head of the main administration of the Security Service of Ukraine in the Autonomous Republic of Crimea, the heads of the administrations of the Security Service of Ukraine in each *oblast* and in the cities of Kyiv and Sevastopol.

The membership of the co-ordinating councils in the regional offices of the Security Service of Ukraine shall be approved, respectively, by the Council of Ministers of the Autonomous Republic of Crimea, the chairmen of the *oblast* state administrations, and the chairmen of the executive organs of the Kyiv and Sevastopol city councils.

The organisational needs of co-ordinating groups shall be provided for by the regional offices of the Security Service of Ukraine.

The Anti-terrorism Centre of the Security Service of Ukraine shall be maintained at the expense of funds allocated for this purpose in a separate item of the State Budget of Ukraine.

Article 8
Co-operation among bodies that are directly responsible for combating terrorism

The bodies that in accordance with this Law are directly responsible for combating terrorism are obligated:

1) to work together to suppress the criminal activity of persons involved in terrorism, including international terrorism, the financing, support or commission of terrorist acts and crimes committed for terrorist purposes;

2) to exchange information about:
   o the possession or threat of possession by terrorist groups (terrorist organisations) of weapons, explosives or other means of mass destruction;
   o the crossing of the state border of Ukraine by her citizens, aliens, and stateless persons for the purpose of committing terrorist acts;
   o the discovery of apparently counterfeit travel documents in the possession of passengers that permit them to travel on means of transport with intercity or international destinations;
   o the use or threat of use by terrorists, terrorist groups or terrorist organisations of means of communication and communication technologies;

3) to help ensure effective border controls and controls over the issuance of identity papers and travel documents in order to prevent the falsification, counterfeiting or illegal use of such documents;

4) to prevent the actions or movement of terrorists, terrorist groups or terrorist organisations, as well as persons suspected of committing terrorist acts or suspected of involvement with international terrorist groups or organisations;

5) to stop attempts by aliens known to be involved in international terrorist groups or organisations to transit the territory of Ukraine.

Article 9
Assistance to bodies conducting the fight against terrorism

State government organs of Ukraine, local self-government bodies, associations of citizens, organisations, and their officials are obligated to assist the bodies that conduct the fight against terrorism and provide them with information that they have obtained about terrorist activity or any other circumstances that can help to prevent, detect and suppress terrorist activity as well as minimise its effects.

Section III
The conduct of anti-terrorist operations

Article 10
Conditions for conducting an anti-terrorist operation

An anti-terrorist operation shall be conducted only if there is a real threat to the life and security of citizens or the interests of society or the state and if this threat cannot be eliminated by any other means.

Article 11
The decision to conduct an anti-terrorist operation

The decision to conduct an anti-terrorist operation shall be made, depending on the degree of the social threat of a terrorist act, by the head of the Anti-terrorism Centre of the Security Service of Ukraine with the written authorisation of the Chairman of the Security Service of Ukraine, or the head of the co-ordinating group of the relevant regional office of the Security Service of Ukraine with the written authorisation of the head of the Anti-terrorism Centre of the Security Service of Ukraine and with the approval of the Chairman of the Security Service of Ukraine. The President of Ukraine shall be immediately informed about the decision to conduct an anti-terrorist operation.

The Anti-terrorism Centre of the Security Service of Ukraine shall conduct an anti-terrorist operation if:
- the terrorist act threatens to result in the death of many people or other serious consequences, or if it is committed simultaneously on the territory of several *oblasts*, *rayons* or cities;
- the situation involving the commission or threat to commit a terrorist act is unclear as to the causes and circumstances producing it and what might happen;
- the commission of the terrorist act affects the international interests of Ukraine and her relations with foreign states;
- the response to the commission of acts which show the hallmark of an act of terrorism falls within the jurisdiction of various law enforcement agencies and other organs of executive power;

- it is obvious that the terrorist act cannot be prevented or suppressed by the forces of law enforcement and local executive-branch bodies in the specific region.

In other cases, the anti-terrorist operation shall be conducted independently, with the approval of the head of the Anti-terrorism Centre of the Security Service of Ukraine, by the co-ordinating group of the relevant regional office of the Security Service of Ukraine or an organ of executive power in accordance with its jurisdiction.

Article 12
Command of an anti-terrorist operation

To exercise direct command over a specific anti-terrorist operation and to direct the forces and means engaged to conduct anti-terrorist measures, a special operations headquarters shall be created, headed by the head of the Anti-terrorism Centre of the Security Service of Ukraine (co-ordinating group of the relevant regional office of the Security Service of Ukraine) or a person deputised by him.

The procedure governing the activity of the operations headquarters in command of an anti-terrorist operation shall be defined on the basis of a statute, approved by the Cabinet of Ministers of Ukraine.

The chief of the operations headquarters shall determine the boundaries of the zone of an anti-terrorist operation, decide what forces and means shall be used to conduct the operation, and, if necessary because of the existence of grounds provided for by law, shall submit a proposal for consideration by the National Security and Defence Council of Ukraine to declare a state of emergency in Ukraine or in certain localities of the country.

Interference with the operational command of an anti-terrorist operation by any person, irrespective of office, is prohibited.

All legal demands made by the participants in an anti-terrorist operation shall be binding on citizens and officials.

Article 13
Forces and means used to conduct an anti-terrorist operation

In conducting an anti-terrorist operation, use shall be made of the forces and means (personnel, specialists, weapons, special and transport means, means of communication, other material and technical means) of the bodies responsible for combating terrorism, as well as those of enterprises, institutions and organisations engaged to participate in an anti-terrorist operation, according to the procedure defined by the statute indicated in paragraph two of Article 12 of this Law. The costs incurred and losses suffered in connection with the conduct of an anti-terrorist operation shall be reimbursed in accordance with acting legislation.

Law enforcement officers, military servicemen and other persons engaged to take part in an anti-terrorist operation shall, for the duration of the conduct of the operation, be subordinate to the authority of the chief of the operations headquarters.

Article 14
Regime in the zone of an anti-terrorist operation

A special regime may be established in the zone of an anti-terrorist operation for the duration of the operation; in particular, a patrol service may be organised and the perimeter may be cordoned off.

The presence of persons not engaged in the conduct of an anti-terrorist operation shall be allowed in the zone in which the operation is being conducted by permission of the chief of the operations headquarters.

With the approval of the managements of enterprises, institutions and organisations located in the zone of an anti-terrorist operation, the work of these bodies may be halted partly or completely during the conduct of the operation. Qualified specialists from these enterprises, institutions and organisations may be engaged, in accordance with established procedure and with their consent, in the conduct of the anti-terrorist operation to perform certain tasks.

Article 15
The rights of persons in the zone of an anti-terrorist operation

Officials in the zone of an anti-terrorist operation, who are engaged to participate in conducting the operation, have the right:

1) to use weapons and special means in accordance with the laws of Ukraine;

2) to detain and hand over to bodies responsible for internal affairs persons who have committed or are committing offences or other acts that hinder the fulfilment of the legal demands of persons engaged in the anti-terrorist operation, or acts involving unsanctioned attempts to penetrate the zone of the anti-terrorist operation and obstruct its conduct;

3) to check the identity documents of citizens and officials, and, in the absence of such documents, to detain them for identification;

4) to conduct a personal search of citizens in the zone of an anti-terrorist operation, a search of their belongings, means of transport and the items they are transporting;

5) to temporarily restrict or prohibit the movement of means of transport and pedestrians on streets and roads, to deny admittance to means of transport, including those belonging to diplomatic representatives and consular offices, and to citizens into certain areas and facilities, to remove citizens from certain areas and facilities, and to tow away means of transport;

6) to enter (penetrate) residential and other premises or plots of land belonging to citizens, during the suppression of a terrorist act and when pursuing persons suspected of committing a terrorist act, and into the territory and premises of enterprises, institutions and organisations, and to inspect means of transport if a delay could cause a real threat to the life and health of people;

7) to use for official purposes means of communication and transport, including special means that belong to citizens (with their consent), enterprises, institutions and organisations, with the exception of the means of transport belonging to diplomatic, consular and other representatives of foreign states and international organisations, in order to prevent a terrorist act, to pursue or detain persons suspected of committing a terrorist act, or to transport people in need of immediate medical attention to medical facilities, as well as to travel to the place of the crime.

Contacts with members of the media in the zone of an anti-terrorist operation shall be conducted by the chief of the operations headquarters or persons designated by him. The measures provided for by this article shall be taken in accordance with acting legislation and shall cease immediately upon the completion of the anti-terrorist operation.

Article 16
Conditions of negotiating with terrorists

In the course of conducting an anti-terrorist operation, negotiations with terrorists shall be permitted in order to save the life or health of people and physical assets, to persuade the terrorists to refrain from committing illegal acts, to exercise a restraining influence on them, or to determine the possibility of putting an end to the terrorist act.

Conducting negotiations shall be entrusted to persons specially authorised to do so by the chief of the operations headquarters.

If the goal of the negotiations with terrorists cannot be achieved because they refuse to halt the terrorist act, and a real threat to the life and health of people remains, the chief of the anti-terrorist operation has the right to make a decision to render harmless the terrorist (or terrorists).

If there is a clear threat of a terrorist act being committed against an object or person and it is impossible to remove this threat by other legal means, the terrorist (or terrorists) may be rendered harmless without warning on the order of the chief of the operations headquarters.

In conducting negotiations, such conditions for halting a terrorist act as the release to the terrorists of any persons, items or substances that can be used directly to commit acts of technological terrorism may not be considered.

Article 17
Informing the public about a terrorist act

The public shall be informed about the commission of a terrorist act by the chief of the operations headquarters or a person authorised by him to maintain relations with the public.

The dissemination of information in the mass media or any other form of media shall be prohibited if it:
- reveals special technical means and tactics used to conduct the anti-terrorist operation;
- could make the conduct of an anti-terrorist operation more difficult, and (or) create a threat to the life and health of hostages and other people located in the zone of an anti-terrorist operation or outside its boundaries;
- has as its goal the propaganda or justification of terrorism, contains statements by persons who offer resistance or call for resistance to the conduct of an anti-terrorist operation;
- contains information about items and substances that can be used directly to commit acts of technological terrorism;
- reveals information about the identity of the members of special units and members of the operations headquarters who are taking part in the conduct of an anti-terrorist operation, as well as about persons who are assisting in the conduct of the operation (without their consent).

Article 18
Conclusion of an anti-terrorist operation

An anti-terrorist operation shall be considered as concluded if the terrorist act has been stopped and threats to life and health of hostages and other people in the zone of operations have been eliminated.

The decision that an anti-terrorist operation has been concluded shall be made by the chief of the operations headquarters in charge of the operation.

When conducting an anti-terrorist operation, the chief of the operations headquarters, together with the relevant organs of executive power and local self-government bodies, shall organise the provision of assistance to victims, determine the measures to be taken to eliminate and minimise the effects of the terrorist act, and organise the implementation of these measures.

Section IV
Compensation of damages caused by terrorist acts
The social rehabilitation of victims of terrorist acts

Article 19
Compensation of damages caused by a terrorist act

Compensation of damages caused to citizens by a terrorist act shall be made at the expense of funds from the state budget of Ukraine in accordance with the law and with the subsequent recovery of the amount paid out in compensation from the persons who inflicted the damage, in accordance with the procedure prescribed by law.

Compensation of damages caused to an organisation, enterprise or institution by a terrorist act shall be made in accordance with the procedure established by law.

Article 20
Social rehabilitation of persons who have suffered as a result of a terrorist act

The social rehabilitation of persons who have suffered as a result of a terrorist act shall be conducted for the purpose of returning them to normal life. If necessary, such persons shall be provided with psychological, medical and professional rehabilitation, legal assistance and housing, and they shall be found employment.

The social rehabilitation of persons who have suffered as a result of a terrorist act, as well as of persons designated in Article 21 of this Law, shall be provided at the expense of funds from the state budget of Ukraine.

The procedure for socially rehabilitating persons who have suffered as a result of a terrorist act shall be established by the Cabinet of Ministers of Ukraine.

Section V
Legal and social protection of persons who take part in the fight against terrorism

Article 21
Persons entitled to legal and social protection

Persons who take part in the fight against terrorism shall be protected by the state. The following are entitled to legal and social protection:

1) military servicemen, employees and officials of central and local organs of executive power who participate (have participated) directly in anti-terrorist operations;

2) persons who on a permanent or temporary basis assist the organs that combat terrorism to prevent, detect, and suppress terrorist activity and minimise its effects;

3) members of the families of persons specified in subsections 1) and 2) of this paragraph if the need for protecting them arises as a result of their participation in the fight against terrorism.

Persons engaged in the conduct of the fight against terrorism shall be provided with social safeguards in accordance with the procedure prescribed by law.

If a person who took part in the fight against terrorism was killed during the conduct of an anti-terrorist operation, the members of his/her family and persons who were his/her dependants, shall be awarded from the funds of the state budget of Ukraine a lump sum payment in the amount of twenty minimum living wages, compensation for the cost of burial of the deceased, a pension in connection with the death of the breadwinner, and any privileges that the deceased had for housing, municipal services and the like shall be retained.

If a person who took part in the fight against terrorism has become disabled as a result of injury sustained in the conduct of an anti-terrorist operation, the person shall be awarded from the funds of the state budget of Ukraine a lump sum payment in the amount of ten minimum living wages and a pension in accordance with the legislation of Ukraine.

If a person who took part in the fight against terrorism sustained in the conduct of an anti-terrorist operation an injury that did not result in disability, the person shall be awarded a lump sum in the amount of five minimum living wages.

Article 22
Exemption from liability for damages

If in the course of conducting an anti-terrorist operation, unavoidable damage occurs to the life, health or property of terrorists, the military servicemen and other persons who participated in the anti-terrorist operation shall be exempt from liability for such damages in accordance with the laws of Ukraine.

Section VI
Legal responsibility for participation in terrorist activity

Article 23
Legal responsibility of persons guilty of terrorist activity

Persons guilty of terrorist activity shall be liable to criminal prosecution in accordance with the procedure provided for by law.

Insubordination or resistance to the legal demands of military servicemen and officials who take part in conducting an anti-terrorist operation, or unlawful interference in their legal activity, shall be prosecuted in accordance with the law.

Article 24
Legal responsibility of organisations for terrorist activity

An organisation responsible for committing a terrorist act and declared by a court decision to be a terrorist organisation shall be subject to liquidation and the confiscation of its property.

If a court of Ukraine declares the activity of an organisation (its division, branch or representation), which is registered outside Ukraine, to be terrorist activity, including in accordance with Ukraine's international legal obligations, the activity of the organisation on the territory of Ukraine shall be prohibited, its Ukrainian division (branch, representation) shall be closed on the basis of a court decision, and its assets and the assets of the designated organisation that are located on the territory of Ukraine shall be confiscated.

Charges of terrorist activity against an organisation shall be brought before the court by, respectively, the Prosecutor General of Ukraine, the prosecutors of the Autonomous Republic of Crimea, of an *oblast*, and of the cities of Kyiv and Sevastopol, in accordance with the procedure established by law.

Article 25
Legal responsibility for supporting terrorist activity

The directors and officials of enterprises, institutions and organisations, as well as citizens, who have provided support for terrorist activity, in particular those who have:

1) financed terrorists, terrorist groups (terrorist organisations);

2) provided or collected funds, directly or indirectly, to be used for the commission of terrorist acts or crimes of a terrorist nature;

3) conducted transactions involving funds or other financial assets for:
   o natural persons, who have committed or tried to commit terrorist acts or crimes of a terrorist nature, or participated in the commission of such acts, or provided assistance in their commission;
   o juridical persons, whose assets are directly or indirectly owned or controlled by terrorists, or persons who support terrorism;
   o juridical and natural persons, who act on behalf of or on instructions from terrorists or persons who support terrorism, including funds received or acquired through the use of objects directly or indirectly owned or controlled by persons who support terrorism, or by juridical and natural persons associated with them;

4) provided funds, other financial assets or economic resources, or services, directly or indirectly, to be used in the interests of natural persons who commit terrorist acts or support or participate in their commission, or in the interests of juridical persons whose assets are owned or controlled, directly or indirectly, by terrorists or persons who support terrorism, as well as of juridical and natural persons, who act on behalf of or on instructions from the persons designated above;

5) provided assistance to persons who participated in the commission of terrorist acts;

6) recruited natural persons to engage in terrorist activity, helped to establish channels for supplying weapons to terrorists or transporting terrorists across the state border of Ukraine;

7) harboured persons, who financed, planned, supported or committed terrorist acts or crimes of a terrorist nature;

8) used the territory of Ukraine in order to prepare or commit terrorist acts or crimes of a terrorist nature against other states or foreigners

– shall be liable to prosecution in accordance with the law.

Section VII
International co-operation of Ukraine in the fight against terrorism

Article 26
Principles of international co-operation in the sphere of combating terrorism

In accordance with the international treaties to which she is party, Ukraine shall co-operate in the fight against terrorism with foreign states, their law enforcement agencies and special services, as well as with international organisations, which are combating international terrorism.

Guided by the interests of ensuring the security of the individual, society and the state, Ukraine shall pursue on her territory persons involved in terrorist activity, including in cases in which terrorist acts or crimes of a terrorist nature were planned or were committed outside the borders of Ukraine but cause harm to Ukraine, and in other instances provided for by Ukraine's international treaties, which have been approved as binding by the Supreme Council of Ukraine.

Article 27
Providing information

Ukraine shall provide information to a foreign state about matters relating to the fight against international terrorism upon request, in conformity with the requirements of the laws of Ukraine and Ukraine's international legal obligations. Such information may be provided even without a prior request from a foreign state, if doing so does not jeopardise the conduct of a pre-trial investigation or a trial and can help the competent authorities of a foreign state to suppress a terrorist act.

Article 28
Participation in joint measures with foreign states in the fight against terrorism

In accordance with international treaties that have been approved as binding by the Supreme Council of Ukraine, Ukraine may take part in joint anti-terrorist actions by providing assistance to a foreign state or an interstate alliance in the redeployment of troops (forces), special anti-terrorist units and the transport of weapons, or by providing her own forces and means in conformity with the provisions of the laws of Ukraine "On the Procedure for Sending Units of the Armed Forces of Ukraine to Other States" and "On the Procedure for Allowing and the Conditions Governing the Presence of Military Units of Other States on the Territory of Ukraine".

Article 29
Extradition of persons who have participated in terrorist activities

The participation of aliens or stateless persons, who are not permanent residents of Ukraine, in terrorist activities may serve as grounds for the extradition of such persons to another state to face criminal proceedings.

The extradition of the persons designated in paragraph one of this article for the purpose of criminal proceedings or the carrying out of a sentence by a foreign state shall be conducted in conformity with the laws of Ukraine and the obligations assumed by Ukraine by the ratification of the European Convention on Extradition (1957), the European Convention on the Suppression of Terrorism (1977), and other international treaties approved as binding by the Supreme Council of Ukraine, as well as on the basis of reciprocity.

Section VIII
Control and oversight of compliance with the law in conducting the fight against terrorism

Article 30
Oversight of the conduct of the fight against terrorism

Control over compliance with legislation in conducting the fight against terrorism shall be exercised by the Supreme Council of Ukraine in accordance with the procedure prescribed by the Constitution of Ukraine (254k/96).

Control over the activity of the bodies responsible for combating terrorism shall be exercised by the President of Ukraine and the Cabinet of Ministers of Ukraine in accordance with the procedure prescribed by the Constitution and laws of Ukraine.

Article 31
Monitoring compliance with the law in the conduct of anti-terrorist actions

Compliance with the requirements of the law by bodies that participate in anti-terrorist actions shall be monitored by the Prosecutor General of Ukraine and the prosecutors authorised by him in accordance with the procedure prescribed by the laws of Ukraine.

Section IX
Closing provisions

1.   This Law shall enter into force on the day of its official publication.
2.   The Cabinet of Ministers, within three months of the day on which this Law enters into force, shall:
- o   approve the normative-legal acts provided for by this Law;
- o   bring all normative-legal acts into conformity with this Law;
- o   ensure a review by ministries and other central organs of executive power of their normative-legal acts and the revocation of any such acts that contravene this Law.

Appendix 4

Law of Ukraine on surveillance activities

Enacted under Resolution of the Supreme Council of Ukraine
No. 2136-12 of 18 February 1992
(Changed and amended in accordance with Laws of Ukraine
No. 2549-12 of 7 July 1992,
No. 2932-12 of 26 January 1993,
No. 3784-12 of 23 December 1993
No. 85/98-yR of 5 February 1998
No. 312-XIV(312-14) of 11 December 1998,
No. 1381-XIV(1381-14) of 13 January 2000,
No. 2181-III (2181-14) of 21 December 2000 –
comes into force as from 1 April 2001,
No. 2246-III (2246-14) of 18 January 2001,
No. 3111-III of 7 March 2002)

(Throughout the text of the law, the words "National Security Service" and "High-Ranking Officials of the Security Department of Ukraine" in all cases have been replaced with the words "Security Service" and "State Guard Directorate of Ukraine" respectively in appropriate cases according to Law of Ukraine No. 2246-III (2246-14) of 18 January 2001.

Article 1
Tasks of Surveillance Activities

The task of surveillance activities shall be to search for and record factual data on the illegal actions of individuals and groups subject to liability under the Criminal Code of Ukraine (2001-05, 2002-05), and intelligence and sabotage activities of the special services of foreign countries and organisations, with the objective of stopping illegal actions and in the interests of criminal justice, as well as to obtain information in the interests of the security of citizens, society and the state. (The article changed according to Law of Ukraine 1381-XIV (1381-14) of 13 January 2000; No. 2246-III (2246-14) of 18 January 2001).

Article 2
Definition of Surveillance Activities

Surveillance activities shall denote public and non-public searching, intelligence and counter-intelligence measures taken with the use of surveillance and technical means of surveillance.

Article 3
Legal Framework of Surveillance Activities

The legal framework of surveillance activities shall be established by the Constitution of Ukraine (888-09), this Law, the Criminal Code (2001-05, 2002-05) and Code of Criminal Procedures (1001-05, 1002-05, 1003-05) of Ukraine, the Laws of Ukraine on the Prosecutor's Office (1789-12), Militia (565-12), Security Service, Frontier Troops (1779-12), the state protection of state authorities of Ukraine and officials, the status of judges, the security of parties to criminal proceedings, the state protection of court and law enforcement officers, other legal acts and international agreements and treaties, to which Ukraine is a party. (The article changed according to Law of Ukraine No. 1381-XIV (1381-14) of 13 January 2000.)

Article 4
Principles of Surveillance Activities

Surveillance activities shall be based upon the principles of law, adherence to human rights and freedoms, interaction with government bodies and residents.

Article 5
Bodies Exercising Surveillance Activities

Surveillance activities shall be exercised by surveillance departments of:

- The Ministry of Internal Affairs of Ukraine: the criminal, transport and special militia, and special units for combating organised crime, ensuring the security of officers of courts, law enforcement bodies and participants in criminal proceedings;
  (Paragraph 2 of Section 1 of Article 5 in the wording of Law No. 3784-12 of 23 December 1993; changed according to Law No. 312-XIV of 11 December 1998; in the wording of Law of Ukraine No. 2246-III (2246-14) of 18 January 2001)

- The Security Service of Ukraine: the intelligence, counter-intelligence, military counter-intelligence, the protection of national statehood, the special units combating corruption and organised crime, the operative equipment, internal security, operative recording and counter-terrorism units, and units protecting participants in criminal proceedings and officers of law enforcement bodies;
  (Paragraph 3 in the wording of Law of Ukraine No. 2246-111(2246-14) of 18 January 2001)

- Border Forces of Ukraine: the intelligence agency of the State Committee for the State Border Protection of Ukraine, operative and surveillance units;

(Paragraph 4 in the wording of Law of Ukraine No. 3111-III of 7 March 2002)

- Department of State Security – ensuring security solely to ensure the security of individuals and facilities guarded by the state;
  (Paragraph 5 changed and amended according to Law of Ukraine No. 2246-III (2246-14) of 18 January 2001)

- Bodies of the State Tax Administration: investigation and surveillance departments of the tax militia;
  (The paragraph added to Part I according to Law of Ukraine No. 85/98-yR (85198-VR) of 5 February 1998)

- Bodies and institutions of the State Correction Administration Department of Ukraine – investigation and surveillance units;
  (The paragraph added to Part I according to Law of Ukraine No. 312-XIV of 11 December 1998)

- The intelligence agency of the Ministry of Defence of Ukraine: surveillance, technical surveillance and own security units.
  (The paragraph added to Part 1 according to Law of Ukraine No. 3111-III of 7 March 2002)
- (Part 1 changed and amended according to Law of Ukraine No. 2932-12 of 26 January 1993)

The exercise of surveillance activities by other departments of the specified bodies, by departments of other ministries, agencies, public, private organisations and individuals is prohibited.
(Part 2 changed according to Law of Ukraine No. 2246-III (2246-14) of 18 January 2001)

Article 6
Grounds for Exercise of Surveillance Activities

The grounds for the exercise of surveillance activities shall be as follows:

1) The availability of sufficient information received according to the procedure specified by law, which requires verification using surveillance actions and facilities, about (Paragraph 1, Item I in the wording of Law of Ukraine No. 2246-III (2246-14) of 18 January 2001) the following:
  o crimes under preparation or crimes committed by unidentified individuals;
  o individuals who are preparing or have committed a crime;
  o individuals escaping from investigation bodies, from a court or from serving a criminal sentence; (Paragraph 4, Item 1 changed and amended according to Law of Ukraine No. 2246-III (2246-14) of 18 January 2001)

- missing individuals; (Paragraph 5, Item I changed and amended according to Law of Ukraine No. 2246-III (2246-14) of 18 January 2001)
- intelligence and sabotage activities of the special services of foreign states, organisations and individuals against Ukraine;
- a real threat to the life, health, housing and property of court and law enforcement officials in connection with their official activities, as well as individuals involved in criminal court proceedings, members of their families and close relatives in order to create the conditions required for the proper administration of justice; officials of intelligence agencies of Ukraine in connection with the official activities of such individuals, their close relatives and individuals who co-operate or have co-operated with intelligence agencies of Ukraine on a confidential basis, and their family members for the purposes of the proper exercise of intelligence activities; (The paragraph added to the Item according to Law of Ukraine No. 1381-XIV (1381-14) of 13 January 2000; in the wording of Law of Ukraine No. 3111-III of 7 March 2002)

2) Requests from authorised state bodies, institutions and organisations for the scrutiny of individuals due to their access to the state, secrets and the work with nuclear materials and on nuclear installations; (Item 2 changed and amended according to Law of Ukraine No. 2246-III (2246-14) of 18 January 2001)

3) The need to obtain intelligence information in the interests of the security of society and the state.

The specified grounds can be contained in applications or notifications of individuals, officials, public organisations, in mass media, in written authorisations and resolutions of an investigator, in a prosecutor's instructions, in court decisions related to the cases in the scope of court's competence, in materials of investigation bodies and other law protection bodies, in requests of surveillance departments of international law protection bodies and organisations of other states, as well as in the requests of authorised state bodies, institutions and organisations specified by the Cabinet of Ministers of Ukraine for the scrutiny of individuals with regard to their access to state, military and service secrets.

It shall be forbidden to take a decision on the exercise of surveillance activities, if the grounds specified in this article are missing.

Article 7
Obligations of Departments Exercising Surveillance Activities

Departments performing surveillance activities shall:

461

1) take the necessary surveillance measures within the scope of their authority in accordance with laws making up the legal framework of surveillance activities, in order to prevent, detect in a timely way, terminate and reveal offences, as well as ascertain reasons and conditions conducive to offences, to prevent a crime or misdemeanour;
(Item I added to the Article according to Law of Ukraine No. 2246-II! (2246-14) of 18 January 2001)

2) obey the investigator's written orders, prosecutor's instructions and court decisions and requests of authorised state bodies, institutions and organisations for surveillance measures;

3) carry out requests of relevant international law protection organisations and law protection bodies of other states on the basis of treaties and agreements;

4) inform the relevant state authorities about facts known to them and data confirming the threat to the security of society and the state, as well as about violations of the legislation related to service activities of officials;
(Item in the wording of Law of Ukraine No. 2246-III (2246-14) of 18 January 2001)

5) interact with one another and with other law protection bodies with the objective of rapid and complete investigation of crimes and identification of culpable individuals;

6) ensure, in co-operation with other units, the safety of court and law enforcement officers, persons assisting and aiding surveillance, persons taking part in criminal proceedings, family members and close relatives.
(Item in the wording of the Law of Ukraine No. 1381-XIV (1381-14) of 13 January 2000)

Article 8
Rights of Departments Performing Surveillance Activities

Surveillance departments shall have the following rights to carry out tasks of surveillance, if there are grounds specified in Article 6 hereof:

1) to interview people with their consent, or use their voluntary help;

2) to undertake the control and operative purchase and supply of commodities, objects and substances, including those whose sale is prohibited, to and from individuals and legal bodies regardless of ownership forms in order to detect and record the facts of illegal actions. The procedure of the operative purchase and controlled supply shall be specified by regulations of the Ministry of Internal Affairs of Ukraine, the tax militia, the Security Service of Ukraine with the agreement of the General Public Prosecution Office of Ukraine and registered with the

Ministry of Justice of Ukraine; (Item 2 in the wording of Law of Ukraine No. 2246-111(2246-14) of 18 January 2001)

3) to raise the issue of performing the inspection of financial and commercial activities of enterprises, institutions and organisations regardless of ownership forms and individuals engaging in business activities or other types of commercial activities on their own according to the procedure established by law, and to take part in such inspections; (Item 3 in the wording of Law of Ukraine No. 2246-III (2246-14) of 18 January 2001)

4) to request, collect and examine documents and data characterising the activities of enterprises, institutions, organisations and lifestyle of individuals suspected of preparing or committing a crime, and the sources and amount of their revenue;

5) to carry out operations for the capture of criminals, termination of crimes, intelligence and sabotage activities of special services of foreign states, organisations and individuals; (Item 5 changed and amended according to Law of Ukraine No. 2246-III (2246-14) of 18 January 2001)

6) to visit dwellings and other rooms with the consent of their owners or tenants in order to determine the circumstances of a committed crime or crime under preparation, as well as to gather information on the illegal activities of suspects or individuals under scrutiny;

7) to detect and record in a non-public manner the traces of a grave crime, documents and other objects that could become evidence of the preparation or committing of such a crime, or to receive intelligence information also by way of penetration by an operative to rooms, vehicles and land plots;

8) to undertake penetration of a criminal group by an undercover operative or a person co-operating with the latter, while ensuring the confidentiality of factual data about their identity. A resolution shall be passed in respect of the need of such penetration; it is to be approved by the head of the relevant authority; (Item 8 in the wording of Law of Ukraine No. 2246-III (2246-14) of 18 January 2001)

9) to collect information from communication channels, and to use other technical facilities of information collection;

10) to monitor telegraph and mail correspondence by way of selection according to certain features;

11) to carry out visual observation in public places using photo or cinema filming and video recording, optical and radio devices, or other technical facilities;

12) to have employees, known and unknown, included in the staffing schedule and those not included in the staffing schedule; (Item 12 changed and amended according to Law of Ukraine No. 2246-III (2246-14) of 18 January 2001)

13) to establish confidential co-operation with individuals on a voluntary basis;

14) to obtain information on crimes, which are under preparation or have been committed, and the threat to the security of society and the state; from legal bodies and individuals, free of charge or against payment;

15) to use rooms, vehicles and other property of enterprises, institutions and organisations subject to the consent of their administration as well as to use housing, other rooms, vehicles and property owned by individuals subject to the consent of the latter;

16) to establish, for purposes of confidentiality, enterprises or organisations, and to use documents concealing an individual or the subordination of members, rooms or vehicles of surveillance departments;

17) to create and use automated information systems;

18) to use means of physical restraint, special means and firearms on the basis and according to the procedures established by the laws on the Militia, Security Service, Frontier Troops, the state guarding of state authorities of Ukraine and officials. (Item 18 changed and amended according to Law of Ukraine No. 2246-III (2246-14) of 18 January 2001)

Concealed penetration of a house or other property of a person, the recording of information on communication channels, the monitoring of mail, telephone conversations, telegrams and other correspondence, and the application of other technical facilities for obtaining information shall be undertaken by court decision made on the basis of a proposal of the head or deputy head of the relevant surveillance unit. The said individuals shall notify the public prosecutor within one day about the obtainment of such a court permit or the refusal thereof. These measures shall be applied solely to prevent an offence or find out the truth while investigating a criminal case, unless it is impossible to obtain the required information otherwise. A protocol with appropriate attachments, to be used as the source of evidence during criminal proceedings, shall be compiled as a result of the said surveillance actions. (Part 2 of Article 8 in the wording of Laws No. 2549-12 of 7 July 1992; No. 2246-III (2246-14) of 18 January 2001)

Exclusively in order to obtain intelligence information for ensuring the external security of Ukraine, or the prevention and termination of intelligence and sabotage encroachments of the special services of foreign states and foreign organisations, the abovementioned actions may be taken according to the procedure agreed upon with the Prosecutor General of Ukraine and the Chairman of the Supreme Court of Ukraine. (Part 3 changed and amended according to Law of Ukraine No. 2246-III (2246-14) of 18 January 2001)

Members of other departments may be involved to carry out certain tasks in the course of surveillance activities.

In case of the performance of surveillance assignments related to the termination of offences in the field of the tax legislation, the rights under this article shall be granted solely to bodies of the tax militia within the framework of their competence. (Part added to the article according to Law of Ukraine No. 2181-III (2181-14) of 21 December 2001)

Article 9
Law Guarantees during Use of Surveillance Activities

In every case, when there are grounds for the use of surveillance activities, a surveillance file shall be initiated. A resolution on the initiation of such a case shall be approved by the head of the body of internal affairs, security service, frontier troops, high-ranking officials of security, investigation and surveillance departments of the tax militia, state correction administration, institution of the intelligence agency of the Ministry of Defence of Ukraine or his authorised deputy. (Part 1, Article 9 changed and amended according to Laws of Ukraine No. 85/98 of 5 February 1998; No. 31 2-XIV of 11 December 1998; No. 2246-III (2246-14) of 18 January 2001; No. 3111-III of 7 March 2002)

Supervision of surveillance activities shall be exercised by the Ministry of the Interior of Ukraine, Security Service of Ukraine, State Committee of Ukraine for State Border Protection, State Guard Directorate of Ukraine, State Tax Administration of Ukraine, State Correction Administration and the intelligence agency of the Ministry of Defence of Ukraine. (Part 2, Article 9 changed and amended according to Laws of Ukraine No. 85/98 of 5 February 1998; No. 312-XIV of 11 December 1998; No. 3111-III of 7 March 2002)

For any individual who is suspected of preparing or committing a crime, escaping from investigation authorities, court or from serving a criminal sentence, or is missing, only one surveillance file shall be initiated. Surveillance actions shall be prohibited without setting up a surveillance case, except for the case covered by Part Four of this article. A resolution to be approved by the head or an authorised deputy head of the internal affairs, security service bodies, border troops unit, the State Security Administration of Ukraine, the intelligence agency of the Ministry of Defence of Ukraine, an operative unit of the tax militia, a penitentiary body or institution shall be passed when setting up a surveillance case. The resolution shall indicate the place and time of its

465

adoption, the position and the name of the person issuing the resolution, grounds for and objectives of setting up the surveillance case. (Part 3, Article 9 changed and amended according to Law of Ukraine No. 2246-III (2246-14) of 18 January 2001; No. 3111-III of 7 March 2002)

No surveillance case shall be set up in cases of clearing individuals in connection with allowing them access to state secrets, or to work with nuclear materials and on nuclear installations. The clearance inspection should not take more than one month. (Part 4, Article 9 in the wording of Law of Ukraine No. 2246-III (2246-14) of 18 January 2001)

When usingsurveillance activities, it shall not be allowed to violate the rights and freedoms of individuals and legal bodies. Individual limitations of these rights and freedoms shall be of an exceptional and temporary nature and may be applied only subject to a court decision in respect of a person whose actions contain indications of a grave offence, as well as in cases specified by the legislation of Ukraine in order to ensure the rights and freedoms of other individuals as well as the security of the society. (Part 5, Article 9 changed and amended according to Law of Ukraine No. 2246-III (2246-14) of 18 January 2001)

If sufficient grounds exist, the permit for the exercise of surveillance activities shall be issued by the head of the relevant surveillance department, who is also liable for the legality of measures being taken in accordance with the current legislation.

When taking surveillance measures, the members of surveillance departments shall take into account their compliance with the degree of social danger of the criminal encroachments and of the threat to the interests of society and the state.

In cases where violation of the rights and freedoms of individuals or legal bodies in the course of surveillance activities, or involvement in a crime of the individual in relation to whom the surveillance measures have been undertaken, is not confirmed, the Security Service of Ukraine, Ministry of Interior of Ukraine, State Frontier Committee of Ukraine, State Guard Directorate of Ukraine, State Tax Administration of Ukraine, State Punishment Administration Department of Ukraine or an intelligence agency of the Ministry of Defence of Ukraine shall restore urgently the violated rights and reimburse for the caused tangible and non-pecuniary damages in full. (Part 8, Article 9 changed and amended according to Laws of Ukraine No. 85/98 of 5 February 1998; No. 312-XIV of 11 December 1998; No. 2246-III (2246-14) of 18 January 2001; No. 3111-III of 7 March 2002)

The citizens of Ukraine and other individuals are entitled (in accordance with the procedure established by law) to receive from bodies entitled to exercise surveillance activities an explanation in writing with regard to the limitation of their rights and freedoms and to appeal against such actions.

It shall be forbidden to transfer or disclose information about security actions and protected persons, non-investigated crimes or such information as could be harmful for the investigation, for the interests of an individual, or for the security of Ukraine. (Part 10 changed and amended according to Law of Ukraine No. 1381-XIV (1381-14) of 13 January 2000)

Departments using automated information systems for surveillance activities shall provide for the possibility of issuing the data for an individual on the request of investigation bodies, prosecutor's office, or court. The information adequacy and reliability of its protection shall be guaranteed in places of information storage.

The data related to the private life, honour and dignity of an individual obtained as a result of surveillance activities shall not be kept and must be destroyed, if they do not contain information on committing illegal actions.

The results of surveillance activities, which are state secrets under the legislation of Ukraine, as well as the data related to the private life, honour and dignity of an individual, shall not be transferred and disclosed. The members of surveillance departments as well as the individuals to whom these data have been assigned in the course of surveillance activities, or who have become aware of these data in the course of work, shall be liable under the current legislation for the transfer and disclosure of such data, except for the cases of disclosing the information on illegal actions violating the human rights. (Part 13 changed and amended according to Law of Ukraine No. 2246-III (2246-14) of 18 January 2001)

The surveillance measures are associated with temporary limitation of human rights, in order to prevent, terminate and investigate grave crimes, search for individuals who are escaping from serving a criminal sentence or missing, protection of life, health, housing and property of court and law enforcement officers and persons participating in criminal proceedings, termination of intelligence and sabotage activities against Ukraine. In case of operative necessity of urgently taking such measures, surveillance departments shall within 24 hours notify the court or the prosecutor of their application and grounds for taking such measures. (Part changed and amended according to Law of Ukraine No. 1381-XIV (1381-14) of 13 January 2000; No. 2246-III (2246-14) of 18 January 2001)

Visual observation may be carried out in order to obtain data on a person and their relations, if there is evidence of such person's preparing or having committed a grave crime, in order to obtain

467

information indicating the signs of such crime, as well as in order to ensure the safety of court and law enforcement officers, persons participating in criminal proceedings, their family members and close relatives. (Part in the wording of Law of Ukraine No. 1381-XIV(1381-14) of 13 January 2000)

It shall be forbidden to use technical means, psychotropics, chemical and other substances, inhibiting the will or causing damage to the health of people and to the environment.

Article 9-1
Period of Surveillance Proceedings

The surveillance proceedings shall take place in respect of:

1) unidentified persons, who are preparing for or have committed a crime, as well as persons who hide from the investigation agencies or the court or evade serving their criminal sentences – until such persons are identified or found; the time for proceedings shall not exceed the limitation period of the criminal liability or the enforcement of an indicting sentence;

2) persons in connection with the investigation of a criminal case in their respect – until the sentence passed on them becomes legally effective, until the court resolves to terminate the proceedings, until the court passes a judgment (resolution) on applying measures of a medical or educational nature, or until the criminal case is terminated by the court, public prosecutor, investigator or an inquest agency;

3) missing people – until they are found or a court decision declaring them missing or deceased becomes legally effective;

4) persons, if there are data on their participation in the preparation or commitment of a crime – up to six months;

5) in cases of intelligence activities aimed at the security of the society and the state – until the intelligence activities are completed or the opportunities for the exercise thereof are exhausted. (Item 5 added to the Article according to Law of Ukraine No. 3111-III of 7 March 2002)

Should data be obtained in the course of surveillance proceedings on the participation of a person in the preparation or commitment of a grave crime, the time for proceedings may be extended to 12 months by heads of main and independent directorates of the Ministry of Interior of Ukraine, the Central Directorate of the Security Service of Ukraine, main directorates and directorates of the Ministry of Interior of Ukraine and the tax militia of the State Tax Administration of Ukraine in the Autonomous Republic of Crimea, an *oblast*, cities of Kyiv and Sevastopol, regional directorates and agencies of the military counter-intelligence of the

Security Service of Ukraine, the Head of the State Border Committee of Ukraine or their deputies.

Further extension of surveillance proceedings up to 18 months may be granted by the Minister of the Interior of Ukraine, the Head of the Security Service of Ukraine, the First Deputy Head of the State Tax Administration of Ukraine being the head of the tax militia, and the Head of the State Border Committee of Ukraine and the Head of the State Guard Directorate of Ukraine.

The extension of surveillance proceedings in respect of foreigners suspected of engaging in intelligence and subversion activities against Ukraine for a period over 18 months shall be granted by the Head of the Security Service of Ukraine in agreement with the Prosecutor General of Ukraine.

The period of the surveillance proceedings shall commence from the date of approval of a resolution on the institution of proceedings by the head or deputy head of the relevant agency and end on the date of the approval of the resolution on the termination of the surveillance proceedings.

This period may be suspended if the person, in whose respect the proceedings have been instituted, has left Ukraine temporarily or is dangerously ill and surveillance activities in respect of such person are not possible.

A substantiated resolution to be approved by the head or deputy head of the relevant agency shall be issued in cases of the suspension and resumption of the period of the surveillance proceedings. (Article 9-1 added to the Law according to Law of Ukraine No. 2246-III (2246-14) of 18 January 2001)

Article 9-2
Termination of Surveillance Proceedings

Surveillance proceedings shall be terminated if:

1) the person, who hid from the investigation agencies or the court, evaded serving the criminal sentence or was missing, has been detected;

2) the court sentence, resolution or judgment has become effective;

3) the criminal proceedings have been terminated by the court, public prosecutor, investigator or inquest authority;

4) the intelligence or counter-intelligence actions have been completed or opportunities for such actions have been exhausted;

5) materials on criminal activities of a person have been disproved according to the established procedure;

6) the person in question has left Ukraine for a place of permanent residence, unless it is possible to undertake surveillance actions in respect of such person;

7) data confirming the availability of indications of a crime in actions of a person have not been ascertained within the time frames specified hereby;

8) a public prosecutor has detected proceedings initiated illegally, in cases of the use of surveillance in the course of such proceedings;

9) if the person, in whose respect the surveillance proceedings were instituted, has died.

A substantiated resolution to be approved by a head or deputy head of the relevant authority shall be issued in case of the termination of surveillance proceedings. If the surveillance actions under such proceedings were performed upon the basis of a court decision, the notice of termination shall be sent to the court within three days.

The retention period for records of terminated surveillance proceedings shall be established in line with the legislation of Ukraine. (Article 9-2 added to the Law according to Law of Ukraine No. 2246-III (2246-14) of 18 January 2001)

Article 10
Use of Materials of Surveillance Activities

The materials of surveillance activities shall be used:

1) as the basis and grounds for bringing a criminal action or conducting urgent investigation actions;

2) for obtaining factual data, which serve as evidence in a criminal case;

3) for the prevention, termination and investigation of crimes, intelligence and sabotage encroachments against Ukraine, search for criminals and missing individuals;

4) to ensure the safety of court and law enforcement officials, and individuals involved in criminal court proceedings, members of their families and close relatives, and officials of intelligence agencies of Ukraine, their close relatives, as well as individuals who co-operate or have co-operated with intelligence agencies of Ukraine on a confidential

basis, and their family members; (Item added to Article 10 according to Law of Ukraine No. 1381-XIV (1381-14) of 13 January 2000; in the wording of Law of Ukraine No. 3111-III of 7 March 2002)

5) for mutual information of departments authorised to exercise surveillance activities as well as other law protection bodies;

6) for informing state authorities according to their competence.

Article 11
Assistance with Exercise of Surveillance Activities

The state authorities shall assist surveillance departments with solving the tasks of surveillance activities.

Subject to the wish of an individual, his co-operation with a surveillance department can be the subject of a written agreement guaranteeing the confidentiality of the co-operation. The agreement on assistance to surveillance departments with their surveillance activities may be concluded with a competent individual. The agreement procedure shall be established by the Cabinet of Ministers of Ukraine.

Individuals involved in surveillance activities shall keep confidential the information they became aware of. The disclosure of these secrets shall result in prosecution according to the current legislation, except for cases of disclosing the information on illegal actions violating the human rights.

It shall be forbidden to involve in the execution of surveillance tasks the medical staff, priests, lawyers, if the individual, in relation to whom they have to take surveillance measures, is their patient or client.

Article 12
Social and Legal Protection of Members of Surveillance Departments

The guarantees of the legal and social protection provided by relevant laws of Ukraine shall apply to officials performing surveillance activities.

Officials who perform surveillance activities are entitled to additional social and financial privileges according to the procedure established by the Cabinet of Ministers of Ukraine.

If there are data on a threat to the life, health or property of an official or his relatives due to his performing surveillance activities in the interests of the security of Ukraine, or of the investigation of a grave crime or exposure of an organised criminal group, the surveillance department shall take special measures to ensure their safety: by change in the personal data, change in the place of residence, work and study or in

471

other data according to the procedure to be established by the Cabinet of Ministers of Ukraine.

A member of a surveillance department shall not be liable for the damage caused by him to the rights, freedoms of an individual, interests of the state in the course of performing surveillance activities, while being in conditions of necessary defence, ultimate necessity or professional risk as well as in connection with the arrest of an individual, whose actions contain indications of a crime.

Article 13
Social and Legal Protection of an Individual Involved in Performance of Tasks of Surveillance Activities

An individual involved in performance of surveillance activities shall be under state protection.

Co-operation of such an individual with the surveillance department shall be included in his overall labour record, if an employment contract has been concluded with such an individual. If such an individual has died or become disabled in connection with the performance of tasks of surveillance activities, he shall be entitled to the privileges envisaged for the officials of surveillance departments.

In case of a danger to the life, health or property of an individual involved in the performance of tasks of surveillance activities, his protection shall be ensured according to the procedure provided by Part 3 of Article 12 hereof.

Article 14
Supervision of Compliance with Laws in the Course of Surveillance Activities

The compliance with laws in the course of surveillance activities shall be supervised by the Prosecutor General of Ukraine, his/her deputies, public prosecutors of the Autonomous Republic of Crimea, *oblasts*, the cities of Kyiv and Sevastopol, public prosecutors and their deputies with the equivalent status, as well as by heads and public prosecutors of directorates and departments of the Public Prosecution Office of Ukraine and prosecution offices of the Autonomous Republic of Crimea, *oblasts* and cities of Kyiv and Sevastopol.

Within the scope of his authority, the public prosecutor shall:

1) enter all premises of agencies engaging in surveillance activities without obstruction;

2) request for inspection the directions, instructions, orders and other acts related to surveillance activities, records of surveillance

proceedings, registration, accounting, reporting, statistical and analytical documents, and other information on the progress of surveillance actions;

3) instruct heads of relevant authorities to undertake inspections in units reporting to them, aiming at the elimination of breaches of the law;

4) issue written instructions to undertake surveillance actions in the interests of the criminal procedure, to search for missing people;

5) give consent to the extension of the time for surveillance activities;

6) receive explanations on the violation of requirements of the law from officials of the surveillance agencies;

7) verify complaints on the violation of laws by surveillance agencies and familiarise himself with the surveillance materials, if necessary thereto;

8) cancel illegal resolutions on the institution or termination of surveillance proceedings, suspension or resumption of surveillance activities or other decisions contradicting the law;

9) take measures aimed at rectifying violations of laws in the course of surveillance activities and making the guilty persons answerable at law;

10) protest against illegal resolutions of courts permitting surveillance actions or refusing such a permit. A protest shall suspend the surveillance actions permitted by the court.

Information about individuals who co-operate or have co-operated with an intelligence agency of Ukraine, the fact of a particular individual's being among the staff officials of intelligence agencies, as well as forms, methods and means of the intelligence activities, and the organisational/staffing structure of intelligence agencies, shall not be the subject of the public prosecutor's supervision. (Part 4 added to the Article according to Law of Ukraine No. 3111-III of 7 March 2002)

(Article 14 in the wording of Law of Ukraine No. 2246-III (2246-14) of 18 January 2001)

Leonid Kravchuk, President of Ukraine
City of Kyiv, 18 February 1992

United Kingdom

1. Please indicate the SITs used in your country, the respective legal framework governing their use and their legal definition, if any.

The Regulation of Investigatory Powers Act (RIPA) 2000 provides a framework compliant with the European Convention on Human Rights for the use of the following special investigation techniques.

Interception of Communications

Part I Chapter I of RIPA defined communications as any communication in the course of its transmission by means of (a) a public postal service; or (b) a public telecommunications system. For more information please see the Interception Code of Practice at the following web link:
 http://www.homeoffice.gov.uk/crimpol/crimreduc/regulation/ioccop.html

Covert Surveillance

Part II of RIPA provides two categories of covert surveillance. Intrusive surveillance is defined as covert surveillance inside residential premises or private vehicles that is carried out by means of a surveillance device or involves a person on the premises on in the vehicle. Directed surveillance is defined as covert surveillance that is not intrusive which is undertaken for a specific investigation or operation that is likely to obtain private information about a person. For more information please see the Covert Surveillance Code of Practice at the following link:
http://www.homeoffice.gov.uk/crimpol/crimreduc/regulation/codeofpractice/surveillance/index.html

Use of Informants and Undercover Officers

Part II of RIPA defines an Informant and Undercover Officer as a Covert Human Intelligence Source (CHIS), which is defined as a person who establishes or maintains a personal or other relationship with a person to covertly obtain and disclose information. A person who is running a 'front store operation (e.g. undercover company)' and a person who carries out 'pseudo-purchases or other "pseudo-offences"' would fall within the definition of a CHIS.

For more information please see the Covert Human Intelligence Source Code of Practice at the following link:
http://www.homeoffice.gov.uk/crimpol/crimreduc/regulation/codeofpractice/humanintell/index.html

Bugging

Part III of the Police Act 1997 provides the lawful basis for the police service and HM Customs and Excise to enter on or interfere with property or with wireless telegraphy. Section 5 of the Intelligence Services Act 1994 provides the lawful basis for the security and intelligence agencies to enter on or interfere with property or with wireless telegraphy.

2. When and under which circumstances (e.g. criminal investigation, preliminary stage, etc.) can SITs be used?

Interception of communications may only be conducted by means of a warrant authorised by the Secretary of State, on application by the police or security and intelligence agencies in the interests of national security, to prevent or detect serious crime or for the purpose of safeguarding the economic well-being of the United Kingdom. The product of an intercepted communication can not be used in evidence.

Intrusive surveillance may only be carried out by the police service and HM Custom and Excise if an independent Surveillance Commissioner approves an authorisation. The authorisation must be necessary on the grounds that it is to prevent or detect serious crime. Intrusive surveillance by the security and intelligence services may only be carried out by means of a warrant authorised by the Secretary of State in the interests of national security, to prevent or detect serious crime or in the interests of the economic well-being of the United Kingdom.

The carrying out of Directed Surveillance and the use of a Covert Human Intelligence Source is authorised internally at a senior level within the police service, HM Customs and Excise and security and intelligence services. An authorisation can be granted if it is necessary and proportionate, if it is in the interests of national security, for the purpose of preventing or detecting crime or preventing disorder, in the interests of the economic well-being of the United Kingdom, in the interests of public safety or for the purpose of protecting public health.

3. Are there any specific features governing the use of SITs in relation to acts of terrorism? If so, please specify.

Not Applicable.

4. How does the legal framework governing the use of SITs guarantee respect for human rights and individual freedoms, the principles of subsidiarity and proportionality? Is the authorisation to use SITs subject to time-limits? Which bodies and procedures are in place to supervise compliance with human rights standards and with the above-mentioned principles in the use of SITs? Is supervision automatic/systematic?

All of the powers covered by RIPA are ECHR-compliant. A three-pronged oversight system is written into the law:

- the principle of considering necessity and proportionality before authorisations are granted, including tight controls on who can intercept communications and carry out intrusive surveillance, safeguards on the interception procedure itself and other rules governing interception by the police, HM Customs and the Security and Intelligence Agencies;
- oversight by independent Commissioners, who are senior serving or retired members of the judiciary, reporting to the Prime Minister annually on the use of interception, covert surveillance and covert human intelligence sources (CHIS); and
- anyone can apply to the Investigatory Powers Tribunal (IPT), an independent tribunal consisting of eight members of the senior serving or retired judiciary. The IPT has jurisdiction to hear human rights complaints in respect of alleged interception of communications, carrying out of covert surveillance and use of CHIS.

5. Which institutions are involved in the use of SITs and what is their role (e.g. law enforcement agencies, prosecutor's office, judicial authorities, etc.)? Which institutions can order and/or authorise the use of SITs? How does co-operation between these institutions work in practice?

Section 6(2) of RIPA defines the following as able to apply to the Secretary of State for an interception warrant:

- The Director-General of the Security Service,
- The Chief of the Secret Intelligence Service,
- The Director of GCHQ,
- The Director General of the National Criminal Intelligence Service,
- The Commissioner of the Metropolitan Police,
- The Chief Constable of the Police Service of Northern Ireland,
- The Chief Constable of any police force in Scotland,
- The Commissioners of Customs and Excise,
- The Chief of Defence Intelligence,
- A person who, for the purposes of any international mutual legal assistance agreement, is the competent authority of a country or territory outside the United Kingdom.

See the answer to question 2 for a list of public authorities which can carry out intrusive surveillance, directed surveillance and use covert human intelligence sources.

6. Are there any specialised counter-terrorism institutions? What is their role in the use of SITs?

The police and Security and Intelligence Agencies work together to combat the threat of terrorism.

7.   Which measures have been adopted in order to facilitate international co-operation (e.g. joint investigation teams)? Can the SITs listed in reply to question 1 be used in cross-border settings?

The EU Framework Decision on Joint Investigation Teams (JITs) has been implemented and the cross-border surveillance provision in Article 40 of the Schengen Implementation Convention is in the process of being implemented.

8.   What use can be made of SIT in the context of mutual legal assistance?

Subject to future ratification of articles 17-22 of the EU convention on mutual legal assistance in criminal matters (MLAC), EU countries may make MLAC requests to the UK to conduct interception of communications to prevent or detect serious crime.

9. How can the use of SITs be improved? Please provide any comments/proposals concerning the implementation of the terms of reference of the PC-TI and in particular the use and regulation of SITs.

Canada

1. Please indicate the SITs used in your country, the respective legal framework governing their use and their legal definition, if any.

General issues

Before discussing special investigative techniques (SITs) in Canadian law from the perspective of this Council of Europe questionnaire, it is important first to clarify a number of general issues:

First, in criminal investigations under the Canadian legal system, there is a firm separation between the role of the police and that of the judiciary. The judiciary does not initiate law enforcement investigations or lead, or form part of, the law enforcement investigative function. The planning, initiation and use of investigative techniques, including SITs, in criminal investigations, is a matter for the police and is not directed by the judiciary. This separation of functions does not mean that the judiciary has no role with respect to ruling on the legality of investigative techniques. General and specific legal requirements and standards govern the use of investigative techniques. Failure to adhere to these requirements and standards may lead to serious consequences for the prosecution – such as judicial rulings disallowing evidence or staying prosecution – during court proceedings against the targets of the investigation. It may also lead to criminal, civil or disciplinary (deontological) proceedings against the law enforcement officials. For certain specific investigative techniques, the judiciary does play a role in authorising, beforehand, use of the technique in individual cases. This procedure, however, is initiated by police and prosecutors by application to the court: the judiciary remains independent in performing this role and does not otherwise become involved in the direction of the investigation.

Second, in respect of the functions of police, there is no organisational distinction between the police role in engaging in preventive law enforcement and the police role in investigating crimes that have been committed. Police forces in Canada have both roles and there is no clear and formal division in Canada between "pro-active investigations" and "reactive investigations".

Third, in Canadian law, there is no separate legislative framework that applies to SITs. Law enforcement in Canada is covered under the general legal framework of criminal law, as well as under legislation governing the establishment and conduct of police forces and other enforcement agencies. Within this framework, specific kinds of SITs are subject to specific legal requirements. It should be emphasised, as well, that laws providing for SITs, and law enforcement activity in using SITs, are subject to review by the courts under the *Canadian Charter of Rights and Freedoms* and in respect of compliance with other general requirements, such as those that govern abuse of process. These matters are further discussed below.

Types of SITs not available

With respect to the specific types of special investigative techniques available in Canada, all of those mentioned in the inventory[1] may be used in Canada, subject to applicable conditions and limitations, with two exceptions.

Cross-border pursuits

There is no general right to engage in international cross-border pursuits in general investigative situations. An ability to engage in "hot pursuit" of suspects – that is, continuation of an active pursuit of suspects – across the US/Canadian border is generally recognised. Beyond this, however, Canadian police do not have any general police officer status outside their jurisdiction. Special exceptional arrangements with other jurisdictions sometimes are made to grant individual officers special status outside Canada, but, in general, Canadian law enforcement must seek the assistance and co-operation of the police in other jurisdictions in respect of investigations which cross international borders.

Agents Provocateurs

The use of *agents provocateurs* is not considered acceptable to the extent that it constitutes "entrapment". Under Canadian law, the practice of "entrapment" by police is considered to be an abuse of process.[2] As stated by the Supreme Court of Canada, entrapment occurs when:

- the authorities provide a person with an opportunity to commit an offence without acting on a reasonable suspicion that this person is already engaged in criminal activity or pursuant to a *bona fide* inquiry;
- although having such a reasonable suspicion or acting in the course of a *bona fide* inquiry, they go beyond providing an opportunity and induce the commission of an offence.[3]

The last six words of the judgment should be noted.

Specific measures applying to individual SITs

Some SITs in Canada, such as general undercover police operations, non-intrusive police observation techniques and use of informants, are not subject to specific provisions of statutory law addressing when and how they can be used. Nevertheless, general legal standards and common law requirements apply.

As discussed elsewhere in this document, police actions are subject to the *Canadian Charter of Rights and Freedoms*. Common law standards (judicially imposed), such as the "abuse of process" doctrine, also come into play: police conduct which is unacceptable as an abuse of process is that which violates a community's sense of decency and fair play, and police use of such abusive techniques may lead to a judicial staying of proceedings against the accused.

It further should be noted that the use of SITs such as undercover operations is also governed by internal police policy and procedures. In addition, comprehensive administration and accountability provisions addressing law enforcement activity are provided by laws addressing the establishment and organisation of police forces, codes of conduct, and internal discipline (deontology), and public complaints.

As previously mentioned, certain SITs under Canadian law do have detailed provisions requiring prior judicial authorisation. In respect of those listed under the inventory, these are electronic (video) surveillance,[4] "bugging" and interception of private communications,[5] and searches.[6] Judicial authorisation requirements also apply to additional special procedures such as the taking of DNA samples,[7] installation of tracking devices[8] and installation of devices recording telephone numbers dialled (and the numbers from which calls are received).[9] Detailed discussion of the individual requirements and procedures in respect of each of these SITs is beyond the scope of this paper.

In respect of SITs in which the police would engage in illegal conduct, the Supreme Court of Canada has ruled that the police have no inherent immunity from liability for unlawful conduct committed in good faith during the course of an investigation.[10] The Supreme Court further noted that, if immunity were necessary, it was for Parliament to provide for it. On the face of it, this restrictive principle could apply, depending on the circumstances, to SITs such as front store operations, controlled deliveries and pseudo-purchases/pseudo-offences,[11] as mentioned in the inventory.

Parliament has, however, adopted certain provisions allowing law enforcement officers to engage in conduct that would otherwise be illegal, for the purpose of investigations and enforcement, subject to controls and limitations. For example, measures under the Criminal Code provide a limited justification[12] for designated law enforcement officers – and others acting at their direction – for acts and omissions that would otherwise be offences. The justification includes a fundamental requirement of "reasonable and proportional" conduct.

Three factors are set out as relevant to determining reasonableness and proportionality: the nature of the act or omission, the nature of the investigation and the reasonable availability of other means for carrying out enforcement duties. Certain conduct that would otherwise be an offence is justified only if a public officer has the prior written authorisation of a senior official responsible for law enforcement or in exigent circumstances. Certain other conduct, such as the intentional causing of death or bodily harm, obstruction of justice, or conduct that would violate the sexual integrity of an individual, is not justified.[13]

2. When and under which circumstances (e.g. criminal investigation, preliminary stage, etc.) can SITs be used?

There is no general principle of Canadian law restricting the use of SITs to situations where it is believed that a crime has already been committed. As discussed above, there is no clear and formal division in Canada between pro-active investigations and reactive investigations. Specific legal provisions address the circumstances under which certain SITs can be used, but, for the most part, these do not prohibit their use in preventive law enforcement activity. Some techniques, such as the interception of private communications, are in fact especially useful during investigations targeted at the planning stages of a crime.

Provisions governing SITs may set different standards under which a SIT can be used in preventive law enforcement, compared to standards for its use where a crime has already been committed. For example, judicial authorisation for a search under Section 487(1)(c) of the Criminal Code permits authorisation where a judge is "satisfied by information on oath … that there are reasonable grounds to believe that there is in a building, receptacle or place … anything that there are reasonable grounds to believe is intended to be used for the purpose of committing any offence against the person for which a person may be arrested without a warrant".

Other provisions of Section 487 meanwhile set less restrictive standards for search warrants where a crime has already been committed: in particular, paragraphs 487.1(a) and (b) apply generally to any offence that has been committed under federal law, not just to certain offences against the person.

3. Are there any specific features governing the use of SITs in relation to acts of terrorism? If so, please specify.

Police engaged in investigations into terrorism have available the full range of techniques and tools, including SITs, that are available in Canada in relation to law enforcement and investigations. However, certain additional special provisions apply to terrorism investigations.

For example, Section 83.28 of the Criminal Code allows for the holding of an investigative hearing in relation to a terrorism offence. Upon application by the police, an investigative hearing may be ordered by a judge for the gathering of information from a person in relation to a terrorism offence where it is reasonably believed that a terrorism offence has been committed or will be committed and there are reasonable grounds to believe that the hearing will provide information about the offence or the whereabouts of a suspect.

It should be noted, however, that this measure is subject to a number of strict conditions and protections. The investigative hearing is held before a judge. The procedure is not a trial of the person for an offence: the person is subject to an order for the gathering of information and is not an accused. No answer given or thing produced – nor any evidence derived from it – can be used against the person in any criminal proceedings against that person, other than for perjury or for giving contradictory evidence. The consent of the Attorney General is required to initiate the process. The witness is accorded legal safeguards including the right to retain and instruct counsel and protection against the disclosure of information subject to privilege under Canadian law.

The Criminal Code, at Section 83.3, also provides for recognisances with conditions (sometimes referred to as "preventive arrest") in the context of anti-terrorist investigations and enforcement. If a police officer believes, on reasonable grounds, that a terrorist activity will be carried out and suspects on reasonable grounds that the arrest of a particular person would prevent it, then that person can be arrested, without a warrant, and brought before a judge. The judge may consider whether restrictions should be imposed on the person's movements and associations and may impose such conditions on release of the person. If the person refuses to accept conditions, the judge may commit the person to prison for up to 12 months.

Save for emergency or exigent circumstances, the consent of the Attorney General is required as a prerequisite for this procedure. The person arrested must initially be brought before a provincial court judge within 24 hours, or as soon as possible, and a maximum further period in detention of 48 hours is allowed prior to the hearing to determine conditions of release. It should be noted that the underlying purpose of this provision is not detention *per se*, but rather to provide for the imposing of conditions on the person to prevent terrorist activity from being carried out.

Special provisions govern an application for an authorisation to intercept communications in respect of terrorism offences. For other criminal offences, the warrant has a maximum statutory validity period of 60 days. In the case of terrorism offences, it may be in effect for a maximum of one full year. Also, unlike general investigative situations, in terrorism investigations there is no requirement to demonstrate that other investigative techniques have been tried and have failed, or are unlikely to succeed, or that urgency would render other techniques impractical. These special extended provisions for interception authorisations also apply to investigations into criminal organisations.[14]

4. How does the legal framework governing the use of SITs guarantee respect for human rights and individual freedoms, the principles of subsidiarity and proportionality? Is the authorisation to use of SITs subject to time-limits? Which bodies and procedures are in place to supervise compliance with human rights standards and with the above-mentioned principles in the use of SITs? Is supervision automatic/systematic?

The *Canadian Charter of Rights and Freedoms* guarantees the rights and freedoms set out in it subject only to such reasonable limits prescribed by law as can be demonstrably justified in a free and democratic society. Furthermore, for a limit to be reasonable and demonstrably justified, two central criteria must be satisfied.

First, the underlying objective of the measures that would limit rights must be pressing and substantial. Second, there must be: (a) a rational connection between the measures adopted and the objective of those measures; (b) minimal impairment of the right or freedom in question; and (c) proportionality between the effects of the measures and the objective which has been identified.[15] The charter is part of Canada's Constitution; and laws providing for SITs, and law enforcement activity in using SITs, are subject to review under charter standards. Judicial supervision with respect to human rights standards is systematic in this manner.

In addition, laws governing individual SITs provide for standards, controls, and limitations. For example, the Criminal Code sets out detailed criteria and procedures governing prior judicial authorisation for searches and interception of private communication, including, among many other matters, time-limits for authorisations for the interception of private communications and consideration of the need for employment of the technique in individual instances.

Use of the law enforcement justification described above (i.e., providing for certain otherwise unlawful conduct by law enforcement officers) is not subject to prior judicial authorisation, but is subject to specific limiting legal criteria, including a designation requirement for individual officers and a requirement for reasonableness and proportionality, as discussed previously. Failure to meet these standards may lead to judicial rulings disallowing evidence or staying prosecution during court proceedings against the targets of the investigation, or even criminal, civil or disciplinary (deontological) proceedings against law enforcement officials. For SITs requiring prior judicial authorisations, law enforcement conduct under the authorisation will be subject to judicial scrutiny, including scrutiny of the sufficiency of the prior judicial authorisation itself, if the legality of law enforcement conduct is challenged in legal proceedings. Judicial supervision of compliance with the standards, controls and limitations governing SITs is thus systemic in this manner.

As has been previously observed, the use of SITs is also governed by internal law enforcement policy. As well, restrictions on and accountability for law enforcement conduct generally are provided by laws addressing the establishment and organisation of police forces, codes of conduct, internal discipline (deontology) and public complaints.

5. Which institutions are involved in the use of SITs and what is their role (e.g. law enforcement agencies, prosecutor's office, judicial authorities, etc.)? Which institutions can order and/or authorise the use of SITs? How does co-operation between these institutions work in practice?

In Canada, operational decisions to initiate, engage in and manage SITs rest fundamentally with the police. Internal law enforcement policies generally place responsibility for internal approval of SITs with senior levels of police forces. The police investigative role is independent of the judiciary.

As indicated above, although prior judicial authorisation is required for the use of certain SITs, judicial authorities do not themselves initiate or participate in, or manage the course of investigations even when such authorisation is required: these functions are left to the police.

This does not mean the judiciary plays no role in respect of SITs. As mentioned, certain SITs require prior judicial authorisation. A fundamental judicial role is also to consider the legality and appropriateness of the use of SITs during any eventual court proceedings against the targets of the investigation. Potentially, judicial consideration of legality of SITs may also take place in the context of criminal or civil proceedings against the law enforcement officials. Non-judicial review bodies, such as disciplinary tribunals and independent public complaints bodies that have been set up in statute with respect to police forces in Canada, also may have a role in the consideration of the legality of SITs during their proceedings.

Lawyers acting for the state have a role in providing legal advice to law enforcement agencies on the use of SITs. Although prosecutors do not authorise investigations, they will recommend against the use of a particular investigative technique if it would negatively impact or otherwise jeopardise the successful prosecution of a case. As an additional role, designated state lawyers are required to make applications, on behalf of police, for judicial authorisations for certain SITs that require these authorisations.

Specified government ministers, who are accountable to Parliament, also have roles in respect of certain SITs. For example, in the case of interception of private communications and in the case of the law enforcement justification provisions, they provide designations of the individual officers and agents who can employ SITs.

With regard to co-operation, the various authorities noted above have specific points of interaction in the course of engaging in their roles with respect to SITs. It is important to emphasise, however, that Canadian law and practice dictates that they each maintain a high degree of independence in these roles.

6. Are there any specialised counter-terrorism institutions? What is their role in the use of SITs?

In Canada, no special police, prosecution or judicial bodies are designated or established with respect to terrorism. Within police forces, individual officers and units may, of course, be dedicated to working specifically on anti-terrorism investigations. Similarly, individual state prosecutors may develop specific expertise with respect to terrorism.

Nevertheless, while specialisation can and does exist at an individual and unit level, anti-terrorism investigations and prosecutions take place within the general institutional structures of law enforcement and criminal prosecutions in Canada.

With regard to security and intelligence functions the Canadian Security and Intelligence Service (CSIS) has the mandate, under the CSIS Act, to collect, analyse and retain information or intelligence on activities that may on reasonable grounds be suspected of constituting threats to the security of Canada and to report to and advise the Government of Canada in that regard. Threats to the security of Canada, as defined under the CSIS Act, can include activity which would be considered as terrorist activity. It is important to emphasise, however, that CSIS does not have law enforcement or prosecution powers.

7. Which measures have been adopted in order to facilitate international co-operation (e.g. joint investigation teams)? Can the SITs listed in reply to question 1 be used in cross-border settings?

The international nature of terrorism requires a high degree of co-operation between states with regard to investigations and prosecutions, including the sharing of information at the law enforcement and security and intelligence levels and the undertaking of operations or investigations at the request of foreign law enforcement. Canada fully participates in international co-operation of all of these types.

With respect to joint law enforcement teams, except where exceptional additional status has been given on an individual basis, police officer status is restricted to the home jurisdiction of each officer. Officers from other countries may nevertheless participate in an advisory capacity in Canadian law enforcement teams, as Canadian officers can similarly participate on teams in other countries. Further, integrated teams with members on each side of the border can ensure that officers' work on their own side of the border takes place as part of a co-ordinated enforcement effort.

Specifically, there exist Integrated Border Enforcement Teams (IBETs) that bring a harmonised approach to Canadian and United States efforts to target cross-border criminal activity, including terrorist activity. IBETs involve six core partner agencies – the Royal Canadian Mounted Police (RCMP), Canada Customs and Revenue Agency, Citizenship and Immigration Canada, US Border Patrol, US Customs Service and US Coast Guard – as well as local governments and law enforcement agencies. In addition to

Canada's participation in these Canada/US border teams, Canadian police and security and intelligence liaison officers are posted on an ongoing basis in other countries around the world and officers are posted in Canada from other countries.

While SITs themselves are not authorised for use across Canadian borders, SITs are used within Canada by various Canadian law enforcement agencies on behalf of agencies from other countries. The reverse also applies. Further detail is provided in the response to Question 8 below.

8. What use can be made of SIT in the context of mutual legal assistance?

Legal assistance can be rendered both formally and informally.

Formal – pursuant to court order

Canada has bilateral and multilateral treaties dealing wholly or partly with mutual legal assistance. Canada's Mutual Legal Assistance in Criminal Matters Act is the legislation which enables Canadian authorities to give effect to treaty requests to obtain search warrants, evidence-gathering orders and other warrants available under the Criminal Code on behalf of a requesting state, assuming the legal and evidential basis for the order exists. Some of the other warrants that may be obtained on behalf of a requesting state include warrants to obtain bodily substances for DNA analysis, warrants to install tracking devices and warrants to record numbers dialled. Canada cannot, however, intercept private communications pursuant to a mutual legal assistance treaty request.

Informal – techniques which do not require court order

At their discretion, police agencies in Canada may be prepared to undertake investigative actions not requiring a court order (such as surveillance, general undercover investigations, etc.) at the request of a foreign state.

9. How can the use of SITs be improved? Please provide any comments/proposals concerning the implementation of the terms of reference of the PC-TI and in particular the use and regulation of SITs.

SITs must be assessed and reviewed from a policy perspective to ensure that they adequately fulfill the investigative function for which they are intended, and also to ensure that they do not inappropriately affect human rights and freedoms.

From a practical perspective, ongoing policy consideration of the general adequacy and appropriateness of SITs can and should take place within law enforcement agencies who use SITs and within the policy centres of government departments responsible for law enforcement. Ultimately, this responsibility rests with government ministers responsible for law enforcement and criminal law. It is also a responsibility of Parliament, which can establish, eliminate or change legislative authorisation for SITs.

Although Parliament may review SITs at any time, specific legislated requirements for parliamentary review for certain new SITs have been created in Canada as part of the legislation authorising these SITs. For example, statutory requirements on the law enforcement justification require that the provisions establishing this SIT and operations under these provisions should be reviewed by a parliamentary committee within three years of the provisions coming into force.

In addition, all of the provisions of Canada's Anti-terrorism Act, which includes the special measures in relation to terrorism described above, are also subject to a review by a parliamentary committee within three years of that Act coming into force. Further the investigative hearing provisions and the preventive arrest provisions are subject to a "sunset clause" under which they will expire after five years. Parliament can, however, extend this expiry period for additional periods of five years on resolutions adopted by a majority of each chamber.

International comparison of SITs provides a useful benchmark for review of the adequacy and appropriateness of SITs. Such comparative exercises, including multilateral reviews such as through the PC-TI, should take fully into account differences in constitutional and legal frameworks in each country, including differences in the functions of various authorities in the legal systems, differences in the nature of relations between the authorities, and differences in methods of control and accountability. Comparisons should be seen as providing a means of examining best practices in other jurisdictions.

Finally, as a matter of general ongoing work, continuing efforts must be made to maintain and improve co-ordination and co-operation among authorities responsible for law enforcement throughout the international community.

---

1. The inventory mentions the following techniques: "opérations sous-couverture [undercover operations]; front store [store front] operations; [use of] informateurs/informants; livraisons surveillées/controlled deliveries; observation; surveillance électronique/electronic, ecoutes/bugging; interception des communications/interception of communication; fouilles et perquisitions/searches; poursuites transfrontières/cross-border pursuits; [use of] agent provocateur; pseudo-achats ou autres pseudo-crimes/ pseudo-purchases or other pseudo-offences".
2. The general doctrine of abuse of process is discussed immediately following under "Specific measures applying to individual SITs". Entrapment, discussed here, is a specific instance under which the general doctrine of abuse of process can be invoked.
3. Supreme Court of Canada decision in R. v. Mack [1988] 2 S.C.R. 903.
4. Where such surveillance takes place in a situation where a person has a reasonable expectation of privacy: subsection 487.01(4) of the Criminal Code.
5. Part VI of the Criminal Code.
6. Sections 487 and 487.01 of the Criminal Code.
7. Section 487.05 of the Criminal Code.

8. Section 492.1 of the Criminal Code.
9. Section 492.2 of the Criminal Code.
10. R. v. Campbell and Shirose [1999] 1 S.C.R. 565.
11. That is, where the police conduct goes beyond just simulation of illegal activity.
12. Sections 25.1 to 25.4 of the Criminal Code.
13. Certain other exemptions and exceptions for specific law enforcement conduct that would otherwise be illegal are provided by separate legal provisions. For example, the Controlled Drugs and Substances Act (Police Enforcement) Regulations governs the use of controlled deliveries and reverse stings in drug investigations. Subsections 354(4) and 462.31(3) of the Criminal Code provide exceptions, respectively, for possession of property obtained by crime and for money laundering where this is done by a law enforcement officer – or a person acting under the direction of a law enforcement officer – for the purpose of an investigation or otherwise in the execution of the law enforcement officer's duties.
14. Subsections 185(1.1), 186(1.1) and Section 186.1 of the Criminal Code. Authorisations may be renewed upon application provided a judge is satisfied the circumstances leading to the granting of the application still exist.
15. The Supreme Court of Canada decision in R. v. Oakes [1986] 1 S.C.R. 103.

United States of America

Introductory remark

The United States is a federal state consisting of federal, state and local jurisdictions that may have varying applicable substantive and procedural provisions in the criminal law area. In responding to this questionnaire, primary reliance has been placed on applicable federal laws and rules. The provisions applicable to non-federal jurisdictions in the United States may vary to some extent from the federal framework.

1 Please indicate the SITs used in your country, the respective legal framework governing their use and their legal definition, if any.

In the United States, forms of most of the SITs may be used in appropriate circumstances (exceptions are described in more detail below). Notwithstanding whether the SIT is controlled by statute or internal policy and/or requires prior judicial approval, it must always be exercised in a manner that comports with the United States Constitution, which, through judicial interpretation and court rulings in specific cases, also places legal limits on the actions of the federal and state governments.

In general, with respect to electronic surveillance methods and search and seizure, there are significant statutory and jurisprudential controls on application. With respect to other SITs, controls are generally imposed as a result of internal agency guidelines.

Thus, for example, US law permits the use of undercover operations/companies to detect and prevent crime (techniques 1-2). These operations are generally governed by internal agency policy (e.g., the US Department of Justice requires pre-approval from agency supervisors or federal prosecutors for certain operations). Depending on the type of operation, there may be additional restrictions. For example, as mentioned above, the use of many types of electronic surveillance during undercover operations is governed by statute, and many require a prosecutor's agreement, prior judicial review and a court order.

Moreover, undercover operations cannot be used to manufacture crimes or otherwise be used in order to entrap targets into committing an offence, and must be tied to legitimate law enforcement investigations, so there are numerous checks on use of this activity (even though the United States concept of "entrapment' is not identical to the concept of the *agent provocateur*, which is also discussed further below).

With respect to the use of informants (technique 3), this technique is dealt with by controls set forth in agency policies, rather than through statutes or jurisprudence. At the same time, jurisprudence has provided certain rules governing the manner in which information obtained from informants may be used by law enforcement agents (e.g., the manner in which information from an informant may be used to establish the level of proof required for an arrest or the issuance of a search warrant).

Controlled delivery (technique 4) follows the same pattern, with controls set forth in agency policies. Jurisprudence provides rules regarding the manner in which controlled delivery must be conducted to ensure the reliability of the technique as evidence of guilt, but the legitimacy of the technique itself is not subject to serious question.

Simple observation (technique 5) is broadly permitted, unless carried out through the use of particularly advanced technology, or the observation has been made from certain types of private areas.

Most strictly controlled are the remaining techniques. Initially, there are significant statutory requirements controlling the use of such techniques, including factual showings that must generally be made to judicial authorities. Thus, non-consensual recording of electronic communications (techniques 6-8) is controlled through statute (in particular Chapters 119 and 206 of Title 18 of the United States Code) and jurisprudence interpreting the applicable provisions of the US. Constitution.

Moreover, guidelines such as those contained in the internal policies of the US Department of Justice, including the United States Attorney Manual, may place further restrictions on such methods, including, in many cases, a requirement that a request for such surveillance be authorised at a high level in the US Department of Justice before judicial authorisation is sought.

On the other hand, it should be noted that rules can be less restrictive where a conversation is covertly recorded by a participant. Federal law specifically authorises one of the parties to a conversation to consent to the monitoring and/or recording of his/her conversations in the course of a federal investigation.

Search and seizure (technique 9) is regulated by both statute (see, e.g., Chapters 109 and 205 of Title 18 of the United States Code; Rule 41 of the Federal Rules of Criminal Procedure) and jurisprudence interpreting the applicable provisions of the US Constitution.

Moreover, in the case of search and seizure, the US Constitution requires a certain level of evidence (i.e., probable cause to believe that a crime has been committed and that evidence of it will be found at the location to be searched), requirements for the contents of search warrants, and rules for exceptions to the warrant requirement, before such an intrusive investigative technique may be carried out.

In addition, pursuits across national boundaries (technique 10) are generally not permitted, although such pursuits may occur across state and local boundaries, depending on the law and policy of the jurisdictions involved. Finally, the use of *agent provocateurs* and pseudo-purchases or other pseudo-offences (techniques 11-12) is limited by US jurisprudence providing that a subject cannot be "entrapped" into committing an offence (i.e., caused by a government agent to commit an offence that he would not otherwise have been predisposed to commit).

2. When and under which circumstances (e.g. criminal investigation, preliminary stage, etc.) can SITs be used?

Some of the SITs do not require any particular legal standard; for example, technique 5.

With regard to undercover operations and the use of informants (techniques 1-3), law enforcement officials deciding whether to approve use of such techniques must consider a number of factors in making their decision.

With respect to non-consensual electronic surveillance (generally techniques 6-8), in addition to the factors provided for under internal agency review, the applicable standards and procedures are set by federal statute and are extremely strict. Chapter 119 of Title 18 of the US Code requires that applications to employ electronic surveillance be made under oath and submitted to a court for approval, followed by continuing judicial oversight. These applications must include, *inter alia*, a full and complete statement of the facts and circumstances that give rise to the need for surveillance; precise details of the offence that has been, is being, or is about to be committed; a description of the exact communications to be intercepted, including naming the subjects whose communications are expected to be intercepted; as well as showing that other less intrusive methods have either failed or would not be effective.

Electronic surveillance is only available for certain serious crimes, and steps must be taken during monitoring to minimise the intrusiveness of the operation and intercept only those communications that are believed to be in furtherance of the target's criminal activities,

With respect to search and seizure (technique 9), there are also strict requirements for the issuance of search warrants, although exceptions to the warrant requirement exist in cases of exigent circumstances (see response to question 1) as well as for judicial supervision regarding the result of the search. Precise details providing sufficient cause for the search and seizure must be provided when a warrant is sought (in the case of an exception to the warrant requirement, the searched party may seek subsequent judicial review).

With respect to *agents provocateurs* and pseudo-purchases, see response to question 1. For remaining techniques, generally they are implemented only once there is evidence that a crime has been or is being committed.

3. Are there any specific features governing the use of SITs in relation to acts of terrorism? If so, please specify.

In general, the rules governing SITs are applied irrespective of the type of crime under investigation; thus, rules are not terrorism-specific. Electronic surveillance, however, is only available for certain listed offences. Terrorism-related offences are generally contained in this list.

In addition, the Foreign Intelligence Surveillance Act, which provides for a special mechanism for electronic surveillance of foreign operatives in the United States, may be useful for the purpose of combating terrorism, although its scope is not limited to solely that category of crime,

4. How does the legal framework governing the use of SITs guarantee respect for human rights and individual freedoms, the principles of subsidiarity and proportionality? Is the authorisation to use SITs subject to time-limits? Which bodies and procedures are in place to supervise compliance with human rights standards and with the above-mentioned principles in the use of SITs? Is supervision automatic/systematic?

With regard to respect for individual freedoms, the US Constitution and interpretive jurisprudence place restrictions on government intrusions into places and relationships where a private person can reasonably expect privacy. Additional restrictions may be embodied in statutes, jurisprudence or internal agency guidelines. For instance, there may be harsh civil, criminal and administrative penalties for the illegal use of electronic surveillance, search and seizure, and other investigative techniques, including possible exclusion of the improperly obtained evidence by the prosecution at trial.

While principles of proportionality and subsidiarity as we understand them to be used under European legal principles generally are not considered in the same way in decisions on the use of SITs in US investigations, resource-allocation decisions that restrict the initiation or expansion of an investigation are based on the seriousness of the offence and nature/extent of the evidence.

In addition, non-consensual interception of wire and/or oral communications is limited by statute to certain enumerated offences that are considered major in nature. The principle of subsidiarity also is a legal requirement with respect to certain forms of technical surveillance, arid is often incorporated as a matter of practice even in the absence of such requirement.

5. Which Institutions are involved in the use of SITs and what is their role (e.g., law enforcement agencies, prosecutor's Office, judicial authorities, etc.)? Which institutions can order and/or authorise the use of SITs? How does co-operation between these institutions work in practice?

in general, it is law enforcement agencies that are involved in the use of SITs. Depending on the type of operation (e.g., some types of undercover operations) and the applicable practices of particular domestic legal systems (in particular, federal v. state), agents may need to seek approvals from supervisors, locally or at headquarters, or from prosecutors. Electronic surveillance and search and seizure also usually need approval by a judge.

6. Are there any specialised counter terrorism institutions? What is their role in the use of SITs?

There are no specialised institutions limited solely to counter-terrorism issues. Various federal agencies, including the US Department of Justice (the chief investigative agency of which is the Federal Bureau of Investigation, which is responsible for counter-terrorism investigations) and the US Department of Homeland Security, have authority over aspects of the investigation and prosecution of terrorism offences.

7. Which measures have been adopted in order to facilitate international co-operation (e.g joint investigation teams)? Can the SITs listed in reply to question 1 be used in cross-border settings?

The United States participates extensively in joint investigation teams, and has also stationed federal law enforcement liaison officers in a number of countries in order to facilitate international co-operation. Most of the SITs listed in reply to question 1 can be used in cross-border settings. However, electronic surveillance, bugging and interception of communicatjons may only be carried out where the USA can assert domestic criminal jurisdiction over the conduct in question. Subject to some exceptions of this nature, SITs can be used on behalf of a joint team under the same circumstances as in a domestic investigation.

8. What use can be made of SITs in the context of mutual legal assistance?

With the exception of the above-described limitations on the ability to provide co-operation for electronic surveillance, bugging and interception of communications, mutual legal assistance in the use of the SITs listed is broadly available. Even here, however, whether such a request can be executed in part or in full depends, of course, on the particular facts and circumstances of each case and the specific provisions of the applicable mutual legal assistance treaty or statute concerned. In addition, with respect to requests for searches and seizures, mutual legal assistance is provided on the basis of the same requirements as provided for under the US Constitution in domestic situations before such an intrusive form of assistance can be provided.

9. How can the use of SITs be improved? Please provide any comments/proposals concerning the implementation of the terms of reference of the PC-TI and in particular the use and regulation of SITs.

The United States believes that the use of SITs can best be improved by practical measures such as increased training and technical assistance to assist countries in understanding the extent and limits of SITs in member and observer states, so that countries may better determine how co-operation might be enhanced in a particular situation.

As a general matter, the United States does not at this time believe it necessary to elaborate a binding instrument on the use of SITs. Such an instrument is unlikely to expand countries' abilities to co-operate. Moreover, given the breadth of approaches among state practice, harmonisation may prove difficult, and an instrument may in fact end up imposing additional restrictions on their use that may be unnecessary for some systems.

UNIVERSITY OF WOLVERHAMPTON
LEARNING & INFORMATION SERVICES

Sales agents for publications of the Council of Europe
Agents de vente des publications du Conseil de l'Europe

AUSTRALIA/AUSTRALIE
Hunter Publications, 58A, Gipps Street
AUS-3066 COLLINGWOOD, Victoria
Tel.: (61) 3 9417 5361
Fax: (61) 3 9419 7154
E-mail: Sales@hunter-pubs.com.au
http://www.hunter-pubs.com.au

BELGIUM/BELGIQUE
La Librairie européenne SA
50, avenue A. Jonnart
B-1200 BRUXELLES 20
Tel.: (32) 2 734 0281
Fax: (32) 2 735 0860
E-mail: info@libeurop.be
http://www.libeurop.be

Jean de Lannoy
202, avenue du Roi
B-1190 BRUXELLES
Tel.: (32) 2 538 4308
Fax: (32) 2 538 0841
E-mail: jean.de.lannoy@euronet.be
http://www.jean-de-lannoy.be

CANADA
Renouf Publishing Company Limited
5369 Chemin Canotek Road
CDN-OTTAWA, Ontario, K1J 9J3
Tel.: (1) 613 745 2665
Fax: (1) 613 745 7660
E-mail: order.dept@renoufbooks.com
http://www.renoufbooks.com

**CZECH REPUBLIC/
RÉPUBLIQUE TCHÈQUE**
Suweco Cz Dovoz Tisku Praha
Ceskomoravska 21
CZ-18021 PRAHA 9
Tel.: (420) 2 660 35 364
Fax: (420) 2 683 30 42
E-mail: import@suweco.cz

DENMARK/DANEMARK
GAD Direct
Fiolstaede 31-33
DK-1171 COPENHAGEN K
Tel.: (45) 33 13 72 33
Fax: (45) 33 12 54 94
E-mail: info@gaddirect.dk

FINLAND/FINLANDE
Akateeminen Kirjakauppa
Keskuskatu 1, PO Box 218
FIN-00381 HELSINKI
Tel.: (358) 9 121 41
Fax: (358) 9 121 4450
E-mail: akatilaus@stockmann.fi
http://www.akatilaus.akateeminen.com

FRANCE
La Documentation française
(Diffusion/Vente France entière)
124, rue H. Barbusse
F-93308 AUBERVILLIERS Cedex
Tel.: (33) 01 40 15 70 00
Fax: (33) 01 40 15 68 00
E-mail: commandes.vel@ladocfrancaise.gouv.fr
http://www.ladocfrancaise.gouv.fr

Librairie Kléber (Vente Strasbourg)
Palais de l'Europe
F-67075 STRASBOURG Cedex
Fax: (33) 03 88 52 91 21
E-mail: librairie.kleber@coe.int

**GERMANY/ALLEMAGNE
AUSTRIA/AUTRICHE**
UNO Verlag
August-Bebel-Allee 6
D-53175 BONN
Tel.: (49) 2 28 94 90 20
Fax: (49) 2 28 94 90 222
E-mail: bestellung@uno-verlag.de
http://www.uno-verlag.de

GREECE/GRÈCE
Librairie Kauffmann
28, rue Stadiou
GR-ATHINAI 10564
Tel.: (30) 1 32 22 160
Fax: (30) 1 32 30 320
E-mail: ord@otenet.gr

HUNGARY/HONGRIE
Euro Info Service
Hungexpo Europa Kozpont ter 1
H-1101 BUDAPEST
Tel.: (361) 264 8270
Fax: (361) 264 8271
E-mail: euroinfo@euroinfo.hu
http://www.euroinfo.hu

ITALY/ITALIE
Libreria Commissionaria Sansoni
Via Duca di Calabria 1/1, CP 552
I-50125 FIRENZE
Tel.: (39) 556 4831
Fax: (39) 556 41257
E-mail: licosa@licosa.com
http://www.licosa.com

NETHERLANDS/PAYS-BAS
De Lindeboom Internationale Publikaties
PO Box 202, MA de Ruyterstraat 20 A
NL-7480 AE HAAKSBERGEN
Tel.: (31) 53 574 0004
Fax: (31) 53 572 9296
E-mail: books@delindeboom.com
http://home-1-worldonline.nl/~lindeboo/

NORWAY/NORVÈGE
Akademika, A/S Universitetsbokhandel
PO Box 84, Blindern
N-0314 OSLO
Tel.: (47) 22 85 30 30
Fax: (47) 23 12 24 20

POLAND/POLOGNE
Głowna Księgarnia Naukowa
im. B. Prusa
Krakowskie Przedmiescie 7
PL-00-068 WARSZAWA
Tel.: (48) 29 22 66
Fax: (48) 22 26 64 49
E-mail: inter@internews.com.pl
http://www.internews.com.pl

PORTUGAL
Livraria Portugal
Rua do Carmo, 70
P-1200 LISBOA
Tel.: (351) 13 47 49 82
Fax: (351) 13 47 02 64
E-mail: liv.portugal@mail.telepac.pt

SPAIN/ESPAGNE
Mundi-Prensa Libros SA
Castelló 37
E-28001 MADRID
Tel.: (34) 914 36 37 00
Fax: (34) 915 75 39 98
E-mail: libreria@mundiprensa.es
http://www.mundiprensa.com

SWITZERLAND/SUISSE
Adeco – Van Diermen
Chemin du Lacuez 41
CH-1807 BLONAY
Tel.: (41) 21 943 26 73
Fax: (41) 21 943 36 05
E-mail: info@adeco.org

UNITED KINGDOM/ROYAUME-UNI
TSO (formerly HMSO)
51 Nine Elms Lane
GB-LONDON SW8 5DR
Tel.: (44) 207 873 8372
Fax: (44) 207 873 8200
E-mail: customer.services@theso.co.uk
http://www.the-stationery-office.co.uk
http://www.itsofficial.net

**UNITED STATES and CANADA/
ÉTATS-UNIS et CANADA**
Manhattan Publishing Company
2036 Albany Post Road
CROTON-ON-HUDSON,
NY 10520, USA
Tel.: (1) 914 271 5194
Fax: (1) 914 271 5856
E-mail: Info@manhattanpublishing.com
http://www.manhattanpublishing.com

Council of Europe Publishing/Editions du Conseil de l'Europe
F-67075 Strasbourg Cedex
Tel.: (33) 03 88 41 25 81 – Fax: (33) 03 88 41 39 10 – E-mail: publishing@coe.int – Website: http://book.coe.int

U.W.E.L. LEARNING RESOURCES